THE STORY OF GOD

PETER SUTTON

Ark House Press
arkhousepress.com

© 2025 Peter Sutton

All rights reserved. Apart from any fair dealing for the purpose of study, research, criticism, or review, as permitted under the Copyright Act, no part may be reproduced by any process without written permission.

Cataloguing in Publication Data:
Title: The Story of God
ISBN: 978-1-7641051-2-5 (pbk)
Subjects: REL067110 RELIGION / Christian Theology / Systematic; REL006700 RELIGION / Biblical Studies / Bible Study Guides; REL006160 RELIGION / Biblical Reference / General.

Design by initiateagency.com

Dedicated to my father Colin

CONTENTS

AN INTRODUCTION ix
A READERS GUIDE xi
BIBLE QUOTES xiii

The Pentateuch

GENESIS 1
EXODUS 27
LEVITICUS 42
NUMBERS 45
DEUTERONOMY 49

The Historical Books

THE BOOK OF JOSHUA 57
THE BOOK OF JUDGES 62
THE BOOK OF RUTH 71
THE BOOKS OF SAMUEL I AND II 73
THE BOOKS OF KINGS I AND II 87
THE BOOKS OF CHRONICLES I AND II 97
THE BOOK OF EZRA AND NEHEMIAH 108
TOBIT 112
JUDITH 116
ESTHER 119
BOOK OF MACCABEES I AND II 122

The Wisdom Books

JOB	215
THE PSALMS	223
THE PROVERBS	234
ECCLESIASTES	242
THE SONG OF SONGS	245
THE BOOK OF WISDOM	251
ECCLESIASTICUS	256

The Prophets

OBADIAH	181
JOEL	183
AMOS	188
JONAH	193
HOSEA	196
ISAIAH	201
MICAH	215
NAHUM	219
ZEPHANIAH	220
HABAKKUK	223
JEREMIAH	226
BARUCH	233
LAMENTATIONS	236
EZEKIEL	241
DANIEL	248
HAGGAI	258
ZECHARIAH	260
MALACHI	265

The New Testament

MATTHEW	269
MARK	303
LUKE	325
JOHN	357
ACTS OF THE APOSTLES	380
ROMANS	402
1 CORINTHIANS	407
2 CORINTHIANS	414
GALATIANS	418
EPHESIANS	422
PHILIPPIANS	426
COLOSSIANS	429
1 THESSALONIANS	432
2 THESSALONIANS	435
1 TIMOTHY	437
2 TIMOTHY	440
TITUS	442
PHILEMON	444
HEBREWS	445
JAMES	455
1 PETER	458
2 PETER	461
1 JOHN	464
2 JOHN	467
3 JOHN	468
JUDE	470
THE BOOK OF REVELATION	472
REFERENCE MATERIALS	487
EXPLANATIONS OF SOME FREQUENT BIBLICAL WORDS	489

AN INTRODUCTION

The Bible is the most popular book in the world, filled with the words of God the Father and Jesus.

For many, the Bible can seem overwhelming due to its size and complex structure. Recognising this, I have set out to create an approachable introduction. *The Story of God* is designed for those who have previously struggled to read the Bible, or never considered it.

In 2018, during a conversation with friends, I had an epiphany: 'Could I help bring the Bible into the consciousness of more people?' I'm not a literary person, and I repeatedly told myself this idea was out of my reach. But no matter how much I doubted, the drive to continue never faded.

Seven years later - after much reading, writing, and editing - *The Story of God* is here.

I hope this book offers a new perspective, inviting readers to explore the wisdom of the Bible in a way that is accessible to all. For anyone new to the Bible, or looking for a guide to better understand it, *The Story of God* strives to provide a starting point to engage with the most influential book of all time.

If anything contained here is opposed to Catholic Church doctrine then let it be known that I willingly withdraw it in favour of the Catholic Church teachings.

> 'If there is anything good in it, let this be
> to the glory and honour of God.'
>
> **St Teresa of Avila**

A READERS GUIDE

I find it beneficial to read the first five books (the Pentateuch) with an understanding of their origins. These books were compiled in a form resembling the present-day version by Israelite priestly scholars during the Babylonian exile[1], a time when the Israelites were confused and dismayed and wondering what or where God was. They are derived from Israelite oral stories handed down over a period of 800 years.

So the first five books allowed the people to revisit their history and see how God had worked among them in the past, and whilst at times he raised his hand against them, he was ultimately always faithful to his original promise.

The history and wisdom books are, in a way, easier to understand, as they are largely straightforward in their dialogue. The prophetic books, however, oscillate between offering clear instructions from God - regarding his expectations and how the Israelites' actions will shape their future - and being enigmatic.

I have rearranged the order of some of the books in the Old Testament. This is intended to present the text in a more chronological sequence, which I believe helps in the understanding.

The New Testament tells the story of Jesus, the Son of God - his life, his teachings, his death, and the coming of the Holy Spirit. These

---

[1] A critical time in the history of the Israelites, and is covered in detail in the books after The Second Book of Kings.

books were written by people who had either known him or had been deeply shaped by his message. Where the Old Testament speaks of God's faithfulness to Israel, the New Testament opens up that promise to everyone. It's a message of hope and grace.

In this work, I've primarily cited the World English Bible (WEB) because it allows me to adhere to copyright laws (see 'Bible Quotes' on the following page). However, my personal preference is the New Jerusalem Bible. I find it more relatable and, as a result, I've occasionally used it to provide a more accessible reading experience.

Reading the Bible is a deeply personal experience, and no two individuals will necessarily share the same interpretation. Even re-reading the same book or chapter can yield different meanings. So, prepare yourself for a lifelong journey of discovery.

BIBLE QUOTES

Unless specifically noted otherwise, the bible verses used in this work are from the World English Bible (WEB), an English translation of the Bible published in 2000. It is an updated revision of the American Standard Version (1901). The World English Bible was created by volunteers using the American Standard Version as the base text as part of the ebible.org project through Rainbow Missions, Inc., a Colorado nonprofit corporation. The World English Bible is public domain.

Where specifically noted with an asterisk (*) after the verse location I have used the New Jerusalem Bible instead as I thought it provided an easier read.

THE PENTATEUCH

GENESIS

The opening chapters of Genesis are profound, setting the narrative that significantly influences subsequent biblical events.

It establishes God as the Creator and master of everything. It chronicles how mankind had it all, a life in God's perfect grace and presence, until 'The Fall' and subsequent separation from God. The rest of the Old Testament is God and man coming to terms with this.

Genesis also sets the scene for the constant struggle, which is to come, between God wanting a holy nation of believers, and mankind getting it wrong and being unfaithful.

In the Beginning

Before God there was nothing, only God. In the beginning God created everything.

On the first day God created light, so there was a difference between light and dark: day and night.

As there was nothing (but God) before creation, on the second day God created the sky and land.

The earth had no form, so on the third day God created the vegetation.

On the fourth day, God created the sun and the moon.

It wasn't until the fifth day that God created the first life - fish for the sea and birds for the sky.

The sixth day was a busy one, God created (from dust of the soil) male and female in the image of himself, he also created all the animals and beasts on the land. God placed man as master of all other living things.

On the seventh day, God rested and made the day a holy day.[2]

There is a second account of creation where God creates man (Adam) alone at first, and after placing him in the Garden of Eden sees he needs a helper. The animals were then created as Adam's helpers, but God saw this was still not good enough, so while Adam slept, he removed one of his ribs and with it created a woman (Eve). Adam said, *"This one at last is bone of my bones and flesh of my flesh! She is to be called woman because she was taken out of Man."* (Gen 2:23)

God created a special place for Adam and Eve to live - a garden called Eden. In the garden was everything they would need to live and be happy. God said there was only one rule, *"You shall not eat of the tree of the knowledge of good and evil; for on the day that you eat of it, you will surely die."* (Gen 2:17)

One of the wild beasts of creation, a serpent[3], questioned Eve, asking if God had in fact said that if they ate from the tree of knowledge, they would die. Eve replied, "Yes." The serpent told Eve this wasn't true, but the real reason God prohibited them from eating from that tree was because God knew if they did, their eyes would be opened, and they would be like gods themselves. This was too tempting for Eve, so she ate from the tree. After eating the fruit, she also offered some to Adam, and yes, their eyes were opened, but all they saw was that they were naked. Immediately, they went to cover themselves using fig leaves.

---

[2] This (Sabbath) day was a Saturday until the time of Jesus when it changed to Sunday in celebration of the day he rose from the dead.
[3] The devil.

Later in the day, as God was walking through the garden, he noticed them hiding in the bushes. When he asked why, Adam replied that it was because they were naked.

"Who told you that you were naked?" asked God, "Did you eat from the tree I told you not to eat from?"

"Eve made me do it," replied Adam.

To which Eve quickly added, "The snake tempted me."

God cursed the snake. The woman would endure exhausting pain during childbirth; the man would forever sweat and suffer working the land for food and, in the end, die, returning to the dust from which he came. And the serpent was condemned beyond all wild beasts, crawling on its belly.

Because God couldn't trust man anymore, and knowing there was one other tree in the garden he needed to be kept away from - the tree of life (which would enable them to live forever) - he made clothes and *sent him out from the garden of Eden, to till the ground from which he was taken. So he drove out the man; and he placed cherubim at the east of the garden of Eden, and a flaming sword which turned every way, to guard the way to the Tree of Life.* (Gen 3:23-24)

Adam and Eve

Adam and Eve conceived a son Cain, followed by a second son, Abel. Cain grew up to be a farmer, and Abel grew up to be a shepherd. Even though they were banished from Eden they were not banished from God, and Cain and Abel would bring offerings to him. As a farmer, Cain brought produce from the soil. As a shepherd, Abel brought a firstborn from his flock. God liked Abel's offering but didn't like Cain's, which Cain could not understand. Angered by God's reaction, Cain invited his brother Abel out into the fields and killed him.

Sometime later, God questioned Cain, asking him if he knew where Abel was. Cain answered, "How should I know? I'm not his keeper; he can look after himself."

God knew the truth however and cursed Cain and the future of his family saying, *"What have you done? The voice of your brother's blood cries to me from the ground. Now you are cursed because of the ground, which has opened its mouth to receive your brother's blood from your hand. From now on, when you till the ground, it won't yield its strength to you. You will be a fugitive and a wanderer on the earth."* (Gen 4:10-12)

Cain protested, complaining he would have no chance of survival, so God put a mark on Cain and declared that anyone who killed Cain would suffer a fate seven times worse. Cain left and settled in Nod.

Adam continued to father children and at the age of one hundred and thirty, a son, Seth, was born. Adam fathered many more sons and daughters before dying at the age of nine hundred and thirty.

Through the line of Seth, and some nine generations later, Noah was born. Noah fathered three sons, Shem, Japheth, and Ham. Noah was five hundred years old.

Noah and the Ark

Over time, the world grew corrupt in the eyes of God, so he resolved to do something about it, and as Noah and his household were the only ones judged to be good, he told Noah, *"I will bring an end to all flesh, for the earth is filled with violence through them. Behold, I will destroy them and the earth."* (Gen 6:13)

"I ... will bring the flood of waters on this earth, to destroy all flesh having the breath of life from under the sky. Everything that is on earth will die. But I will establish my covenant with you. You shall come into the ship, you, your sons, your wife, and your sons' wives with you. Of every living thing of all flesh, you shall bring two of every sort into the ship, to keep them alive with you. They shall be male and female." (Gen 6:17-19)

Noah built the ark; exactly as God commanded him.

Like the story of creation, the story of Noah and the flood has two similar yet different tellings. In the second telling, God mentions:

"Of all the clean animals, you must take seven of each kind, both male and female; of the unclean animals, you must take two, a male and its female (and of the birds of heaven also, seven of each kind, both male and female), to propagate their kind over the whole earth." (Gen 7:2-3)

Noah was six hundred years old when he entered the ark with his wife and three sons Shem, Japheth, and Ham, plus their three wives. God closed the doors behind them and opened the heavens to bring down forty days and forty nights of rain.[4]

Everything living on land died; all that remained were Noah and his family.

The flood waters caused by the forty days and forty nights of rain lasted for one hundred and fifty days. On the seventh day of the seventh month the ark came to rest on the mountain of Ararat.[5]

The waters continued to subside before eventually the mountain peaks started to appear. Forty days later, hoping to find dry land, Noah sent out a dove. On the first attempt the dove returned unsuccessfully, however when Noah tried again seven days later it was a success. The dove returned with a new olive branch, signalling to Noah there was dry land. To be sure, seven days later he sent the dove out again, and this time it didn't return. So, on the first day of the first month Noah opened the doors, and he saw the earth was dry. Yet it wasn't until the

---

[4] Generally speaking, the number forty has been considered to be used in the bible as a rounded number. It was used to express a complete period of time rather than expressions like 'many' or 'some'. It would be similar to referring to a number of years ranging from eight to twelve as 'about a decade'. In this case, the number forty is being used instead of saying 'a few days' or 'a few decades'. When we see the number forty used to denote time in the bible, we are being told that something extraordinary and definitive is happening. 'Get Catholic Answers, catholic.com/.'

[5] Current day Mt Ararat is a snow-covered volcano in Turkey.

twenty-seventh day of the second month that God said to Noah, *"Go out of the ship, you, your wife, your sons, and your sons' wives with you. Bring out with you every living thing that is with you of all flesh, including birds, livestock, and every creeping thing that creeps on the earth, that they may breed abundantly, and be fruitful, and multiply on the earth."* (Gen 8:16-17)

Once on land, Noah built an altar to God and made an animal sacrifice, which pleased God. In turn, God made a covenant with Noah, declaring, *"I will not again curse the ground any more for man's sake because the imagination of man's heart is evil from his youth. I will never again strike every living thing, as I have done."* (Gen 8:21)

The sign of this covenant is the rainbow.[6]

After leaving the ark and setting up home again, God instructed Noah and his family to be fruitful and multiply, and he once again placed man above all other living things, just as he did with Adam and Eve. However, this time he specifically stated, *"Whoever sheds man's blood, his blood will be shed, for God made man in his own image."* (Gen 9:6)

From Noah's three sons, Shem, Japheth, and Ham (to become Canaan's ancestors) and their descendants, nations were born and dispersed over all the earth.

Noah died at nine hundred and fifty.

God Calls Abram

Shem, the eldest son of Noah, bore many sons and daughters, as did his descendants. After ten generations, Abram was born (soon to be known as Abraham).

---

[6] This is God's first covential sign. We will see two more in the Old Testament. The second is circumcision, and the third is the Sabbath day.

Abram was seventy-five when God told him, *"Leave your country, your relatives, and your father's house, and go to the land that I will show you. I will make you a great nation. I will bless you and make your name great. You will be a blessing. I will bless those who bless you, and I will curse him who treats you with contempt. All the families of the earth will be blessed through you."* (Gen 12:1-3)

Abram did what was asked of him and left with his wife Sarai, his nephew Lot, and all his possessions. On the journey, they travelled through the land of the Canaanites (descendants of Ham, son of Noah), where God promised Abram these lands would be for him and his (many) descendants. Abram built an altar there and made a sacrifice to God, and God appeared to him.

Since being called by God, Abram had grown very prosperous. So too had his nephew Lot. In fact, it reached the point where, together, they were too big for any one place. To avoid any potential conflicts over grazing lands, Abram suggested to Lot that they split up. Abram ended up settling in the land of Canaan,[7] while Lot settled among the cities of the plain on the outskirts of Sodom.

Soon after Lot departed, God said to Abram, *"Now, lift up your eyes, and look from the place where you are, northward and southward and eastward and westward, for I will give all the land which you see to you and to your offspring forever. I will make your offspring as the dust of the earth, so that if a man can count the dust of the earth, then your offspring may also be counted. Arise, walk through the land in its length and in its width; for I will give it to you."* (Gen 13:14-17)

Abram settled in Hebron, and there he built another altar to God.

---

[7] The land of Ham's descendants and also what will be known as the Promised Land to the Hebrews being led by Moses through the desert.

A Covenant Between God and Abram

Sometime later God spoke to Abram, telling him again that he was his protector, and his reward would be great. Abram, however, was not as sure, asking God, "How can this be when I haven't fathered any children? Who will be my descendants and heirs?"

God took Abram outside, telling him to look up at the stars in the sky, "Start counting them, if you can," said God, "Your descendants will be as many as there are stars, and I will make you heir to this land you are on."

Abram put his faith in God, yet still he remained unsure, asking God, "How am I to know I will inherit this land?"

God instructed Abram to get some animals, cut them in half, and lay them out. As the sun was setting Abram dozed off into a terror-filled sleep. God spoke again to him. *"Know for sure that your offspring will live as foreigners in a land that is not theirs, and will serve them. They will afflict them for four hundred years. I will also judge that nation, whom they will serve. Afterward they will come out with great wealth; but you will go to your fathers in peace. You will be buried at a good old age."* (Gen 15:13-15)

When the sun had set, a smoking furnace, and a piece of burning wood appeared between the halves of the animals laid out by Abram. A covenant was made on that day between God and Abram. *That day Yahweh made a Covenant with Abram in these terms:*

> *"To your descendants I give this land,*
> *from the wadi of Egypt to the Great River."* (Gen 15:18*)

Birth of Ishmael, Abram's First Son

At this time Abram had settled in Canaan and his wife Sarai was becoming despondent as she was not able to bear children, so she devised a plan. She went to Abram, proposing he take her slave girl Hagar as his wife, and thus father children. Abram agreed, and soon Hagar was pregnant.

However, as soon as Hagar knew she was pregnant with Abram's child, she stopped paying any obedience to Sarai. Sarai went to Abram, complaining that he needed to do something about it. Abram, instead, told Sarai that the fate of Hagar was in her hands, and she could do whatever she wanted to her. Sarai treated Hagar so badly that she ran away.

Stopping near a spring, an angel asked Hagar, "Where have you come from and where are you going?" She said she was running away from her terrible mistress. The angel told her to go back and submit to Sarai, promising that her own descendants would be too numerous to count.[8] Hagar returned and gave birth to a son, Ishmael.

The Covenant of Circumcision

When Abram was ninety-nine, God appeared to him, renewing the covenant he made - making him the father of nations. God also changed Abram's name to Abraham.[9] To ratify the covenant, God ordered that all males, eight days and older, be circumcised.[10] God then changed Sarai's name to Sarah and promised her a son of her own.

Abraham scoffed at God, questioning his ability to father a child with a wife who was ninety. He went as far as to say his son Ishmael would be the better person to continue the line, but God said no. He told Abraham he would have a son with Sarah, he was to name him Isaac, and Isaac would take the place of Abraham when he died.

When God left, Abraham quickly gathered all the males in his household and had them circumcised.

---

[8] The Ishmaelites.
[9] The conferring of a name is an act of power and an assertion of ownership. A change of name indicates a change of state or condition, the beginning of a new existence. Brown, Raymond E., et al. The Jerome Biblical Commentary. Prentice-Hall, 1968. [77:6]
[10] The second of three covenential signs.

Sodom and Gomorrah

One day, while sitting outside his tent, Abraham saw three men approaching.[11] He offered them food to eat and water to wash. At the end of the meal, they stated they would return in one year, at which time Sarah would have a son. Sarah, who was just inside the tent, overheard this and laughed to herself, murmuring, "Not at my age, I am no longer able."

God asked Abraham why Sarah was laughing at the proposal of having a child, reminding him he was God and could do anything he wanted. Sarah overheard the conversation and quickly denied saying it.

"Yes, you did," replied God.

Abraham offered to help the three men find their way onwards, and they were soon within sight of Sodom. God debated how much he should tell Abraham about his plans for the township; yet reasoned that because he had singled out Abraham as the father of nations and entrusted him to live an upright life, he should be told. *"Because the cry of Sodom and Gomorrah is great, and because their sin is very grievous, I will go down now and see whether their deeds are as bad as the reports which have come to me. If not, I will know."* (Gen 18:20-21)

So, the two men (angels) went on into the city while Abraham stayed back with God.

Feeling bold, Abraham questioned God, *"Will you consume the righteous with the wicked? What if there are fifty righteous within the city? Will you consume and not spare the place for the fifty righteous who are in it?..."*

God said, *"If I find in Sodom fifty righteous within the city, then I will spare the whole place for their sake."*

Abraham answered, *"See now, I have taken it on myself to speak to Yahweh, although I am dust and ashes. What if there will lacks five of the fifty righteous? Will you destroy all the city for lack of five?"*

He said, *"I will not destroy it if I find forty-five there."*

---

[11] Two angels and God.

He spoke to him yet again, and said, "What if there are forty found there?"
He said, "I will not do it for the forty's sake."
He said, "Oh don't let Yahweh be angry, and I will speak. What if there are thirty found there?"
He said, "I will not do it if I find thirty there."
He said, "See now, I have taken it on myself to speak to Yahweh. What if there are twenty found there?"
He said, "I will not destroy it for the twenty's sake."
He said, "Oh don't let Yahweh be angry, and I will speak just once more. What if ten are found there?"
He said, "I will not destroy it for the ten's sake."
God went his way as soon as he had finished communing with Abraham, and Abraham returned to his place.[12] (Gen 18:23-33)

Lot is Saved

As the two angels approached the gates of Sodom, they encountered Lot, who was sitting at the gate. He bowed before them, enjoining them to come into his home and eat.[13]

After dinner, there was a commotion outside Lot's front door. Opening it, Lot saw a rabble from the town demanding he hand over the two strangers so they could sodomise them. Lot would not agree, instead he offered to send out his two young daughters.[14] *"See now, I have two virgin daughters. Please let me bring them out to you, and you may*

---

[12] St Augustine saw Abraham's intercession as a model of prayer and mercy, admiring Abraham's humility and boldness in approaching God.

[13] At the time, there was a sacred duty to hospitality. Some sources say the host would receive guests as if they were sent directly by God; other sources say it was more cultural than religious, but in either case, the duty of the homeowner to provide safety and shelter was as unwavering as the duty of the guest to not bring any harm to the owner.

[14] At that time, the honour of a woman was considered less important than hospitality to a guest.

do to them what seems good to you. Only don't do anything to these men, because they have come under the shadow of my roof." (Gen 19:8)

The two angels pulled Lot back into the house and struck down the rabble with blindness so they could not find their way inside. They let Lot know that it was God who sent them, *"Because the outcry against (Sodom) has grown so great before God that God has sent us to destroy it."* (Gen 19:13)

They asked Lot to gather all his household (which comprised his wife, two daughters, and his two future sons-in-law) and they would be safely escorted out of town and far enough away so they would not be destroyed, along with the town. The two future sons-in-law did not believe Lot, and consequently remained in the town to suffer the same fate as the rest.

As the sun rose the next day, the angels took Lot, his wife and two daughters outside the city-gates to safety, with strict instructions to, *"Escape for your life! Don't look behind you, and don't stay anywhere in the plain. Escape to the mountains, lest you be consumed!"* (Gen 19:17)

Then God rained on Sodom and on Gomorrah, sulphur, and fire from the sky. He overthrew those cities, all the plain, all the inhabitants of the cities, and that which grew on the ground. (Gen 19:24-25)

Regrettably, Lot's wife looked back at the destruction of the towns and was turned into a pillar of salt.

At the age of one hundred, Abraham and Sarah finally had a son of their own, he was named Isaac.

Abraham is Tested

Sometime later, God spoke to Abraham, *"Now take your son, your only son, Isaac, whom you love, and ... offer him there as a burnt offering on one of the mountains, which I will tell you of."* (Gen 22:2)

Abraham obediently rose early the next morning and, together with some servants, took Isaac into the mountains to make the sacrifice to God. After three days climbing, Abraham told his servants to wait while he continued alone with Isaac, who was carrying the chopped wood for the sacrifice. Abraham carried the fire and the knife. Isaac, unaware he was to be the sacrifice, spoke.

"*My father?*"

He said, "Here I am, my son."

He said, "Here is the fire and the wood, but where is the lamb for a burnt offering?"

Abraham said, "God will provide himself the lamb for a burnt offering, my son." (Gen 22:7-8)

Arriving at the place God revealed to him, Abraham built an altar, arranged the wood, and bound his son Isaac on the altar. As he was raising the knife in readiness to kill his son, an angel of God appeared, saying, *"Don't lay your hand on the boy or do anything to him. For now I know that you fear God, since you have not withheld your son, your only son, from me."*

Abraham lifted up his eyes and saw that behind him was a ram caught in the thicket by his horns. Abraham went and took the ram, and offered it up for a burnt offering instead of his son. (Gen 22:12-13)

God's angel called to Abraham a second time out of the sky, and said, "'I have sworn by myself,' says God, 'because you have done this thing, and have not withheld your son, your only son, that I will bless you greatly, and I will multiply your offspring greatly, like the stars of the heavens, and like the sand which is on the seashore. Your offspring will possess the gate of his enemies. All the nations of the earth will be blessed by your offspring, because you have obeyed my voice.'" (Gen 22:15-18)

Isaac and Rebekah

God continued to bless Abraham as he grew old. Sometime later (after Sarah's death), Abraham called in one of his servants, making him promise under oath he would ensure his son Isaac would marry a girl from his own native land and family.[15] The servant agreed and set off as instructed. Arriving at the town of Haran, he came across a well where many women were drawing water. The servant, mindful of wanting to please Abraham, prayed to God, *"Let it happen, that the young lady to whom I will say, 'Please let down your pitcher, that I may drink,'* (will say in reply), *'Drink, and I will also give your camels a drink,' – let her be the one you have appointed for your servant Isaac. By this I will know that you have shown kindness to my master."* (Gen 24:14)

He had not even finished praying when a woman, Rebekah, (who turned out to be the daughter of one of Abraham's nephews) came to him behaving as the servant had prayed. He knew God had chosen her to be the wife of his master, Isaac. The servant gave her a gold ring and two arm bracelets. She hurried back home to tell the story of the man she met at the well. Her brother Laban, returned to the well to find the servant and brought him home. When he arrived, the servant told them who he was and why he was there, just as Abraham had told him. Hearing what the servant had to say, Laban and his father proposed they call Rebekah to hear the story. Rebekah agreed to go back with the man and marry Isaac. The family gave her their blessing.

Abraham died at the age of one hundred and seventy-five, after marrying again and fathering more sons and daughters. He gave all his possessions to Isaac.

Isaac, Esau, and Jacob

Isaac was forty when he married Rebekah, and he prayed to God to lift her barrenness. God heard his prayer and soon she was pregnant with twins. It was an uncomfortable pregnancy, as the twins fought with each other in utero. The first to be born was Esau (who was very hairy, like he was wrapped in a hairy coat). The second was Jacob.

---

[15] Haran.

Many years later, as adults, Esau was returning home after spending the day in the fields when he saw Jacob preparing a meal. Esau asked for some food and Jacob said no. Esau continued to press him, saying, "Yet here I am at death's door."

Jacob devised a plan, that if Esau gave up his birthright as the firstborn son of Isaac, he would give him some food. Esau unwittingly agreed.

When Esau was forty, he married a woman. Neither Isaac nor Rebekah approved.

Jacob and Rebekah Deceive Isaac

As Isaac grew older, his eyesight started to fail. One day he summoned his eldest son Esau, revealing he was soon to die, and needed to give him a final blessing first. In preparation for the blessing, Isaac sent Esau out to hunt some game so they could prepare a meal. Rebekah became aware of this (Esau was always Isaac's favourite, but Rebekah's favourite was Jacob), telling Jacob what was about to take place. She told him to quickly go and kill some goats, and return with them to her, and they would also prepare a meal.

To trick Isaac and secure the first son's blessing for Jacob, Rebekah dressed him in some of Esau's clothes (including covering parts of his body with the fur of a goat), so he would smell and feel like Esau. Everything went to plan - Isaac was fooled, and Jacob received the blessing meant for Esau.[16]

> *"Behold, the smell of my son*
> *is as the smell of a field which God has blessed.*
> *God give you of the dew of the sky,*
> *of the fatness of the earth, and plenty of grain*
> *and new wine.*

---

[16] God preferring or choosing the younger brother to continue the family name is an occurrence repeated with Jacob and Joseph.

> *Let peoples serve you,*
> *and nations bow down to you.*
> *Be lord over your brothers.*
> *Let your mother's sons bow down to you.*
> *Cursed be everyone who curses you.*
> *Blessed be everyone who blesses you."* (Gen 27:27-29)

Infuriated by the betrayal, Esau promised himself he would kill Jacob. Luckily for Jacob, Rebekah realised this and quickly made plans to send him off to Haran (her birthplace).

Jacob Marries Rachel and Leah

Like the finding of Rebekah (as a wife for Isaac), Jacob approached a well to water his stock. While there, he came across other herdsmen who turned out to be from Haran (where he was heading). Jacob asked if they knew his uncle Laban (his mother Rebekah's brother), and they replied, "Indeed we do."

Laban's daughter Rachel came to the well often. As soon as Jacob saw Rachel, he was smitten and told her who he was and all about his journey. Jacob returned with Rachel to meet Laban.

Jacob stayed on for a month, working for Laban without payment. Eventually, Laban became uncomfortable with the situation and told Jacob he wanted to pay him. Jacob (who was in love with Rachel) offered to continue to work without pay for seven years, if in the end he would be allowed to marry Rachel. Laban agreed, and after seven years, the marriage was agreed. When night came and Jacob retired to his matrimonial bed, Laban sent in Leah (the eldest daughter) instead of Rachel. Jacob slept with Leah and when he discovered the deception in the morning, screamed at Laban, "What have you done? We had an agreement. Why did you trick me?"

Laban explained it away by saying, "I could not let you marry my younger daughter before I married my eldest daughter."

So they came to a new agreement. If Jacob could work another seven years, he would be allowed to marry Rachel the following week. Jacob agreed.

Birth of the Twelve Sons of Jacob

Jacob did not love Leah as he loved Rachel, and God knew it, so he made Rachel barren and Leah fertile. Leah gave birth to four sons - Reuben, Simeon, Levi, and Judah. Rachel was naturally upset with these events, and questioned Jacob about it, to which Jacob said, "Am I God? How is it my fault you can't fall pregnant?"

Rachel then offered Jacob her slave-girl Bilhah to sleep with. This union was successful (twice), and sons Dan and Naphtali were born. Leah became jealous that Jacob wasn't sleeping with her anymore, so she sent her slave-girl Zilpah to sleep with Jacob, and two other sons, Gad, and Asher, were born.

One day, as Leah and her first-born son Reuben were in the fields harvesting corn, Reuben gave her some mandrakes he had picked. In the distance, Rachel saw them and asked if she could have some.
"No," protested Leah, "Why should I? You have stolen my husband."

Rachel, seemingly desperate for the mandrakes, said, "What if I let you sleep with Jacob again? Will you give me some then?"

"Yes," replied Leah.

Entering his bed that night, Leah explained why she was there, and another son, Issachar was born. Another son, Zebulun, followed, then finally a daughter, Dinah.[17]

Soon God felt pity for Rachel and opened her womb, and she gave birth to her first son, Joseph (of the coat of many colours).

---

[17] Leah was now the mother to Reuben, Simeon, Levi, Judah, Issachar, Zebulun, and Dinah. Bilhah had two sons, Dan, and Naphtali. Zilpah also had two sons, Gad, and Asher.

Jacob Becomes Israel, the Father of the Twelve Tribes

Eventually, Jacob felt it was time to leave the home and lands of Laban and return to his own country, Hebron. Getting close to home, an unknown man appeared and wrestled with Jacob throughout the night.[18] In the morning, still unable to beat Jacob, the unknown man resorted to dislocating his hip.

Jacob would still not let him go, saying, *"I won't let you go unless you bless me."*

He said to him, *"What is your name?"*

He said, *"Jacob."*

He said, *"Your name will no longer be called Jacob, but Israel*[19]*; for you have fought with God and with men, and have prevailed."* (Gen 32:26-28)

Before arriving back in Hebron, one more son was to be born to Rachel and Israel, Benjamin. Rachel died giving birth.

These are the twelve sons of Jacob.[20] *The sons of Leah: Reuben (Jacob's firstborn), Simeon, Levi, Judah, Issachar, and Zebulun. The sons of Rachel: Joseph and Benjamin. The sons of Bilhah (Rachel's servant): Dan and Naphtali. The sons of Zilpah (Leah's servant): Gad and Asher.* (Gen 35:23-26)

Joseph is Sold into Slavery

Joseph was seventeen when he had a dream. In the dream, he was binding sheaves of grain with his brothers in the field. His sheaf rose up and stood tall, and his brothers' sheaves gathered around and bowed down. His brothers, who already hated him because their father, Israel,

---

[18] Either an Angel or God himself.
[19] Yet another account of God renaming one of his chosen.
[20] To be known as the 12 tribes of Israel.

loved him above them,[21] mocked the dream, saying, "So you want to lord it over us?"

Joseph had a second dream, this time, it was the sun and the moon and eleven stars bowing to him. Even Israel, on hearing the dream, scolded him. *"What is this dream that you have dreamed? Will I and your mother and your brothers indeed come to bow ourselves down to the earth before you?"* (Gen 37:10)

There came a time when Joseph's brothers were out tending to their father's flock. Israel asked Joseph, who had not gone with them, to go out to them and bring back word. So off he set. His brothers could see him coming from a distance, as he was wearing a special long-sleeved coat which their father had given him.[22] Because they hated him, they schemed between themselves, *"Let's kill him, and cast him into one of the pits, and we will say, 'An evil animal has devoured him.' We will see what will become of his dreams."* (Gen 37:20)

Reuben was not happy with the plan and wanted to stop them, so told his brothers that whatever they do, they must not shed any of his blood (thus hoping he could somehow save him from the fate they had in store for him). When Joseph reached his brothers, they attacked him, pulled his coat off, and threw him into an empty well. They then casually sat down to eat.

Looking up from their meal, they saw a group of men approaching. Judah suggested to his brothers, *"Let's sell him to the Ishmaelites, and not let our hand be on him; for he is our brother, our flesh."* (Gen 37:27)

They sold Joseph for twenty pieces of silver and watched him taken off to Egypt. Reuben, who wasn't there when the sale took place, was distressed when he discovered Joseph was gone. To cover their tracks, the brothers took Joseph's coat and covered it in the blood of a slaughtered

---

[21] Being the first born son of his wife Rachel.
[22] A special coat that no other brother received, this was the fabled technicolour dream coat.

goat, with the plan to tell their father there was a terrible accident and Joseph had fallen prey to an animal. When Israel heard the news, he was beyond consolation.

Joseph in Egypt

After arriving in Egypt, Joseph was sold to Potiphar, an official of Pharaoh. Potiphar and his household flourished while Joseph was there. Noticing *that God was with him, and that God made all that he did prosper in his hand, Joseph found favour in his sight. He ministered to him, and Potiphar made Joseph overseer of his house, and all that he had he put into his hand.* (Gen 39:3-4)

Potiphar's wife had eyes for Joseph and continually tried to seduce him - but he refused, for he knew the esteem with which they held him, and he didn't want to do anything to dishonour himself, or lose the trust placed in him. Determined not to give up, one day when few people were around, she tried again, this time grabbing him by his clothes and dragging him towards her. Joseph wriggled free and ran away. Left clutching his tunic in her hand, and ashamed by being rejected again, she screamed out for help, claiming Joseph had tried to seduce her. When Potiphar found out, he was enraged. He had Joseph arrested and locked up.

Two of Pharaoh's servants were also in jail with Joseph. One was the Pharaoh's cupbearer, the other the Pharaoh's chief baker. Joseph, because he had God's favour, had been elevated to jail supervisor and was assigned to attend to them both. One night both men had dreams and were still troubled by them in the morning when Joseph arrived. He asked them why they were so gloomy, and they answered they had dreams they couldn't understand and had no one to interpret them. Joseph offered to help.

After both men recounted their dreams, Joseph explained. He told the cupbearer his dream meant that in three days Pharaoh would release him from jail and he would be restored to his position as cupbearer.

After interpreting the dream, Joseph asked the cupbearer to use his freedom to try and have him released.

Hearing the interpretation, the chief baker was filled with hope for his own dream. Sadly, it wasn't good news. Joseph told him that in three days he would also leave prison, but in his case, it was to be hanged. In three days' time both dreams came to pass but the cupbearer completely forgot about Joseph.

Two years later, Pharaoh had a dream that greatly disturbed him. In the dream he saw seven fat and healthy cows eating by the river, and they were joined by seven other cows, but these were sickly and thin. The seven sickly and thin cows ate the seven fat and healthy cows. Another dream followed. This time, he saw a stalk with seven healthy ears of grain that were full and ripe. Behind this grew another stalk with seven meagre and scorched ears of grain. The scanty ears of grain swallowed the healthy ones. In the morning Pharaoh called his magicians and wise men, but none could interpret his dreams, until the cupbearer remembered the young Hebrew in jail who interpreted his dream. Pharaoh sent for Joseph immediately.

Joseph interpreted the dreams:

"*The dream of Pharaoh is one. What God is about to do he has declared to Pharaoh. The seven good cattle are seven years; and the seven good heads of grain are seven years. The dream is one. The seven thin and ugly cattle that came up after them are seven years, and also the seven empty heads of grain blasted with the East wind; they will be seven years of famine.*" (Gen 41:25-27)

"*The dream was doubled to Pharaoh, because the thing is established by God, and God will shortly bring it to pass.*" (Gen 41:32)

"*Now therefore let Pharaoh look for a discreet and wise man and set him over the land of Egypt. Let Pharaoh do this, and let him appoint overseers over the land, and take up the fifth part of the land of Egypt's produce in the seven plenteous years. Let them gather all the food of these good years that come, and store grain under the hand of Pharaoh for food in the cities and let them keep it. The food will be to supply the land against the seven years of famine, which will be in the land of Egypt; so that the land will not perish through the famine."* (Gen 41:33-36)

Pharaoh was so impressed with Joseph and his abilities he appointed him as his chancellor to oversee all aspects of protecting Egypt from this famine. Joseph was elevated above everyone else in Egypt, except Pharaoh himself. Joseph was thirty years of age.

Joseph took a wife, and her name was Asenath. He travelled throughout Egypt, overseeing every aspect of grain growth. Nothing was done in Egypt without Joseph's approval. During the seven years of plenty, the crops were harvested and stored in amounts never seen before. During these seven years Joseph had two sons, Manasseh, and Ephraim. Once the famine started, people from all over the world came to Egypt to buy grain from Joseph.

Joseph's Brothers Journey to Egypt

The famine eventually hit the land of Canaan and the home of Israel. Hearing the news that grain could be bought in Egypt, he sent ten of his sons there.[23] Arriving in Egypt the brothers were brought before Joseph, and they bowed their heads low as a sign of respect. Joseph immediately recognised them - but they did not recognise him. Joseph remembered the dream he had when he was seventeen and accused them of being spies. His brothers vehemently denied the accusations, saying they had only come to buy grain. "No," said Joseph, "you are spies!"

"We, your servants, are twelve brothers, the sons of one man in the land of Canaan; and behold, the youngest is today with our father, and one is no more." (Gen 42:13)

---

[23] Still reeling from losing his favourite son Joseph, Israel kept his youngest son Benjamin at home with him.

Joseph locked them up for three days.

On the third day Joseph spoke to his brothers demanding, that if they were honest men as they say and not spies, to leave one of their number behind while the rest return home with the grain they need; but they must immediately return with the youngest brother. Reuben was troubled hearing this, telling his brothers God was holding them accountable for what they did to their brother Joseph. At this time, they were speaking in their own language, believing no one could understand them, but Joseph could. He left them and wept. When he returned, he chose Simeon as the brother to remain.

Joseph ordered that they receive all the grain they needed. He also secretly had the money they gave as payment for the grain put back into their sacks. Camping the first night on the return journey, one brother discovered the money. Their hearts collectively sank, as they once again assumed they were being punished by God. Returning to their father they gave a full account of what had happened, and Israel said to them, *"You have bereaved me of my children! Joseph is no more, Simeon is no more, and you want to take Benjamin away. All these things are against me."*

Reuben spoke to his father, saying, "Kill my two sons, if I don't bring him to you. Entrust him to my care, and I will bring him to you again." (Gen 42:36-37)

Despite their pleas, Israel would not relent, but as the famine got worse, he tried again to send them back without Benjamin. They explained to their father how the man who released them was resolute that unless they returned with their youngest brother, they would not be allowed in his presence. Eventually Israel had no choice but to send Benjamin back with them.

Joseph's Brothers Return to Egypt Again

Arriving back in Egypt with Benjamin, they presented themselves again to Joseph, who, on seeing them, whispered to one of his men to take them to his home and to prepare a feast for them. Still not knowing it was their brother Joseph, they were all terrified, thinking they were about to be punished for having the money in their sacks, and spoke to Joseph's servant.

"*Oh, my lord, we indeed came down the first time to buy food. When we came to camp, we opened our sacks, and behold, each man's money was in the mouth of his sack... We have brought it back in our hand. We have brought down other money in our hand to buy food. We don't know who put our money in our sacks.*"

He said, "Peace be to you. Don't be afraid. Your God, and the God of your father, has given you treasure in your sacks. I received your money." He brought Simeon out to them. (Gen 43:20-23)

Joseph came to meet them and asked numerous questions about them and their father, but when he saw Benjamin, he was overcome by sentiment and needed to excuse himself as he didn't want them to see him cry.[24] He gave an order to fill their sacks with as much grain as they could carry, and to again send the money back. This time he also hid a silver cup in Benjamin's sack.

Not long after they left to return home, Joseph sent a servant after them with orders to ask them why they would repay his kindness with theft. When the servant caught up with the brothers, they were indignant, assuring him there was no way they would ever steal anything from Joseph. They were so confident, they agreed that if it was found, the person responsible would return to Egypt as a slave. When the cup was found in Benjamin's sack, they all returned to Egypt to beg Joseph not to enslave Benjamin, saying it would kill their father to lose a second son. Reuben spoke up and pleaded again, explaining to Joseph he had placed his own two children's lives as surety for the safe return of Benjamin.

---

[24] Benjamin was Joseph's only 'full blood' brother.

Joseph Reveals Himself

Overcome with emotion, Joseph asked his servants to leave the room so he could speak to the brothers in private. Once they were alone Joseph revealed himself to them. *"I am Joseph! Does my father still live?"*

His brothers couldn't answer him; for they were stunned. Joseph said to his brothers, "Come near to me, please."

They came near. He said, "I am Joseph, your brother, whom you sold into Egypt. Now don't be grieved, nor angry with yourselves, that you sold me here, for God sent me before you to preserve life... God sent me before you to preserve for you a remnant on earth... So know it wasn't you who sent me here, but God, and he has made me a father to Pharaoh, lord of all his house, and ruler over all the land of Egypt. Hurry, and go to my father, and tell him, 'This is what your son Joseph says, God has made me lord of all Egypt. Come down to me. Don't wait.'" (Gen 45:3-9)

He threw his arms around Benjamin and wept. He forgave and kissed all his brothers.

By this stage Pharaoh had become aware of what was happening, and told Joseph to send for the rest of his family and bring them all to Egypt, where he would bestow on them the finest lands to settle in. He even told them to leave behind all their belongings, for the best Egypt offered was theirs.

Returning home to Canaan, the brothers told their father the good news about Joseph.

Israel Moves his Family to Egypt

On his way to Egypt, God spoke to Israel again, reassuring him of his divine plan for him and his family.

Seeing Joseph, Israel said he could die happy knowing he was alive and well. Pharaoh was true to his word and allowed them to settle in Egypt.

The famine continued, and eventually there was no money left for anyone to buy grain, so Joseph began taking livestock as payment. When the livestock was gone, he took land. Eventually Pharaoh owned everything and still there was famine. Joseph told the people he would give them seed to sow their land, but in return one-fifth of all the produce must be returned to Pharaoh as tax. The Egyptians agreed, effectively becoming serfs to Pharaoh.

Israel died at one hundred and forty-seven years old. When he died, Joseph and his brothers stayed on in Egypt and prospered. Joseph died at one hundred and ten.

EXODUS

Moses is a pivotal figure of the Old Testament. He is responsible for liberating the Hebrews from Egypt and leading them to the Promised Land. He is also the first person God directly reveals himself to. Moses didn't have an easy life. In the forty years he was wandering through the desert between Egypt and Canaan, he had to deal with a rebellious, hard-nosed, quarrelsome group of people, with short memories.

Repeatedly throughout their time in the desert, the Hebrews turned away from God, doubting him, rebelling against him and being problematic. Time and time again Moses petitioned on their behalf, as God would seek revenge on their godless ways. If not for Moses the Old Testament could not be, (this makes the fact that Moses' exclusion from ever entering the Promised Land particularly poignant, considering he made only one mistake during the four decades.)

Moses was also the one chosen by God to be given the Ten Commandments. In fact, he was entrusted with passing down all the foundational laws God prescribed for his people to live by.

Moses

As the years passed, Pharaoh died and with him the favour and protection that Joseph had won for his family and people. Their population was growing fast and strong, and the new Pharaoh saw them as a threat, and feared an uprising. So, he forced them into slavery and ordered his slave drivers to work them hard and wear them down in the hope they would not have the energy to revolt against him.

Pharaoh's fear of the Hebrews got to the point where he decided, in order to control their numbers, he would have all male babies killed at birth. This was accomplished by issuing an order to the Hebrew midwives to kill all boys. The midwives, however, did not obey the orders, telling Pharaoh their women were strong and gave birth without the help of a midwife.

Pharaoh decreed all boys born to the Hebrews were to be thrown into the river.

During this decree, a baby boy was born to the tribe of Levi. The mother kept the birth secret for three months, but fearing he would be found, she put him in a basket and sent him out onto the river. Secretly watching on was the baby's older sister.

Pharaoh's daughter[25] was down by the river bathing when she spotted the floating basket. Telling a maid to retrieve it, she found the child wrapped in a Hebrew cloth. She decided to keep the baby as her own. Seeing the events unfold, the baby's sister, who was an attendant to Pharaoh's daughter, quickly offered to find a suitable wet nurse from among the Hebrews. The wet nurse found was the babies mother. The baby was named Moses, and was treated as a son by Pharaoh's daughter.

When Moses was an adult, he went to visit his fellow Hebrews[26] and while he was out he came across an Egyptian who was beating a slave. Enraged, Moses killed the Egyptian. The following day he saw two Hebrews fighting. Approaching them, he pulled them apart and asked them why they were fighting. They replied, *"Who made you a prince and a judge over us? Do you plan to kill me, as you killed the Egyptian?"* (Ex 2:14)

---

[25] Believed to be called Bithiah.
[26] The Hollywood portrayal of Moses incorrectly suggests that neither Moses nor the Pharaoh's daughter knew of his true heritage.

This frightened Moses (thinking the news would reach Pharaoh), so he fled Egypt for Midian.

Resting by a well, Moses watched seven women (daughters of Jethro, the priest of Midian) drawing water from a well when some shepherds came along and pushed them out of the way so they could water their stock. Moses came to the women's defence.

Returning home, the women told their father what happened. When he heard how an Egyptian came to their aid, he sent for him. Moses ended up staying with the family in Midian and marrying one of the daughters, Zipporah. They had a son, Gershom.

Meanwhile, back in Egypt, *the children of Israel sighed because of the bondage, and they cried, and their cry came up to God because of the bondage. God heard their groaning, and God remembered his covenant with Abraham, with Isaac, and with Jacob. God saw the children of Israel, and God understood.* (Ex 2:23-25)

Moses is Called by God

One day, as Moses was attending his flock he encountered a burning bush, but it was no ordinary fire, for while there was a flame the bush itself was not being burnt. Intrigued by this, he walked closer and then heard the voice of God.

"*Don't come close. Take off your sandals, for the place you are standing on is holy ground.*" He said, "*I am the God of your father, the God of Abraham, the God of Isaac, and the God of Jacob.*"

Moses hid his face because he was afraid to look at God.

God said, "I have surely seen the affliction of my people who are in Egypt, and have heard their cry because of their taskmasters, for I know their sorrows. I have come down to deliver them out of the land of the Egyptians, and to bring them up out of that land to a good and large land, to a land flowing with milk and honey...Come now and I will send you to Pharaoh, that you may bring my people, the children of Israel, out of Egypt." (Ex 3:5-10)

Moses' first reaction was to reject the call, claiming he was not worthy, not capable, and afraid. He worried specifically about why the Hebrews in Egypt would even listen to him.

He said to God, *"When I come to the children of Israel, and tell them, 'The God of your fathers has sent me to you,' and they ask me, 'What is his name?' What should I tell them?"*[27]

God said to Moses, *"I AM WHO I AM"*[28], and he said, *"You shall tell the children of Israel this: 'I AM has sent me to you.'" God said to Moses, "You shall tell the children of Israel this, 'Yahweh, the God of your fathers, the God of Abraham, the God of Isaac, and the God of Jacob, has sent me to you.' This is my name forever, and this is my memorial to all generations."* (Ex 3:13-15)

Still not convinced he was suitable for the job, he challenged God again, asking, "What if they don't believe me?"

God gave Moses a sign to help - telling him to throw his shepherd's staff onto the ground. Obeying, Moses saw the staff turn into a snake, and when he picked it up, it reformed back into his staff. Moses was headstrong though and needed further convincing. This time God said to place his hand on his chest inside his tunic. When he pulled his hand

---

[27] In those days, to have no name is to have no existence in reality: when one's name is blotted out, one ceases to exist. To give a name is to confer identity and not merely to distinguish from other individuals or species: when God creates, he gives a name to each object of his creation. Brown, Raymond E., et al. The Jerome Biblical Commentary. Prentice-Hall, 1968. [77:6]

[28] The revelation of the name Yahweh to Israel through Moses represented a new and fuller revelation of the personal reality of Yahweh. Israel knows it's God by this name and no further definition or qualification is needed. By this name he is proclaimed as the personal divine being who has revealed himself to Israel. The distinctive name Yahweh indicates that he is a personal being whose essence and attributes can be shared by no other being. Brown, Raymond E., et al. The Jerome Biblical Commentary. Prentice-Hall, 1968. [77:13]

out it was covered with leprosy. When he put his hand back and withdrew it again, it was restored to normal.

Sensing Moses might need even more convincing, God said that if the first two signs were not enough to convince the Hebrews that Moses was sent by God to free them, then he was to use a jug to draw water from the river and pour it onto the ground. The water from the jug would pour as blood onto the ground.

Moses continued to debate with God, complaining he wasn't good at speaking to large groups of people and wondering if he wasn't right for the task. Getting angry with Moses, God told him to get his brother Aaron to be his spokesman to the Hebrews, and Moses would be the spokesman for God.

Moses, Aaron In Egypt

Moses and Aaron left for Egypt to meet with Pharaoh. Moses told Pharaoh what God wanted - which was to let the Hebrews leave Egypt for three days so they could make a sacrifice to God, at the same time warning him that a refusal would cause the wrath of God to fall on him. Not only did Pharaoh refuse, but he ordered his slave masters to drive the Hebrews even harder than before. As a result, the Hebrews turned on Moses. Moses turned to God, asking him why he was making life so difficult for them.

This was all part of God's plan - to make Pharaoh stubborn, so when he was finished, no one would ever doubt God and his love for his people.

Moses and Aaron returned to petition Pharaoh again, this time showing him the marvel of turning his staff into a snake, but Pharaoh summoned his magicians, who performed the same transformation.

The First Plague

Returning once more to Pharaoh, Aaron held his staff over the river, and the water turned to blood, and the fish died, making it impossible to drink. Pharaoh turned to his magicians, who again were able to perform the same feat. Pharaoh stayed stubborn.

Seven days later, God sent Moses and Aaron back to Pharaoh with the message, *"Let my people go, that they may serve me."* (Ex 8:1)

The Second Plague

Pharaoh refused, so God told Moses that Aaron should stretch out his hand over the lands, and a plague of frogs covered Egypt. Pharaoh's magicians did the same. However, this time he said to Moses that if his God would rid them of the frogs, he would let his people leave to make a sacrifice. Moses prayed to God and God answered. As soon as Pharaoh saw the frogs die away, he became stubborn again and would not let the Hebrews leave.

The Third Plague

On their next visit, Aaron was told to strike the ground with his staff, creating a swarm of mosquitoes like the world had never seen. They attacked both man and beast. Pharaoh's magicians could not replicate this plague and finally admitted this to Pharaoh, but as God had foretold, Pharaoh refused to listen.

The Fourth Plague

Next, God told Moses to go out and meet Pharaoh and inform him that if he continued to refuse to listen, the ensuing plague would be horseflies, which would infest and infect everyone and everything. But as a sign of God's power, he would set apart the land where the Hebrews lived, so Pharaoh could witness for himself how God can punish the Egyptians but not his people.

Pharaoh called Moses to him to plead with him to remove the horseflies. In return he would let the people travel for a three-day journey from Egypt to sacrifice to God. But, as before, once the plague subsided, Pharaoh went back on his word and would not let them go.

The Fifth Plague

The next act of God was the death of all livestock owned by the Pharaoh and the Egyptians. Everything died; nothing survived except the Hebrews' livestock, where none died.

The Sixth Plague

God then sent a plague of boils, which broke out on all the Egyptians.

Calling Moses to him, Pharaoh (again) admitted defeat, but as soon as God stopped the boils, he reneged.

The Seventh Plague

Next, God brought an intense hailstorm on Egypt, like nothing ever seen before. Accompanied by thunder and lightning, hail struck every man and beast, ruined crops, and split trees in half.

The Eighth Plague

God said to Moses, "Go to Pharaoh, for I have hardened his heart..., that I may show these my signs among them; and that you may tell in the hearing of your son, and of your son's son, what things I have done to Egypt, and my signs which I have done among them; that you may know that I am God."

Moses and Aaron went to Pharaoh, and said to him, "This is what Yahweh, the God of the Hebrews, says: 'How long will you refuse to humble yourself before me? Let my people go, that they may serve me. Or else, if you refuse to let my people go, behold, tomorrow I will bring locusts into your country, and they shall cover the surface of the earth, so that one won't be able to see the earth. They shall eat the residue of that which has escaped, which remains to you from the hail, and shall eat every tree which grows for you out of the field. Your houses shall be filled, and the houses of all your servants, and the houses of all the Egyptians, as neither your fathers nor your fathers' fathers have seen, since the day that they were on the earth to this day.''' (Ex 10:1-6)

Pharaoh, seemingly realising he was on the losing side, agreed to let them go and worship God, but he would not let everyone go; (he wanted only the men to go, leaving the women and children, for he feared they would never return otherwise). So, the locust plague was brought down on Egypt.

Again, Pharaoh agreed to let the Hebrews go until a strong wind removed the plague, and he went back on his word.

The Ninth Plague

Next, God created a darkness over all Egypt, where no one could see or move about for three days, but where the Hebrews lived, there was light. Pharaoh softened and allowed them all to go, but he drew the line at taking their livestock. Moses explained there could be no sacrifice to God without livestock. Pharaoh refused, this time adding that if they came back to him again, he would kill them.

The Tenth and Final Plague

God had one last disaster in store for Pharaoh and Egypt - all the first-borns in the land of Egypt would die. There would be no distinction between Pharaoh, servants, and livestock. All Egyptians would suffer the same fate, but to prove God discriminates, no Hebrew would suffer death.

God gave the Hebrews specific and detailed instructions on how they were to avoid the plague of death he was going to send. Part of which was to kill a year-old sheep or goat and use their blood to paint their doorposts and lintels, as a sign for death not to enter, or to Passover.[29]

When death came, terror filled every Egyptian home, including Pharaoh's. In the morning, Pharaoh summoned Moses and exclaimed, *"Rise up, get out from among my people, both you and the children of Israel; and go serve God, as you have said! Take both your flocks and your herds, as you have said, and be gone; and bless me also!"* (Ex 12:31-32)

Departure from Egypt

When Pharaoh had let the people go, God did not let them take the road to the land of the Philistines, although that was the nearest way. God thought that the prospect of fighting would make the people lose heart and turn back to Egypt. Instead, God led the people by the roundabout way of the wilderness to the Sea of Reeds. (Ex 13:17-18*)

As they left Egypt, God guided them by a pillar of cloud during the day, and a pillar of fire at night. Not finished humiliating Pharaoh, God instructed Moses to make camp beside the sea, so Pharaoh and his spies would think they were lost and would come to pursue them, allowing God one more chance to show his power. Then all Egypt would know that he is God.

Pharaoh set off to capture and destroy the Hebrews. Encamped by the sea, the Hebrews saw Pharaoh approaching in the distance and turned on Moses saying, *"Because there are no graves in Egypt, have you*

---

[29] The sacrifice of Jesus is seen as the fulfilment of the Passover. Jesus is often referred to as the 'Lamb of God', highlighting the parallels between the Passover lamb and his role in salvation. Just as the blood of the lamb protected the Israelites from death, the blood of Jesus, shed on the cross, provided spiritual deliverance and protection. Both the Passover and Jesus' sacrifice show God's love and plan to save his people, connecting the Old Testament and New Testament with stories of deliverance. *(unknown source)*

taken us away to die in the wilderness? Why have you treated us this way, to bring us out of Egypt? Isn't this the word that we spoke to you in Egypt, saying, 'Leave us alone, that we may serve the Egyptians?' For it would have been better for us to serve the Egyptians than to die in the wilderness." (Ex 14:11-12)

Moses reassured them that God had a plan, and they would escape the clutches of Pharaoh and Egypt forever. *"Have no fear! Stand firm, and you will see what Yahweh will do to save you today: the Egyptians you see today, you will never see again. Yahweh will do the fighting for you: you have only to keep still."* (Ex 14:13-14)

The Parting of the Red Sea

Instructed by God, Moses held his staff out over the sea, and an extreme wind blew up, which divided it into two, leaving a dry stretch of land for the Hebrews to cross. In the distance, Pharaoh could see what was happening. He gave chase and followed the Hebrews into the divided sea. Once the Hebrews were through and safely on the other side, Moses again raised his staff and the water flowed back, collapsing onto the Egyptians. None survived.

Seeing the might and power of God, the Hebrews believed and put their faith in God.

Bread from Heaven

As Moses led the Hebrews away into the desert, it didn't take long for them to return to their complaining.

"We wish that we had died by God's hand in the land of Egypt, when we sat by the meat pots, when we ate our fill of bread, for you have brought us out into this wilderness to kill everyone with hunger?" (Ex 16:3)

To feed them and prove he would meet all their needs, God made it rain down bread from heaven in the evenings, while in the mornings, quail covered the ground. Along with the food, there also came strict

Building of the Sanctuary

God prescribed explicit and meticulous instructions on the building of a sanctuary - a Tent of Meeting - the place in which the Ark of the Covenant was located.

Moses continued to lead the people through the desert, always preceded by the cloud of God, which would appear outside the Tent of Meeting.

At every stage of their journey, whenever the cloud rose from the tabernacle the sons of Israel would resume their march. If the cloud did not rise, they waited and would not march until it did. For the cloud of Yahweh rested on the tabernacle by day, and a fire shone within the cloud by night, for all the House of Israel to see. And so it was for every stage of their journey. (Ex 40:36-38*)

LEVITICUS

There are numerous references to sacrifice in the Old Testament. The meaning behind them all is complex, but for the purposes here, regard it as a means by which the Israelites could give God a gift. They chose something they owned and that was valuable to them, such as an animal from their flock, or produce from their fields - items they could have consumed themselves. Similarly with incense, it was a pleasing smell that they offered to God in the hope that it would bring him joy.

Leviticus also examines in great detail the laws pertaining to many aspects of Israelite life and is widely believed to have been written during the exile of the House of Judah in Babylon; to assist the people on their return to Jerusalem by ensuring they had access to the Laws of God needed to re-establish themselves.

God Continues his Law Giving

In the laws and rules set down by God, some significant ones were related to sacrifices. God set specific and detailed instructions on the different types of ritual sacrifice and the different reasons for them.

The first type of sacrifice mentioned was Holocaust.[33] This was a burnt offering of a male animal from the herd, or if there was no herd, it was to be a male lamb or goat. It could also be a turtledove or a young

---

[33] Lev 1

pigeon. Whatever the animal was, there were strict instructions that none of the fat or the blood of the animal was to be eaten. They were to be burnt on the altar as an offering to God.

The second type was Oblation.[34] This was a sacrifice of agricultural produce, either wheaten flour on which wine and incense were poured, or unleavened bread, broken and poured over with oil.

Third, was a Communion sacrifice, or peace offering.[35] This was very similar to the burnt offering, but only the liver and kidneys were burnt.

Next was the sacrifice for sin,[36] which had differing requirements depending on whether it related to sins of the high priest, the community, the leaders, or individuals.

God instructed Moses to bring his brother Aaron, and all his sons, to the Tent of Meeting, for he was going to bless them and confer on them and the tribe of Levi the position of priests.

"They shall be holy to their God, and not profane the name of their God, for they offer the offerings of Yahweh made by fire, the bread of their God. Therefore, they shall be holy.

"They shall not marry a woman who is a prostitute. A priest shall not marry a woman divorced from her husband; for he is holy to his God. Therefore, you shall sanctify him, for he offers the bread of your God. He shall be holy to you, for I Yahweh, who sanctify you, am holy." (Lev 21:6-8)

God continued to hand down many laws that contained great details.[37] There were laws covering clean and unclean animals; anything from the sea, birds, insects, rodents, and lizards. There were laws covering the purification of a woman after childbirth, leprosy, boils, burns, skin disease, rashes, loss of hair and the bodily discharges of men and women.

---

[34] Lev 2
[35] Lev 3
[36] Lev 4
[37] 613 in total.

God banned all the sexual practices which were rife in Egypt. Specifically, he forbade intercourse between brothers and sisters, with one's father or mother, with one's son or daughter, with one's father-in-law or mother-in-law, with any aunts, uncles, or cousins, with anyone of the same sex, or with animals.[38]

Other laws included men not cutting off their beards, standing for people with grey hair, not sending their daughters into prostitution, and not molesting strangers.

Solemn feasts were established, particularly covering how to honour and keep holy the Sabbath Day and the Passover.

---

[38] Lev 20

NUMBERS

Numbers is about God dwelling among his people. It underscores God's unwavering commitment to his people (despite their disobedience and unfaithfulness). It also affirms that despite God's love and faithfulness, he will punish wrongdoings.[39]

The first eight chapters primarily focus on recording a census of the tribes of Israel.

The Census of the Israelites

Moses was commanded by God to take a census of all the *children of Israel, by their families, by their fathers' houses, according to the number of the names from twenty years old and upward, all who are able to go out to war in Israel.* (Nm 1:2-3)

The names of the families were: Reuben, Simeon, Judah, Issachar, Zebulun, Ephraim, and Manasseh (from Joseph), Benjamin, Dan, Asher, Gad, and Naphtali.

The family of Levi was not counted in the census, as God set them apart to be priests, saying, *"They shall keep God's requirements, and the requirements of the whole congregation before the Tent of Meeting, to do the service of the tabernacle. They shall keep all the furnishings of the Tent of Meeting, and the obligations of the children of Israel, to do the service of the tabernacle."* (Nm 3:7-8)

---

[39] Power, F.J., Pujolas, M., McLarnon, D.H. Guide to Reading the New Testament. Messenger of the sacred heart, 1978.

The Passover and Departure

In the second year of the exodus in the wilderness, God instructed Moses to commemorate the Passover. *Moses told the children of Israel that they should keep the Passover. They kept the Passover in the first month, on the fourteenth day of the month at evening, in the wilderness of Sinai. According to all that Yahweh commanded Moses, so the children of Israel did.* (Nm 9:4-5)

Throughout the journey through the Sinai wilderness, God remained with his people in the form of a cloud above the tabernacle. While ever the cloud remained stationary above the tabernacle, the people camped and worshipped. When it lifted away, they broke camp until the cloud settled again.

The People Complain

As time passed, the people strayed in their faithfulness. One day they *were complaining in the ears of Yahweh. When Yahweh heard it, his anger burned; and Yahweh's fire burned among them and consumed some outskirts of the camp.* (Nm 11:1)

The people appealed to Moses to save them, and he went to ask God. *"Why have you treated your servant so badly? Why haven't I found favour in your sight, that you lay the burden of all this people on me? Have I conceived all this people? Have I brought them out, that you should tell me, 'Carry them in your bosom, as a nurse carries a nursing infant, to the land which you swore to their fathers?'... I am not able to bear all this people alone, because it is too heavy for me. If you treat me this way, please kill me right now..."* (Nm 11:11-15)

God instructed Moses to gather seventy elders from the families of Israel, saying he would pass onto them some of the spirit that he had, until now, only placed on Moses.

Soon after, Aaron complained to Moses that it was unfair that God spoke to him only. God overheard this and was quick to intercede, not holding back on the truth of the matter. *"Now hear my words. If there is a prophet among you, I, Yahweh, will make myself known to him in a vision. I will speak with him in a dream. My servant Moses is not so. He is faithful in all my house. With him, I will speak mouth to mouth, even plainly, and not in riddles; and he shall see Yahweh's form. Why then were you not afraid to speak against my servant, against Moses?"* (Nm 12:6-8)

The First Sight of The Promised Land

As they continued their journey, Moses chose twelve men from among the tribes of Israel to be led by Joshua to reconnoitre the land of Canaan - the land promised by God. They were to see what type of land it was, who the inhabitants were, whether they were strong or weak, many or few, and whether there were any fortifications. After forty days, they returned to Moses, declaring the land 'flowed with milk and honey', yet at the same time the towns were well fortified, and the people were big and strong. In fact, they described the inhabitants as being giants, adding that they felt as small as grasshoppers in comparison. There were many discussions and arguments between those who were sent to reconnoitre the land as to whether they could be defeated or not.

Threats of Revolt

Many of the reconnaissance party (who were not in favour of attacking the towns for fear of defeat) went among the people to stir up trouble. Hearing the stories, the people again doubted the ability of God to protect them, so much so that they started making overtures about going back to Egypt. Moses, Aaron, and Joshua pleaded with the people not to abandon God and his plans for them, saying that with God at their side, no one could defeat them. The people instead wanted to stone them to death. This enraged God.

"How long will this people despise me? How long will they not believe in me, for all the signs which I have worked among them? I will strike them

with pestilence, and disinherit them, and will make of you a nation greater and mightier than they." (Num 14:11-12)

Moses, yet again, interceded for the Israelites and pleaded with God not to punish them. Again, God consented, but with the condition that none of the people who had disobeyed him would ever get to settle in the promised land of Canaan. Those of the advanced reconnaissance party who stirred the people up were put to death. Only Joshua and Caleb were saved, for they never doubted God.

The banned people could not accept that they would not get to see the promised land, so some of them set off on their own to claim the land. Moses appealed to them not to go, saying that without God at their side they would have no chance. They did not listen and were soundly defeated.

Although the Israelites often insulted God, Moses and Aaron had always been righteous - but for one fateful day. It followed another instance of the Israelites complaining to Moses about the lack of water. Hearing their plea, God instructed Moses and Aaron to stand by a rock and command that water flow from it. They did, but they also hit the rock twice with a staff, and this hadn't been ordered by God. Their punishment for not completely relying on God was to be banned from ever reaching the promised land. They would both die in the desert.

Yahweh said to Moses, "Go up into this mountain of Abraham, and see the land which I have given to the children of Israel. When you have seen it, you also shall be gathered to your people, as Aaron your brother was gathered; because in the strife of the congregation, you rebelled against my word in the wilderness of Zin, to honour me as holy at the waters before their eyes." (Nm 27:12-14)

Yahweh said to Moses, "Take Joshua the son of Nun, a man in whom is the Spirit, and lay your hand on him... You shall give authority to him, that all the congregation of the children of Israel may obey... At his word they shall go out, and at his word they shall come in, both he and all the children of Israel with him, even all the congregation." (Nm 27:18-21)

DEUTERONOMY

As the Israelites' journey progressed towards Canaan, they encountered many towns and people whose land they had to cross to continue onwards. These crossings were considered as trespasses and many battles ensued, but when God was with them, they always triumphed.

Rev Michael Duggan wrote in 'The Consuming Fire', that Deuteronomy is the last will and testament of Moses.[40] His message and plea to the people is summed up in Dt 6:4-9.

"Listen, Israel: Yahweh our God is the one Yahweh. You shall love Yahweh your God with all your heart, with all your soul, with all your strength. Let these words I urge on you today be written on your heart. You shall repeat them to your children and say them over to them whether at rest in your house or walking abroad, at your lying down or at your rising; you shall fasten them on your hand as a sign and on your forehead as a circlet; you shall write them on the doorposts of your house and on your gates."

Moses' Final Words

Knowing he would not live in the promised land along with his fellow Israelites, Moses meticulously retold the exodus story to the people, reminding them of God's call, promises, expectations, and punishments.

---

[40] p137

Beginning at Horeb, where God gave them the Ten Commandments, Moses recounted all their trials, tribulations, and falls from faith, ending with, *"Know therefore today, and take it to heart, that Yahweh himself is God in heaven above and on the earth beneath. There is no one else. You shall keep his statutes and his commandments which I command you today, that it may go well with you and with your children after you, and that you may prolong your days in the land which Yahweh your God gives you for all time."* (Dt 4:39-40)

He then moved on to elaborate the salient points of the Ten Commandments.

1. *You shall have no other gods before me.*
2. *You shall not make a carved image for yourself... You shall not bow yourself down to them, nor serve them, for I, Yahweh your God, am a jealous God, visiting the iniquity of the fathers on the children and on the third and on the fourth generation of those who hate me, and showing loving kindness to thousands of those who love me and keep my commandments.*
3. *You shall not misuse the name of Yahweh your God; for Yahweh will not hold him guiltless who misuses his name.*
4. *Observe the Sabbath day, to keep it holy, as Yahweh your God commanded you. You shall labour six days and do all your work; but the seventh day is a Sabbath to Yahweh your God, in which you shall not do any work.*
5. *Honour your father and your mother, as Yahweh your God commanded you, that your days may be long and that it may go well with you in the land which Yahweh your God gives you.*
6. *You shall not murder.*
7. *You shall not commit adultery.*
8. *You shall not steal.*
9. *You shall not give false testimony against your neighbour.*

10. *You shall not covet your neighbour's wife. Neither shall you desire your neighbour's house, his field… or anything that is your neighbour's.* (Dt 5:7-21)

"Remember all the ways which Yahweh your God has led you these forty years in the wilderness, that he might humble you, to test you, to know what was in your heart, whether you would keep his commandments or not. He humbled you, allowed you to be hungry, and fed you with manna, which you didn't know, neither did your fathers know, that he might teach you that man does not live by bread only, but man lives by every word that proceeds out of Yahweh's mouth."[41] (Dt 8:2-3)

Moses warned the people that it isn't anything good in them that caused God to bring them to a safe place but rather, it was the wickedness of everyone else. *"Not for your righteousness or for the uprightness of your heart do you go in to possess their land; but for the wickedness of these nations Yahweh your God does drive them out from before you, and that he may establish the word which Yahweh swore to your fathers, to Abraham, to Isaac, and to Jacob. Know therefore that Yahweh your God doesn't give you this good land to possess for your righteousness, for you are a stiff-necked people."* (Dt 9:5-6)

Three times during his discourse Moses paraphrases one pertinent point. *"Now, Israel, what does Yahweh your God require of you, but to fear Yahweh your God, to walk in all his ways, to love him, and to serve Yahweh your God with all your heart and with all your soul."*[42] (Dt 10:12)

Moses moves on to say, *"The statutes and the ordinances which you shall observe to do in the land which Yahweh, the God of your fathers, has given you to possess, all the days that you live on the earth."* (Dt 12:1)

---

[41] Jesus was to quote this line of Scripture during his forty days in the desert.
[42] See also Dt 6:4: Dt 10:12

These include.

"You shall surely destroy all the places in which the nations that you shall dispossess served their gods." (Dt 12:2)

"You must seek Yahweh your God only in the place he himself will choose from among all our tribes." (Dt 12:5*)

"Do not imitate any other gods you come upon."

"Beware of false prophets, and live by the rule that if they say, 'Let's go after other gods' (which you have not known) 'and let's serve them,' you shall not listen to the words of that prophet, or to that dreamer of dreams; for Yahweh your God is testing you, to know whether you love Yahweh your God with all your heart and with all your soul." (Dt 13:2-3)

Moses mentioned clean and unclean animals and annual tithes of all that their land yields (to be eaten alongside a firstborn from their flock or herd). Every three years, the tithe is not to be eaten but given to the Levites who had no land or livestock.

The importance of the observance of Passover and Unleavened Bread was emphasised.

Many other rules and regulations concerning the Levitical priests, prophets, murderers, captured towns and slaves, adultery, fornication, and divorce were handed down.

He also outlined how the lands of Canaan would be divided up among them, and he handed his leadership mantle to Joshua.

When he was finished, all his words were written into the Book of Law and given to the Levites to be placed beside the Ark of the Covenant. He then said, *"For I know that after my death you will utterly corrupt yourselves, and turn away from the way which I have commanded you; and evil will happen to you in the latter days, because you will do that which is evil in Yahweh's sight, to provoke him to anger through the work of your hands."* (Dt 31:29)

Moses was one hundred and twenty when he died. *Since then, there has not arisen a prophet in Israel like Moses, whom Yahweh knew face to face, in all the signs and the wonders which Yahweh sent him to do in the land of Egypt, to Pharaoh, and to all his servants, and to all his land, and in all the mighty hand, and in all the awesome deeds, which Moses did in the sight of all Israel.* (Dt 34:10-12)

THE HISTORICAL BOOKS

THE BOOK OF JOSHUA

Succeeding Moses, Joshua led the Israelites across the Jordan into the Promised Land of Canaan. This was neither a quick nor simple journey though, as numerous towns and Kingdoms resisted their advance.

God ensured their success, and each tribe was allotted land to settle down and begin their new lives, but not before Joshua warns them to stay faithful to God, who has given them so much.

The book covers a period of 1220 - 1200 BC.

Entering The Promised Land

Joshua, now in charge of the Israelites, is instructed by God to prepare everyone to cross the Jordan[43] and enter the Promised Land.

"*Moses my servant is dead. Now therefore arise, go across this Jordan, you and all these people, to the land which I am giving to them, even to the children of Israel. I have given you every place that the sole of your foot will tread on, as I told Moses....*

"*No man will be able to stand before you all the days of your life. As I was with Moses, so I will be with you. I will not fail you nor forsake you....*

"*Be careful to observe and to do according to all the Law which Moses my servant commanded you. Don't turn from it to the right hand or to the left, that you may have good success wherever you go....*

---

[43] They were on the East side and would cross to the West side.

"Be strong and courageous. Don't be afraid. Don't be dismayed, for Yahweh your God is with you wherever you go." (Jos 1:2-9)

Preparing to Cross the Jordan

Early on the day of crossing the Jordan, God told Joshua, *"Today I will begin to magnify you in the sight of all Israel, that they may know that as I was with Moses, so I will be with you."* (Jos 3:7)

The tribes of Israel[44] lined up behind the Ark of the Covenant and began their march towards Jericho. The priests carrying the ark were instructed to stop at the edge of the Jordan, and by doing so, the waters stopped flowing so all could cross over safely. The towns towards which they were marching had heard of the victories the Israelite God had brought them, and they feared them. When they heard about the drying up of the River Jordan, they were terrified.

Once across the river, they camped just outside Jericho in a place called Gilgal, where God renewed his covenant with the Israelites. As they had been wandering for so long, all the men initially circumcised were either dead or barred from entering the Promised Land, so God commanded all the men to be circumcised. The feast of Passover was then celebrated, and from that day forward, the manna from heaven, which had been falling, stopped, as they were now going to end their journey and plant their own crops.

And the Walls Come Tumbling Down

God sent an angel to Joshua and gave him instructions on how to be triumphant in the campaign of Jericho.

---

[44] At this stage there were only ten tribes left as the tribes of Reuben and Gad decided to stay on the eastern side of the River Jordan, citing that as they had the largest herds, the land on the East was best for them.

He was ordered to gather all the men who could fight and parade them in a column quietly behind the Ark of the Covenant, with a vanguard of trumpeters. For six days, the procession did one circuit around the walls of Jericho. On the seventh day, they marched around the walls seven times. On the seventh time, all the trumpets blew, and all the men gave up an ear-splitting war cry. When this happened, the walls of the city of Jericho collapsed. The fighting men raced in and conquered and stripped the town of all its gold and silver in preparation to burn it to the ground, with everyone still in it, but were under strict instructions not to take anything as booty.

Israel Take Ownership of the Land West of the Jordan

News of the Israelites', their God, and how he protected them to overcome all forces before them continued to spread to all the lands near the Jordan. One such town was Gibeon, which came up with a unique plan to save themselves. They conspired to trick the Israelites by leaving their town and travelling toward them in old worn clothes, with stale bread and broken wineskins, dragging their feet as if they had travelled a long distance, thus fooling them into thinking they were not local and therefore no threat. They even hoodwinked Joshua into negotiating a non-aggression treaty. By the time Joshua discovered the ruse, it was too late, and he wouldn't go back on his word.

The town of Gibeon was a principal town in the region, so when five of the local Kings[45] heard of their treaty, they resolved to sack the city themselves. The Gibeonites cried out to the Israelites to honour their treaty, so Joshua sent in fighting men and God brought them an easy victory. Some tried to retreat, and God rained down hailstones on them, killing them all. Those who were left in the town met an interesting end

---

[45] Amorite Kings of Jerusalem, Hebron, Jarmuth, Lachish, and Eglon.

- Joshua essentially gave God an order, telling him to keep the sun and moon still in the sky, while he and his troops could wreak havoc.

Joshua then took his army to the towns of the five kings and devastated each of them. News of the victories continued to spread and while resistance continued, every town that stood against the Israelites was defeated and the people put to death.

So Joshua took the entire land,[46] *according to all that Yahweh spoke to Moses; and Joshua gave it for an inheritance to Israel according to their divisions by their tribes. Then the land rested from war.* (Jos 11:23)

All that remained was to divide the territories up among the remaining nine tribes of Israel.[47] (The tribes of Reuben and Gad and the half-tribe of Manasseh had already received their allotment to the east of the Jordan).

Additionally, towns were set aside for the Levites, and for foreigners.

Joshua Reminds the Israelites of God's Divine Goodness

The years passed, and Joshua grew old. Before he died, he gathered all the tribal leaders together and reminded them how steadfast God had been, and even though all the kings and lands had been delivered to them, there was still much to conquer. He also gave them a warning.

"Just as every promise of good made to you by Yahweh your God has been fulfilled for you, so also will Yahweh fulfil against you all his threats of evil, even to driving you out of the good land that Yahweh your God has given you. For if you violate the covenant which Yahweh your God has demanded of you, if you go and serve other gods and bow down before them, then Yahweh's anger

---

[46] All the lands North, South and West of the Jordan, exceeding thirty five Kingdoms.
[47] While there were ten tribes left, the tribe of Levi was all priests and therefore were granted no land, they would live by the grace of God and through the tithes of land and money made by the remaining tribes of Israel. The nine remaining tribes were Asher, Dan, Judah, Naphtali, Simeon, Zebulan, Issachar, Joseph, Benjamin.

will be roused against you and you will quickly vanish from the good land that he has given you." (Jos 23:15-16*)

"...For he is a holy God. He is a jealous God. He will not forgive your disobedience nor your sins. If you forsake Yahweh, and serve foreign gods, then he will turn and do you evil, and consume you, after he has done you good."

The people said to Joshua, "No, but we will serve Yahweh." Joshua said to the people, "You are witnesses against yourselves that you have chosen Yahweh yourselves, to serve him."

They said, "We are witnesses." (Jos 24:19-22)

Nothing failed of any good thing which Yahweh had spoken to the house of Israel. All came to pass. (Jos 21:45)

THE BOOK OF JUDGES

Much of the Old Testament up to this point has been about God choosing a people to be his. In doing so, he expected loyalty and obedience, both to him and the laws he passed down through Moses.

As we have already seen, the Israelites repeatedly succumbed to idolatry, abandoning him for pagan rituals and ways of life. Providentially for them they had Moses and Joshua to intercede and plead for them, and God remained constant to his original promise to protect them and multiply them. Unfortunately, once Joshua died the Israelites returned to their old ways. As they sacked new towns, they failed to obey God and destroy all the temples of other gods. Instead, they favoured them and intermingled with the pagan peoples.

While this behaviour is not unique to the story of the Israelites, it is the first time they did not have a leader amongst them, a leader who would intercede to God for them and ask for forgiveness. They were about to learn the consequences of not being faithful to God.

The book covers a period of about 1200 - 1025 BC.

Israel Struggles with Faithfulness

After Joshua died, the tribes of Israel got together to plan the continuing assaults on the remaining towns. Things began well, with the houses of Judah, Simeon, Joseph, and Benjamin sacking their allotted cities and abiding by the laws of God. The rest, however, did not act as steadfastly and worshipped the pagan gods. God sent an angel with a message. "'I brought you out of Egypt and have brought you to the land which I swore to give your fathers. I will never break my covenant with you. You shall make no covenant with the inhabitants of this land. You shall break down their altars. But you have not listened to my voice. Why have you done this? Therefore, I also said, "I will not drive them out from before you; but they shall be your oppressors, and their gods will be a snare to you."'" (Jg 2:1-3)

Realising their wrongdoings, the Israelites cried out to God who then chose Othniel[48] to be a judge[49] over them. Under Othniel, Israel was again obedient to God and enjoyed peace, but when he died, they fell back into their old ways and angered God. Eventually they realised their wrongdoings and prayed to God for help. God appointed another judge - Ehud.[50] Peace and triumph followed until he died.

The Israelites repeated the cycle of turning to the local pagan gods, only to realise their transgressions and ask God for help. The following Judge was Shamgar,[51] after whom came Deborah.[52] Finding peace again, the Israelites soon fell back into paganism after her death. (Is this theme sounding familiar?)

Gideon

The next judge to be called by God was Gideon.[53] He proved harder to convince than the previous judges, requiring a sign first.[54] He received

---

[48] Othniel - the first Judge of Israel.
[49] Judges would rule over Israel for about 175 years (between 1200 - 1025 BC).
[50] Ehud - the second Judge of Israel.
[51] Shamgar - the third Judge of Israel.
[52] Deborah - the fourth Judge of Israel.
[53] Gideon - the fifth Judge of Israel.
[54] In a common theme, as God chooses his prophets, Gideon is surprised that he is called because his clan is the weakest in the tribe (Manasseh), and he is the least important in the family. God chooses this way to ensure it is known that it is he doing all the miraculous work and not the person. All that Gideon needs to do is listen, act and be faithful.

it as a miraculous consumption by fire of an offering he was preparing for God.

Gideon's first act was to destroy the altars built in honour of the pagan god Baal. This action not only upset some Israelites, but it also particularly enraged the towns of Midian and Amalek, whose god was Baal.

God informed Gideon that he would deliver Midian and Amalek to the Israelites, but Gideon needed convincing.

"If you will save Israel by my hand, as you have spoken, behold, I will put a fleece of wool on the ground. If there is dew on the fleece only, and it is dry on all the ground, then I'll know that you will save Israel by my hand, as you have spoken."

It was so; for he rose up early on the next day, and pressed the fleece together, and wrung the dew out of the fleece, a bowl full of water.

Gideon said to God, "Don't let your anger be kindled against me, and I will speak but this once. Please let me make a trial just this once with the fleece. Let it now be dry only on the fleece, and on all the ground let there be dew."

God did so that night; for it was dry on the fleece only, and there was dew on all the ground. (Jg 6:36-40)

So Gideon called all the men together to make plans for the attack, but before he got underway, God intervened, saying the force was too big.

"The people who are with you are too many for me to give the Midianites into their hand, lest Israel brag against me, saying, 'My own hand has saved me.'" (Jg 7:2)

At this stage, there were thirty-two thousand men. At first, God told Gideon to send home anyone who feared the upcoming attack. Twenty-two thousand left, leaving ten thousand. God said it was still too many. He then sent them down to the river for a drink. Three hundred men drank the water while standing up, but the remaining drank by getting down on their knees first. God chose the three hundred men to attack.

Israel was in awe of the many achievements of Gideon and welcomed him as their new leader/judge.

After Gideon's death, a man not anointed by God stood up. He was a man of few good qualities. He was Abimelech, who was one of Gideon's seventy-one sons.[55] He spoke to his clan to convince them he alone should succeed Gideon - rather than any or all of his seventy brothers, saying, "Would you rather be ruled by seventy people or just one?"

"Just one," they answered.

So, Abimelech collected silver from them and hired a mercenary army to find and kill all seventy of his brothers. They killed all but one brother, Jotham, who was furious and cursed Abimelech and all who supported him.

The judges who followed Abimelech were Tola[56] and Jair.[57] After Jair, the Israelites rebelled against God again. For eighteen years, they were under the oppression of the Philistines[58] until they turned back to God, but he needed to be heard first. *"Didn't I save you from the Egyptians, and from the* (other nations who) *oppressed you; and you cried to me, and I saved you out of their hand? Yet you have forsaken me and served other gods. Therefore, I will save you no more. Go and cry to the gods which you have chosen. Let them save you in the time of your distress!"*

The children of Israel said to Yahweh, "We have sinned! Do to us whatever seems good to you; only deliver us, please, today." They put away the foreign gods from among them and served Yahweh; and his soul was grieved for the misery of Israel. (Jg 10:11-16)

---

[55] Gideon was very productive. Abimelech was the only one born by a concubine of Gideon and not one of his many wives.
[56] Tola - the sixth Judge of Israel.
[57] Jair - the seventh Judge of Israel.
[58] A region and people of Palestine. First emerging around 1196 - 1165 BC. They were superior in arms and military structure. Also known as 'the uncircumcised' and enemies of Israel.

Jephthah[59] was chosen to be the new leader, and he gathered the tribes together to attack the Ammonites. Approaching the battle lines, Jephthah made a vow to God, proclaiming, *"If you deliver the Ammonites into my hands, then the first person to meet me from the door of my house when I return in triumph from fighting the Ammonites shall belong to Yahweh, and I will offer him up as a holocaust".* (Jg 11:30-31*)

Sadly for Jephthah, that person was his one and only daughter; who accepted the consequence, asking only for two months to mourn her virginity with her friends in the mountains.

Following Jephthah as judges, were, Ibzan,[60] Elon,[61] and Abdon.[62]

Again, the Israelites began doing what was evil in God's eyes. In time, an angel of God visited the wife of Manoah (from the tribe of Dan), telling her, *"See now, you are barren and childless; but you shall conceive and bear a son. Now therefore please beware and drink no wine nor strong drink, and don't eat any unclean thing; for, behold, you shall conceive and give birth to a son. No razor shall come on his head, for the child shall be a Nazirite[63] to God from the womb. He shall begin to save Israel out of the hand of the Philistines."* (Jg 13:3-5)

When she went to tell Manoah, he didn't believe her, so he prayed to God that the man[64] who spoke to his wife would come back and speak to him as well. The angel returned and spoke the message again. Manoah also asked for guidance on how the boy should be raised. The angel reiterated what he said before. He was to drink no wine or fermented

---

[59] Jephthah - the eighth Judge of Israel.
[60] Ibzan - the ninth Judge of Israel.
[61] Elon - the tenth Judge of Israel.
[62] Abdon - the eleventh Judge of Israel.
[63] One who is set apart.
[64] He didn't know yet that it was an Angel.

liquor, eat nothing unclean, and never cut his hair.[65] The boy born was called Samson.

Samson

As Samson grew older, he grew fond of a Philistine girl from the town of Timnah, eventually asking his parents to secure her for his wife. His parents were troubled though, and questioned Samson, "Why can't you choose a wife from your own people rather than from the uncircumcised Philistines?"

"Because she is the one I want," Samson replied.

What neither Samson nor his parents knew, was that this was all part of God's plan. He was looking for a way to punish the Philistines, who for too long had oppressed the Israelites.

Soon afterwards, as Samson was heading towards the village of Timnah, where the girl he liked lived, he came across a young lion. With no weapon to defend himself, but strengthened by the spirit of God, Samson ripped the lion apart with his bare hands. Leaving it by the side of the road, he continued into the village to talk to his intended wife. Returning by the same path, he saw the lion carcass was now covered in a swarm of bees and honey. He ate a handful of the honey and took some home for his parents.

Eventually Samson and the girl married and a seven-day celebration with thirty of the young men from Timnah (the girl's hometown) began. On the first day, Samson challenged them all with a riddle and a prize of thirty pieces of fine linen and thirty coloured robes if they could solve it. They accepted.

So, he gave them the riddle: *"Out of the eater came food. Out of the strong came sweetness,"* (Jg 14:14) giving them seven days to answer. After three days they were no closer to solving the riddle, and fearful of being

---

[65] Like Samuel and John the Baptist.

shown up by Samson, they pressured his wife into finding the answer. She was reluctant at first but eventually succumbed to helping the local men solve the riddle - much to Samson's irritation.

Seized by the Spirit of God, Samson went to the nearby town of Ashkelon, killed thirty men, took their clothes, and returned them to the other men as payment for the riddle. Incensed at being betrayed by his new wife, he stormed off back to his hometown.

Eventually Samson calmed down and returned to his wife with a peace offering, only to find out she had been given as a wife to his best man as her father believed Samson would never return. Samson wanted revenge. Catching three hundred foxes, he paired them up with torches in their tails and sent them into the Philistines' crops and vines, which were destroyed in the fire. When the men of the town found out what Samson did, they took retribution on the girl and her father by burning them to death. Samson would not let this rest.

While Samson came from the tribe of Dan, the Philistines went to the tribe of Judah looking to continue their retribution against Samson. The men of Judah dutifully went in search of Samson. Finding him they yelled and argued, telling him they were going to hand him over to the Philistines. Samson agreed to be taken back if they promised they would not kill him themselves. This was agreed. Bound up, they took him to the Philistines. As they saw him coming, their rage was uncontrollable, and they ran forward to kill him. The spirit of God entered Samson and *the ropes that were on his arms became as flax that was burned with fire; and his bands dropped from off his hands. He found a fresh jawbone of a donkey, ... took it, and struck a thousand men with it.* (Jg 15:14-15)

Samson ruled as a virtuous judge over Israel for the next twenty years.

In time, Samson fell in love with another woman, a Philistine named Delilah. After they were married, the Philistines, still eager for revenge, approached Delilah offering her eleven hundred shekels of silver[66] to find out the source of his immense power. She accepted the offer.

One night, as they were alone, Delilah asked Samson what the source of his power was and if it could be bound and tamed.

"If they bind me with seven green cords that were never dried, then shall I become weak, and be as another man." (Jg 16:7)

Delilah reported this to the Philistines and returned with seven new bowstrings along with some Philistines to capture him. Binding him up as he slept, Delilah called out to Samson that the Philistines were coming for him. Samson easily broke the bindings, and the Philistines retreated in fear.

It upset Delilah that Samson lied to her, so she pressed him again.

"If they only bind me with new ropes with which no work has been done, then shall I become weak, and be as another man." (Jg 16:11)

Delilah went back to the Philistines, and they gave her men and the new ropes. She again bound Samson and called out, "The Philistines are here!"

Samson again quickly broke the new rope, and the men fled.

Enraged, Delilah pestered Samson for the truth on how he could be bound, so he told her. *"If you weave the seven locks of my head with the fabric on the loom."* (Jg 16:13)

Returning once more to the Philistines, they again gave her what was needed, but again she was thwarted. She would not give up though. Eleven hundred shekels of silver was a lot of money. She spoke to Samson, *"How can you say, 'I love you' when your heart is not with me? You have mocked me these three times and have not told me where your great strength lies."*

When she pressed him daily with her words and urged him, his soul was troubled to death. He told her all that was on his heart and said to her, "No razor has ever come on my head; for I have been a Nazirite to God from my

---

[66] Probably $100,000 in today's value.

mother's womb. If I am shaved, then my strength will go from me and I will become weak and be like any other man." (Jg 16:15-17)

This time they had him. They captured him, sent him to prison in Gaza, and for good measure plucked out both his eyes. While in prison though, his hair eventually grew back.

Proud of themselves for capturing Samson, the Philistines assembled for a grand feast to their god Dagon. The people called out, asking for Samson to be brought to them so they could ridicule him. After being dragged out into the square, he spoke to one of his handlers (because he had no eyes, he needed men to lead him around) asking if they could take him to a pillar supporting the building so he could rest. Once there, he cried out to God, asking for his strength to be returned to him so he could be avenged. Using all his might, he pushed against the pillar and caused the building to collapse, killing everyone there, including himself.

Samson was the last of the twelve Judges of Israel.

THE BOOK OF RUTH

Believed to be a work of fiction, the book of Ruth celebrates the heroism of two women (Ruth and Naomi). Despite being a Moabite[67], Ruth gains God's favour and becomes an ancestor of both David and Jesus.[68]

The book covers the time of the Judges (1200 - 1025 BC) but is believed to have been written after the return of the exiles, about 430 - 420 BC.

During the times of the Judges when famine was rife, a man called Elimelech moved his wife Naomi and two sons from Bethlehem of Judah to Moab. Elimelech died and soon after, his two sons married Moabite girls named Ruth and Orpah.

In time, both the sons died, and Naomi decided to return to Bethlehem to live out her remaining years. Hearing the news, Naomi's daughter-in-law Ruth, would not leave her side, saying, *"Don't urge me to leave you, and to return from following you, for where you go, I will go; and where you stay, I will stay. Your people will be my people, and your God my God. Where you die, I will die, and there I will be buried. May Yahweh do so to me, and more also, if anything but death parts you and me."* (Rt 1:16-17)

---

[67] The Moabites were descendants of Lot, not Abraham, Isaac, or Jacob, and were not part of God's covenant people of Israel.
[68] Matt 1:5

Once back in Bethlehem, Ruth went out into the fields to scavenge some corn. While there, she was noticed by the landowner, a man called Boaz, who was from the same clan as Elimelech. Boaz recognised her and knew how she had forsaken her own family to stay with Naomi. He allowed Ruth to gather as much corn as she wanted, saying, *"I have been told all about what you have done for your mother-in-law since the death of your husband, and how you have left your father, your mother, and the land of your birth, and have come to a people that you didn't know before. May Yahweh repay your work, and a full reward be given to you from Yahweh, the God of Israel, under whose wings you have come to take refuge."* (Rt 2:11-12)

In time, Naomi felt it right to help Ruth remarry and start a life and family. She told her to go and lie with Boaz, for he was from the same clan as her husband. When Ruth made her intentions known to Boaz he was flattered as he was much older than Ruth.

"May Yahweh bless you, my daughter," said Boaz, *"for this last act of kindness of yours is greater than the first, since you have not gone after young men, poor or rich. Have no fear then, my daughter, I will do whatever you ask, for the people of Bethlehem all know your worth. But, though it is true I have right of redemption over you, you have a kinsman closer than myself. Stay here for tonight, and in the morning if he wishes to exercise his right over you, very well, let him redeem you. But if he does not wish to do so, then as Yahweh lives, I will redeem you. Lie here till morning."* (Rt 3:10-13*)

When Boaz went to speak to the closer kinsmen about Ruth, he declined, so Boaz was free to marry Ruth himself.

They had a son, Obed, who became the grandfather of King David.

THE BOOKS OF SAMUEL I AND II

A proper title of the Book of Samuel could be 'The origin of the Davidic Monarchy'. It is what the books relate to, and it was probably what the scribes, whose work lies at the basis of the book, were commissioned to write.[69]

Written during the time of the divided Kingdoms of Israel and Judah.

Samuel (1040 - 1020 BC)

Samuel was born to Elkanah and Hannah. Hannah was barren most of her life and suffered years of torment because of it. One day, despairing of her fate, she prayed outside the Temple of God,[70] pleading to be heard and be given a child. In her prayer, she vowed that if given a son, she would consecrate him to God and no razor would touch his head.[71] The priest Eli saw her praying and spoke to her, promising that God would answer her.

---

[69] McKenzie, John L. Dictionary of the Bible. 1965. [p772].
[70] Where the Ark of the Covenant was kept.
[71] Same as Samson and John the Baptist.

The following year Samuel was born, and after he was weaned, Hannah took him back to the Temple of God. After making a sacrifice, she found the priest Eli and handed her son over to God.

Samuel grew up under the watchful eye of Eli, who was also raising his own two sons in the service of God.[72] Eli's sons however were immoral and did not follow the laws of God, often abusing their power. Samuel though was good and proper his whole life. News of Eli's sons' sinful ways ultimately became known to him. He was devastated, saying, *"If one man sins against another, God will judge him; but if a man sins against Yahweh, who will intercede for him?" Notwithstanding, they didn't listen to the voice of their father, because Yahweh intended to kill them.* (1Sam 2:25)

A man of God spoke to Eli, informing him that his sons were stealing meat from the sacrifices at the altar, which angered God, especially since their family had been favoured among many. Because of the sins of his two sons, Eli and his family would be punished, they would be wiped out, forgotten, and a new priest would be found, one that would be devoted, one that would walk in the presence of God, one that would be God's anointed one forever.

One night in the sanctuary of God, both Samuel and Eli were asleep when God called, "Samuel, Samuel."

Rising, Samuel went to Eli and said, "Here I am; you called me."

"I didn't call you," said Eli. "Go back to sleep."

Drifting off again, God called a second time, "Samuel, Samuel."

Samuel rose and went to Eli, "Here I am; you called me."

"I didn't call you," said Eli. "Go back and lie down."

Because God had not spoken to his people this directly for so long, neither Samuel nor Eli understood what was happening. A third time God called out to Samuel. "Samuel, Samuel."

Samuel went to Eli and said, "Here I am, you called me."

---

[72] Hophni and Phinehas.

"I didn't call you," said Eli, but he then understood, telling Samuel, "If you are called again, this time respond saying, 'Here I am Lord, your servant is listening.'"

God called him again and Samuel answered, God said, *"Behold, I will do a thing in Israel... In that day I will act against Eli all that I have spoken concerning his house, from the beginning even to the end. For I have told him I will judge his house forever for the iniquity which he knew, because his sons brought a curse on themselves, and he didn't restrain them. Therefore, I have sworn to the house of Eli that the iniquity of Eli's house shall not be removed with sacrifice or offering forever."* (1Sam 3:11-14)

In the morning Samuel lay still, not wanting to wake Eli, as he feared telling him what God said, but when Eli woke, he insisted he be told. Samuel recounted all that God had said, and Eli accepted it.

Meanwhile, the Philistines had assembled their forces and were inflicting a massive defeat on Israel. The Israelites were confused, wondering why God was not bringing them victory as in the past. They decided to send Eli's two sons to Shiloh and return with the Ark of the Covenant believing victory would accompany their return. When they returned with the ark, the Israelites shouted with joy, so much so, that the Philistines could hear them from their camp. Realising why they were cheering, and feeling anxious (as they knew the stories of the tremendous victories the Israelites' God had won), they mustered the courage to attack. Despite the presence of the ark, the Israelites were again beaten. Eli's two sons were killed, and the Ark of the Covenant was captured.

One man (a Benjaminite) escaped and fled back to Shiloh with the terrible news. When Eli, now ninety-eight, heard the news of the defeat, the death of his sons, and the capture of the ark, he collapsed and died.

The Philistines were pleased with themselves after capturing the ark. They believed they could now defeat the Israelites at will. They were wrong. Wherever they placed the ark, it brought nothing but misery and disease. They moved it from town to town hoping for relief, but everywhere it went the wrath of God followed. Finally, they called the local priests for help. They advised them to send the Ark of the Covenant back, and with it, some guilt offerings to appease the God of the Israelites.

With the ark returned, and with Samuel now God's anointed leader, the Israelites enjoyed many years of peace and safety from the Philistines.

As Samuel grew old, he knew he needed to appoint someone to continue after him, so he chose his two sons, Joel and Abijah. Sadly, both boys quickly fell into the ways of corruption, and abused their positions.[73]

The Elders of Israel came to Samuel to complain that his sons were not as good as he was, begging him instead to give them a king to rule over them, like all the surrounding nations had. This worried Samuel, so he turned to God, who replied, *"Listen to the voice of the people in all that they tell you; for they have not rejected you, but they have rejected me as the king over them. According to all the works which they have done since the day that I brought them up out of Egypt even to this day, in that they have forsaken me and served other gods, so they also do to you. Now therefore, listen to their voice. However, you shall protest solemnly to them, and shall show them the way of the king who will reign over them."* (1Sam 8:7-9)

Samuel informed the people what it was going to mean to have the king they wanted. "A king will have total control over you. A king will take your sons and daughters, your crops and produce and make you all as his own slaves. Eventually you will tire of being treated this way and will pray to God to save you - but God will not listen to you!" Yet they were determined to have a king.

---

[73] The same as Eli's sons.

Saul - The First king of Israel (1030 - 1010 BC)

From the tribe of Benjamin, there was a man called Saul. He was tall and handsome. One day, his father instructed him to go out and find some donkeys that had gone missing, so he headed out with a servant in search of them. No matter how hard they searched they couldn't find any trace of them. In fact, they were out looking for so long that Saul feared his father would worry about him. The servant then spoke up and mentioned he had heard of a great and wise man (Samuel) in a nearby town who should be able to tell them where to look.

As Saul entered the town, Samuel was already waiting for him, for the previous night God had told him that a man called Saul would come looking for him and he was to anoint him as the king the people of Israel so desperately wanted. When they met up, Samuel indicated to Saul the great honour awaiting him. Saul came back with an answer almost identical to the call of Gideon, the first of the Judges.

"Am I not a Benjaminite, of the smallest of the tribes of Israel? And my family the least of all the families of the tribe of Benjamin? Why then do you speak to me like this?" (1Sam 9:21)

Samuel replied, *"Hasn't Yahweh anointed you to be prince over his people Israel? You are the man who must rule Yahweh's people, and who must save them from the power of the enemies surrounding them. This shall be the sign for you that Yahweh has appointed you prince of his heritage."* (1Sam 10:1*) Samuel then proceeded to foretell how and when Saul would find the missing donkeys.

Samuel told Saul to go to the town of Gibeah, where he would meet with the local prophets, *"Then Yahweh's Spirit will come mightily on you, then you will prophesy with them and will be turned into another man. Let it be, when these signs have come to you, that you do what is appropriate for the occasion; for God is with you."* (1Sam 10:6-7)

Samuel called all the tribes of Israel to him and said, *"You have today rejected your God, who himself saves you out of all your calamities and your distresses; and you have said to him, 'No! Set a king over us!'"* (1Sam 10:19)

To satisfy the needs of the people, Samuel drew lots from among the tribes to choose the new king. The first lot fell to the tribe of Benjamin, the second to the clan of Matri, and the final lot fell to Saul, son of Kish. The people acclaimed, "Long live the king!"

Before Samuel anointed Saul, he addressed the people once more. He reminded them of God's faithfulness from Moses through to the present time. He refreshed their memories of how they had sinned against God, but he had always remained loyal. Then he reminded them again of the pain they caused God by demanding a king to rule over them when they already had God as their King.

Saul's first attempt at leading the Israelites into battle went poorly. After amassing his army and moving on the Philistines, he initially had success but as the Philistines regrouped and moved forward against him, he became fearful and retreated. Samuel had previously told Saul that after seven days of battle he would join him, but when the seventh day came with no sight of him, Saul offered a burnt offering to God to bring him victory. As the offering was ending, Samuel arrived and was angry. *"What have you done?"*

Saul said, *"Because I saw the people were scattered from me, and that you didn't come within the days appointed, and that the Philistines assembled themselves together at Michmash, therefore I said, 'Now the Philistines will come down on me to Gilgal, and I haven't entreated the favour of Yahweh.' I forced myself therefore and offered the burnt offering."*

Samuel said to Saul, *"You have done foolishly. You have not kept the commandment of Yahweh your God, which he commanded you; for now Yahweh would have established your kingdom over Israel forever. But now your kingdom will not continue. Yahweh has sought for himself a man after his own heart, and Yahweh has appointed him to be prince over his people, because you have not kept that which Yahweh commanded you."* (1Sam 13:11-14)

Saul continued to battle all those before him, inflicting great humiliation on the Philistines. When the Israelites invaded one town for its booty, some men stole sheep and oxen, then slaughtered and ate them even as they dripped with blood.[74]

As a sign of thanks to God for their triumph, Saul decreed that no one was to eat anything before evening. Jonathan, the son of Saul, had been bravely fighting among the Israelites, and as he was returning, he came across some honey, which he helped himself to. Those around him were shocked, but Jonathan said he did not hear of his father's order and therefore would not be held accountable. He was wrong.

Saul prayed to God, asking if he should continue the plunder of the Philistines, but God did not answer - which concerned Saul. Summoning all the people before him, he announced that someone must have sinned against God, and this was the reason why he did not answer. He prayed to God to deliver the sinner to him, decreeing he would put them to death. God delivered his son, Jonathan. However, because Jonathan was well liked and admired, the people petitioned successfully to spare his life.

Saul pressed on, leading his army into war, but eventually his time came to an end. God told Samuel, *"It grieves me that I have set up Saul to be king, for he has turned back from following me, and has not performed my commandments."* (1Sam 15:11)

Samuel sent for Saul, telling him what God had said, but Saul was confused, as he thought he was being faithful to God. Saul thought that by offering sacrifices and holocausts to God, he was observing the rules of faith, but what God wanted was obedience, and Saul had failed when he let the booty be eaten.

---

[74] This is against one of God's laws.

Samuel told Saul, *"Because you have rejected Yahweh's word, he has also rejected you from being king."* (1Sam 15:23)

Saul was devastated, pleading with Samuel to give him another chance, but he would not hear it. As Samuel left him, Saul acted in desperation to keep him there, tearing at the hem of his garment. Samuel turned, saying, *"Yahweh has torn the Kingdom of Israel from you today, and has given it to a neighbour of yours who is better than you."* (1Sam 15:28)

David - The Second king of Israel (1010 - 970 BC)

Immortalised by Michelangelo, David is a key figure of the Old Testament. Not just for the slaying of Goliath, but because God drew a line in the sand with him. Prior to David, God would always go back to the names of Abraham, Isaac, and Jacob as the founding fathers of the Israelites. From here on, it becomes David.

It took Samuel some time to get over the fall of Saul, until one day God told him it was time to move on and find a new king to replace Saul when he died. God had already chosen someone from the house of Jesse of Bethlehem. Samuel wasn't eager about the journey ahead of him though, as he was worried that if Saul heard about it, he would try to stop him.

Arriving at Bethlehem, he went to find Jesse and his sons. When he saw Eliab, the eldest of the sons, who was tall and strong, he thought to himself, "He must be the one," but God quickly corrected him.

"Don't look on his face, or on the height of his stature, because I have rejected him; for I don't see as man sees. For man looks at the outward appearance, but Yahweh looks at the heart." (1Sam 16:7)

Jesse presented seven of his sons to Samuel one by one. All were rejected. Confused, Samuel asked Jesse if this was all his sons, and Jesse told him there was one other, the youngest, who was out looking after the sheep. Samuel asked Jesse to send for his son. When the youngest son David arrived, God immediately instructed Samuel to anoint him

- he was the one, *and the spirit of Yahweh seized on David and stayed with him from that day on.* (1Sam 16:13*)

David Kills Goliath

Saul was still ruling, and soon the Philistines waged war on the Israelites again. Standing across a field staring at each other in readiness, a Philistine by the name of Goliath stepped forward and challenged them. *"Choose a man for yourselves and let him come down to me. If he can fight with me and kill me, then will we be your servants; but if I prevail against him and kill him, then you will be our servants and serve us."* (1Sam 17:8-9)

    Now Goliath was an enormous man, bigger than anyone had ever seen, and the sight of him brought fear to all the army of Israel, so no one accepted. Each day Goliath repeated the challenge.

    Meanwhile, David was asked by his father to go to the front lines and check on his three sons, who were fighting alongside Saul.[75] When David got there, he saw Goliath and heard his challenge, and was both surprised and ashamed that no one had the courage to face him, so he volunteered. When Saul found out, he ridiculed him, telling him he was only a boy and not a warrior.[76] David didn't listen. Saul finally agreed and instructed David to be fitted with a suit of armour. However, David found it too heavy and cumbersome, so he did not wear it when he went to face Goliath.

    Seeing David approach, Goliath was incensed, questioning, "Who is this boy you send against me; am I a dog that you come at me with sticks?"

    With only his staff, sling, and a bag of five stones, David answered him, *"You come to me with a sword, with a spear, and with a javelin; but I come to you in the name of Yahweh… Today, Yahweh will deliver you into my hand. I will strike you and take your head from off you. I will give the dead bodies of the army of the Philistines today to the birds of the sky and to the*

---

[75] Eliab, Abinadab, Shammah.
[76] Saul did not yet know about David's anointing.

wild animals of the earth, that all the earth may know that there is a God in Israel." (1Sam 17:45-46)

David ran at Goliath swinging his sling and flung a stone at him, striking him on the forehead. Goliath stopped in his tracks, fell on his face, and died. Seeing what took place, the Philistine army hastily turned and ran away, and the Israelites pursued them. From that time, Saul kept David by his side as if he were his own son. In fact, his own son Jonathan and David became inseparable. Saul soon put David in charge of all the fighting men, and victory followed them everywhere.

Returning home after a battle, the townspeople came out to meet the returning king and his armies. Saul was disturbed to hear them chanting. *"Saul has slain his thousands, and David his tens of thousands!"* (1Sam 18:7) This started a rage and jealousy in Saul that plagued him for the remainder of his life. He sensed that the favour of Yahweh had left him and was now with David. Deciding he needed to keep David close, Saul offered him his daughter Michal's hand in marriage,[77] on the proviso David promised to continue fighting for him. David accepted, but then Saul added another condition. David had to pay a settlement of one hundred Philistine foreskins. (Saul was banking on David getting killed in the hunt.) David accepted, and to Saul's dismay returned not with one hundred, but two hundred foreskins. So, while David was now his son-in-law, Saul was even more fearful of him, and the favour God showed him.

Saul was filled with hatred for David. Summoning all his household, he made it known he intended to kill David. Among the household was his son Jonathan, who loved David as his own flesh, and he pleaded with his father not to go through with it. He reminded him how David saved the army when he killed Goliath, and of the many victories he had won since that day. Saul weakened and promised he would not go through with it.

---

[77] The first proposal was for his daughter Merab, but that fell through, the second proposal was for Michal.

The promise was quickly broken, though, and after some unsuccessful attempts to kill him, Michal, David's wife, urged him to run away, leaving her and all he owned behind. Like a man possessed, Saul remained relentless in his pursuit of him.

Hearing a rumour that David was hiding in a cave, Saul went out to find and kill him. While searching in a cave, Saul needed to urinate, and while he was doing so, David snuck up behind him, and instead of killing him, cut off a piece of his cloak. On returning to his men, David was interrogated for not killing Saul when he had the chance, but David's view was different, as he still believed Saul was God's anointed one and wasn't to be harmed.

Seeing Saul leave the cave, David sprang up yelling, *"Behold, today your eyes have seen how Yahweh has delivered you today into my hand in the cave. Some urged me to kill you, but I spared you. I said, 'I will not stretch out my hand against my lord, for he is Yahweh's anointed.' Moreover, ... see the skirt of your robe in my hand; for in that I cut off the skirt of your robe and didn't kill you, know and see that there is neither evil nor disobedience in my hand. I have not sinned against you, though you hunt for my life to take it. May Yahweh judge between me and you, and may Yahweh avenge me of you; but my hand will not be on you. As the proverb of the ancients says, 'Out of the wicked comes wickedness'; but my hand will not be on you."* (1Sam 24:10-13)

Saul was overcome with sadness and tears as he realised his wrongdoing. He told David he was more upright than he, for he had repaid his evil with kindness. He accepted David as the rightful future king of Israel.

Saul did not keep to his word though, and again plotted against David. So, David fled, this time finding refuge among the Philistines. Saul stopped his pursuit, and David fought for the Philistines against his own people.

During the ongoing fighting between the Philistines and the Israelites, Saul and his sons were killed. Notwithstanding all the evil Saul directed at David, the death of Saul saddened him.

Now, while Samuel had anointed David as the heir apparent to Saul, this was not common knowledge among the people of Israel, so David asked God for guidance. God told him to go to Hebron, a town in the tribe of Judah, where the men of the town would annoint him as their king. At the same time, however, Ishbaal, another of Saul's sons, was also being anointed king; meaning David was only recognised and supported as king within the house of Judah.

For the first time in their history, the Israelites fought between themselves: the House of Judah against the House of Israel.

In the House of Israel,[78] whilst Ishbaal was king, the real power lay with Abner, who was Saul's commander, but soon these two fought and drifted apart. Seeing no way out, Abner went to parley with David to suggest an alliance to defeat Ishbaal. Fatally for Abner though, as he was returning home, Joab, a fighter loyal to David, saw him, and thinking he was still the enemy, killed him. Knowing his death could jeopardise the new alliance, two other men loyal to David took it on themselves to sneak into Ishbaal's tent one night and cut off his head.

After seven years and six months as only the king of Judah,[79] David became the one king of all Israel.[80] One of his first moves was to march on Jerusalem.[81] Once he captured the city, he went to live there, calling it the City of David. (Becoming the capital of the Kingdom of Israel).

---

[78] At this stage the House of Israel consisted of the (10) Houses of Reuben, Simeon, Levi, Issachar, Zebulun, Joseph, Dan, Naphtali, Gad, and Asher.
[79] At this stage the House of Judah consisted of the Tribes of Judah and Benjamin.
[80] Both Houses of Israel and Judah.
[81] Up until then the city was held by the Jebusites, a tribe of the Canaanites, who were there before Joshua crossed the Jordan.

Now that Jerusalem was his, David moved the Ark of the Covenant to Jerusalem. Along the route they stopped and offered sacrifices and holocausts to God. They also sang and danced before it. As David was rejoicing and dancing around the ark in rapturous joy and celebration of Yahweh, his wife Michal saw him and was horrified. *"How glorious the king of Israel was today, who uncovered himself today in the eyes of his servants' maids, as one of the vain fellows shamelessly uncovers himself!"*

David said to Michal, *"It was before Yahweh, who chose me above your father, and above all his house, to appoint me prince over the people of Yahweh, over Israel."* (2Sam 6:20-21)

David, now at rest from his enemies,[82] decided to build a house for the Ark of the Covenant, surmising that because he himself had a house, why not God? So, he approached the prophet Nathan for guidance, who told him to go ahead, but he also gave David a divine prophecy concerning his legacy. *"'Yahweh will make you a house. When your days are fulfilled and you sleep with your fathers, I will set up your offspring after you, who will proceed out of your body, and I will establish his kingdom. He will build a house for my name, and I will establish the throne of his kingdom forever. I will be his father, and he will be my son. If he commits iniquity, I will chasten him with the rod of men and with the stripes of the children of men; but my loving kindness will not depart from him, as I took it from Saul, whom I put away before you. Your house and your kingdom will be made sure forever before you. Your throne will be established forever.'"* (2Sam 7:11-16)

Bathsheba

One night, David was on his rooftop getting some fresh air when he noticed a striking woman bathing across the road. The following day he made enquiries and found that her name was Bathsheba. She was

---

[82] The Philistines were finally defeated.

married to Uriah, a friend of David's. Sending for her, they soon slept together, and she fell pregnant.

Finding out she was with child David began an elaborate plan to save face. He sent for Uriah, who was away with the army, on the pretext that he wanted to ask him how the fighting was going. After they met, David sent him back to the fighting with a sealed letter to be given to his commander, Joab. The letter stated that on the next assault, Uriah was to be placed on the front line. Joab complied, and Uriah was killed in the battle. Bathsheba mourned when she heard the news, and when her time of mourning was over, David brought her into his home and married her. God was not pleased, so he sent the prophet Nathan to David.

Nathan told David that God was angry, having given him everything he could ever want. Nothing was held back, so why would he plot to kill Uriah and take Bathsheba as his wife? As punishment, God would stir up trouble for David from within his own house. While David had plotted in the dark, God would have his retribution in the day, so all of Israel would see it. David acknowledged his sin, and God forgave him, but there would still be a punishment meted out - God would not allow the child of Bathsheba to live and David would no longer be the one to build the Temple of God.

In time, David and Bathsheba would have another child, a son called Solomon.

As time passed and David grew old, he performed a ceremony so that Solomon would be his rightful successor.

THE BOOKS OF KINGS I AND II

The way God communicates with his people changes now. In the past he has primarily used personal visitations, dreams, or sent angels. Now he uses prophets who speak on his behalf. The role of the prophets becomes crucial in the way God 'shows' himself.

During this period of the Old Testament the prophets foretell future events, some minor, others far more complex, even pertaining to winning wars.

The books cover the rise and fall of the kings of the two tribes of the divided Kingdoms of Judah and Israel. There are overlaps with The Book of Chronicles.

Solomon - The Third king of Israel (970 - 931 BC)

Solomon became king of Israel, four hundred and eighteen years after the Israelites were taken out of Egypt. He reigned between 970 - 931 BC.

One night as Solomon slept, he had a dream. In it he spoke to God.

"Now, Yahweh my God, you have made your servant king instead of David my father. I am just a little child… Give your servant therefore an understanding heart to judge your people, that I may discern between good and evil; for who is able to judge this great people of yours?"

This request pleased Yahweh, that Solomon had asked this thing. God said to him, "Because you have asked this thing, and have not asked for yourself long life, nor have you asked for riches for yourself, nor have you asked for the life of your enemies…, behold, I have done according to your word. Behold, I have given you a wise and understanding heart, so that there has been no one like you before you, and after you none will arise like you. I have also given you that which you have not asked, both riches and honour, so that there will not be any among the kings like you for all your days. If you will walk in my ways, to keep my statutes and my commandments, as your father David walked, then I will lengthen your days." (1Kg 3:7-14)

The Wisdom of Solomon

Then two women who were prostitutes came to the king and stood before him. The one woman said, "Oh, my lord, I, and this woman dwell in one house. I delivered a child with her in the house. The third day after I delivered, this woman delivered also. We were together. There was no stranger with us in the house, just us two in the house. This woman's child died in the night, because she lay on it. She arose at midnight, and took my son from beside me while your servant slept, and laid it in her bosom, and laid her dead child in my bosom. When I rose in the morning to nurse my child, behold, he was dead; but when I had looked at him in the morning, behold, it was not my son whom I bore."

The other woman said, "No! But the living one is my son, and the dead one is your son."

The first one said, "No! But the dead one is your son, and the living one is my son." They argued like this before the king.

Then the king said, "One says, 'This is my son who lives, and your son is the dead;' and the other says, 'No! But your son is the dead one, and my son is the living one.'"

The king said, "Get me a sword." So they brought a sword before the king.

The king said, "Divide the living child in two, and give half to the one, and half to the other."

Then the woman whose the living child was, spoke to the king, for her heart yearned over her son, and she said, "Oh, my lord, give her the living child, and in no way kill him!"

But the other said, "He shall be neither mine nor yours. Divide him."

Then the king answered, "Give the first woman the living child, and definitely do not kill him. She is his mother."

All Israel heard of the judgement which the king had judged; and they feared the king, for they saw that the wisdom of God was in him to do justice. (1Kg 3:16-28)

Four years into his reign, Solomon began to build the Temple of God.[83] The Ark of the Covenant was to be placed inside the temple in a place called the Holy of Holies.

When completed, the people of Israel formed a glorious and holy procession to bring the ark into its new home, as Solomon said, "*Listen to the supplication of your servant, and of your people Israel, when they pray toward this place. Yes, hear in heaven, your dwelling place; and when you hear, forgive.*" (1Kg 8:30)

He added. "*Blessed be Yahweh... who granted rest to his people Israel, keeping all his promises... of good that he made through Moses his servant, not one has failed.*" (1Kg 8:56*)

Solomon continued his prayer and blessing of the people. "*May Yahweh our God be with us as he was with our fathers. Let him not leave us or forsake us, that he may incline our hearts to him, to walk in all his ways, and to keep his commandments, his statutes, and his ordinances, which he commanded our fathers... that he may maintain the cause of his servant and the cause of his people Israel, as every day requires; that all the peoples of the earth may know that Yahweh himself is God. There is no one else.*

"*Let your heart therefore be perfect with Yahweh our God, to walk in his statutes, and to keep his commandments, as it is today.*" (1Kg 8:57-61)

---

[83] The temple his father David wanted to build but didn't because God forbade him. 966 BC.

God replied, *"I have heard your prayer and your supplication that you have made before me. I have made this house holy, which you have built, to put my name there forever; and my eyes and my heart shall be there perpetually. As for you, if you will walk before me as David your father walked, in integrity of heart and in uprightness, to do according to all that I have commanded you, and will keep my statutes and my ordinances, then I will establish the throne of your kingdom over Israel forever, as I promised to David your father, saying, 'There shall not fail from you a man on the throne of Israel.'*

"But if you turn away from following me, you or your children, and not keep my commandments and my statutes which I have set before you, but go and serve other gods and worship them, then I will cut off Israel out of the land which I have given them; and I will cast this house, which I have made holy for my name, out of my sight; and Israel will be a proverb and a byword among all peoples. Though this house is so high, yet everyone who passes by it will be astonished and hiss; and they will say, 'Why has Yahweh done this to this land and to this house?' and they will answer, 'Because they abandoned Yahweh their God, who brought their fathers out of the land of Egypt, and embraced other gods, and worshipped them, and served them. Therefore, Yahweh has brought all this evil on them.'" (1Kg 9:3-9)

Solomon then embarked on building a palace of his own, which took another thirteen years.

Sadly, Solomon would also sin against God, taking up the worship of some pagan gods of his seven hundred wives. God became angry and was swift in his response, telling Solomon his kingship of all of Israel would not be passed down to his son, Rehoboam. Instead, the kingdom would be divided into the House of Israel and the House of David and Judah.

Jeroboam would become the first king of Israel, and as a sign of the fondness God held for Solomon and his promise to David, he would allow his son, Rehoboam, to become the king of Judah and the House of David[84] only, and they would be separated from the rest of Israel.

Over the following eighty years, the two kingdoms[85] went through a series of kings. All of them (with the exception of Asa of Judah) were immoral and did not follow the word of God.[86]

Elijah and Elisha - Prophets Of God

During the reign of Ahab,[87] a remarkable prophet by the name of Elijah lived. God sent him to visit Ahab, so that God could show his displeasure.[88] Once there, Elijah challenged Ahab and his three hundred and fifty prophets of Baal, to see whose god was the greatest. Elijah suggested they each select a cow from the herd, dismember it, and lay it on a pile of wood, but not to light it. Each prophet would then pray to their god to start the fire. Whoever started the fire was the real god. Ahab and his prophets haughtily accepted.

The prophets of Baal went first, and after preparing the cow, cried out to Baal to light the fire, but there was no answer. Cheekily, Elijah suggested they call louder, as their god might be busy or otherwise occupied. They cried out again and again. There was no answer.

Elijah then stepped up, and after preparing the cow and the wood, asked the surrounding people to wet the cow and wood with water. Three times he told them to saturate the cow and the wood. He stepped forward and asked God to light the fire, and instantly the fire of God fell upon the cow and wood and consumed it. The people were astonished,

---

[84] Jesus would come from the line of the House of David.
[85] The House of Israel to be referred to as the Northern Kingdom, and The House of Judah as the Southern Kingdom.
[86] Israel Kings were Jeroboam, Nadab, Baasha, Elah, Zimri, Omri, Ahab. Judah Kings were Rehoboam, Abijah, Asa.
[87] King of Israel.
[88] Under the influence of his wife Jezebel, Ahab abandoned the worship of God in favour of pagan gods.

and they cried out, "The god of Israel is God!" Elijah then killed all the false prophets of Baal.

Elijah is Taken up to Heaven

Eventually God chose that it was time for Elijah to die - but it would not be like anyone before him. Elisha, who was a follower of Elijah, asked that when he succeeded Elijah, he might possess double his share of the spirit. Elijah responded that if Elisha saw him being taken up to God, then his prayer will be granted. Then, before his eyes, Elisha saw a chariot of fire led by horses of fire come and take Elijah up into heaven. Elisha was honoured among the people like Elijah and was blessed by God.

Elisha performed a multitude of miracles, including bringing a dead boy back to life.[89] Another time, they gave him some bread to eat, and he wanted to share it among those around him but was told there wasn't enough. He insisted, however, and it was shared around, and it fed one hundred people. There was even some left over.[90] Later, Elisha was approached by Naaman, an army commander who had leprosy, and he cured him.[91]

Continuation of the Time of the Kings

During this time, the Israelites remained divided. The House of Israel had been through another king - Ahaziah, who continued to do what was displeasing to God. After Asa, the House of Judah was ruled over by Jehoshaphat and Jehoram. While Jehoshaphat was devoted, Jehoram was not (he was more like the kings of Israel), but God did not punish him, for he still favoured his servant, David.

---

[89] Jesus was to replicate this.
[90] Jesus was to replicate this.
[91] Jesus was to replicate this.

Soon, God had had enough of the kings of Israel, and sent Elisha to anoint a new king - Jehu (the previous few kings of Israel were sons of the outgoing king, God was about to break this chain). Once anointed, Jehu killed the reigning King Jehoram, his mother Jezebel, then Ahaziah, the king of Judah. He then went into the city and summoned all the prophets of Baal on the pretext of offering a sacrifice to Baal, then had all the prophets put to death.

Over the ensuing fifty years, both houses went through a cycle of leaders. In the House of Israel after Jehoash came, Jeroboam II, then Zechariah, Shallum, Menahem, Pekahiah, Pekah, and Hoshea.[92]

Whilst Hoshea ruled the House of Israel, it was defeated by the king of Assyria and the people were deported from Samaria to Assyria.[93] The king of Assyria then repopulated the town of Samaria with people from Babylon and other towns.

These new residents, the Samaritans, did not worship Yahweh; so Hoshea said to the king of Assyria that he would kill them unless a priest was sent back from the deported Israelites to teach the new people how to worship Yahweh. But they did not follow Yahweh and continued to worship their old gods.

The End (Of Jerusalem) is Near

After destroying the House of Israel, the king of Assyria turned his attention to Jerusalem, (the capital city for the House of Judah). The people were afraid because the king of Assyria had defeated all before him and seemed unstoppable. So, King Hezekiah consulted the prophet Isaiah,[94] who assured him that God would bring them victory. Then one

---

[92] Between 732- 724 BC.
[93] This is the first of two exiles/deportations.
[94] See the book of Isaiah.

night, the angel of God went into the Assyrian camp striking down one hundred and eighty-five thousand men.

Not long after, Isaiah appeared to Hezekiah[95] with a prophecy of a deportation for the House of Judah (as had happened to the House of Israel).

"*Hear Yahweh's word. 'Behold, the days come that all that is in your house, and that which your fathers have laid up in store to this day, will be carried to Babylon. Nothing will be left,' says Yahweh. 'They will take away some of your sons who will issue from you, whom you will father; and they will be eunuchs in the palace of the king of Babylon.'*"[96] (2Kg 20:17-18)

Many years later, under orders from King Josiah,[97] a high priest found the lost Book of Law[98] in the Temple of God. When the contents were read to Josiah, it saddened him. He realised these were the laws God had decreed in the days of Moses, the laws they were meant to live by to please and honour God, the laws that had been forgotten! Consulting another prophet, Josiah soon realised God intended to carry out all the punishments the book laid down for all the sins that had been committed in the past.

Josiah called all the people together and told them of the book, their sins, and God's prophecy. He began a religious reform urging everyone to repent and follow the decrees and laws as prescribed. All the people acceded. All the idols and temples to Baal were destroyed. Houses of prostitution were torn down. Passover was celebrated for the first time in nearly four hundred years.[99] No king had ever turned to God so staunchly with all his heart and soul, and no king ever would. Josiah ruled for thirty-one years.

---

[95] 13th king of Judah
[96] This would happen in about one hundred years.
[97] 16th king of Judah
[98] Thought to be the book Deuteronomy.
[99] Since the judges ruled Israel and never during the reign of Kings.

Sadly, thirteen years later, when Jehoiakim became king,[100] everything fell back into the ways of old. All the reforms Josiah had brought were abandoned. This decline was continued by the next king, Jehoiachin.[101] During his reign a famous king of Babylon, Nebuchadnezzar, was rising to power and eventually invaded Jerusalem. He forced the surrender of King Jehoiachin (who had only succeeded Jehoiakim three months earlier) and all his royal retinue. Many were exiled throughout the Kingdom of Babylon.[102]

Taking his place was Zedekiah[103] (the last king of Judah). He lasted only a year before King Nebuchadnezzar returned to complete the sacking of Jerusalem. The House of Judah was finally defeated and deported from their land,[104] one hundred and thirty-five years after the defeat of the House of Israel.

---

[100] 18th king of Judah - 609 BC
[101] 19th king of Judah - 598 BC
[102] Known as the first deportation.
[103] 598 BC
[104] The second exile/deportation.

Reign	House of Judah Southern Kingdom	Hose of Israel Northern Kingdom
930 - 913	Rehoboam	
931 - 910		Jeroboam
913 - 910	Abijah	
910 - 869	Asa	
910 - 909		Nadab
909 - 886		Baasha
886 - 885		Elah
885		Zimri
885 - 874		Omri
874 - 853		Ahab
869 - 848	Jehoshaphat	
853 - 852		Ahaziah
848 - 841	Jehoram	
841	Ahaziah	
841 - 835	Athaliah	
841 - 814		Jehu
835 - 796	Joash	
814 - 798		Jehoahaz
798-783		Jehoash
796 - 781	Amaziah	
781 - 740	Uzziah	
740 - 736	Jotham	
736 - 716	Ahaz	
783 - 743		Jeroboam II
743		Zachariah
743		Shallum
743 - 738		Menahem
738 - 737		Pekahiah
737 - 732		Pekah
732 - 721		Hoshea
731		Exile to Assyria
716 - 687	Hezekiah	
687 - 642	Manasseh	
642 - 640	Amon	
640 - 609	Josiah	
609	Jehoahaz	
609 - 598	Jehoiakim	
598	Jehoiachin	
598 - 587	Zedekiah	
598 - 587	Deportation to Babylon	

THE BOOKS OF CHRONICLES I AND II

The Book of Chronicles overlaps with the Book of Kings, only told from a different perspective. It begins with a detailed 'chronicling' of the genealogy of Israel, beginning with Adam right up until Saul, covering the time of David in detail, then onto Solomon. I chose not to retell the stories or to broaden the stories with new details in 1 Chronicles.

2 Chronicles is different however, as it covers the years of the king's ruling over Judah (931 - 587 BC), overlapping in parts with the Book of Kings. It is a snapshot of most of the Old Testament journey. How God continually tries to inspire and lead his chosen people, and they continually stray. A central theme that emerges here more than in any other book is how the fate of the people rests on the faithfulness (or lack thereof) of the reigning king.

Rehoboam 931 - 913 BC

At the death of his father Solomon, Rehoboam went to Shechem, where the Kings of Israel were proclaimed, but he was to come up against Jeroboam, who also wanted to claim the Kingship.

The people went to Rehoboam to plead with him not to be as harsh as his father, but after consulting his advisors he said it would not be possible.

"My father made your yoke heavy, but I will add to it. My father chastised you with whips, but I will chastise you with scorpions."

So the king didn't listen to the people; for it was brought about by God, that Yahweh might establish his word. (2Ch 10:14-15)

When all Israel heard these words they sent Rehoboam away from the city.

"What portion do we have in David? We don't have an inheritance in the son of Jesse! Every man to your tents, Israel! Now see to your own house, David." (2Ch 10:16)

Israel and the House of Judah were separated and existed in a love-hate relationship all throughout their history.[105] Jeroboam became the first king of Israel.

Rehoboam wanted to attack Israel but was warned not to by the prophet Shemaiah. Instead, he stayed in Jerusalem rebuilding the towns around it.

Rehoboam did a lot of good in the eyes of God, but eventually abandoned the Law of Yahweh when he consulted the many gods of his wives.

The prophet Shemaiah once again spoke to Rehoboam.

"Yahweh says, 'You have forsaken me, therefore I have also left you in the hand of Shishak.'" (2Ch 12:5)

Rehoboam immediately repented, and God softened his stance on the city being completely sacked by Shishak.[106] Adding, "However, Jerusalem *will be his servants, that they may know my service, and the service of the kingdoms of the countries."* (2Ch 12:8)

---

[105] Duggan, Michael W. The Consuming Fire: a Christian Introduction to the Old Testament. Ignatius Press, 1991. [p17].
[106] The king of Egypt.

Shishak indeed plundered the city, taking with him a myriad of treasures from the Temple of God.

Rehoboam *reigned seventeen years in Jerusalem, the city which Yahweh had chosen out of all the tribes of Israel to put his name there.* (2Ch 12:13)

Abijah 913 - 911 BC (Son of Rehoboam)

Abijah ruled for only three short years, and in his time he concentrated on attacking Israel. Mustering together an army of four hundred thousand, he marched on King Jeroboam of Israel, and his eight hundred thousand. Abijah won a crushing victory.

Asa 911 - 870 BC (Son of Abijah)

Asa did what was right in the eyes of Yahweh. One day, as he prayed to God, a Cushite by the name of Zerah attacked with his one million strong force (against Asa's three hundred thousand). Asa prayed, *"Yahweh, there is no one besides you to help, between the mighty and him who has no strength. Help us, Yahweh our God; for we rely on you, and in your name we come against this multitude. Yahweh, you are our God. Don't let man prevail against you."* (2Ch 14:11)

Yahweh brought about a crushing defeat of the Cushites.

In the thirty-fifth year of his reign, as he was being attacked by King Baasha of Israel and needed support, Asa made an alliance with a king in Damascus. God was not happy with this lack of faith and sent the prophet Hanani with a message.

"Weren't the Ethiopians and the Libyans a huge army, with chariots and exceedingly many horsemen? Yet, because you relied on Yahweh, he delivered them into your hand. For Yahweh's eyes run back and forth throughout the whole earth, to show himself strong on behalf of them whose heart is perfect toward him. You have done foolishly in this; for from now on you will have wars." (2Ch 16:8-9)

Jehoshaphat 870 - 848 BC (Son of Asa)

Yahweh was with Jehoshaphat because he was good and faithful like his father (in his early years). He amassed glorious wealth and honour, and eventually married the daughter of King Ahab of Israel.[107] This resulted in Ahab asking Jehoshaphat to join him in battle. Jehoshaphat wanted the prophets to be consulted. One prophesied it would be a victory, but Micaiah said it would be a defeat. Ahab dismissed Micaiah because he always gave dire prophecies.

Ahab went ahead with the battle, but to protect himself against the prophecy of Micaiah he rode into battle out of uniform, making Jehoshaphat ride in full regalia. The commander of the invading forces gave orders not to attack anyone of rank except the king. When they saw Jehoshaphat they attacked, but God saved him. Then a random arrow hit Ahab in the chest and killed him. Jehoshaphat returned safely home to Jerusalem.

Another time the Ammonites and Moabites planned to attack Jehoshaphat. Seeking God, Jehoshaphat and all the men of Judah were assured a victory, but with a condition, they would not even need to fight. As the attacking army approached Jerusalem, they came upon the mountain people of Seir whom they destroyed. They then turned on themselves. By the time Jehoshaphat reached them they were all dead. *So the realm of Jehoshaphat was quiet, for his God gave him rest all around.* (2Ch 20:30)

Jehoram 848 - 841 BC (Son of Jehoshaphat)

Jehoram was thirty-two when he came to the throne and *followed the example ... of Ahab...*, *having married one of Ahab's daughters; and he did*

---

[107] King Ahab ruled between 874 - 853 BC. He was the 7th king of Israel.

what is displeasing to Yahweh. Yahweh however did not intend to destroy the House of David.* (2Ch 21:6-7*)

One day a prophecy made by Elijah was bought to him, it read: *"Because you have not walked in the ways of Jehoshaphat your father, nor in the ways of Asa king of Judah, but have walked in the way of the kings of Israel, and have made Judah and the inhabitants of Jerusalem to play the prostitute like Ahab's house did, and also have slain your brothers of your father's house, who were better than yourself, behold, Yahweh will strike your people with a great plague, including your children, your wives, and all your possessions"* (2Ch 21:12-14)

The Philistines and Arabs defeated Jehoram.

Ahaziah 841 BC (Son of Jehoram)

Ahaziah was twenty-two years old when he came to rule and followed the wicked ways of Ahab's family, since his mother was Ahab's daughter. He also joined forces with Israel, and one day, while visiting King Jehoram of Israel,[108] was killed by Jehu (the Israelite king-in-waiting), who had been anointed by God to stop the evil reigns of Jehoram and Ahaziah.

Athaliah 841 - 835 BC (Mother Of Ahaziah)

After Ahaziah died, his mother quickly stepped in to seize power. He had one son, Joash, who was hidden away from harm by his aunt Jehosheba for six years, while his grandmother Athaliah ruled.

In the seventh year Jehosheba's husband, a priest, rallied together many of the influential families and planned to overthrow Queen Athaliah and replace her with Joash.

---

[108] 123 This is the ninth king of Israel, not to be confused with Ahaziah's great-great-great-grandfather Jehoram, the fifth king of Judah.

Joash 835 - 796 BC (Son Of Athaliah)

Joash was seven when he came to power and ruled as a faithful king under the watchful eye of the priest Jehoiada, but after Jehoiada's death Joash became unfaithful and abandoned the Temple of God. God soon sent a prophet, the son of Jehoiada. *"Why do you disobey Yahweh's commandments, so that you can't prosper? Because you have forsaken Yahweh, he has also forsaken you."* (2Ch 24:20)

They stoned the prophet in the court of the Temple of God.

Soon Judah and Jerusalem were attacked and defeated by Arameans, and Joash was murdered by his own people, for they blamed his treatment of the prophet for their defeat.

Amaziah 796 - 781 BC (Son of Joash)

Amaziah was twenty-five when he came to the throne and was mostly pleasing to God.

Once the kingdom was firmly under his control, he gathered all the men who were party to the assassination of his father and had them killed, but he did not kill their sons, as the Law stated: *'Fathers shall not die for the children, neither shall the children die for the fathers; but every man shall die for his own sin.'* (2Ch 25:4)

Uzziah 781 - 740 BC (Son Of Amaziah)

Uzziah was sixteen when he came to power and was given prosperity while he devoutly sought God. He went on a rebuilding campaign, and *his name spread far abroad, because he was marvellously helped until he was strong.* (2Ch 26:15)

In a common theme however, as his power increased, so did his pride, and he soon found himself on the wrong side of God. One day he entered the Temple of God, which was forbidden - only Levitical priests were allowed inside the Temple. While the priests were rebuking him, he broke out in leprosy and lived the rest of his life confined to his room. His son Jotham ruled in his stead.

Jotham 740 - 736 BC (Son Of Uzziah)

Jotham was twenty-five when he came to the throne. He was devoted to God, building the Upper Gate of the Temple of God, and fighting battles against the Ammonites.

Ahaz 736 - 716 BC (Son Of Jotham)

Ahaz was twenty when he started to rule. He also turned away from the laws of God and was more like the people from Israel who followed Baal. Because of that, God delivered Judah into the hands of the Arameans and Israel. But even in their defeat, God would not wipe them out.

The Israelites took two hundred thousand Judeans as captives, causing God to stir in the heart of the prophet Oded and deliver a stern message. *"Behold, because Yahweh, the God of your fathers, was angry with Judah, he has delivered them into your hand, and you have slain them in a rage which has reached up to heaven. Now you intend to degrade the children of Judah and Jerusalem as male and female slaves for yourselves. Aren't there even with you trespasses of your own against Yahweh your God? Now hear me therefore, and send back the captives that you have taken captive from your brothers, for the fierce wrath of Yahweh is on you."* (2Ch 28:9-11)

The Israelites listened to the prophet and released the prisoners.

Yahweh continued to humble Judah by allowing the Edomites and Philistines to invade and defeat them. However, *in the time of his distress, he trespassed yet more against Yahweh, this same King Ahaz. For he sacrificed to the gods of Damascus, which had defeated him. He said, "Because the gods of the kings of Syria helped them, I will sacrifice to them, that they may help me." But they were the ruin of him and of all Israel. Ahaz gathered together the vessels of God's house, cut the vessels of God's house in pieces, and shut up the doors of Yahweh's house; and he made himself altars in every corner of Jerusalem. In every city of Judah, he made high places to burn incense to other gods, and provoked Yahweh, the God of his fathers, to anger.* (2Ch 28:22-25)

Hezekiah 716 - 686 BC (Son Of Ahaz)

Hezekiah was twenty-five when he came to the throne and was an obedient servant of God. In the first year of his reign, he ordered the Temple of God to be repaired and re-sanctified with a view to holding a great Passover event. So strong was his zeal for God that he even resolved to send a proclamation to the House of Israel inviting all to attend. There was great joy and celebration, as not since the time of David had such a gathering occurred.

After Hezekiah's multiple loyal acts, the king of Assyria began looking to attack, but Hezekiah was confident in God. The king ridiculed the people for their 'false' hope.

God saved Judah by sending one of his angels to strike the army down, sending the king back to Assyria in defeat and despair.

Manasseh 686 - 642 BC (Son Of Hezekiah)

Manasseh was twelve when he came to the throne and undid all the good work his father had done. He worshipped all manner of gods and even practised witchcraft and soothsaying. To punish him, God sent the king of Assyria back to attack him, capturing and dragging him off to Babylon in chains.

Praying to God to save and forgive him, God relented and allowed him to return to Jerusalem, where he had a change of heart and began to worship Yahweh alone as the only true God.

Amon 642 - 640 BC (Son Of Manasseh)

Amon was twenty-two when he came to reign and he was like his father, Manasseh. God quickly saw to his demise, with his own officers plotting his death.

Josiah 640 - 609 BC (Son Of Amon)

Josiah was only eight years old when he took the throne from his father. He was a good and steadfast king and followed the example of David.

During his reign, the Book of Law[109] was rediscovered lying within the Temple of God. *(See Book of Kings I and II.)*

On hearing word that King Neco from Egypt was moving towards an Israelite town near him, he went to meet him in battle. The king questioned Josiah about why he was interfering with his attack plans since it was not a Judaean town and had nothing to do with him. Besides, the king was under direct orders from God.

"What have I to do with you, you king of Judah? I come not against you today, but against the house with which I have war. God has commanded me to make haste. Beware that it is God who is with me, that he may not destroy you." (2Ch 35:21)

Josiah did not listen, and as a result, he was wounded in battle and died soon afterwards in Jerusalem.

Jehoahaz 609 - 609 BC (Son Of Josiah)

Jehoahaz was twenty-three years old when he began to reign; and he reigned for three months in Jerusalem. The king of Egypt removed him from office at Jerusalem and fined the land one hundred talents of silver and a talent of gold. The king of Egypt made Eliakim his brother king over Judah and

---

[109] The book of Deuteronomy.

Jerusalem and changed his name to Jehoiakim. Neco took Jehoahaz his brother, and carried him to Egypt. (2Ch 36:2-4)

Jehoiakim 609 - 598 BC (Son Of Josiah, Brother Of Jehoahaz)

Twenty-five when he came to the throne, Jehoiakim did what was displeasing to Yahweh, and Nebuchadnezzar attacked the city, captured him, and took him off in chains back to Babylon. He also ransacked the Temple of God, taking part of the furnishings to put them in his own palace in Babylon. This first of three separate deportations to Babylon occurred circa 605 BC.

Jehoiachin 598 - 598 BC (Son Of Jehoiakim)

Jehoiachin was eight years old when he began to reign, and he reigned three months and ten days in Jerusalem. He did that which was evil in Yahweh's sight. At the return of the year, King Nebuchadnezzar sent and brought him to Babylon, with the valuable vessels of Yahweh's house, and made Zedekiah his brother king over Judah and Jerusalem. (2Ch 36:9-10)

Zedekiah 598 - 587 BC (Son Of Josiah, Brother Of Jehoiakim), And The Last In The Davidic Line Of Kings

Zedekiah was twenty-one years old when he reigned, and he reigned eleven years in Jerusalem. He did that which was evil in Yahweh his God's sight. He didn't humble himself before Jeremiah the prophet, speaking from Yahweh's mouth. He also rebelled against King Nebuchadnezzar, who had made him swear by God; but he stiffened his neck and hardened his heart against turning to Yahweh, the God of Israel. (2Ch 36:11-13)

The rest of Jerusalem and Judah were uniformly as sinful, even the priests had sinned against God with shameful practices.

Time and time again, Yahweh sent them messengers *because he had compassion on his people and on his dwelling place; but they mocked the messengers of God, despised his words, and scoffed at his prophets, until Yahweh's wrath arose against his people, until there was no remedy.* (2Ch 36:15-16)

God handed them all over to the king of the Chaldeans. *All the vessels of God's house, great and small, and the treasures of Yahweh's house, and the treasures of the king and of his princes, all these he brought to Babylon. They burned God's house, broke down the wall of Jerusalem, burned all its palaces with fire, and destroyed all of its valuable vessels. He carried those who had escaped from the sword away to Babylon, and they were servants to him and his sons until the reign of the Kingdom of Persia, to fulfil Yahweh's word by Jeremiah's mouth, until the land had enjoyed its Sabbaths. As long as it lay desolate, it kept Sabbath to fulfil seventy years.* (2Ch 36:18-21)

The second and third deportation to Babylon occurred in 597 BC and 587 BC.

The book then jumps seventy years until the end of the time of deportation in Babylon and the beginning of the reign of King Cyrus of Persia, who, roused by the spirit of God, allowed the people of God (now to be known as Jews) to return to Jerusalem.

THE BOOK OF EZRA AND NEHEMIAH

We find in these books what is considered to be the 'beginning of Judaism'. From this point onwards, 'the Jews' would no longer be a collective noun for a nation, or an ethnic group, or language and culture, but rather defined as those who were obedient to the Laws of Moses.

The book covers a period after the exile, c. 538 - 400 BC

After fifty years of exile and captivity in Babylon, there came along a new king of Persia, known as King Cyrus, who, roused by the word of God, overthrew Babylon and set the remnant of the House of Judah free to return to Jerusalem.[110] At the same time, he also returned all the stolen items, artefacts and precious stones for use in the reconstruction of the Temple of God.

Cyrus King of Persia says, "Yahweh, the God of heaven, has given me all the kingdoms of the earth; and he has commanded me to build him a house in Jerusalem, which is in Judah. Whoever there is among you of all his people, may his God be with him, and let him go up to Jerusalem, which is in Judah, and build the house of Yahweh, the God of Israel (he is God), which is in Jerusalem. Whoever is left, in any place where he lives, let the men of his place

---

[110] After about 50 years, c. 539 BC.

help him with silver, with gold, with goods, and with animals, in addition to the free will offering for God's house which is in Jerusalem." (Ezr 1:2-3)

The people did not get too far into the restoration, though. Those who had repopulated Jerusalem (the Samaritans)[111] after the House of Israel were driven out, felt aggrieved they were not invited to take part in the rebuilding, so they went to the new king, Artaxerxes, to stir up trouble, telling him the returning Jews had a history of being rebellious and wicked. They urged him to put a stop to it and he did.

The Jews[112] of Jerusalem appealed to the king to go back into his records to find the decree written by the former King Cyrus saying he had given permission for them to return and rebuild, (even going as far as to say the Persian kingdom would help financially). The Persian King Darius, found the evidence and reversed the earlier decision and the building ban was overturned.

At this time, the prophets Haggai and Zechariah began to prophesy.

The temple re-construction was completed c.515BC and the Israelites celebrated Passover and *joyfully dedicated this Temple of God*, (Ezr 6:16*) with a sacrifice of rams, lambs, and he-goats.

Some sixty years later, a scribe by the name of Ezra came up from Babylon and was given instructions by King Artaxerxes (who God was moving in) to *make inspection of Judah and Jerusalem according to the Law of your God...*(and to)...*carry the silver and gold which the king and his consellors have voluntarily offered to the God of Israel who dwells in Jerusalem.* (Ezr 7:14-15*)

He was also commissioned *to appoint scribes and judges...* (and)...*teach those who do not know* (the Law of God). (Ezr 7:25*)

---

[111] While not technically Jews, they had been taught the ways of Yahweh.
[112] After their exile and captivity the Houses of Judah and Israel were no more, instead the people became one nation again, this time adopting the name Jew.

As a scribe dedicated to the Law of Yahweh, Ezra reintroduced the original laws of Moses, which had again been forgotten. One law that was expressly enforced was against all the men and women who had married outside of the Jewish community. The guilty were rounded up and sent away.

At the same time, Nehemiah (a cup-bearer for the king of Persia) heard of the return of his people to Jerusalem. Inspired by God to rebuild the walls and gates around Jerusalem, he sought and was granted, a release to go back home.

Gathering together builders, he oversaw the repair and rebuilding of the gates and walls of Jerusalem. His efforts we soon noticed by the neighbouring pagan towns who quickly conspired to attack. On ten occassions the Jews (under the protection of God) were able to defend the city and repel the attacks.

When the walls were completed, it became apparent how large and extensive the city was, but the population was small. Nehemiah then began to find and return the exiles. Eventually over forty-two thousand people regathered in Jerusalem.

When the seventh month came, all the people gathered as one man on the square before the Water Gate. They asked Ezra the scribe to bring the Book of the Law of Moses which Yahweh had prescribed for Israel. Accordingly Ezra the priest brought the Law before the assembly, consisting of men, women, and children old enough to understand. (Neh 7:72-8:2*)

Each day, from the first day to the last, Ezra read from the Book of the Law of God. They celebrated the feast for seven days; on the eighth day, as prescribed, there was a solemn assembly. (Neh 8:18*)

On the twenty-fourth day of this month the Israelites, in sackcloth and with dust on their heads, assembled for a fast. Those of Israelite stock separated themselves from all those of foreign origin; they stood confessing their sins and the transgressions of their ancestors. (Neh 9:1-2*)

As one they prayed for atonement.

> *"Blessed be you, Yahweh our God,*
> *from everlasting to everlasting.*
> *And blessed be your name of glory*
> *that surpasses all blessing and praise.*
> *Yahweh, you are the only one.*
> *You made the heavens, the heaven of heavens, with all*
> *their array,*
> *the earth and all it bears,*
> *the seas and all they hold.*
> *To all of these you give life*
> *and the array of the heavens bow down before you."*
> (Neh 9:6-7*)

They also resolved to recommit themselves to the Laws of God that had been forgotten. *"In particular: we will not give our daughters to the natives of the land nor take their daughters for our sons.*

"If the natives of the land bring goods or any foodstuff whatever to sell on the Sabbath day, we will buy nothing from them on the Sabbath or holy day.

"We will forgo the fruits of the soil in the seventh year, and all debts." (Neh 10:30-31*)

They promised to recognise the obligations for sacrifices, oblations, holocausts; the first fruits of food and livestock, and tithes for the Levitical priests. *"We will no longer neglect the Temple of our God."* (Neh 10:40*)

TOBIT

This book was written before the time of Maccabees, so probably around 200 BC (but set in 720 BC). It was written for the Jewish people who were living outside of Jerusalem, and in foreign countries (unlike those exiled in Babylon).

It was written as an encouragement on how to remain faithful to God and his laws in a city and culture that did not share the same beliefs.

At Nineveh in Assyria, there lived a man called Tobit, who was upright and devoted to the laws of God. He always gave alms and watched over those less fortunate. He would even have pity on and bury his countrymen who had died and were tossed over the city walls instead of being properly buried. All the while he was being righteous, he was raising the ire of those around him who did not care for what he did.

One night, when celebrating the feast of Pentecost, he sent his son Tobias to find a less fortunate person to share their meal. While out looking, Tobias found a fellow countryman who had been murdered. Returning to tell his father, Tobit left his table and went out to collect the body to bury it. Later in the day, after bathing himself, he was sitting outside in the sun when a sparrow's droppings hit him in the eyes, causing spots and eventually sending him blind.

Tobit suffered for four years and became distraught and prayed for death. Starting to worry about his mortality, his family, and how he could provide for them, he called his son Tobias to him. He made him promise he would lead a good and righteous life and always watch over his mother, Anna. He also instructed him to collect some money that was due to them. It was from a man called Gabael.

Tobias, being a dutiful son, accepted his father's charge and began by looking for a travelling companion, someone who knew how to get to the town of Media, where Gabael lived. The companion he found was a man called Azariah (who was in fact Raphael, an angel of God, but this was hidden from Tobias).

Not long after departing, they stopped for a break beside a river where Tobias cooled his feet. Without warning, a fish surfaced and bit him. Tobias yelled in pain. Raphael came to him and told him to catch the fish, cut it open, and save the gall, heart, and liver, claiming they had healing powers.

Confused, Tobias questioned the angel, *"Brother Azariah, of what use is the heart, the liver, and the bile of the fish?"*

"About the heart and the liver: If a demon or an evil spirit troubles anyone, we must burn those and make smoke of them before the man or the woman, and the affliction will flee. But as for the bile, it is good to anoint a man that has white films in his eyes, and he will be healed." (Tob 6:6-8)

As they continued on to Media, Raphael told Tobias about a girl in a nearby town who he should marry. He explained to Tobias how she was from his own family line and therefore a suitable match, and she would surely please his father. Her name was Sarah,[113] but Tobias had heard things about her - and they weren't good.

Sarah was a widow to seven husbands, and all seven had died on their wedding night. Raphael assured Tobias it would not happen to him, telling him that on the night of their marriage, when they were in their

---

[113] On the same day that Tobit prayed to God for death, Sarah also prayed to God, asking for death because of the sorrow she had brought on her family with the death of her seven husbands.

room alone together, he was to use the heart and liver of the fish he caught and burn them with incense. The smell would make the demon responsible for the previous seven deaths leave Sarah. Tobias did as instructed and after the demon had fled, they both prayed to God for grace and protection.

At the same time, Sarah's father, Raguel, was outside expectantly digging a new grave. He then sent a maid into the room to see if Tobias was dead. When the report came back that he was alive, he quickly filled in the grave, hoping no one would know.

Everyone was euphoric: Sarah and her parents, Raguel, and Edna, because this husband didn't die, and Tobias, that he was still alive. They celebrated for many days.

In due course, Tobias remembered he had been away from his father for some time and that he would be anxious about his safe return. He called Raphael to ask him to continue the journey to Media, find Gabael, and get the money.

Returning home with his new wife, servants, and the money, Raphael asked Tobias if it would be better if the two of them set out ahead of the rest to see his father and prepare him to meet Sarah.

Entering the room where Tobit was, Tobias (under instructions from Raphael) had the fish gall in his hand, which he blew over and into the eyes of his father. A thin film appeared, and when Tobias wiped it away, his father's sight returned. They all feasted in celebration.

Tobit called Tobias to him, telling him he should pay Azariah for his assistance. Tobias agreed, but added he deserved more than what they agreed to at the start. Tobias called Raphael to him and gave him half of all the money collected, in thanks for Sarah and his father.

Raphael couldn't accept, and he decided it was time to reveal himself. *"I am going to tell you the whole truth, hiding nothing from you... So you must know that when you and Sarah were at prayer, it was I who offered your supplications before the glory of the Lord and who read them; so too when you were burying the dead. When you did not hesitate to get up and leave the table to go and bury a dead man, I was sent to test your faith, and at the same time God sent me to heal you and your daughter-in-law Sarah. I am Raphael, one of the seven angels who stand ever ready to enter the presence of the glory of the Lord."* (Tob 12:11-15*)

Everyone there fell onto their faces in terror, but the angel said, *"Don't be afraid. You will all have peace; but bless God forever. For I came not of any favour of my own, but by the will of your God. Therefore bless him forever. All these days I appeared to you. I didn't eat or drink, but you all saw a vision. Now give God thanks, because I ascend to him who sent me. Write in a book all the things which have been done."* (Tob 12:17-20)

JUDITH

Judith is a militant heroine from the period after the Jews had returned to their homeland. It is believed to have been written around 100 BC. The author 'sought to strengthen the faith of his people in God's abiding presence among them...and take to heart that God was still the Master of history, who could save Israel from her enemies'.[114]

Within a few years of the Jews returning from captivity there came a king of Assyria, Nebuchadnezzar, who was fanatical about taking over the world. He sent word out to all the towns within his domain, demanding that men be sent to join his armies. Most of the towns refused. This infuriated him, and he vowed to wipe them all out.

His campaign began in the North and was an overwhelming success, so much so that he soon slowed down to celebrate his victories. Tired of the fighting, he summoned his second-in-charge - Holofernes, who was singularly evil, to finish the plundering of the more southern towns. Like the kings before him, the towns surrendered without a fight, until they came to Judah. Because the people had only recently resettled there, they were not going to leave without a fight.

Holofernes was baffled as to why this town wasn't surrendering, so he called an advisor to find out. The advisor, Achior, returned with what

---

[114] Introduction to The Book of Judith NAB Catholic Biblical Association 1969.

he had discovered, telling Holofernes the history of the Israelites from leaving Egypt up to the present time. He explained they had a god like no other and he shouldn't be tested. He did, however, tell him that if the Israelites had sinned against their god, then the city could be easily taken. If they had not however, then it would be suicide to attack as they would be defeated. Holofernes laughed at the report and banished Achior to the city of Judah to meet the same end as the rest of the city.

When the Israelites found Achior lurking outside the city walls, they brought him in to be questioned. He recounted everything he said to Holofernes, and they believed him.

The one hundred and thirty-thousand troops of Holofernes were prepared for war, but first an advance party was sent out. They discovered that while the city was only defended by a small number, its defences were well built, and large numbers of men would be killed trying to capture the strongholds. Instead, it was recommended they encircle the city, stopping trade in and out, thus defeating the city by starvation.

Eventually, the morale of the Jews waned, and after a month of diminishing food and water they began to consider surrender. When Judith, a widow, heard about this, she admonished the leaders for their lack of faith in God, and after praying took matters into her own hands.

Leaving the town, Judith set out to the camp of Holofernes; as she approached, a crowd of men formed. They were fascinated by her beauty.

"Who would despise these people, who have among them such women? For it is not good that one man of them be left, seeing that, if they are let go, they will be able to deceive the whole earth." (Jud 10:18)

They took her to meet Holofernes, who was captivated by her beauty. One night, she was left alone in the tent with Holofernes. He had so much to drink that he collapsed. Judith seized the chance to attack. Striking twice, she cut off his head.

Returning to the town with the head of Holofernes, everyone rejoiced at her exceptional deeds, and they gave praise to God. *"Praise God! Praise* him! Praise God, who has not taken away his mercy from the house of Israel, but has destroyed our enemies by my hand tonight!"* (Jud 13:14)

The high priests and elders praised her. *"You are the exaltation of Jerusalem! You are the great glory of Israel! You are the great rejoicing of our race! You have done all these things by your hand. You have done with Israel the things that are good, and God is pleased with it. May you be blessed by the Almighty Lord forever!"* (Jud 15:10-12)

When Holofernes' men discovered what had happened, they fled in panic.

ESTHER

This book tells the story of a devout and heroic Jewess, who, through her own cleverness saves her fellow Jews from mass annihilation - brought on by an all too familiar hatred of their way of life. Interestingly God is not mentioned once.

The book is set in Persia around 470 BC, and probably written around mid 3/4th Century BC.

There was a king called Ahasuerus, who was looking for a new queen, and decided the surest way to find her would be to hold a pageant. At the time, there was a Jew called Mordecai in the king's court who was raising his uncle's daughter, Esther. He encouraged her to join the pageant, which she did and won, becoming Queen Esther.

Sometime later, Mordecai heard about a plot to kill the king, telling Esther so that she could bring it to the king. Two of the king's eunuchs, Bigthan and Teresh, were discovered, tortured, and swiftly sent to their death.

Shortly afterward, King Ahasuerus promoted a man called Haman to be in charge of his palace and pronounced that all should bow before him when in his presence, as he would be second only to the king himself. Mordecai could not bow before him though, as he was a proud Jew. When Haman heard of his insolence, he was infuriated and promptly made up his mind to kill him and his whole family. He also swore to wipe out the entire race of the Jews.

News of this reached Esther and Mordecai. Esther prayed, *"O Lord, don't surrender your sceptre to those who don't exist, and don't let them laugh at our fall, but turn their counsel against themselves, and make an example of him who has begun to injure us.*

"Remember us, O Lord! Manifest yourself in the time of our affliction. Encourage me, O King of gods, and ruler of all dominion!

"Put harmonious speech into my mouth before the lion, and turn his heart to hate him who fights against us, to the utter destruction of those who agree with him.

"But deliver us by your hand, and help me who is alone and have no one but you, O Lord." (Est 4:39-42)

Esther devised a plan to save her race. She invited her husband King Ahasuerus and Haman to a banquet. The king was so overwhelmed by her and the banquet she had prepared in his honour that he told her he would give her anything she wanted, even up to half of his kingdom.[115] Not yet prepared to ask for what she wanted, Esther instead invited them both back the following night for another feast, at which time she would make her request.

Meanwhile, Mordecai was sitting in the corner. When Haman saw him, he was filled with loathing. Later that night he began to plot his death. He even ordered gallows to be prepared in anticipation of his hanging.

That night, the king couldn't sleep, so he picked up a copy of the City Chronicles. In it he discovered Mordecai was the person responsible for alerting the palace about the assassination attempt by Bigthan and Teresh.

---

[115] A similar pledge was made by King Herod which resulted in the death of John the Baptist.

While he was still reading, Haman came to his door (wanting to ask for permission to hang Mordecai), but before he could speak the king posed him a question.

"What would be a fitting way to honour a man who has the king's favour?"

Haman assumed the king must be speaking about him, so answered, "They should buy him royal robes, and he should be paraded through the city on horseback with a crown on his head."

The king replied, "Let it be done as you say - the man is Mordecai."

While Haman was crestfallen, he obeyed and did as the king ordered.

The following night when they both attended the second banquet, the king again pressed Esther to make her request. This time she did. She said all she wanted was for her people (The Jews) to be saved from someone who wanted to destroy them. When the king asked who it was, she named Haman. The king promptly ordered him to be hanged. As fate would have it, it was on the exact same gallows he had prepared for Mordecai.

Esther explained to the king that Haman had already sent out letters to every province of the realm ordering the pogrom of the Jewish people. King Ahasuerus told his queen to write again, in his name, to all these provinces reversing the decree, and to leave all the Jews safe and unharmed.

BOOKS OF MACCABEES I AND II

The two Maccabees books offer a historical account of the Jewish people during a tumultuous period. As a backdrop to the seemingly never-ending cycle of attacks on the Jewish people, we encounter a time when the Hellenistic influence is affecting the people of Judah, and see the rise of one family that restores the fortunes of the Jewish people.

Written c. 100 BC, the books primarily cover the period 175 - 140 BC.

After the time of Alexander the Great (during the reign of Antiochus IV),[116] there was a growing number of Jews who were moving away from the laws of Yahweh and towards Hellenism (the culture of the Greeks). This was manifested by the building of a gymnasium, disguising their circumcisions, and abandoning their covenant.

Antiochus, looking to expand his kingdom, turned his attention to the Jews, and in particular the riches to be found in Jerusalem. He sacked the sanctuary and took off with *the golden altar and the lampstand for the light with all its fittings, together with the table for the loaves of offering,*

---

[116] 175 BC

the libation vessels, the cups, the golden censers, the veil, the crowns, and the golden decoration on the front of the Temple. (1Mac 1:23-24*)

Unfortunately for the Jews, Antiochus returned two years later to bring greater carnage - killing many people, taking women and children hostage, and setting fire to the city. He also claimed the City of David's fortress as his own citadel, where he garrisoned a portion of his army to safeguard the plunder he had amassed.

Antiochus next proclaimed that all people (within his kingdom) must unify under his religion. Many Jews accepted and *consented to his worship, sacrificed to the idols, and profaned the Sabbath.* (1Mac 1:43) Anyone found with a copy of the covenant or practising their Jewish beliefs was put to death. Even babies found to be circumcised were killed, along with their mothers.

Among the people of Israel, though, there were those who remained devout and rebelled. These were led by a priest from Modein called Mattathias, who, on seeing the blasphemies around him said, *"Woe is me! Why was I born to see the destruction of my people and the destruction of the holy city, and to dwell there when it was given into the hand of the enemy, the sanctuary into the hand of foreigners?... Her vessels of glory are carried away into captivity. Her infants are slain in her streets. Her young men are slain with the enemy's sword... Behold, our holy things, our beauty, and our glory are laid waste. The Gentiles have profaned them. Why should we live any longer?"* (1Mac 2:7-13)

Banding together as many supporters as he could, Mattathias left his hometown and went to hide in the hills, as he knew they would be hunted down.

This remnant of obedient Jews was soon joined by another group - the Hasideans[117], who were strong supporters of the Law. Their joining

---

[117] It was widely agreed the Hasideans were the forebears of the Pharisees that we have come to know in the New Testament times of Jesus.

inspired others as well. Together with his new army, Mattathias enforced the Law among their people and cities, hunting down and killing transgressors. But Mattathias was nearing the end of his life, so he appointed his son Judas[118] as the new general of the army, and his other son Simon to be the leader of the people.

Judas was soon to meet the armies of Antiochus in battle, and with the support of God, easily won. News of the losses inflamed Antiochus, and he quickly sent another of his generals, Lysias, to crush the Jews. Lysias chose three men, Ptolemy, Nicanor, and Gorgias, to lead the assaults. As the armies faced off, Judas caught sight of the size of their force and knew he was hopelessly outnumbered. Turning to God for help and guidance, Judas set time aside to pray and fast. He assembled all before him and said, *"Arm yourselves and be valiant men! Be ready in the morning, that you may fight with these Gentiles who are assembled together against us to destroy us and our holy place. For it is better for us to die in battle than to see the evils of our nation and the holy place. Nevertheless, as may be the will in heaven, so shall he do."* (1Mac 3:58-60)
God delivered a glorious victory.

Lysias was furious when he heard the 'impossible' news of his massive force being defeated, so the following year he amassed an even bigger army that he himself commanded. But God and the Jews were victorious again, sending Lysias back to Antioch, demoralised and defeated.

While all this was happening, Antiochus, who was occupied fighting other battles, heard about Lysias' defeat. Rushing to be at his side, he fell off his chariot and was fatally injured.

On his deathbed, Antiochus had an epiphany. *"I said in my heart, 'To what suffering I have come! How great a flood it is that I'm in, now! For I was gracious and loved in my power.' But now I remember the evils which I*

---

[118] Judas was to become known as Maccabee, the titular character of the Book of Maccabees.

did at Jerusalem, and that I took all the vessels of silver and gold that were in it, and sent out to destroy the inhabitants of Judah without a cause. I perceive that it is because of this that these evils have come upon me. Behold, I am perishing through great grief in a strange land." (1Mac 6:11-13)

Antiochus had appointed his friend Philip as his successor, but when Lysias heard of the death, he appointed Antiochus' nine-year-old son to the throne, thus becoming Antiochus V.

In the meantime, Judas and his brothers decided it was time to restore, purify, and rededicate the sanctuary at Jerusalem, which had been defiled by Antiochus.

First, he appointed new and faithful priests. Then it was agreed that the altar of holocausts needed to be completely pulled down for fear it might remain stained by the objects of pagan worship. A new altar was erected, and three years to the day after it was destroyed, and among much joy and celebration, it was rededicated to God according to the Law.[119]

Sadly for the Jews, they were still not to find peace. As news of the temple's restoration reached the neighbouring regions, they became hostile and *took counsel to destroy the race of Jacob that was amid them.* (1Mac 5:2)

Before long, Judas decided the garrison left at the City of David had to be overthrown. During the attack, some of the garrison, along with a few renegade Jews, escaped and made their way to the king[120] to plead for support.

A vast force, led by Lysias, was mustered and advanced towards Jerusalem. The Jews put up determined resistance but eventually faded

---

[119] This time and event is still celebrated by the Jews today as Hanukkah.

[120] King Antiochus V was probably only about eleven, so it was more likely Lysias was calling the shots.

as they ran out of provisions, for it was a sabbatical year.[121] At the very point of victory Antiochus V heard how Philip (the one appointed by his father to succeed him), was planning to take control of the government at Antioch. As Lysias needed to return to Antioch to deal with Philip, he stopped the attack on Jerusalem. A peace was agreed, but once the city gates were opened and Lysias saw the diminished strength of the Jewish defences, he broke his pact and ordered the encircling city walls to be destroyed.

When Lysias reached Antioch, he found Philip was already victorious, but he didn't stand long against his arriving forces.

Interestingly, Antiochus V and his regent Lysias were soon to meet their end - at the hand of Demetrius, an uncle of Antiochus IV. He had just escaped imprisonment in Rome and returned to Antioch to proclaim himself rightful king.

Once all the renegade Jews heard of the new king, they went to stir up more trouble, telling him, *"Judas and his kindred have destroyed all your friends, and have scattered us from our own land. Now, therefore, send a man whom you trust, and let him go and see all the havoc which he has made of us, and of the king's country, and how he has punished them and all who helped them."* (1Mac 7:6-7)

Nicanor and his army returned and eventually marched into Jerusalem, where he issued a warrant for the capture and arrest of Judas, with a threat he would burn the place down if they did not bring him to him.

Judas was not given up. Nicanor sent for reinforcements, and they fought a battle at Adasa, where Nicanor was among the first to die.

---

[121] The sabbatical year was a year of rest for the land. The observance was to remind the Israelites that the land belonged to God and that in his eyes they were living there only as strangers. No field was to be cultivated or sown: no garden, no fruit tree was to receive attention. Whatever grew without any action on the part of man became common property. Schoenberg, M. (1966). Old Testament reading guide: The first and the second books of the Maccabees. p41

On receiving this news, King Demetrius sent more men. During the defence, all was going well until Judas was killed, sending his army to retreat in fear.

When news of Judas' death got out, it gave new hope to the nefarious and Hellenistic Jews. Bacchides (a general of King Demetrius) seized on this opportunity to appoint loyal governors to all the provinces in Judah. *There was great suffering in Israel, such as was not since the time that no prophet appeared to them.* (1Mac 9:27) The people then chose Judas' brother Jonathan to become their new leader.[122]

Jonathan and Bacchides met in battle on the banks of the Jordan. Jonathan was outnumbered and could not win, so he fled with his forces across the River Jordan. Bacchides returned to Jerusalem as victor and began building his own strongholds.

Feeling confident his fortifications and forces remaining were secure enough, Bacchides felt safe to return home to Antioch. And while Judah remained occupied, it enjoyed two years of peace.

The demanding Hellenistic Jews were still looking to inflict a final blow on the ardent Jews, so they went to petition Bacchides with what they believed was a surefire plan. Bacchides was only too pleased to listen and respond. Things did not go well though. Jonathan, knowing of the impending attack, had ample time to set up his defences. Bacchides arrived expecting a walk in the park (as promised by those who came to petition him), yet what he discovered was anything but. Infuriated, he corralled those pesky petition makers and had them killed. He then negotiated peace terms with Jonathan, which included him agreeing to never again come to their borders.

Thus the sword ceased from Israel. Jonathan lived at Michmash. Jonathan began to judge the people; and he destroyed the ungodly out of Israel. (1Mac 9:73)

---

[122] The youngest of the sons of Mattathias.

Jonathan became a virtuous and respected leader, ultimately dying in battle. His brother Simon took over the leadership. He also oversaw the evacuation of the last of the garrisoned men in the Citadel and reopened it up as a holy place of God.

Simon ultimately met his death at the hand of Ptolemy, the Governor of Jericho.

THE WISDOM BOOKS

JOB

This is a story of an innocent man who is made to suffer. It is a story about temptation, but importantly it lets us know that temptation doesn't come from God, but from evil. It also readies us to know that temptation will be a fact of life for us, for God does allow it - but not beyond our own limitations to bear it. The light at the end of the tunnel is, if we stay obedient to, and trust in God, we will prevail.

Likely to have been written sometime in the 6th Century BC.

Poor Job, always an honest, devout, and upright man. Blessed with seven sons and three daughters, and master of many sheep, goats, and cattle. One day, God and Satan got into a conversation. God expressed his delight in Job and his confidence that Job was faithful and beyond temptation. The Devil scoffed, saying Job is only obedient because he has everything he wants. So, God allowed Satan to try and turn him from God.

At first Satan slaughtered all Job's cattle, destroyed all his crops, and finally killed all his children. As if that wasn't enough, he returned and struck him down with ulcers, sores, and scabs. Job was wrecked. His wife questioned him, *"Do you still maintain your integrity? Renounce God, and die."* (Job 2:9)

But Job was strong and replied, *"What? Shall we receive good at the hand of God, and shall we not receive evil?"* (Job 2:10)

However, Job did not know how long he was to be inflicted with suffering, nor the pain and suffering that was to come. Soon he began to lament his life.

> "Let the day perish in which I was born,
> the night which said, 'There is a boy conceived.'
> Let that day be darkness,
> don't let God from above seek for it,
> neither let the light shine on it." (Job 3:3-4)

Some of Job's friends heard of his plight and came to call on him, to offer some wisdom and help if they could. They were Eliphaz, Bildad, Zophar, and Elihu.

Eliphaz spoke first, beginning with a challenge.

> "Behold, you have instructed many,
> you have strengthened the weak hands.
> Your words have supported him who was falling,
> you have made the feeble knees firm.
> But now it has come to you, and you faint.
> It touches you, and you are troubled.
> Isn't your piety your confidence?
> Isn't the integrity of your ways your hope?" (Job 4:3-6)

Eliphaz counselled to submit all to God.

> "For affliction doesn't come out of the dust,
> neither does trouble spring out of the ground;
> but man is born to trouble,
> as the sparks fly upward.
> But as for me, I would seek God.
> I would commit my cause to God,

> *who does great things that can't be fathomed."* (Job 5:6-9)

Job responds, saying he'd rather be dead than go through any more pain, especially because he has no idea why he is suffering as he is.

> *"Oh that my anguish were weighed,*
> *and all my calamity laid in the balances!*
> *For now it would be heavier than the sand of the seas,*
> *therefore my words have been rash.*
> *For the arrows of the Almighty are within me,*
> *my spirit drinks up their poison.*
> *The terrors of God set themselves in array against me."*
> (Job 6:2-4)

> *"Even that it would please God to crush me;*
> *that he would let loose his hand, and cut me off!*
> *Let it still be my consolation,*
> *yes, let me exult in pain that doesn't spare,*
> *that I have not denied the words of the Holy One."*
> (Job 6:9-10)

Bildad now chimes in, essentially saying God doesn't make mistakes.

> *"How long will you speak these things?*
> *Shall the words of your mouth be a mighty wind?*
> *Does God pervert justice?*
> *Or does the Almighty pervert righteousness?*
> *If you were pure and upright,*
> *surely now he would awaken for you,*
> *and make the habitation of your righteousness prosperous."*
> (Job 8:2,3,6)

Job replies, acknowledging God is just.

> "Truly I know that it is so,
> but how can man be just with God?
> ...
> God is wise in heart, and mighty in strength,
> who has hardened himself against him and prospered?
> He removes the mountains, and they don't know it,
> when he overturns them in his anger.
> He shakes the earth out of its place,
> its pillars tremble.
> He commands the sun and it doesn't rise,
> and seals up the stars.
> He alone stretches out the heavens,
> and treads on the waves of the sea." (Job 9:2-8)

Now Zophar speaks, having a jibe at Job, saying God is always right, just, and merciful, and men are not blameless.

> "For you say, 'My doctrine is pure,
> I am clean in your eyes.'
> But oh that God would speak,
> and open his lips against you,
> that he would show you the secrets of wisdom!
> For true wisdom has two sides,
> know therefore that God exacts of you less than your iniquity deserves." (Job 11:4-6)

> "For he knows false men,
> he sees iniquity also, even though he doesn't consider it."
> (Job 11:11)

Job still can't understand why this is happening to him.

> "I was at ease, and he broke me apart.
> Yes, he has taken me by the neck, and dashed me to pieces,
> he has also set me up for his target." (Job 16:12)

He goes on complaining how everyone now shuns him: his family, his friends, even the local children avoid him.

> "Have pity on me.
> Have pity on me, you my friends,
> for the hand of God has touched me.
> Why do you persecute me as God,
> and are not satisfied with my flesh?" (Job 19:21-22)

Eliphaz chimes in again, telling Job that if he repents, God will relent.

> "If you return to the Almighty, you will be built up.
> …
> The Almighty will be your treasure,
> and precious silver to you.
> For then you will delight yourself in the Almighty,
> and will lift up your face to God.
> You will make your prayer to him, and he will hear you,
> you will pay your vows." (Job 22:23-27)

Elihu has been silent until now, but he needs to say something too; that is, God is God, and he will do what he wants, how he wants, when he wants.

> "Surely you have spoken in my hearing,
> I have heard the voice of your words, saying,
> 'I am clean, without disobedience,
> I am innocent, neither is there iniquity in me.

> *Behold, he finds occasions against me,*
> *he counts me for his enemy.*
> *He puts my feet in the stocks,*
> *He marks all my paths.'*
> *Behold, I will answer you. In this you are not just,*
> *for God is greater than man.*
> *Why do you strive against him,*
> *because he doesn't give account of any of his matters?*
> *For God speaks once,*
> *yes twice, though man pays no attention."* (Job 33:8-14)

> *"Then he shows them their work,*
> *and their transgressions,*
> *that they have behaved themselves proudly."* (Job 36:9)

It is now God's turn to set them all straight.

> *"Who is this who darkens counsels,*
> *by words without knowledge?*
> *Brace yourself like a man,*
> *for I will question you, then you answer me!*
> *Where were you when I laid the foundations of the earth?*
> *Declare, if you have understanding.*
> *Who determined its measures, if you know?*
> *Or who stretched the line on it?*
> *What were its foundations fastened on?*
> *Or who laid its cornerstone?*
> *Or who shut up the sea with doors,*
> *when it broke out of the womb,*
> *and said, 'You may come here, but no further.*
> *Your proud waves shall be stopped here?'"*

> "Have you commanded the morning in your days,
> and caused the dawn to know its place?" (Job 38:2-6, 8, 11, 12)

> "Does the rain have a father?
> Or who fathers the drops of dew?
> Whose womb did the ice come out of?
> Who has given birth to the grey frost of the sky?
> The waters become hard like stone,
> when the surface of the deep is frozen." (Job 38:28-30)

Job replies to Yahweh, admitting his defeat.

> "Behold, I am of small account. What will I answer you?
> I lay my hand on my mouth.
> I have spoken once, and I will not answer;
> yes, twice, but I will proceed no further." (Job 40:4-5)

Job's final words on the matter are:

> "I know that you can do all things,
> and that no purpose of yours can be restrained.
> You asked, 'Who is this who hides counsel without knowledge?'
> Therefore I have uttered that which I didn't understand,
> things too wonderful for me, which I didn't know.
> You said, 'Listen, now, and I will speak;
> I will question you, and you will answer me.'
> I had heard of you by the hearing of the ear,
> but now my eye sees you.
> Therefore I abhor myself,
> and repent in dust and ashes." (Job 42:2-6)

In the end, Job is cured, and all his fortunes are restored. In fact, his new wealth and holdings are double what he lost. He went on to father seven more sons and three more daughters.

THE PSALMS

These are hymns, songs, poems, lamentations, prayers, expressions of sorrow, love, thanksgiving, and praise. Of the 150 Psalms, 73 are attributed to David. They cover a period from the time of David until after the return from exile in Babylon.

The Psalms play a meaningful part in the New Testament where both Jesus and Mary reference them.

When reading or praying the Psalms, we are communicating with God using the same words to express the same feelings that all the people of the Old Testament used, thus connecting us with them in prayer.

Psalm 1

> *Blessed is the man who doesn't walk in the counsel of*
> *the wicked,*
> *nor stand on the path of sinners,*
> *nor sit in the seat of scoffers;*
> *but his delight is in Yahweh's law.*
> *On his Law he meditates day and night.*
>
> *He will be like a tree planted by the streams of water,*
> *that produces its fruit in its season,*
> *whose leaf also does not wither.*

Whatever he does shall prosper.

The wicked are not so,
but are like the chaff which the wind drives away.
Therefore the wicked shall not stand in the judgement,
nor sinners in the congregation of the righteous.
For Yahweh knows the way of the righteous,
but the way of the wicked shall perish.

Psalm 6

Yahweh, don't rebuke me in your anger,
neither discipline me in your wrath.
Have mercy on me, Yahweh, for I am faint.
Yahweh, heal me, for my bones are troubled.
My soul is also in great anguish.
But you, Yahweh – how long?

Return, Yahweh. Deliver my soul,
and save me for your loving kindness' sake.
For in death there is no memory of you.
In Sheol, who shall give you thanks?

I am weary with my groaning.
Every night I flood my bed.
I drench my couch with my tears.
My eye wastes away because of grief.
It grows old because of all my adversaries.

Depart from me, all you workers of iniquity,
for Yahweh has heard the voice of my weeping.
Yahweh has heard my supplication.
Yahweh accepts my prayer.

May all my enemies be ashamed and dismayed.
They shall turn back, they shall be disgraced suddenly.

Psalm 13

Will you forget me forever?
How long will you hide your face from me?
How long shall I take counsel in my soul,
having sorrow in my heart every day?
How long shall my enemy triumph over me?
Behold, and answer me, Yahweh, my God.

Give light to my eyes, lest I sleep in death;
lest my enemy say, "I have prevailed against him;"
lest my adversaries rejoice when I fall.
But I trust in your loving kindness.
My heart rejoices in your salvation.
I will sing to Yahweh,
because he has been good to me.

Psalm 15

Lord, who shall dwell in your sanctuary?
Who shall live on your holy hill?

He who walks blamelessly and does what is right,
and speaks truth in his heart;
he who doesn't slander with his tongue,
nor does evil to his friend,

nor casts slurs against his fellow man;
in whose eyes a vile man is despised,
but who honours those who fear Yahweh;

*he who keeps an oath even when it hurts, and
doesn't change;
he who doesn't lend out his money for usury,
nor take a bribe against the innocent.*

He who does these things shall never be shaken.

Psalm 40

*I waited patiently for Yahweh.
He turned to me,
and heard my cry.*

*He brought me up also out of a horrible pit,
out of the miry clay.
He set my feet on a rock,
and gave me a firm place to stand.*

*He has put a new song in my mouth,
even praise to our God.
Many shall see it, and fear,
and shall trust in Yahweh.*

*Blessed is the man
who makes Yahweh his trust,
and doesn't respect the proud,
nor such as turn away to lies.*

*Many, Yahweh, my God,
are the wonderful works which you have done,
and your thoughts which are toward us.
They can't be declared back to you.*

If I would declare and speak of them,
they are more than can be counted.

Sacrifice and offering you didn't desire.
You have opened my ears.
You have not required burnt offering and sin offering.
Then I said, "Behold, I have come."

It is written about me in the book in the scroll.
I delight to do your will, my God.
Yes, your Law is within my heart.

I have proclaimed glad news of righteousness
in the great assembly.
Behold, I will not seal my lips,
Yahweh, you know.

I have not hidden your righteousness within my heart.
I have declared your faithfulness and your salvation.
I have not concealed your loving kindness
and your truth from the great assembly.

Don't withhold your tender mercies from me, Yahweh.
Let your loving kindness and your truth
continually preserve me.

For innumerable evils have surrounded me.
My iniquities have overtaken me, so that I am not able
to look up.
They are more than the hairs of my head.
My heart has failed me.

Be pleased, Yahweh, to deliver me.

Hurry to help me, Yahweh.
Let them be disappointed and confounded
together who seek after my soul to destroy it.

Let them be turned backward and brought to dishonour
who delight in my hurt.

Let them be desolate by reason of their shame
that tell me, "Aha! Aha!"

Let all those who seek you
rejoice and be glad in you.
Let such as love your salvation
say continually, "Let Yahweh be exalted!"

But I am poor and needy.
May Yahweh think about me.
You are my help and my deliverer.
Don't delay, my God.

Psalm 56

Be merciful to me, God, for man wants to swallow me up.
All day long, he attacks and oppresses me.
My enemies want to swallow me up all day long,
for they are many who fight proudly against me.

When I am afraid,
I will put my trust in you.
In God, I praise his word.
In God, I put my trust.
I will not be afraid.
What can flesh do to me?

All day long they twist my words.
All their thoughts are against me for evil.
They conspire and lurk,
watching my steps.
They are eager to take my life.

Shall they escape by iniquity?
In anger cast down the peoples, God.
You count my wanderings.
You put my tears into your container.
Aren't they in your book?
Then my enemies shall turn back on the day that I call.

I know this: that God is for me.
In God, I will praise his word.
In Yahweh, I will praise his word.
I have put my trust in God.
I will not be afraid.
What can man do to me?

Your vows are on me, God.
I will give thank offerings to you.
For you have delivered my soul from death,
and prevented my feet from falling,
that I may walk before God in the light of the living.

Psalm 62

My soul rests in God alone.
My salvation is from him.
He alone is my rock, my salvation, and my fortress.
I will never be greatly shaken.

How long will you assault a man?
Would all of you throw him down,
like a leaning wall, like a tottering fence?

They fully intend to throw him down from his lofty place.
They delight in lies.
They bless with their mouth, but they curse inwardly.

My soul, wait in silence for God alone,
for my expectation is from him.
He alone is my rock and my salvation, my fortress.
I will not be shaken.
My salvation and my honour are with God.
The rock of my strength, and my refuge, is in God.

Trust in him at all times, you people.
Pour out your heart before him.
God is a refuge for us.

Surely men of low degree are just a breath,
and men of high degree are a lie.
In the balances they will go up.
They are together lighter than a breath.
Don't trust in oppression.
Don't become vain in robbery.
If riches increase,
don't set your heart on them.

God has spoken once;
twice I have heard this,
that power belongs to God.
Also to you, Lord, belongs loving kindness,
for you reward every man according to his work.

Psalm 67

May God be merciful to us, bless us,
and cause his face to shine on us.
That your way may be known on earth,
and your salvation among all nations.

Let the peoples praise you, God.
Let all the peoples praise you.

Oh let the nations be glad and sing for joy,
for you will judge the peoples with equity,
and govern the nations on earth.

Let the peoples praise you, God.
Let all the peoples praise you.

The earth has yielded its increase.
God, even our own God, will bless us.
God will bless us.
All the ends of the earth shall fear him.

Psalm 96

Sing to Yahweh a new song!
Sing to Yahweh, all the earth.
Sing to Yahweh!
Bless his name!
Proclaim his salvation from day to day!
Declare his glory among the nations,
his marvellous works among all the peoples.

For Yahweh is great, and greatly to be praised!

He is to be feared above all gods.
For all the gods of the peoples are idols,
but Yahweh made the heavens.

Honor and majesty are before him.
Strength and beauty are in his sanctuary.
Ascribe to Yahweh, you families of nations,
ascribe to Yahweh glory and strength.

Ascribe to Yahweh the glory due to his name.
Bring an offering, and come into his courts.
Worship Yahweh in holy array.
Tremble before him, all the earth.

Say among the nations, "Yahweh reigns."
The world is also established.
It can't be moved.
He will judge the peoples with equity.

Let the heavens be glad, and let the earth rejoice.
Let the sea roar, and its fullness!
Let the field and all that is in it exult!
Then all the trees of the woods shall sing for joy
before Yahweh; for he comes,
for he comes to judge the earth.
He will judge the world with righteousness,
the peoples with his truth.

Psalm 150

Praise Yahweh!

Praise God in his sanctuary!

Praise him in his heavens for his acts of power!
Praise him for his mighty acts!
Praise him according to his excellent greatness!
Praise him with the sounding of the trumpet!
Praise him with harp and lyre!
Praise him with tambourine and dancing!
Praise him with stringed instruments and flute!
Praise him with loud cymbals!
Praise him with resounding cymbals!
Let everything that has breath praise Yahweh!

Praise Yahweh!

THE PROVERBS

Most of this book is attributed to King Solomon, a man of legendary wisdom. Much of it is familiar to us today.

While the proverbs were important to the Israelites in the time of the Old Testament, Christians see Jesus as the fulfilment of the wisdom embodied in Proverbs

The first nine chapters present a father commending Wisdom to his son (with Wisdom herself even intervening).[123] These are followed by a collection of Proverbs of Solomon.

The purpose of the Book of Proverbs is summed up in the first few verses:

> *to know wisdom and instruction;*
> *to discern the words of understanding;*
> *to receive instruction in wise dealing,*
> *in righteousness, justice, and equity;*
> *to give prudence to the simple,*
> *knowledge and discretion to the young man –*
> *that the wise man may hear, and increase in learning;*
> *that the man of understanding may attain to*
> *sound counsel;*
> *to understand a proverb and parables,*
> *the words and riddles of the wise.* (Pr 1:2-6)

---

[123] Jerusalem Bible (Introduction to Proverbs).

How to Acquire Wisdom

> *My son, don't forget my teaching,*
> *but let your heart keep my commandments,*
> *for they will add to you length of days,*
> *years of life, and peace.*
> *Don't let kindness and truth forsake you,*
> *bind them around your neck.*
> *...*
> *Trust in Yahweh with all your heart,*
> *and don't lean on your own understanding.*
> *In all your ways acknowledge him,*
> *and he will make your paths straight.*
> *Don't be wise in your own eyes,*
> *fear Yahweh, and depart from evil.*
> *...*
> *Honour Yahweh with your substance,*
> *with the first fruits of all your increase;*
> *so your barns will be filled with plenty,*
> *and your vats will overflow with new wine.*
> *My son, don't despise Yahweh's discipline,*
> *neither be weary of his correction;*
> *for whom Yahweh loves, he corrects,*
> *even as a father reproves the son in whom he delights.*
> (Pr 3:1-12)

The Joys of Wisdom

> *Happy is the man who finds wisdom,*
> *the man who gets understanding.*
> *For her good profit is better than getting silver,*
> *and her return is better than fine gold.*
> *She is more precious than rubies,*

> *none of the things you can desire are to be compared to her.*
> (Pr 3:13-15)
>
> *Don't withhold good from those to whom it is due,*
> *when it is in the power of your hand to do it.*
>
> *Don't say to your neighbour, "Go, and come again;*
> *tomorrow I will give it to you," when you have it by you.*
>
> *Don't devise evil against your neighbour,*
> *since he dwells securely by you.*
>
> *Don't strive with a man without cause,*
> *if he has done you no harm.*
>
> *Don't envy the man of violence,*
> *choose none of his ways.*
> *For the perverse is an abomination to Yahweh,*
> *but his friendship is with the upright.*
> *Yahweh's curse is in the house of the wicked,*
> *but he blesses the habitation of the righteous.* (Pr 3:27-33)

On Choosing Wisdom

> *Wisdom is supreme. Get wisdom,*
> *yes, though it costs all your possessions, get understanding.*
> *Esteem her, and she will exalt you,*
> *she will bring you to honour when you embrace her.*
> *She will give to your head a garland of grace,*
> *she will deliver a crown of splendour to you.* (Pr 4:7-9)

Wisdom Speaks

*I, wisdom, have made prudence my dwelling,
find out knowledge and discretion.
The fear of Yahweh is to hate evil,
I hate pride, arrogance, the evil way, and the perverse mouth.
Counsel and sound knowledge are mine,
I have understanding and power.
...
I love those who love me,
those who seek me diligently will find me.
With me are riches, honour,
enduring wealth, and prosperity.
My fruit is better than gold, yes, than fine gold,
my yield better than choice silver.
I walk in the way of righteousness,
in the middle of the paths of justice,
that I may give wealth to those who love me,
I fill their treasuries.* (Pr 8:12-21)

Wisdom: God's Eternal Companion

*Yahweh possessed me in the beginning of his work,
before his deeds of old.
I was set up from everlasting, from the beginning,
before the earth existed.*

*When there were no depths, I was born,
when there were no springs abounding with water.
Before the mountains were settled in place,
before the hills, I was born;
while as yet he had not made the earth, nor the fields,*

> nor the beginning of the dust of the world.
>
> When he established the heavens, I was there.
>
> When he set a circle on the surface of the deep,
> when he established the clouds above,
> when the springs of the deep became strong,
> when he gave to the sea its boundary,
> that the waters should not violate his commandment,
> when he marked out the foundations of the earth,
> then I was the craftsman by his side.
> I was a delight day by day,
> always rejoicing before him,
> rejoicing in his whole world.
> My delight was with the sons of men. (Pr 8:22-31)

The Proverbs of Solomon

> Treasures of wickedness profit nothing,
> but righteousness delivers from death.
> Yahweh will not allow the soul of the righteous to
> go hungry,
> but he thrusts away the desire of the wicked. (Pr 10:2-3)
>
> He who walks blamelessly walks surely,
> but he who perverts his ways will be found out. (Pr 10:9)
>
> Hatred stirs up strife,
> but love covers all wrongs. (Pr 10:12)
>
> The fear of Yahweh prolongs days,
> but the years of the wicked shall be shortened. (Pr 10:27)

*The way of Yahweh is a stronghold to the upright,
but it is a destruction to the workers of iniquity.*
(Pr 10:29)

*The righteousness of the upright shall deliver them,
but the unfaithful will be trapped by evil desires.* (Pr 11:6)

*One who brings gossip betrays a confidence,
but one who is of a trustworthy spirit is one who keeps a
secret.* (Pr 11:13)

*Wicked people earn deceitful wages,
but one who sows righteousness reaps a sure reward.*
(Pr 11:18)

*Whoever loves correction loves knowledge,
but he who hates reproof is stupid.* (Pr 12:1)

*The fool's talk brings a rod to his back,
but the lips of the wise protect them.* (Pr 14:3)

*The fear of Yahweh is a fountain of life,
turning people from the snares of death.* (Pr 14:27)

*A gentle answer turns away wrath,
but a harsh word stirs up anger.* (Pr 15:1)

*Yahweh's eyes are everywhere,
keeping watch on the evil and the good.* (Pr 15:3)

*Better is little, with the fear of Yahweh,
than great treasure with trouble.* (Pr 15:16)

Yahweh is far from the wicked,
but he hears the prayer of the righteous. (Pr 15:29)

Yahweh has made everything for its own end -
yes, even the wicked for the day of evil. (Pr 16:4)

How much better it is to get wisdom than gold!
Yes, to get understanding is to be chosen rather than silver.
(Pr 16:16)

Pride goes before destruction,
and an arrogant spirit before a fall.
It is better to be of a lowly spirit with the poor,
than to divide the plunder with the proud. (Pr 16:18-19)

Whoever rewards evil for good,
evil shall not depart from his house. (Pr 17:13)

Don't say, "I will pay back evil."
Wait for Yahweh, and he will save you. (Pr 20:22)

Every way of a man is right in his own eyes,
but Yahweh weighs the hearts.
To do righteousness and justice
is more acceptable to Yahweh than sacrifice. (Pr 21:2-3)

Whoever stops his ears at the cry of the poor,
he will also cry out, but shall not be heard. (Pr 21:13)

The rich and the poor have this in common:
Yahweh is the maker of them all. (Pr 22:2)

If your enemy is hungry, give him food to eat,

if he is thirsty, give him water to drink;
for you will heap coals of fire on his head,
and Yahweh will reward you. (Pr 25:21-22)

Don't boast about tomorrow;
for you don't know what a day may bring.
Let another man praise you,
and not your own mouth;
a stranger, and not your own lips. (Pr 27:1-2)

ECCLESIASTES

This is an interesting book that provides somewhat of a divergence from the previous 'wisdom' books of the Bible. It is the story of a clever and wealthy man who wants for nothing, yet equally isn't happy.

He is searching for the meaning of life. The why? He mentions repeatedly the vanity and folly of life.

Written c. 250 BC.

The words of the Ecclesiastes, the son of David, king in Jerusalem. ...Vanity of vanities, all is vanity. What does man gain from all his labour in which he labours under the sun? (Ecc 1:1-3)

The writer questions why we go along acquiring riches - to what end? If we gain them for our heirs, that is one thing, but will they benefit from them? If we are alone in the world, then why do we spend so much time working hard to gain wealth that will not be handed down to anyone? There is no value in storing up riches.

> *He who loves money never has money enough,*
> *he who loves wealth never has enough profit;*
> *this, too, is vanity.*
> *Where goods abound,*
> *parasites abound.* (Ecc 5:9-10*)

He mentions that our efforts are a folly, for we work in a timeline we know nothing about. The way we measure time, and the way God measures time are completely different. We never know when our last minute will be upon us, yet we carry on as if it is not within reach. God will choose when and where to deliver his blessings or adjudications or the end.

Death will come to us all, yet we live as if it will not reach us.

> *For everything there is a season,*
> *and a time for every purpose under heaven:*
> *a time to be born,*
> *and a time to die;*
> *a time to plant,*
> *and a time to pluck up that which is planted;*
> *a time to kill,*
> *and a time to heal;*
> *a time to break down,*
> *and a time to build up;*
> *a time to weep,*
> *and a time to laugh;*
> *a time to mourn,*
> *and a time to dance;*
> *...*
> *a time to keep silence,*
> *and a time to speak;*
> *a time to love,*
> *and a time to hate;*
> *a time for war,*
> *and a time for peace.* (Ecc 3:1-8)

We are urged to find the happiness in each day - in what we eat and drink, the way we live, in the lot God has given us.

The writer says we are no different to the beasts, both coming from nothing and returning to the same. We both breathe the same air. We have no real advantage over them.

Who really has the best life? The man who lives but is living under oppression; the wealthy man who thinks he has it all but isn't happy; the dead man who has already endured all there is to endure and now knows some peace? Or is it the unborn child who is still to know the evil that lurks in the world?

We must learn to live with and accept the good times and the bad, for God sends them both.

This is the end of the matter. All has been heard. Fear God and keep his commandments; for this is the whole duty of man. For God will bring every work into judgement, with every hidden thing, whether it is good, or whether it is evil. (Ecc 12:13-14)

THE SONG OF SONGS

The Song of Songs is a set of five poems written by and about a bride and bridegroom. In it, they lavishly, and at times sensually, describe each other and their feelings toward each other, and what love means to them. It is the only book of the bible where there is no direct mention of God.

Some theorise the interchange between the bridegrrom and the bride is an allegory of God and his church.

The First Poem - Awakening of Love

The Bride

> *Don't stare at me because I am dark,*
> *because the sun has scorched me.*
> *My mother's sons were angry with me,*
> *they made me keeper of the vineyards.*
> *I haven't kept my own vineyard.*
>
> *Tell me, you whom my soul loves,*
> *where you graze your flock,*
> *where you rest them at noon;*
> *for why should I be as one who is veiled*
> *beside the flocks of your companions?* (Sgs 1:5-7)

The Bridegroom

> *I have compared you, my love,*
> *to a steed in Pharaoh's chariots.*
> *Your cheeks are beautiful with earrings,*
> *your neck with strings of jewels.* (Sgs 1:9-10)

The Second Poem - Seeking of love

The Bride

> *The voice of my beloved!*
> *Behold, he comes,*
> *leaping on the mountains,*
> *skipping on the hills.*
>
> *My beloved is like a roe or a young deer.*
> *Behold, he stands behind our wall!*
> *He looks in at the windows.*
> *He glances through the lattice.* (Sgs 2:8-9)
>
> *By night on my bed,*
> *I sought him whom my soul loves.*
> *I sought him, but I didn't find him.*
>
> *I will get up now, and go about the city;*
> *in the streets and in the squares I will seek him whom my soul loves.*
> *I sought him, but I didn't find him.* (Sgs 3:1-2)

The Third Poem - Union of Love

The Bridegroom

Behold, you are beautiful, my love.
...
Your eyes are like doves behind your veil,
your hair is as a flock of goats,
that descend from Mount Gilead.

Your teeth are like a newly shorn flock,
which have come up from the washing,
where every one of them has twins.
None is bereaved among them.

Your lips are like scarlet thread.
your mouth is lovely.
Your temples are like a piece of a pomegranate behind
your veil.

Your neck is like David's tower built for an armoury,
on which a thousand shields hang,
all the shields of the mighty men.

Your two breasts are like two fawns
that are twins of a roe,
which feed among the lilies. (Sgs 4:1-5)

The Fourth Poem - Loss and Search for Love

The Bride

I was asleep, but my heart was awake.
It is the voice of my beloved who knocks:
"Open to me, my sister, my love, my dove, my undefiled;
for my head is filled with dew,
and my hair with the dampness of the night."

> I have taken off my robe. Indeed, must I put it on?
> I have washed my feet. Indeed, must I soil them?
> My beloved thrust his hand in through the latch opening,
> my heart pounded for him.
> ...
> I opened to my beloved;
> but my beloved left, and had gone away.
> My heart went out when he spoke,
> I looked for him, but I didn't find him,
> I called him, but he didn't answer.
>
> I adjure you, daughters of Jerusalem,
> If you find my beloved,
> that you tell him that I am faint with love. (Sgs 5:2-8)

The Fifth Poem - Triumph of Love

The Bridegroom

> My dove, my perfect one, is unique.
> She is her mother's only daughter.
> She is the favourite one of her who bore her.
> The daughters saw her, and called her blessed.
> The queens and the concubines saw her, and they praised her. (Sg 6:8-9)
>
> Your body is like a round goblet,
> no mixed wine is wanting.
> Your waist is like a heap of wheat,
> set about with lilies.
>
> Your two breasts are like two fawns,
> that are twins of a roe.

The hair of your head like purple.
The king is held captive in its tresses.

How beautiful and how pleasant you are,
love, for delights!
This, your stature, is like a palm tree,
your breasts like its fruit.

I said, "I will climb up into the palm tree,
I will take hold of its fruit."
Let your breasts be like clusters of the vine,
the smell of your breath like apples.

Your mouth is like the best wine,
that goes down smoothly for my beloved,
gliding through the lips of those who are asleep.
(Sgs 7:2-9)

The Bride

Oh that you were like my brother,
who nursed from the breasts of my mother!
If I found you outside, I would kiss you;
yes, and no one would despise me.

I would lead you, bringing you into the house of my mother,
who would instruct me.
I would have you drink spiced wine,
of the juice of my pomegranate.

His left hand would be under my head.
His right hand would embrace me.

*I adjure you, daughters of Jerusalem,
that you not stir up, nor awaken love,
until it so desires.* (Sgs 8:1-4)

THE BOOK OF WISDOM

Believed to be written in Egypt during a time of crisis in faith for the Jews, especially those living in Alexandria among the pagans. The book focuses on wisdom as a divine gift, and offers guidance and reassurance.

Sometimes known as The Book of Solomon. The Church Fathers largely accept that it is Solomon himself who is the speaker.

Seek Wisdom and Shun Evil

Love righteousness, all you who are judges of the earth,
think of Yahweh with a good mind.
Seek him in singleness of heart,
because he is found by those who don't put him to the test,
and is manifested to those who trust him. (Wis 1:1-2)

Wisdom will not enter into a soul that devises evil,
nor dwell in a body that is enslaved by sin.
For a holy spirit of discipline will flee deceit,
and will depart from thoughts that are without understanding,
and will be ashamed when unrighteousness has come in.
For wisdom is a spirit who loves man,
and she will not hold a blasphemer guiltless for his lips,
because God is witness of his inmost self,

and is a true overseer of his heart,
and a hearer of his tongue. (Wis 1: 4-6)

Don't court death in the error of your life,
don't draw destruction upon yourselves by the works of
your hands;
because God didn't make death,
neither does he delight when the living perish.
For he created all things that they might have being,
the generative powers of the world are wholesome,
and there is no poison of destruction in them,
nor has Hades royal dominion upon earth;
for righteousness is immortal. (Wis 1:12-15)

The Folly of Life Without Hope

Our life is short and sorrowful,
there is no healing when a man comes to his end,
Because we were born by mere chance,
and hereafter we will be as though we had never been.
(Wis 2:1-2)

Our name will be forgotten in time,
no one will remember our works. (Wis 2:4)

For our allotted time is the passing of a shadow,
and our end doesn't retreat,
because it is securely sealed, and no one turns it back.
Come therefore and let's enjoy the good things that exist,
let's use the creation earnestly as in our youth.
Let's fill ourselves with costly wine and perfumes,
and let no spring flower pass us by.
Let's crown ourselves with rosebuds before they wither,

> let none of us go without his share in our proud revelry.
> Let's leave tokens of mirth everywhere,
> because this is our portion, and this is our lot. (Wis 2:5-9)

The Godless are Mistaken

> They didn't know the mysteries of God,
> neither did they hope for wages of holiness,
> nor did they discern that there is a prize for blameless souls.
> Because God created man for incorruption,
> and made him an image of his own everlastingness;
> but death entered into the world by the envy of the devil,
> and those who belong to him experience it. (Wis 2:22-24)

Testing of God

> But the souls of the righteous are in the hand of God,
> and no torment will touch them.
> In the eyes of the foolish they seemed to have died,
> their departure was considered a disaster,
> and their travel away from us ruin,
> but they are in peace.
> For even if in the sight of men they are punished,
> their hope is full of immortality.
> Having borne a little chastening, they will receive great good;
> because God tested them, and found them worthy of himself.
> He tested them like gold in the furnace,
> and he accepted them as a whole burnt offering.
> in the time of their visitation they will shine,
> they will run back and forth like sparks among stubble.
> (Wis 3:1-7)

Choosing Wisdom Above all

> *For this cause I prayed,*
> *and understanding was given to me,*
> *I asked, and a spirit of wisdom came to me.*
> *I preferred her before sceptres and thrones,*
> *I considered riches nothing in comparison to her.*
> *Neither did I liken to her any priceless gem,*
> *because all gold in her presence is a little sand,*
> *and silver will be considered as clay before her.*
> *I loved her more than health and beauty,*
> *and I chose to have her rather than light,*
> *because her bright shining is never laid to sleep.*
> *All good things came to me with her,*
> *and innumerable riches are in her hands.*
> *And I rejoiced over them all because wisdom leads them;*
> *although I didn't know that she was their mother.*
> *As I learned without guile, I impart without grudging,*
> *I don't hide her riches.*
> *For she is a treasure for men that doesn't fail,*
> *and those who use it obtain friendship with God,*
> *commended by the gifts which they present through discipline.* (Wis 7:7-14)

The Divine Image of Wisdom

> *For she is a breath of the power of God,*
> *and a pure emanation of the glory of the Almighty,*
> *therefore nothing defiled can find entrance into her.*
> *For she is a reflection of everlasting light,*
> *an unspotted mirror of the working of God,*
> *and an image of his goodness.* (Wis 7:25-26)

Seeking Wisdom

Wisdom is with you and knows your works,
and was present when you were making the world,
and understands what is pleasing in your eyes,
and what is right according to your commandments.
Send her from the holy heavens,
and ask her to come from the throne of your glory,
that being present with me she may work,
and I may learn what pleases you well.
For she knows all things and understands,
and she will guide me prudently in my actions.
She will guard me in her glory,
so my works will be acceptable.
I will judge your people righteously,
and I will be worthy of my Father's throne. (Wis 9:9-12)

ECCLESIASTICUS

Written by Ben Sira, a scribe and teacher. This book reflects his concern over how his people's faith was being eroded away by the Greeks and their Hellenist culture.

Written c. 180 BC for the Jews living in Judea. Also known as the Book of Sirach.

Whereas many and great things have been delivered to us by the Law and the prophets, and by the others that have followed in their steps, for which we must give Israel the praise for instruction and wisdom; my grandfather Jesus, having much given himself to the reading of the law, and the prophets, and the other books of our fathers, and having gained great familiarity with them, was also drawn on himself to write somewhat pertaining to instruction and wisdom, in order that those who love learning, and are devoted to these things, might make progress much more by living according to the law. You are entreated therefore to read with favour and attention, and to pardon us, if in any parts of what we have laboured to interpret, we may seem to fail in some of the phrases. (Sir Forward)

Wisdom from Eternity

> *All wisdom comes from Yahweh,*
> *and is with him forever.*
> *Who can count the sand of the seas,*
> *the drops of rain, and the days of eternity?*

Who will search out the height of the sky,
the breadth of the earth, the deep, and wisdom?
Wisdom has been created before all things,
and the understanding of prudence from everlasting.
(Sir 1:1-4)

The Fear of God

The fear of Yahweh is glory, exultation,
gladness, and a crown of rejoicing.
The fear of Yahweh will delight the heart,
and will give gladness, joy, and length of days.
Whoever fears Yahweh, it will go well with him at the last.
He will be blessed on the day of his death.
To fear Yahweh is the beginning of wisdom,
she was created together with the faithful in the womb,
she laid an eternal foundation with men,
she will be trusted among their offspring.
To fear Yahweh is the fullness of wisdom,
she inebriates men with her fruits.
She will fill all her house with desirable things,
and her storehouses with her produce.
The fear of Yahweh is the crown of wisdom,
making peace and perfect health to flourish.
He both saw and measured her.
He rained down skill and knowledge of understanding,
and exalted the honour of those who hold her fast.
To fear Yahweh is the root of wisdom,
her branches are length of days. (Sir 1:11-20)

Seek Wisdom with a Humble Heart

If you desire wisdom, keep the commandments,

and Yahweh will give her to you freely;
for the fear of Yahweh is wisdom and instruction.
Faith and humility are his good pleasure. (Sir 1:26-27)

Don't exalt yourself,
lest you fall and bring dishonour upon your soul.
Yahweh will reveal your secrets
and will cast you down in the midst of the congregation,
because you didn't come to the fear of Yahweh
and your heart was full of deceit. (Sir 1:30)

Trust in God

My son, if you come to serve Yahweh,
prepare your soul for temptation.
Set your heart aright, constantly endure,
and don't make haste in time of calamity.
Cling to him, and don't depart,
that you may be increased at your latter end.
Accept whatever is brought upon you,
and be patient when you suffer humiliation.
For gold is tried in the fire,
and acceptable men in the furnace of humiliation.
Put your trust in him, and he will help you.
Make your ways straight, and set your hope on him.
(Sir 2:1-6)

Humility

My son, be gentle in carrying out your business,
and you will be better loved than a lavish giver.
The greater you are, the more you should behave humbly,

and then you will find favour with the Lord.
(Sir 3:17-19*)

The Sin and Shame of Pride

Pride is hateful before Yahweh and men,
arrogance is abhorrent in the judgement of both. (Sir 10:7)

It is the beginning of pride when a man departs
from Yahweh,
his heart has departed from him who made him.
For the beginning of pride is sin,
he who keeps it will pour out abomination. (Sir 10:12-13)

Miscellaneous Advice

Let those that are at peace with you be many,
but your advisers one of a thousand. (Sir 6:6)

Do no evil, so no evil will overtake you,
depart from wrong, and it will turn away from you.
(Sir 7:1-2)

Don't be faint-hearted in your prayer,
don't neglect to give alms. (Sir 7:10)

Also stretch out your hand to the poor man,
that your blessing may be complete. (Sir 7:32)

Don't commend a man for his good looks,
don't abhor a man for his outward appearance. (Sir 11:2)

Don't blame before you investigate,

> *understand first, and then rebuke.*
> *Don't answer before you have heard,*
> *don't interrupt while someone else is speaking.*
> *Don't argue about a matter that doesn't concern you,*
> *don't sit with sinners when they judge.* (Sir 11:7-9)

> *Forgive your neighbour the hurt that he has done,*
> *and then your sins will be pardoned when you pray.*
> (Sir 28:2)

Don't Envy the Sinner

> *Good things and bad, life and death,*
> *poverty and riches, are from Yahweh.* (Sir 11:14)

> *Don't marvel at the works of a sinner,*
> *but trust Yahweh and stay in your labour;*
> *for it is an easy thing in the sight of Yahweh*
> *to swiftly and suddenly make a poor man rich.*
> *Yahweh's blessing is in the reward of the godly,*
> *he makes his blessing flourish in an hour that comes swiftly.*
> (Sir 11:21-22)

> *Don't say, "I have enough,*
> *what harm could happen to me now?"*
> *In the day of good things,*
> *bad things are forgotten,*
> *in the day of bad things,*
> *a man will not remember things that are good.*
> (Sir 11:24-26)

Free to Choose

Before man is life and death,
whichever he likes, it will be given to him.
For the wisdom of Yahweh is great,
he is mighty in power, and sees all things.
His eyes are upon those who fear him,
he knows every act of man.
He has not commanded any man to be ungodly,
he has not given any man license to sin. (Sir 15:18-20)

Man's Purpose and God's Patience

What is mankind, and what purpose do they serve?
What is their good, and what is their evil?
The number of man's days at the most are a hundred years.
As a drop of water from the sea, and a pebble
from the sand,
so are a few years in the day of eternity.
For this cause Yahweh was patient over them,
and poured out his mercy upon them.
He saw and perceived their end, that it is evil,
therefore he multiplied his forgiveness.
The mercy of a man is on his neighbour;
but the mercy of Yahweh is on all flesh:
reproving, chastening, teaching,
and bringing back, as a shepherd does his flock.
He has mercy on those who accept chastening,
and that diligently seek after his judgements. (Sir 18:8-14)

Happiness

Don't give your soul to sorrow,

don't afflict yourself deliberately.
Gladness of heart is the life of a man,
cheerfulness of a man lengthens his days,
Love your own soul, and comfort your heart.
remove sorrow far from you,
for sorrow has destroyed many,
and there is no profit in it.
Envy and wrath shorten life,
anxiety brings old age before its time.
Those who are cheerful and merry
will benefit from their food. (Sir 30:21-25)

Gladness in Generosity

Glorify Yahweh with generosity,
don't reduce the first fruits of your hands.
In every gift show a cheerful countenance,
and dedicate your tithe with gladness.
Give to the Most High according as he has given,
as your hand has found, give generously.
For Yahweh repays,
and he will repay you sevenfold. (Sir 35:8-11)

THE PROPHETS

OBADIAH

This book covers a prophecy regarding the punishment and treatment by God against Edom - 'a mountain dwelling nation whose founding father was Esau (Isaac's eldest son)',[124] who had become arrogant in the faith. Written c. 430 BC.

A Vision of Obadiah Concerning Edom

I have made you small among the nations. You are greatly despised. The pride of your heart has deceived you ... Though you mount on high as the eagle, and though your nest is set among the stars, I will bring you down from there, says Yahweh.

If thieves came to you, if robbers by night - oh, what disaster awaits you - wouldn't they only steal until they had enough? If grape pickers came to you, wouldn't they leave some gleaning grapes? How Esau will be ransacked! How his hidden treasures are sought out!... The men who were at peace with you have deceived you, and prevailed against you. Friends who eat your bread lay a snare under you. There is no understanding in him.

Won't I in that day, says Yahweh, destroy the wise men out of Edom. ... Your mighty men, Teman, will be dismayed, to the end that everyone may be cut off from the mountain of Esau by slaughter. For the violence done to your brother Jacob, shame will cover you, and you will be cut off forever. On the day that you stood on the other side, on the day that strangers carried away his

---

[124] Book of Obadiah - wikipedia.

substance and foreigners entered into his gates and cast lots for Jerusalem, even you were like one of them.

But don't look down on your brother on the day of his disaster, and don't rejoice over the children of Judah on the day of their destruction.

Don't speak proudly on the day of distress.

Don't enter into the gate of my people on the day of their calamity.

Don't look down on their affliction on the day of their calamity, neither seize their wealth on the day of their calamity.

Don't stand on the crossroads to cut off those of his who escape.

Don't deliver up those of his who remain on the day of distress. For the day of Yahweh is near all the nations!

As you have done, it will be done to you. Your deeds will return upon your own head. For as you have drunk on my holy mountain, so all the nations will drink continually. Yes, they will drink, swallow down, and will be as though they had not been. But in Mount Zion, there will be those who escape, and it will be holy. The house of Jacob will possess their possessions. The house of Jacob will be a fire, the house of Joseph a flame, and the house of Esau for stubble. They will burn among them and devour them. There will not be any remaining to the house of Esau. Indeed, Yahweh has spoken. (Ob 1:2-18) (with editing)

JOEL

The Book of Joel is written to the people of Judah, and focuses on a devastating locust plague that serves as an allegory for divine judgment. This plague is not only seen as a natural disaster, but as a wake-up call to repentance, urging Judah to return to God with sincere hearts.

Central to Joel's message is the concept of the 'Day of the Lord', a time of both judgment and salvation.

Written around a time after the Babylonian exile, as the people are still floundering.

Speaking through Joel, God calls attention to a locust plague as a destructive symbol of Judah's fall.

> *"Hear this, you elders,*
> *And listen, all you inhabitants of the land!*
> *Has this ever happened in your days,*
> *or in the days of your fathers?*
>
> *"Tell your children about it,*
> *and have your children tell their children,*
> *and their children, another generation.*
>
> *"What the swarming locust has left, the great locust has eaten.*
> *What the great locust has left, the grasshopper has eaten.*

> What the grasshopper has left, the caterpillar has eaten.
>
> "Wake up, you drunkards, and weep!
> Wail, all you drinkers of wine, because of the sweet wine,
> for it is cut off from your mouth.
>
> "For a nation has come up on my land, strong, and without number.
> His teeth are the teeth of a lion,
> and he has the fangs of a lioness.
>
> "He has laid my vine waste,
> and stripped my fig tree.
> He has stripped its bark, and thrown it away.
> Its branches are made white." (Jl 1: 2-7)

Through Joel, God calls for repentance.

> "'Sanctify a fast.
> Call a solemn assembly.
> Gather the elders
> and all the inhabitants of the land
> to the house of the Yahweh your God,
> and cry to Yahweh.
>
> 'Alas for the day!
> For the day of Yahweh is at hand,
> and it will come as destruction from the Almighty.'" (Jl 1:14-15)

God foretells of his salvation.

> "They rush on the city.
> They run on the wall.
> They climb up into the houses.

They enter in at the windows like thieves.

"The earth quakes before them.
The heavens tremble.
The sun and the moon are darkened,
and the stars withdraw their shining.

"Yahweh thunders his voice before his army,
for his forces are very great;
for he is strong who obeys his command;
for the day of Yahweh is great and very awesome,
and who can endure it?" (Jl 2:9-11)

God repeats his calls for repentance

"Gather the people.
Sanctify the assembly.
Assemble the elders.
Gather the children, and those who nurse from breasts.
Let the bridegroom go out of his room,
and the bride out of her chamber.

"Let the priests, the ministers of Yahweh,
weep between the porch and the altar,
and let them say, 'Spare your people, Yahweh,
and don't give your heritage to reproach,
that the nations should rule over them.
Why should they say among the peoples,
"Where is their God?"''" (Jl: 2:16-17)

The locust plague ceases.

Yahweh answers his people,

> "Behold, I will send you grain, new wine, and oil,
> and you will be satisfied with them;
> and I will no more make you a reproach among the nations.
> But I will remove the northern army far away from you,
> and will drive it into a barren and desolate land." (Jl 2:19-20)

Joel continues to speak as a prophet of God.

> "Be glad then, you children of Zion,
> and rejoice in Yahweh, your God;
> for he gives you the early rain in just measure,
> and he causes the rain to come down for you,
> the early rain and the latter rain, as before." (Jl 2:23)

> "And you will know that I am in the middle of Israel,
> that I am Yahweh your God, with none equal to me.
> My people will not be disappointed any more." (Jl 2:27*)

God speaks of the outpouring of his Holy Spirit.[125]

> "It will happen afterward, that I will pour out my Spirit on all flesh;
> and your sons and your daughters will prophesy.
> Your old men will dream dreams.
> Your young men will see visions.
> And also on the servants and on the handmaids in those days,
> I will pour out my Spirit.

> "I will show wonders in the heavens and on the earth:
> blood, fire, and pillars of smoke."

> "The sun will be turned into darkness,

---

[125] To be fulfilled at Pentecost - see Acts of the Apostles.

and the moon into blood,
before the great and terrible day of Yahweh comes." (Jl 2:28-31)

Joel tells of the glorious Day of the Lord.

"Yahweh roars from Zion,
makes his voice heard from Jerusalem;
heaven and earth tremble.

"But Yahweh will be a shelter for his people,
a stronghold for the sons of Israel.

"'You will learn then that I am Yahweh your God,
dwelling in Zion, my holy mountain.
Jerusalem will be a holy place,
no alien will ever pass through it again. (Joel 4:16-17*)

"When that day comes,
the mountains will run with new wine
and the hills flow with milk,
and all the river beds of Judah
will run with water." (Joel 4:18*)

AMOS

Amos prophesied for only a short period around the time when Jeroboam II was ruling the Northern Kingdom of Israel - c. 750 BC. This was some 30 years before their defeat and exile.

The book emphasises the importance of social justice, genuine worship, and the need for a sincere relationship with God.

John L McKenzie. in 'Dictionary of the Bible', calls Amos, 'a prophet of judgement'. He adds that Amos presents 'the relationship between God and His people as a union of will, not of nature'.

Yahweh Speaks to Israel

Amos begins boldly, with dire predictions of doom for Israel.

> *"I will not turn away* (Israel's) *punishment,*
> *because they have sold the righteous for silver,*
> *and the needy for a pair of sandals;*
> *They trample the heads of the poor into the dust*
> *of the earth*
> *and deny justice to the oppressed.*
> *A man and his father use the same maiden,*
> *to profane my holy name.*
> *They lay themselves down beside every altar*
> *on clothes taken in pledge.*
> *In the house of their god they drink the wine*

> *of those who have been fined.*
>
> ...
>
> *"Also I brought you up out of the land of Egypt
> and led you forty years in the wilderness,
> to possess the land of the Amorites.
> I raised up some of your sons for prophets,
> and some of your young men for Nazirites[126].*
>
> ...
>
> *"Behold, I will crush you in your place,
> as a cart crushes that which is full of grain.
> Flight will perish from the swift.
> The strong won't strengthen his force.
> The mighty won't deliver himself."* (Amos 2:6-14)

Israel's punishment for this will be. (Foretelling of the exile to come).

> *"An adversary will overrun the land;
> and he will pull down your strongholds,
> and your fortresses will be plundered."* (Amos 3:11)

God lets Israel know he has seen their injustices, how they tried to cover it up and how he tried other measures of correction before choosing this final one of destruction and exile.

> *"Go and sin as you please.
> Bring your sacrifices every morning,
> your tithes every three days,
> offer a sacrifice of thanksgiving of that which is leavened,
> and proclaim free will offerings and brag about them;
> for this pleases you, you children of Israel,"* says Yahweh.
>
> ...

---

[126] A consecrated male. Samson was a Nazirite.

> "I also have withheld the rain from you,
> when there were yet three months to the harvest;
> and I caused it to rain on one city,
> and caused it not to rain on another city.
> One field was rained on,
> and the field where it didn't rain withered.
> So two or three cities staggered to one city to drink water,
> and were not satisfied;
> yet you haven't returned to me," says Yahweh.
> ...
> "I sent plagues among you like I did Egypt.
> I have slain your young men with the sword,
> and have carried away your horses.
> I filled your nostrils with the stench of your camp,
> yet you haven't returned to me," says Yahweh.
> ...
> "Therefore I will do this to you, Israel;
> because I will do this to you,
> prepare to meet your God, Israel." (Amos 4:4-12)

Through Amos, God lets the Israelites know that faithfulness and devotion to him aren't only about going through the motions of sacrifice and chants, it is about what is in their hearts. It is their purity that God sees. He reminds them that they survived in the desert for forty years without any sacrifices, but by being faithful and true.

> "I hate, I despise your feasts,
> and I can't stand your solemn assemblies.
> Yes, though you offer me your burnt offerings and meal offerings,
> I will not accept them;
> neither will I regard the peace offerings of your fat animals.
> Take away from me the noise of your songs!

> *I will not listen to the music of your harps.*
> *But let justice roll on like rivers,*
> *and righteousness like a mighty stream.*
> *Did you bring to me sacrifices and offerings in the wilderness forty years,*
> *House of Israel?"* (Amos 5:21-25)

When the destruction and exile come, Israel will also be silenced from hearing the word of God.

> *"Behold, the days come, says Yahweh,*
> *that I will send a famine on the land,*
> *not a famine of bread,*
> *nor a thirst for water,*
> *but of hearing Yahweh's words."* (Amos 8:11)

As always God never completely shuts the door, instead he lets his people know that the righteous will survive his anger.

"Behold, I will command, and I will sift the house of Israel among all the nations as grain is sifted in a sieve, yet not the least kernel will fall on the earth. All the sinners of my people will die by the sword, who say, 'Evil won't overtake nor meet us.'

"In that day I will raise up the tent of David who is fallen and close up its breaches, and I will raise up its ruins, and I will build it as in the days of old, that they may possess the remnant of Edom and all the nations who are called by my name," says Yahweh who does this.

...

> *"I will bring my people Israel back from captivity,*
> *and they will rebuild the ruined cities, and inhabit them;*
> *and they will plant vineyards, and drink wine from them.*
> *They shall also make gardens,*
> *and eat their fruit.*

*I will plant them on their land,
and they will no more be plucked up out of their land
which I have given them," says Yahweh your God.* (Amos 9:9-15)

JONAH

The Book of Jonah tells the tale of a reluctant prophet, who tries to flee from his responsibilities. Notwithstanding that, in the end, he complies and is perplexed by the successful outcome. Set c. 800 BC, written c. 330 BC.

Jonah Rebels Against his Mission

While living in Joppa, Jonah is visited by God, telling him to go to the people of the Assyrian city of Nineveh and tell them of their sinfulness. Jonah, like so many called by God before, wasn't eager, but unlike the others, he runs away and boards a ship bound for Tarshish.

While asleep on the ship, a violent storm lashed at the boat, and everyone onboard soon feared for their lives. Each petitioned their god to be delivered from the storm. During the commotion, Jonah was found sound asleep, causing the crew to suspect he might be the cause of their current misfortune.

Questioning him, they discovered he was an Israelite and worshipped Yahweh (a god they were familiar with), so when Jonah disclosed he was running away from Yahweh, they concluded he was the cause of the storm - even Jonah agreed.

Encouraged by Jonah himself, they threw him overboard, hoping it would appease God and the storm would abate. It did.

Awash in the sea, God directed a fish to swallow Jonah, and he lived for three days and nights in the fish's belly.

While in the belly of the fish Jonah repented and prayed. He was eventually spat out onto the shore, where God again ordered him to go to Nineveh. This time he obeyed.

The Conversion of Nineveh

Arriving in Nineveh, Jonah's message was blunt.

"In forty days, Nineveh will be overthrown!" (Jon 3:4)

All the town listened and believed and immediately went about changing their ways, hoping God would not destroy them, thinking *who knows whether God will not turn and relent, and turn away from his fierce anger, so that we might not perish?*

God saw their works, that they turned from their evil way. God relented of the disaster which he said he would do to them, and he didn't do it. (Jon 3:9-10)

Jonah sulks

Jonah took the town's repentance rather unusually, complaining to God, *"Wasn't this what I said* (would happen) *when I was still in my own country? Therefore, I hurried to flee to Tarshish, for I knew that you are a gracious God and merciful, slow to anger, and abundant in loving kindness, and you relent from doing harm. Therefore now, Yahweh, take, I beg you, my life from me, for it is better for me to die than to live."* (Jon 4: 2-3)

Feeling sorry for himself, Jonah left the city to sulk. God caused a vine to grow above where he sat to provide shade and to ease his ill humour. Overnight however the vine withered and died, leaving Jonah to suffer in the terrible heat. Jonah begged for death again, *"It is better for me to die than to live."*

God said to Jonah, "Is it right for you to be angry about the vine?"

He said, "I am right to be angry, even to death."

Yahweh said, "You have been concerned for the vine, for which you have not laboured, neither made it grow; which came up in a night and perished in a night. Shouldn't I be concerned for Nineveh, that great city, in which are more than one hundred twenty-thousand persons who can't discern between their right hand and their left hand, and also many animals?" (Jon 4: 8-11)

HOSEA

Hosea prophesied for 25 years, from the infamous reign of King Jeroboam II (750 BC) until the exile of the House of Israel. At this time, the Northern Kingdom of Israel was at its political height, but a series of lacklustre and unfaithful kings saw the kingdom become dominated by Assyria,[127] which included having to pay heavy tributes. This is the mood and the times of the message.

The central theme of the Book of Hosea is the symbolic relationship between God and Israel, portrayed as a marriage. Hosea is instructed by God to marry a woman, who becomes unfaithful to him. This marital relationship serves as an allegory for the covenantal relationship between God and the people of Israel. Gomer's (Hosea's wife) unfaithfulness symbolises Israel's idolatry and disobedience to God.

A large part of the book is set aside to list the innumerable ways in which Israel has lived apart from the teachings of God.

Hosea is the first prophet to compare God's covenant with Israel to a marriage.[128]

---

[127] 106 A kingdom to their North to which they had subjugated themselves during the reign of Hoshea.
[128] Flanagan, Neal. The Books of Amos Hosea and Micah. The Liturgical Press, 1968.

Hosea's Marriage

Yahweh said to Hosea, "Go, take for yourself a wife of prostitution and children of unfaithfulness; for the land commits great adultery, forsaking Yahweh." (Hos 1:2)

Hosea did as he was asked by God, and married Gomer. They soon had children. The first was called 'Jezreel'.

The second was called 'Unloved', and God said, *"For I will no longer have mercy on the house of Israel, that I should in any way pardon them. But I will have mercy on the house of Judah, and will save them by Yahweh their God, and will not save them by bow, sword, battle, horses, or horsemen."* (Hos 1:6-7)

The third, 'No People of Mine', God saying, *"For you are not my people, and I will not be yours."* (Hos 1:9)

Yahweh and his Unfaithful wife

God talks of Israel as his unfaithful wife, a whore, *"For she is not my wife nor am I her husband. Let her rid her face of her whoring and her breasts of adultery."* (Hos 2:2*) He will not love the children of a whore. He will withdraw all the provisions he has given her and make her pay for her turning away, but when she has had enough, he will call her back and,

> *"I will sow her to me in the earth;
> and I will have mercy on her who had not obtained mercy;
> and I will tell those who were not my people, 'You are
> my people;'
> and they will say, 'You are My God!'"* (Hos 2:23)

> *"I will betroth you to myself for ever,
> betroth you with integrity and justice,
> with tenderness and love."* (Hos 2:19*)

Hosea's wife Gomer became unfaithful and they separated, prompting God to tell Hosea, *"Go again, love a woman loved by another, and an adulteress, even as Yahweh loves the children of Israel, though they turn to other gods, and love cakes of raisins."* (Hos 3:1)

Hosea paid fifteen shekels for her, God told Hosea to say to her, *"'You shall stay with me many days. You shall not play the prostitute, and you shall not be with any other man. I will also be so toward you.' For the children of Israel shall live many days without king, without prince, without sacrifice, without sacred stone, and without ephod or idols. Afterward the children of Israel shall return and seek Yahweh their God, and David their king, and shall come with trembling to Yahweh and to his blessings in the last days."* (Hos 3:3-5)

The Crimes and Punishment of the House of Israel

Hosea spoke Gods message to the house of Israel, telling them that they have brought all their current sufferings on themselves by their sins.

> *"Hear Yahweh's word, you children of Israel,*
> *for Yahweh has a charge against the inhabitants*
> *of the land:*
> *Indeed there is no truth, nor goodness,*
> *nor knowledge of God in the land.*
> *There is cursing, lying, murder, stealing, and committing adultery;*
> *they break boundaries, and bloodshed causes bloodshed.*
> *Therefore the land will mourn,*
> *and everyone who dwells in it will waste away,*
> *with all living things in her,*
> *even the animals of the field and the birds of the sky;*
> *yes, the fish of the sea also die."* (Hos 4:1-3)
>
> *"Yes, I am going to return to my dwelling place*

> *until they confess their guilt and seek my face;*
> *they will search for me in their misery."* (Hos 5:15*)

Israel's Short Memory

Yet, even as God accepts the repentant return of Israel, they believe they can keep on sinning and God will keep on forgiving them.

> *"Come, let us return to Yahweh.*
> *He has torn us to pieces, but he will heal us;*
> *he has struck us down, but he will bandage our wounds;*
> *after a day or two he will bring us back to life,*
> *on the third day he will raise us*
> *and we shall live in his presence.*
> *Let us set ourselves to know Yahweh;*
> *that he will come is as certain as the dawn;*
> *his judgement will rise like the light,*
> *he will come to us as showers come,*
> *like spring rains watering the earth."* (Hos 6:1-3*)

God speaks:

> *"What am I to do?..*
> *This love of yours is like a morning cloud,*
> *like the dew that quickly disappears.*
> *This is why I have torn them to pieces by the prophets,*
> *why I have slaughtered them with words from my mouth,*
> *since what I want is love, not sacrifice;*
> *knowledge of God, not holocausts."* (Hos 6:4-6*)

But even though God is angered by the way he is treated, he still loves Israel and ultimately wants them for himself.

> *"How can I hand you over, Israel?*
> *…*
> *My heart is turned within me,*
> *my compassion is aroused.*
> *I will not execute the fierceness of my anger.*
> *I will not return to destroy Ephraim,*
> *for I am God, and not man - the Holy One among you.*
> *I will not come in wrath."* (Hos 11:8-9)

Concluding words of Hosea,
> *"Let the wise man understand these words.*
> *Let the intelligent man grasp their meaning.*
> *For the ways of Yahweh are straight,*
> *and virtuous men walk in them,*
> *but sinners stumble."* (Hos 14:9*)

ISAIAH

Isaiah was a prophet around the time of 740 - 700 BC. He comes from the House of Judah, but the House of Israel is also included in his prophecies. His task was to guide Judah through one of the most critical periods in her history. Israel was being conquered by Assyria, causing many to doubt the power of God to protect them.[129]

In what is a typical manner, the prophecies seesaw between:

- God lamenting about the ingratitude and unfaithfulness of his people and how he is going to punish and purify them,
- to him expressing a loving regret and sorrow for their actions,
- to forgiving them and calling them back to him,
- and finally announcing a bright and fruitful salvation for a remnant - through the arrival of a messiah.

Throughout the book however, this seesaw tips many times.

God Calls Isaiah

Isaiah is called by God through a majestic vision where he sees God, and *above him stood the seraphim.*[130] *Each one had six wings. With two he covered his face. With two he covered his feet. With two he flew.* (Is 6:2)

---

[129] The Jerome Biblical Commentary p265.
[130] An Angel.

Completely overawed by the sight, Isaiah asked how it was possible that such a sinful man should be allowed to see God. Next, an angel flew to him and touched his lips with a burning coal, removing his sinfulness. God then gave Isaiah his mission.

> *"Go, and tell this people,*
> *'You hear indeed, but don't understand.*
> *You see indeed, but don't perceive.'*
>
> *"Make the heart of this people fat.*
> *Make their ears heavy, and shut their eyes;*
> *lest they see with their eyes,*
> *hear with their ears,*
> *understand with their heart,*
> *and turn again, and be healed."* (Is 6:9-10)

Judgement and Hope for Judah

Isaiah's prophecies begin with a series of judgements and hope directed toward Judah and Jerusalem.

> *Hear, heavens,*
> *and listen, earth; for Yahweh has spoken:*
> *"I have nourished and brought up children*
> *and they have rebelled against me.*
> *The ox knows his owner,*
> *and the donkey his master's crib;*
> *but Israel doesn't know.*
> *My people don't consider.*
> *Ah sinful nation,*
> *a people loaded with iniquity,*
> *offspring of evildoers,*
> *children who deal corruptly!*

> They have forsaken Yahweh.
> They have despised the Holy One of Israel.
> They are estranged and backward." (Is 1:2-4)

Isaiah tells the people that God isn't impressed anymore by their sacrifices and holocausts because they are done by rote rather than with the heart.

> "What are the multitude of your sacrifices to me?"
> says Yahweh.
> "I have had enough of the burnt offerings of rams,
> and the fat of fed animals.
> I don't delight in the blood of bulls,
> or of lambs,
> or of male goats." (Is 1:11)

> "Wash yourselves. Make yourself clean.
> Put away the evil of your doings from before my eyes.
> Cease to do evil.
> Learn to do well.
> Seek justice.
> Relieve the oppressed.
> Defend the fatherless.
> Plead for the widow." (Is 1:16-17)

God leaves them with hope.

> "If you are willing to obey,
> you shall eat the good things of the earth.
> But if you persist in rebellion,
> the sword shall eat you instead.
> The mouth of Yahweh has spoken." (Is 1:19-20*)

Isaiah tells a rather easy-to-interpret parable of Judah as a vineyard.

> *Let me sing to my friend*
> *the song of his love for his vineyard.*
> *My friend had a vineyard*
> *on a fertile hillside.*
> *He dug the soil, cleared it of stones,*
> *and planted choice vines in it.*
> *In the middle he built a tower,*
> *he dug a press there too.*
> *He expected it to yield grapes,*
> *but sour grapes were all that it gave.*
> *And now, inhabitants of Jerusalem*
> *and men of Judah,*
> *I ask you to judge*
> *between my vineyard and me.*
> *What could I have done for my vineyard*
> *that I have not done?*
> *I expected it to yield grapes.*
> *Why did it yield sour grapes instead?*
> *Very well, I will tell you*
> *what I am going to do to my vineyard:*
> *I will take away its hedge for it to be grazed on,*
> *and knock down its wall for it to be trampled on.*
> *I will lay it waste, unpruned, undug;*
> *overgrown by the briar and the thorn.*
> *I will command the clouds*
> *to rain no rain on it.*
> *Yes, the vineyard of Yahweh*
> *is the House of Israel,*
> *and the men of Judah*
> *that chosen plant.*

> *He expected justice, but found bloodshed,*
> *integrity, but only a cry of distress.* (Is 5:1-7*)

The Sign of Immanuel

Whilst delivering a message to King Ahaz of Judah,[131] who was being attacked by Rezin, the king of Aram, Isaiah is gifted with a most beautiful and epic prophecy of a messianic era to come; after the remnant has been fortified.

> *Listen now, house of David. Is it not enough for you to try the patience of men, that you will try the patience of my God also? Therefore Yahweh himself will give you a sign. Behold, the virgin will conceive, and bear a son, and shall call his name Immanuel.* (Is 7:13-14*)

> *For there is a child born for us,*
> *a son given to us*
> *and dominion is laid on his shoulders;*
> *and this is the name they give him:*
> *Wonder Counsellor, Mighty God,*
> *Eternal Father, Prince of Peace.*
> *Wide is his dominion*
> *in a peace that has no end,*
> *for the throne of David*
> *and for his royal power,*
> *which he establishes and makes secure*
> *in justice and integrity.*

---

[131] The message was that although Aram would attack Jerusalem, it would not be victorious. But this would come to pass only if they stood beside God faithfully; otherwise, 'you will not stand at all!' (Is 7:9).

> *From this time onward and forever,*
> *the jealous love of Yahweh will do this.* (Is 9:6-7*)

> *A shoot will come out of the stock of Jesse,[132]*
> *and a branch out of his roots will bear fruit.*
> *Yahweh's Spirit will rest on him:*
> *the spirit of wisdom and understanding,*
> *the spirit of counsel and might,*
> *the spirit of knowledge and of the fear of Yahweh.*
> *His delight will be in the fear of Yahweh.*
> *He will not judge by the sight of his eyes,*
> *neither decide by the hearing of his ears;*
> *but he will judge the poor with righteousness,*
> *and decide with equity for the humble of the earth.*
> *He will strike the earth with the rod of his mouth;*
> *and with the breath of his lips he will kill the wicked.*
> *Righteousness will be the belt around his waist,*
> *and faithfulness the belt around his waist.* (Is 11:1-5)

Over the next 25 chapters God berates his people and many of the neighbouring cities (Babylon, Assyria, Philistine, Moab, Damascus, Cush, Egypt, Tyre) denouncing them for their evil ways, pausing to say something poignant for his people:

> *"Now go and write this on a tablet,*
> *write it in a book,*
> *that it may serve in the time to come*
> *as a witness for ever*

> *"This is a rebellious people,*
> *they are lying sons,*

---

[132] Line of David.

> *sons who will not listen
> to Yahweh's orders."* (Is 30:8-9*)

In the year 702 BC (the 14th year of the reign of Hezekiah), the king of Assyria laid siege to the outlying towns of Judah.[133] Sitting outside the city walls, the king sent an envoy to petition for the city's surrender (for his army far outnumbered Hezekiah's army). Despite the overwhelming odds, Hezekiah's trust in God would not be shaken. He prayed.

"It is true, Yahweh, that the kings of Assyria have exterminated all the nations and their countries, they have thrown their gods on the fire, for these were not gods but the work of men's hands, wood and stone, and hence they have destroyed them. But now, Yahweh our God, save us from his hand, and let all the kingdoms of the earth know that you alone are God, Yahweh." (Is 37:18-20*)

Isaiah swiftly gave God's response to the prayer of Hezekiah.

> *"He will not enter this city,
> he will let fly no arrow against it,
> confront it with no shield,
> throw up no earthwork against it.
> By the road that he came on he will return;
> he shall not enter this city. It is Yahweh who speaks.
> I will protect this city and save it
> for my own sake and for the sake of my servant David."*
> (Is 37:33-35*)

That night an angel of God destroyed one hundred and eighty-five thousand Assyrian troops.

With the demise of the Assyrian king, a new power was on the horizon, that of Babylon. Hezekiah had grown older and had recovered (through

---

[133] Assyria had already conquered the House of Israel and exiled them from Samaria.

the grace of God) from a deathly illness. Hearing of his recovery, the king of Babylon sent a messenger with gifts and well wishes. Hezekiah, caught up in his own self-importance and invulnerability, naively showed all his wealth and defences to the king's messengers. When Isaiah got wind of this, he labelled it an 'act of stupidity', adding, *"Behold, the days are coming when all that is in your house, and that which your fathers have stored up until today, will be carried to Babylon. Nothing will be left," says Yahweh. "They will take away your sons who will issue from you, whom you shall father, and they will be eunuchs in the king of Babylon's palace."* (Is 39:6-7)

Hezekiah however was completely blind to this warning and instead read the message as good news! *"Yahweh's word which you have spoken is good."* He said moreover, *"For there will be peace and truth in my days."* (Is 39:8)

It has become commonly accepted that chapters 40 onwards were not written by Isaiah himself but rather an 'unknown' author,[134] and at a much later date (around 200 years). After the return from exile, sometimes called Second Isaiah.

The ability of the Israelites to swing from God fearing to Godlessness, shows no signs of abating. Even after they return from exile (as the remnant, foretold by Isaiah), they still manage to be blind to the hand of God.

God's faithfulness is up to the task though.

A 'mysterious servant'[135] is poetised in four Songs of the Servant, but first God restates his authority and kingship as the ONE and ONLY God, the God of the past, present, and future, a God with no rivals, a God with a plan for life after exile.

> *Who has measured the waters in the hollow of his hand,*
> *and marked off the sky with his span,*

---

[134] But no less inspired by God.
[135] NJB 42a. p 1209.

and calculated the dust of the earth in a measuring basket,
and weighed the mountains in scales,
and the hills in a balance?

Who has directed Yahweh's Spirit,
or has taught him as his counsellor?
Who did he take counsel with,
and who instructed him,
and taught him in the path of justice,
and taught him knowledge,
and showed him the way of understanding?
...
All the nations are like nothing before him.
They are regarded by him as less than nothing, and vanity.
(Is 40:12-17)

Haven't you known?
Haven't you heard?
Haven't you been told from the beginning?
Haven't you understood from the foundations of the earth?
It is he who sits above the circle of the earth,
and its inhabitants are like grasshoppers;
who stretches out the heavens like a curtain,
and spreads them out like a tent to dwell in,
who brings princes to nothing,
who makes the judges of the earth meaningless.
(Is 40:21-23)

Seek Yahweh while he may be found.
Call on him while he is near.
Let the wicked forsake his way,
and the unrighteous man his thoughts.
Let him return to Yahweh, and he will have mercy on him,

to our God, for he will freely pardon.

*"For my thoughts are not your thoughts,
and your ways are not my ways," says Yahweh.
"For as the heavens are higher than the earth,
so are my ways higher than your ways,
and my thoughts than your thoughts.
For as the rain comes down and the snow from the sky,
and doesn't return there, but waters the earth,
and makes it grow and bud,
and gives seed to the sower and bread to the eater;
so is my word that goes out of my mouth:
it will not return to me void,
but it will accomplish that which I please,
and it will prosper in the thing I sent it to do."*
(Is 55:6-11)

First Song of the Servant[136]

Yahweh Speaks

*"Behold, my servant, whom I uphold,
my chosen, in whom my soul delights:
I have put my Spirit on him.
He will bring justice to the nations.
He will not shout,
nor raise his voice,
nor cause it to be heard in the street.
He won't break a bruised reed.
He won't quench a dimly burning wick.
He will faithfully bring justice.*

---

[136] The identity of the Servant has been heavily debated, but the most common interpretation is that the Servant is Jesus.

He will not fail nor be discouraged,
until he has set justice on the earth,
and the islands wait for his law." (Is 42:1-4)

Second Song of the Servant

The Servant Speaks

"Yahweh called me before I was born,
from my mother's womb he pronounced my name.
He made my mouth a sharp sword,
and hid me in the shadow of his hand.
He made me into a sharpened arrow,
and concealed me in his quiver.

"He said to me, 'You are my servant (Israel)
in whom I shall be glorified;'
while I was thinking, 'I have toiled in vain,
I have exhausted myself for nothing;'
and all the while my cause was with Yahweh,
my reward with my God.
I was honoured in the eyes of Yahweh,
my God was my strength.

"And now Yahweh has spoken,
he who formed me in the womb to be his servant,
to bring Jacob back to him,
to gather Israel to him:
It is not enough for you to be my servant,
to restore the tribes of Jacob
and bring back the survivors of Israel;
I will make you the light of the nations
so that my salvation may reach to the ends of the earth."
(Is 49:1-6*)

Third Song of the Servant

Yahweh has given me
a disciple's tongue.
So that I may know how to reply to the wearied
he provides me with speech.
Each morning he wakes me to hear,
to listen like a disciple.
Yahweh has opened my ear.

For my part, I made no resistance
neither did I turn away.
I offered my back to those who struck me,
my cheeks to those who tore at my beard;
I did not cover my face
against insult and spittle. (Is 50:4-6*)

Fourth Song of the Servant

Surely he has borne our sickness
and carried our suffering;
yet we considered him plagued,
struck by God, and afflicted.
But he was pierced for our transgressions.
He was crushed for our iniquities.
The punishment that brought our peace was on him;
and by his wounds we are healed.
All we like sheep have gone astray.
Everyone has turned to his own way;
and Yahweh has laid on him the iniquity of us all.

He was oppressed,
yet when he was afflicted he didn't open his mouth.

As a lamb that is led to the slaughter,
and as a sheep that before its shearers is silent,
so he didn't open his mouth. (Is 53:4-7)

Yet it pleased Yahweh to bruise him.
He has caused him to suffer.
When you make his soul an offering for sin,
he will see his offspring.
He will prolong his days
and Yahweh's pleasure will prosper in his hand.
After the suffering of his soul,
he will see the light and be satisfied.
My righteous servant will justify many by the knowledge
of himself;
and he will bear their iniquities. (Is 53:10-11)

From Chapter 56 onwards begins Third Isaiah, and focuses on the 'New Jerusalem', where all nations and believers are welcome - not just Israelites.

"To the eunuchs[137] who keep my Sabbaths, choose the things that please me, and hold fast to my covenant, I will give them in my house and within my walls a memorial and a name better than that of sons and of daughters. I will give them an everlasting name that will not be cut off.

"Also the foreigners[138] who join themselves to Yahweh to serve him, and to love Yahweh's name, to be his servants, everyone who keeps the Sabbath from profaning it, and holds fast my covenant, I will bring these to my holy mountain, and make them joyful in my house of prayer. Their burnt offerings and their sacrifices will be accepted on my altar; for my house will be called a house of prayer for all peoples.

---

[137] The use of the word eunuch can be interpreted as symbolic for any and all people that are marginalised or excluded.

[138] Non Israelites, akin to the Pagan's of the New Testament.

> "Yahweh, who gathers the outcasts of Israel, says, 'I will yet gather others to him, in addition to his own who are gathered.'" (Is 56:4-8)

The book of Isaiah draws to its end with a significant and momentous oracle on the mission of the prophet, which Jesus will cite when he begins his own public ministry.

> *Yahweh's Spirit is on me,*
> *because Yahweh has anointed me to preach good news to*
> *the humble.*
> *He has sent me to bind up the broken hearted,*
> *to proclaim liberty to the captives*
> *and release to those who are bound,*
> *to proclaim the year of Yahweh's favour*
> *and the day of vengeance of our God,*
> *to comfort all who mourn.* (Is 61:1-2)

MICAH

The prophet Micah covers a similar discourse to the prophets Amos and Hosea, with one distinction - he is focused more on the Southern Kingdom - the House of Judah, than the Northern Kingdom - House of Israel.

He goes over the sins and transgressions, the impending doom, but also the salvation at the end.

He was around before the deportation - in the time of Jotham, Ahaz and Hezekiah c. 740 - 690 BC.

The book begins with a judgement from God for the North and South Kingdoms (Samaria and Jerusalem).

> *"Hear, you peoples, all of you!*
> *Listen, O earth, and all that is therein.*
> *Let Yahweh be witness against you,*
> *the Lord from his holy temple.* (Mic 1:2)

> *"All this is for the disobedience of Jacob,*
> *and for the sins of the house of Israel.*
> *What is the disobedience of Jacob?*
> *Isn't it Samaria?*
> *And what are the high places of Judah?*
> *Aren't they Jerusalem?*

> "Therefore I will make Samaria like a rubble heap of
> the field,
> like places for planting vineyards;
> and I will pour down its stones into the valley,
> and I will uncover its foundations.
>
> "All her idols will be beaten to pieces,
> all her temple gifts will be burned with fire,
> and I will destroy all her images;
> for of the hire of a prostitute has she gathered them,
> and to the hire of a prostitute shall they return.
> (Mic 1:5-7)
>
> "There is no healing for the blow Yahweh strikes:
> it reaches into Judah,
> it knocks at the very door of my people,
> reaches even into Jerusalem." (Mic 1:9*)

So often after God expresses his anger, he follows it up with love and hope.

> "Yes, I am going to gather all Jacob together,
> I will gather the remnant of Israel,
> bring them together like sheep in the fold;
> like a flock in its pasture
> they will fear no man." (Mic 2:12*)

Micah goes on to vent God's condemnation of the corrupt rulers and false prophets who oppress the people.

He also brings to light the glorious future and restoration God has planned.

> In the latter days,
> it will happen that the mountain of Yahweh's temple

> will be established on the top of the mountains,
> and it will be exalted above the hills;
> and peoples will stream to it.
>
> Many nations will go and say,
> "Come! Let's go up to the mountain of Yahweh,
> and to the house of the God of Jacob;
> and he will teach us of his ways,
> and we will walk in his paths."
> For the Law will go out of Zion,
> and Yahweh's word from Jerusalem. (Mic 4:1-2)
>
> "In that day," says Yahweh,
> "I will assemble that which is lame,
> and I will gather that which is driven away,
> and that which I have afflicted;
> and I will make that which was lame a remnant,
> and that which was cast far off a strong nation:
> and Yahweh will reign over them on Mount Zion
> from then on,
> even forever." (Mic 4:6-7)

God again challenges Israel, saying:

> "My people, what have I done to you?
> How have I burdened you?
> Answer me!
> For I brought you up out of the land of Egypt,
> and redeemed you out of the house of bondage.
> I sent before you Moses, Aaron." (Mic 6:3-4)
>
> "What is good has been explained to you, man;
> this is what Yahweh asks of you:

> *only this, to act justly,*
> *to love tenderly*
> *and to walk humbly with your God."* (Mic 6:8*)

Micah speaks on behalf of Israel.

> *Don't rejoice against me, my enemy.*
> *When I fall, I will arise.*
> *When I sit in darkness,*
> *Yahweh will be a light to me.*
> *I will bear the indignation of Yahweh,*
> *because I have sinned against him,*
> *until he pleads my case and executes judgement for me.*
> *He will bring me out to the light.*
> *I will see his righteousness.*
> *Then my enemy will see it,*
> *and shame will cover her who said to me,*
> *"Where is Yahweh your God?"*
> *My eyes will see her.*
> *Now she will be trodden down like the mire of the streets.*
> (Mic 7:8-10)

NAHUM

This book covers the fall of Nineveh, the capital of the Assyrian Empire (much like the Book of Jonah), which is a long-time enemy of the Israelites. It was written between 660 BC and 650 BC.

The Fall of Nineveh

Woe to the bloody city! It is all full of lies and robbery - no end to the prey. The noise of the whip, the noise of the rattling of wheels, prancing horses, and bounding chariots, the horseman charging, and the flashing sword, the glittering spear, and a multitude of slain, and a great heap of corpses, and there is no end to the bodies. They stumble on their bodies because of the multitude of the prostitution of the alluring prostitute, the mistress of witchcraft, who sells nations through her prostitution, and families through her witchcraft.

"Behold, I am against you," says Yahweh of Armies, "and I will lift your skirts over your face. I will show the nations your nakedness, and the kingdoms your shame. I will throw abominable filth on you and make you vile, and will make you a spectacle. It will happen that all those who look at you will flee from you, and say, 'Nineveh is laid waste! Who will mourn for her?' Where will I seek comforters for you?" (Nah 3:1-7)

There is no healing your wound, for your injury is fatal. All who hear the report of you clap their hands over you, for who hasn't felt your endless cruelty? (Nah 3:19)

ZEPHANIAH

God speaks to Zephaniah with a message (to the House of Judah), which is severe and blunt. God means to establish his sovereignty over all people, and singles out idol worshippers, rulers, and unbelievers. He lived during the reign of Josiah, c. 630 BC.

The book begins with an utterance of God's Judgement, 'The Day of the Lord'.

> *"I will utterly sweep away everything*
> *from the surface of the earth", says Yahweh.*
> *"I will sweep away man and animal.*
> *I will sweep away the birds of the sky,*
> *the fish of the sea,*
> *and the heaps of rubble with the wicked.*
> *I will cut off man from the surface of the earth.*
> *I will stretch out my hand against Judah*
> *and against all the inhabitants of Jerusalem."* (Zep 1:2-4)

> *"I will search Jerusalem with lamps,*
> *and I will punish the men who are settled on their dregs,*
> *who say in their heart, 'Yahweh will not do good,*
> *neither will he do evil.'*
> *Their wealth will become a plunder,*
> *and their houses a desolation.*

> *Yes, they will build houses,*
> *but won't inhabit them.*
> *They will plant vineyards,*
> *but won't drink their wine."* (Zep 1:12-13)

God goes on to paint a grim picture of what the Day of the Lord will look like.

> *"The great day of Yahweh is near.*
> *It is near and hurries greatly,*
> *the voice of the day of Yahweh.*
> *The mighty man cries there bitterly.*
> *That day is a day of wrath,*
> *a day of distress and anguish,*
> *a day of trouble and ruin,*
> *a day of darkness and gloom,*
> *a day of clouds and blackness,*
> *a day of the trumpet and alarm against the fortified cities*
> *and against the high battlements.*
> *I will bring such distress on men*
> *that they will walk like blind men*
> *because they have sinned against Yahweh.*
> *Their blood will be poured out like dust*
> *and their flesh like dung.*
> *Neither their silver nor their gold*
> *will be able to deliver them in the day of Yahweh's wrath,*
> *but the whole land will be devoured*
> *by the fire of his jealousy;*
> *for he will make an end,*
> *yes, a terrible end, of all those who dwell in the land."*
> (Zep 1:14-18)

But as always God wants faithfulness and is always willing to accept repentance, even from the unbelievers and pagans.

> *"Seek Yahweh, all you humble of the land,*
> *who have kept his ordinances.*
> *Seek righteousness.*
> *Seek humility.*
> *It may be that you will be hidden*
> *on the day of Yahweh's anger."* (Zep 2:3)

> *"For then I will purify the lips of the peoples,*
> *that they may all call on Yahweh's name,*
> *to serve him shoulder to shoulder.*
> *From beyond the rivers of Cush,*
> *my worshippers,*
> *even the daughter of my dispersed people,*
> *will bring my offering.*
> *In that day you will not be disappointed*
> *for all your doings in which you have transgressed*
> *against me;*
> *for then I will take away out from among you your proudly*
> *exulting ones,*
> *and you will no more be arrogant in my holy mountain."*
> (Zep 3:9-11)

HABAKKUK

Habakkuk's relationship with God seems quite audacious. Confronted by the impending Babylonian invasion and Judah's oppression, he has the brazenness to question God's actions of choosing the oppressors of his people. Written for the House of Judah c. 600 BC, and during Nebuchadnezzar's reign.

Habakkuk opens by boldly asking God why he allows oppression and injustice, why is there so much violence and hatred, why does the wicked man succeed over the upright man?

> *How long will I cry, and you will not hear?*
> *I cry out to you "Violence!" and will you not save?*
> *Why do you show me iniquity,*
> *and look at perversity?*
> *For destruction and violence are before me.*
> *There is strife, and contention rises up.*
> *Therefore the Law is paralysed,*
> *and justice never prevails;*
> *for the wicked surround the righteous;*
> *therefore justice comes out perverted.* (Hab 1:2-4)

God replies with the news that he is stirring up a nearby nation to become his instrument of action.

> *"Behold, I am raising up the Chaldeans,[139]*
> *that bitter and hasty nation*
> *who march through the width of the earth,*
> *to possess dwelling places that are not theirs."* (Hab 1:6)
>
> *"All of them come for violence.*
> *Their hordes face forward.*
> *They gather prisoners like sand."* (Hab 1:9)

Habakkuk goes on to question God again, asking why he chooses people who are even more wicked to deliver his wrath on his chosen people.

> *Aren't you from everlasting,*
> *Yahweh my God, my Holy One?*
> *Who will not die.*
> *Yahweh, you have appointed them for judgement.*
> *You, Rock, have established him to punish.*
> *You who have purer eyes than to see evil,*
> *and who cannot look on perversity,*
> *why do you tolerate those who deal treacherously*
> *and keep silent when the wicked swallows up the man*
> *who is more righteous than he?* (Hab 1:12-13)

God replies by telling Habakkuk to just listen.

> *"Woe to him who increases that which is not his,*
> *and who enriches himself by extortion."* (Hab 2:6)
>
> *"Woe to him who gets an evil gain for his house,*
> *that he may set his nest on high,*
> *that he may be delivered from the hand of evil!"* (Hab 2:9)

---

[139] Rulers of Babylon.

> *"Woe to him who builds a town with blood,*
> *and establishes a city by iniquity!"* (Hab 2:12)

> *"Woe to him who gives his neighbour drink,*
> *pouring your inflaming wine until they are drunk,*
> *so that you may gaze at their naked bodies!"* (Hab 2:15)

Habakkuk accepts God's judgement.

> *Yahweh, I have heard of your fame.*
> *I stand in awe of your deeds, Yahweh.*
> *Renew your work in the middle of the years.*
> *In the middle of the years make it known.*
> *In wrath, you remember mercy.* (Hab 3:2)

> *You uncovered your bow.*
> *You called for your sworn arrows,*
> *you split the earth with rivers.*
> *The mountains saw you, and were afraid.*
> *The storm of waters passed by.*
> *The deep roared and lifted up its hands on high.*
> (Hab 3:9-10)

> *Yet I will rejoice in Yahweh.*
> *I will be joyful in the God of my salvation!*
> *Yahweh, the Lord, is my strength,*
> *he makes my feet like deer's feet,*
> *and enables me to go in high places.* (Hab 3:18-19)

JEREMIAH

In Jeremiah, we see a change in the way God displays himself. Previously, we have seen him as being exacting and vengeful. Now we see a different side to him, one that is deeply hurt by the way he has been treated, one that questions why he isn't being loved as he should. Dare I say, he becomes human in his feelings and is torn between being merciful, but also demanding respect and faithfulness. For while he can be extremely benevolent, he can also be strict and punishing. Jeremiah prophesied during Judah's decline, from the reign of Josiah around 620 BC until the Babylonian exile in 587 BC.

God called Jeremiah to be a prophet during the last thirty years of the House of Judah, before the fall and exile, saying,

> "Before I formed you in the womb, I knew you.
> Before you were born, I sanctified you.
> I have appointed you a prophet to the nations." (Jer 1:5)

But Jeremiah was reluctant to accept. Like many before him, he told God he felt inadequate.

> "Ah, Lord Yahweh! Behold, I don't know how to speak; for I am a child." (Jer 1:6)

"Don't say, 'I am a child'; for you must go to whomever I send you, and you must say whatever I command you. Don't be afraid because of them, for I am with you to rescue you," says Yahweh. (Jer 1:7-8)

Once he accepted the call of God, Jeremiah boldly spoke his word to the people of Judah. His calling was a hard one though, as God had chosen him to speak out against all the sins of the people and not only that, but also to outline the wrath God was sending their way. Consequently, he was hated and despised and even targeted to be killed several times, once by people from his own hometown.[140] Because his message was a hard one, other prophets emerged and began telling different stories, ones that were easier to hear, ones that played down the extent of the judgement that was coming their way. This made Jeremiah's task much harder, as God pointed out.

"It will happen, when you tell this people all these words, and they ask you, 'Why has Yahweh pronounced all this great evil against us?' or 'What is our iniquity?' or 'What is our sin that we have committed against Yahweh our God?' then you shall tell them, 'Because your fathers have forsaken me,' says Yahweh, 'and have walked after other gods, have served them, have worshipped them, have forsaken me, and have not kept my law. You have done evil more than your fathers, for behold, you each walk after the stubbornness of his evil heart, so that you don't listen to me. Therefore, I will cast you out of this land into the land that you have not known, neither you nor your fathers. There you will serve other gods day and night, for I will show you no favour.'" (Jer 16:10-13)

There were times when Jeremiah tried to convince God to leave him be.

> Yahweh, you have persuaded me, and I was persuaded.
> You are stronger than I, and have prevailed,
> I have become a laughingstock all day.
> Everyone mocks me.

---

[140] In the New Testament we will see Jesus being confronted with the same situation.

> *For as often as I speak, I cry out;*
> *I cry, "Violence and destruction"!*
> *because Yahweh's word has been made a reproach to me,*
> *and a derision, all day.* (Jer 20:7-8)

God reminds Israel how faithful they once were and goes on to ask what he did to deserve their turning from him, saying,

> *"I remember for you the kindness of your youth,*
> *your love as a bride,*
> *how you went after me in the wilderness,*
> *in a land that was not sown.*
> *Israel was holiness to Yahweh,*
> *the first fruits of his increase.*
> *All who devour him will be held guilty.*
> *Evil will come on them."* (Jer 2:2-3)

> *"For my people have committed two evils:*
> *they have forsaken me, the spring of living waters,*
> *and cut out cisterns for themselves:*
> *broken cisterns that can't hold water."* (Jer 2:13)

God next spoke to Jeremiah about how the sins of Israel were being copied by Judah, so much so that in comparison, Israel looked good. But as always, God was open and ready to accept their repentant return.

"Have you seen that which backsliding Israel has done? She has gone up on every high mountain and under every green tree, and has played the prostitute there. I said after she had done all these things, 'She will return to me;' but she didn't return, and her treacherous sister Judah saw it. I saw when, for this very cause, that backsliding Israel had committed adultery, I had put her away and given her a certificate of divorce, yet treacherous Judah, her sister, had no fear, but she also went and played the prostitute. Because she took her prostitution lightly, the land was polluted, and she committed adultery with

(idols). *Yet for all this her treacherous sister, Judah, has not returned to me with her whole heart, but only in pretence," says Yahweh.*

Yahweh said to me, "Backsliding Israel has shown herself more righteous than treacherous Judah. Go, and proclaim these words toward the north, and say, 'Return, you backsliding Israel,' says Yahweh; 'I will not look in anger on you, for I am merciful,' says Yahweh. 'I will not keep anger forever. Only acknowledge your iniquity, that you have transgressed against Yahweh your God, and have scattered your ways to the strangers under every green tree, and you have not obeyed my voice,' says Yahweh." (Jer 3:6-13)

God told Jeremiah to buy a loincloth and put it around his waist. Next God told him to go down to the river, take it off, and hide it under a rock. Jeremiah did all of this. Several days later, God sent him back to the river to retrieve the loincloth. When Jeremiah did as directed, he found the loincloth had spoiled and was useless. God explained to him that just as the loincloth had spoiled, so had Judah and Jerusalem spoiled. For just as a loincloth is made to cling to the waist, so too was the House of Judah formed to cling to God.

Jeremiah then proclaimed to the people of Judah,

> *Hear, and give ear.*
> *Don't be proud,*
> *for Yahweh has spoken.*
> *Give glory to Yahweh your God,*
> *before he causes darkness,*
> *and before your feet stumble on the dark mountains,*
> *and while you look for light,*
> *he turns it into the shadow of death,*
> *and makes it deep darkness.*
>
> *But if you will not hear it,*
> *my soul will weep in secret for your pride.*
> *My eye will weep bitterly,*

and run down with tears,
because Yahweh's flock has been taken captive.
(Jer 13:15-17)

"Therefore, I will scatter them
as the stubble that passes away
by the wind of the wilderness.
This is your lot,
the portion measured to you from me," says Yahweh,
"because you have forgotten me,
and trusted in falsehood.
Therefore, I will also uncover your skirts on your face,
and your shame will appear." (Jer 13:24-26)

Jeremiah foretells the impending deportation and exile for the House of Judah.

For twenty-three years, from the thirteenth year of Josiah son of Amon, king of Judah, until today, the word of Yahweh has been addressed to me and I have persistently spoken to you (but you have not listened. Furthermore, Yahweh has persistently sent you all his servants the prophets, but you have not listened, or paid attention). The message was this, "Turn back, each of you, from your evil behaviour and your evil actions, and you will stay on the soil Yahweh long ago gave to you and to your ancestors forever. (And do not follow alien gods to serve and worship them, do not provoke me by what your own hands have made; then I will not harm you.) But you have not listened to me (it is Yahweh who speaks – so that you have now provoked me by what your own hands have made, and thus harmed yourselves)." (Jer 25:3-7*)

"Because you (Judah) *have not heard my words, behold, I will send for all the clans of the North,... and I will send to Nebuchadnezzar (the king of Babylon, my servant), and* (I) *will bring them against this land, and against its inhabitants, and against all these nations around. I will utterly destroy them... Moreover, I will take from them the voice of mirth and the voice of gladness, the voice of the bridegroom and the voice of the bride, the sound of*

the millstones, and the light of the lamp. This whole land will be a desolation, and an astonishment; and these nations will serve the king of Babylon for seventy years.

"It will happen, when seventy years are accomplished, then I will punish the king of Babylon and that nation, for their iniquity." (Jer 25:8-12)

Jeremiah, who had remained living in Jerusalem after the exile of Judah, sent a letter to those who had been carried off, informing them that God had not forgotten them, but they would still need to endure seventy years of exile. The letter informed them that God had decreed they should work hard and support themselves during this time. They should continue to have children, and their children should marry and have children of their own. At the end of their time in exile, God would fulfil his original promise and bring them back. Then when they called out his name, he would answer.

But he also warned them that he would not send any prophets to them during exile, so anyone saying they were speaking on his behalf was a false prophet and not to be listened to.

God again spoke to Jeremiah,

"Behold, the days come," says Yahweh, *"that I will make a new covenant[141] with the house of Israel, and with the house of Judah, not according to the covenant that I made with their fathers on the day that I took them by the hand to bring them out of the land of Egypt, which covenant of mine they broke, although I was a husband to them,"* says Yahweh. *"But this is the covenant that I will make with the house of Israel after those days,"* says Yahweh:

---

[141] The New Jerusalem Bible comments that 'The old covenant has been violated', so 'an everlasting covenant will be made'. This covenant is 'new' in three respects: 1. God's spontaneous forgiveness of sin, 2. Individual responsibility and retribution, 3. Interiorisation of religion: the Law is no longer to be a code regulating external activity but an inspiration working on the heart of man.

> "I will put my Law in their inward parts,
> and I will write it in their heart
> I will be their God,
> and they shall be my people.
> They will no longer each teach his neighbour,
> and every man teach his brother, saying, 'Know Yahweh;'
> for they will all know me,
> from their least to their greatest," says Yahweh,
> "For I will forgive their iniquity,
> and I will remember their sin no more." (Jer 31:31-34)

Finally, after exile, God promises through Jeremiah, that he will besiege the city of Babylon, and return the remnant of the sons of Israel to Jerusalem.

> "I will bring Israel again to his pasture,
> and he will feed on Carmel and Bashan.
> His soul will be satisfied on the hills of Ephraim and in Gilead.
> In those days, and in that time," says Yahweh,
> "The iniquity of Israel will be sought for,
> and there will be none,
> also the sins of Judah,
> and they won't be found;
> for I will pardon them whom I leave as a remnant."
> (Jer 50:19-20)

BARUCH

Baruch was a companion of Jeremiah and is mentioned in the Book of Jeremiah. This book is thought to have been written c. 582 BC by Baruch in Babylon (he was among the first to be exiled) and sent to those still living in Jerusalem.

It provides comfort, hope, and spiritual guidance during a time of great hardship and exile.

While exiled in Babylon, Baruch read aloud the contents of a book to Jeconiah.[142] When the words were heard, all those present wept, fasted, and prayed. They took a collection for the priests and people still back in Jerusalem. They sent the collection along with the book, and a message.

"*We have disobeyed him and have not listened to the voice of the Lord our God, to walk in the commandments of the Lord that he has set before us. Since the day that the Lord brought our fathers out of the land of Egypt to this present day, we have been disobedient to the Lord our God, and we have been negligent in not listening to his voice. Therefore, the plagues have clung to us, along with the curse which the Lord declared through Moses his servant in the day that he brought our fathers out of the land of Egypt to give us a land that flows with milk and honey, as at this day. Nevertheless, we didn't listen to the voice of the Lord our God, according to all the words of the prophets whom he sent to us, but we each walked in the imagination of his own wicked heart,*

---

[142] The last ruling king of Judah.

to serve strange gods and to do what is evil in the sight of the Lord our God." (Bar 1:18-22)

A prayer is offered on behalf of Israel.

Hear O Lord, and have mercy; for you are a merciful God. Yes, have mercy upon us, because we have sinned before you. For you are enthroned forever, and we keep perishing. O Lord Almighty, you God of Israel, hear now the prayer of the dead Israelites, and of the children of those who were sinners before you, who didn't listen to the voice of you, their God; because of this, these plagues cling to us. (Bar 3:2-4)

Here Jerusalem is speaking to her 'children', urging them to call on God's mercy.

"Be of good cheer, my people, the memorial of Israel. You were not sold to the nations for destruction, but because you moved God to wrath, you were delivered to your adversaries. For you provoked him who made you by sacrificing to demons and not to God. You forgot the everlasting God who brought you up." (Bar 4:5-8)

"For the sins of my children, I am left desolate, because they turned away from the law of God and had no regard for his statutes. They didn't walk in the ways of God's commandments or tread in the paths of discipline in his righteousness. Let those who dwell near Zion come and remember the captivity of my sons and daughters, which the Everlasting has brought upon them. For he has brought a nation upon them from afar, a shameless nation with a strange language, who didn't respect old men or pity children. They have carried away the dear beloved sons of the widow, and left her who was alone desolate of her daughters." (Bar 4:12-16)

"Take courage, O Jerusalem, for he who called you by name will comfort you. Miserable are those who afflicted you and rejoiced at your fall. Miserable are the cities which your children served. Miserable is she who received your sons. For as she rejoiced at your fall and was glad of your ruin, so she will be grieved at her own desolation." (Bar 4:30-33)

"Take off the garment of your mourning and affliction, O Jerusalem, and put on forever the beauty of the glory from God. Put on the robe of the righteousness from God. Set on your head a diadem of the glory of the Everlasting. For God will show your splendour everywhere under heaven. For your name will be called by God forever 'Righteous Peace, Godly Glory.'" (Bar 5:1-4)

Though they left on foot, with enemies for an escort, now God brings them back to you like royal princes carried back in glory. (Bar 5:6*)

The Letter of Jeremiah[143]

A message from God given to Jeremiah for the House of Judah and those about to be led away into captivity.

Because of the sins which you have committed before God, you will be led away captives to Babylon by Nebuchadnezzar, king of the Babylonians. So when you come to Babylon, you will remain there many years, and for a long season, even for seven generations. After that, I will bring you out peacefully from there. But now you will see in Babylon gods of silver, gold, wood carried on shoulders, which cause the nations to fear. Beware therefore that you in no way become like these foreigners. Don't let fear take hold of you because of them when you see the multitude before them and behind them, worshipping them. But say in your hearts, "O Lord, we must worship you." (Bar 6:1-5)

---

[143] The 'Letter of Jeremiah' is considered to be a separate work, but is included as Chapter 6 in this book.

LAMENTATIONS

A lamentation is a passionate expression of grief and sorrow. This book has historically been attributed to the prophet Jeremiah, but recent scholars now question this. It covers the period from 597 BC up to the destruction of Jerusalem and the deportation to Babylon (587 BC).

The Jerome Biblical commentary writes that the author 'emphasises Yahweh's part in Jerusalem's destruction', adding 'if Jerusalem's fall is evidence of a mute Yahweh, then Jerusalem can only despair. But if Jerusalem's fall is evident of Yahweh's wrath, then it is evidence too of his…personal interest in (its) correction and well-being'.

First Lamentation

On the desolation of Jerusalem.

> *How the city sits solitary,*
> *that was full of people!*
> *She has become as a widow,*
> *who was great among the nations!*
> *She who was a princess among the provinces*
> *has become a slave!* (Lam 1:1)
>
> *Judah has gone into captivity because of affliction,*

> *and because of great servitude.*
> *She dwells among the nations.*
> *She finds no rest.*
> *All her persecutors overtook her in her distress.* (Lam 1:3)

> *Jerusalem has grievously sinned.*
> *Therefore she has become unclean.*
> *All who honoured her despise her,*
> *because they have seen her nakedness.*
> *Yes, she sighs and turns backward.* (Lam 1:8)

> *All her people sigh.*
> *They seek bread.*
> *They have given their pleasant things*
> *for food to refresh their soul.*
> *"Look, Yahweh, and see,*
> *for I have become despised."* (Lam 1:11)

> *For these things I weep.*
> *My eye, my eye runs down with water,*
> *because the comforter who should refresh my soul is*
> *far from me.*
> *My children are desolate,*
> *because the enemy has prevailed.* (Lam 1:16)

Second Lamentation

God's Judgement.

> *Yahweh has swallowed up*
> *all the dwellings of Jacob without pity.*
> *He has thrown down in his wrath*
> *the strongholds of the daughter of Judah.*

> He has brought them down to the ground.
> He has profaned the kingdom and its princes. (Lam 2:2)
>
> He has violently taken away his tabernacle,
> as if it were a garden.
> He has destroyed his place of assembly.
> Yahweh has caused solemn assembly
> and Sabbath to be forgotten in Zion.
> In the indignation of his anger,
> he has despised the king and the priest. (Lam 2:6)
>
> Yahweh has done that which he planned.
> He has fulfilled his word that he commanded
> in the days of old.
> He has thrown down,
> and has not pitied.
> He has caused the enemy to rejoice over you.
> He has exalted the horn of your adversaries. (Lam 2:17)

Third Lamentation

Hope for Mercy, Petition for Relief.

> Yahweh is good to those who wait for him,
> to the soul who seeks him.
> It is good that a man should hope
> and quietly wait for the salvation of Yahweh.
> It is good for a man that he bears the yoke in his youth.
> Let him sit alone and keep silence,
> because he has laid it on him. (Lam 3:25-28)
>
> Let us search and try our ways,
> and turn again to Yahweh.

> *Let's lift up our heart with our hands to God in*
> *the heavens.*
> *"We have transgressed and have rebelled.*
> *You have not pardoned."* (Lam 3:40-42)

> *I called on your name, Yahweh,*
> *out of the lowest dungeon.*
> *You heard my voice:*
> *"Don't hide your ear from my sighing,*
> *and my cry."*
> *You came near on the day that I called on you.*
> *You said, "Don't be afraid."* (Lam 3:55-57)

Fourth Lamentation

Present Misery of Jerusalem v Her Past Glory.

> *How the gold has become dim!*
> *The most pure gold has changed!*
> *The stones of the sanctuary are poured out*
> *at the head of every street.* (Lam 4:1)

> *Those who ate delicacies are desolate on the streets.*
> *Those who were brought up in purple embrace dunghills.*
> *For the iniquity of the daughter of my people*
> *is greater than the sin of Sodom,*
> *which was overthrown as in a moment.*
> *No hands were laid on her.* (Lam 4:5-6)

Fifth Lamentation

Suffering of the Vanquished, Petition for Release.

Our inheritance has been turned over to strangers,
our houses to aliens.
We are orphans and fatherless.
Our mothers are as widows. (Lam 5:2-3)

Our pursuers are on our necks.
We are weary, and have no rest. (Lam 5:5)

Our fathers sinned, and are no more.
We have borne their iniquities. (Lam 5:7)

The joy of our heart has ceased.
Our dance is turned into mourning.
The crown has fallen from our head.
Woe to us, for we have sinned! (Lam 5:15-16)

You, Yahweh, remain forever.
Your throne is from generation to generation.
Why do you forget us forever,
and forsake us for so long a time?
Turn us to yourself, Yahweh, and we will be turned.
Renew our days as of old.
But you have utterly rejected us.
You are very angry against us. (Lam 5:19-22)

EZEKIEL

Ezekiel was a priest among the group of people deported from Jerusalem in 597 BC, and his ministry was active between 593 BC and 571 BC.

He received unambiguous visions from God depicting the sins of Jerusalem and the Israelites, and why God had no choice but to send them into the wilderness again (like the Exodus Hebrews), where they could contemplate their sins. The visions were God's way of saying he 'authoured' the first exile, and will also allow Jerusalem to be destroyed. The visions also promise hope and redemption.

On many occasions, Ezekiel is referred to as the 'son of man', which is a way of calling Ezekiel a regular person with an important job from God to speak to others on behalf of humanity.

The Vision of Yahweh

In the year 593 BC, while in Babylon,, the hand of God touched Ezekiel, and he received a vision of four animals in human form. Each had four faces: one was human, one an eagle, one a lion, and one a bull. The four faces were facing the four quarters of the world. Each of the animals had four wings, and under each wing were human hands. Over their heads was a vault, and high in the vault was a throne that looked like a sapphire, and on the throne sat what looked like a man. He looked like the glory of Yahweh.

Ezekiel was handed a scroll labelled 'lamentation and wailing and woe' and was told to eat it. The man in the vision said, *"Son of man, go to the house of Israel, and speak my words to them. For you are not sent to a people of a strange speech and of a hard language, but to the house of Israel... Surely, if I sent you to them, they would listen to you. But the house of Israel will not listen to you, for they will not listen to me; for all the house of Israel are obstinate and hard-hearted... Don't be afraid of them, neither be dismayed at their looks, though they are a rebellious house."* (Ez 3:4-9)

Ezekiel was then led by the hand of God into a valley where he was struck dumb and told, *"I will make your tongue stick to the roof of your mouth so that you will be mute and will not be able to correct them, for they are a rebellious house. But when I speak with you, I will open your mouth, and you shall tell them, 'This is what the Lord God says.' He who hears, let him hear; and he who refuses, let him refuse; for they are a rebellious house."* (Ez 3:26-27)

The Siege of Jerusalem Foretold

God instructed Ezekiel to take a brick, place it on the ground and write the name of Jerusalem on it. Around the brick he was to dig a trench, pitch camps and besiege it with battering rams. God explained to Ezekiel that he was preparing to surround Jerusalem with foreign nations because she had sinned against him, even more than the pagan foreign nations had.

"This is Jerusalem. I have set her in the middle of the nations, and countries are around her. She has rebelled against my ordinances in doing wickedness more than the nations, and against my statutes more than the countries that are around her; for they have rejected my ordinances, and as for my statutes, they have not walked in them." (Ez 5:5-6)

"My eye won't spare, and I will have no pity. A third of you will die with the pestilence, and they will be consumed with famine within you. A third will fall by the sword around you. A third I will scatter to all the winds, and will draw out a sword after them." (Ez 5:11-12)

"Moreover, I will make you a desolation and a reproach among the nations that are around you, in the sight of all that pass by. So it will be a reproach and a taunt, an instruction and an astonishment, to the nations that are around you, when I execute judgements on you in anger and in wrath, and in wrathful rebukes." (Ez 5:14-15)

The Sins and Punishment of Jerusalem

A year later, around 592 BC Ezekiel received another vision from God. It was of a man made of half fire and half polished bronze. He took Ezekiel into the air (by his hair) to the inner north gate of Jerusalem, where he saw the glory of God.

"Son of man, do you see what they do? Even the great abominations that the house of Israel commit here." (Ez 8:6)

Ezekiel was then taken to the entrance of the court and told to break a hole through the wall and look inside. *"Son of man, have you seen what the elders of the house of Israel do in the dark, every man in his rooms of imagery? For they say, 'Yahweh doesn't see us. Yahweh has forsaken the land.'"* (Ez 8:12)

Next Ezekiel saw six men, who were ordered by God to go into the city and mark with the sign of a cross, all who were faithful and devout. To the others, God said, *"Don't let your eye spare, neither have pity. Kill utterly the old man, the young man, the virgin, little children and women; but don't come near any man on whom is the mark."* (Ez 9:6)

This disturbed Ezekiel and he couldn't help but ask God, *"Ah Lord Yahweh! Will you destroy all the residue of Israel in your pouring out of your wrath on Jerusalem?"* (Ez 9:8)

God replied, *"The iniquity of the house of Israel and Judah is exceedingly great, and the land is full of blood, and the city full of perversion; for they say, 'Yahweh has forsaken the land, and Yahweh doesn't see.' As for me also, my eye won't spare, neither will I have pity, but I will bring their way on their head."* (Ez 9:9-10)

Yahweh spoke to Ezekiel again, telling him to say to the House of Israel, *"I know the things that come into your mind. You have multiplied your slain in this city, and you have filled its streets with the slain.*

"You have feared the sword; and I will bring the sword on you," says Yahweh. *"I will bring you out of the middle of it, and deliver you into the hands of strangers, and will execute judgements among you. You will fall by the sword. I will judge you in the land of Israel. Then you will know that I am Yahweh."* (Ez 11:5-10)

Ezekiel was again troubled by this and asked God if it was his plan to wipe out all that was left of Israel. Yahweh responded, *"I will gather you from the peoples, and assemble you out of the countries where you have been scattered, and I will give you the land of Israel.*

"They will come there, and they will take away all its detestable things and all its abominations from there. I will give them one heart, and I will put a new spirit within them. I will take the stony heart out of their flesh, and will give them a heart of flesh, that they may walk in my statutes, and keep my ordinances, and do them. They will be my people, and I will be their God." (Ez 11:17-20)

An Account of Israel's Infidelities

During the next year, 591 BC, some elders of Israel came to consult Yahweh (through Ezekiel) and Yahweh didn't hold back.

"In the day when I chose Israel, and swore to the offspring of the house of Jacob, and made myself known to them in the land of Egypt, when I swore to them, saying, 'I am Yahweh your God;' on that day I swore to them to bring them out of the land of Egypt into a land that I had searched out for them, flowing with milk and honey, which is the glory of all lands. I said to them, 'Don't defile yourselves with the idols of Egypt. I am Yahweh your God.'

"But the house of Israel rebelled against me in the wilderness. They didn't walk in my statutes and they rejected my ordinance...they greatly profaned my Sabbaths...

"*I also swore to them in the wilderness that I would not bring them into the land which I had given them, flowing with milk and honey, which is the glory of all lands, because they rejected my ordinances, and didn't walk in my statutes, ... Nevertheless, my eye spared them, and I didn't destroy them. I didn't make a full end of them in the wilderness. I said to their children in the wilderness, 'Don't walk in the statutes of your fathers. Don't observe their ordinances or defile yourselves with their idols. I am Yahweh your God. Walk in my statutes, keep my ordinances, and do them. Make my Sabbaths holy. They shall be a sign between me and you, that you may know that I am Yahweh your God...'*

"*Therefore, tell the house of Israel,... 'Do you pollute yourselves in the way of your fathers?... When you offer your gifts, when you make your sons pass through the fire, do you pollute yourselves with all your idols to this day? Should I be inquired of by you, house of Israel?' As I live, says Yahweh, I will not be inquired of by you!*

"*As I live, says Yahweh, surely with a mighty hand, with an outstretched arm, and with wrath poured out, I will be king over you.*

"*As for you, house of Israel, Yahweh says, '...I will accept them, and there I will require your offerings and the first fruits of your offerings, with all your holy things. I will accept you as a pleasant aroma when I bring you out from the people and gather you out of the countries in which you have been scattered. I will be sanctified in you in the sight of the nations. You will know that I am Yahweh when I bring you into the land of Israel, into the country which I swore to give to your fathers. There you will remember your ways, and all your deeds in which you have polluted yourselves. Then you will loathe yourselves in your own sight for all your evils that you have committed. You will know that I am Yahweh, when I have dealt with you for my name's sake, not according to your evil ways, nor according to your corrupt doings, you house of Israel.'" Says Yahweh.* (Ez 20:5-44) (with editing)

There was also a warning for the priests of Israel who spend more time worrying about themselves than the people entrusted to them. God will appoint a new shepherd over the flock of his people, one who won't lead them astray, one who won't let any be lost.

"Woe to the shepherds of Israel who feed themselves! Shouldn't the shepherds feed the sheep? You eat the fat. You clothe yourself with the wool. You kill the fatlings, but you don't feed the sheep. You haven't strengthened the diseased. You haven't healed that which was sick. You haven't bound up that which was broken. You haven't brought back that which was driven away. You haven't sought that which was lost, but you have ruled over them with force and with rigour." (Ez 34:2-5)

"I myself will be the shepherd of my sheep, and I will cause them to lie down," says Yahweh. *"I will seek that which was lost, and will bring back that which was driven away, and will bind up that which was broken, and will strengthen that which was sick; but I will destroy the fat and the strong. I will feed them in justice."* (Ez 34:15-16)

"I will set up one shepherd over them, and he will feed them, even my servant David. He will feed them, and he will be their shepherd. I, Yahweh, will be their God, and my servant David will be prince among them."[144] (Ez 34:23-24)

God Promises to make Judah and Israel one Kingdom again

Ezekiel was instructed to collect two sticks, on one he was to write Judah (which was for all in the House of Judah and those loyal), on the other he was to write Joseph (which was for all in the House of Israel and those loyal).

Next, he was told to join the sticks together, making one stick, then God explained, *"I will make them one nation in the land, on the mountains of Israel. One king will be king to them all. They will no longer be two nations. They won't be divided into two kingdoms any more at all. They won't defile themselves any more with their idols, nor with their detestable things, nor*

---

[144] Pointing to Jesus.

with any of their transgressions; but I will save them out of all their dwelling places in which they have sinned, and will cleanse them. So they will be my people, and I will be their God." (Ez 37:22-23)

"My servant David will be king over them. They all will have one shepherd. (Ez 37:24) *'I will be their God, and they will be my people."* (Ez 37:27)

The Return of Yahweh

In the year 572 BC - or the twenty-fifth year of his captivity in Babylon; Ezekiel received a final vision from God. In this vision, God showed him a new city and a new temple[145] and the altar he was preparing for the House of Israel. He also emphasised new feasts for the Passover and Sabbath.

'Son of man, this is the place of my throne and the place of the soles of my feet, where I will dwell among the children of Israel forever. The house of Israel will no more defile my holy name, neither they nor their kings.' (Ez 43:7)

'Let them put away their prostitution, and the dead bodies of their kings far from me. Then I will dwell among them forever.' (Ez 43:9)

'You, son of man, show the house to the house of Israel, that they may be ashamed of their iniquities; and let them measure the pattern.' (Ez 43:10)

---

[145] The Second Temple. It was built between 520 - 515 BC.

DANIEL

Written c. 160 BC yet set during the exile in Babylon (600 - 540 BC). Daniel is written to encourage the persecuted Kingdom of Judah who were living under foreign rule. It covers the theme of faith, persecution, and torture under a Hellenistic influence, followed by salvation by the hand of God.

In the third year of the reign of Jehoiakim, king of Judah,[146] King Nebuchadnezzar (by God's will) overthrew Jerusalem. Among his booty, he chose four young Israelites to be brought to him in Shinar, where they were to be raised and groomed to enter his service. The four chosen were Daniel, Hananiah, Mishael, and Azariah, whose names were promptly changed to Belteshazzar, Shadrach, Meshach, and Abednego.

These four quickly found themselves on the wrong side of Nebuchadnezzar's chief eunuch, when they refused to eat the food set out for them on the royal table (because it was ritually unclean). Knowing the eunuch would not easily go against his king's wishes, Daniel asked him to allow the four of them a ten-day trial of eating and drinking only vegetables and water, and if after that time they looked malnourished, they would acquiesce to eating the royal food. The eunuch agreed, and after the ten days, the four Israelites looked stronger and healthier than anyone else and were allowed to eat only clean food.

---

[146] 606 BC

During this time, God favoured the four men with knowledge, wisdom, and intellect, so much so that the king soon noticed, and they were honoured among the sages attending the king.

The King's Dream

In the second year of King Nebuchadnezzar's reign, an upsetting dream came to him. Summoning his sages, he ordered them to not only interpret the dream, but also to describe the dream. They immediately panicked and asked how could they interpret the dream if the king didn't tell them what the dream was? Realising charlatans surrounded him, he commanded they be taken away and killed.

While the guards were marching them to their demise, they passed by Daniel, who quickly spoke up, curious as to what was happening. When he found out, he requested for them to be spared and asked to be taken to the king, where he would tell the king what his dream was, and also interpret it.

Brought before the king, Daniel interpreted the king's dream of a great image representing a series of kingdoms, ending with a divided kingdom overthrown by an eternal one.

"*You, O king, saw a great image. This image, which was mighty,… its head was of fine gold, its breast and its arms of silver, its belly and its thighs of bronze, its legs of iron, its feet part of iron and part of clay. You watched until a stone broke away and struck the image on its feet that were of iron and clay, and broke them in pieces. Then the iron, the clay, the bronze, the silver, and the gold were broken in pieces together, and became like the chaff… The wind carried them away, so that no place was found for them. The stone that struck the image became a great mountain and filled the whole earth.*

"*This is the dream;… You, O king, are king of kings, to whom the God of heaven has given the kingdom, the power, the strength, and the glory… You are the head of gold.*

"*After you, another kingdom will arise that is inferior to you; and another third kingdom of bronze, which will rule over all the earth. The fourth kingdom will be strong as iron,… Whereas you saw the feet and toes, part of potters' clay and part of iron, it will be a divided kingdom; but there will be in it of the strength of the iron, because you saw the iron mixed with miry clay. As the toes of the feet were part of iron, and part of clay, so the kingdom will be partly strong and partly brittle. Whereas you saw the iron mixed with miry clay, they will mingle themselves with the seed of men; but they won't cling to one another, even as iron does not mix with clay.*

"In the days of those kings the God of heaven will set up a kingdom which will never be destroyed, nor will its sovereignty be left to another people; but it will break in pieces and consume all these kingdoms, and it will stand forever. Because you saw that a stone was cut out of the mountain without hands, and that it broke in pieces the iron, the bronze, the clay, the silver, and the gold, the great God has made known to the king what will happen hereafter. The dream is certain, and its interpretation sure." (Dn 2:31-45)

The king was amazed and elevated Daniel to the position of governor of Babylon and the head of all the sages.

Daniel's Three Companions put into a Furnace

Soon, King Nebuchadnezzar ordered a colossal golden statue to be built. He proclaimed that all people should prostrate themselves and worship it. Anyone failing to do so would be thrown into a furnace.

Among the people at the time were those who disliked the Jews living amongst them and wanted them gone. They brought to the king's attention that three men in particular refused to worship the statue, staying faithful to their God alone. These three men were Daniel's companions - Shadrach, Meshach, and Abednego.

Brought before the king, they were questioned if the allegations were true and were warned of the furnace that awaited them if they were. They said, *"If it happens, our God whom we serve is able to deliver us from the burning fiery furnace; and he will deliver us out of your hand, O king. But if not, let it be known to you, O king, that we will not serve your gods or worship the golden image which you have set up."* (Dn 3:17-18)

Infuriated, the king ordered that they be thrown into the furnace. Voluntarily walking into the furnace, the three men began to pray to God:

> "All honour and blessing to you, Lord, God of our ancestors,
> may your name be held glorious forever.
> In all that you have done your justice is apparent:
> your promises are always faithfully fulfilled,
> your ways never deviate,
> your judgements are always true.
> You have given a just sentence
> in all the disasters you have brought down on us
> and on Jerusalem, the holy city of our ancestors,
> since it is for our sins that you have treated us like this,
> fairly and as we deserved." (Dn 3:26-28*)

On and on they prayed to God, all the while the servants of the king were stoking the fire with oil, pitch, and brushwood until the heat was too much even for them.

Then from inside the fire, the three men could be heard singing.

> "May you be blessed, Lord, God of our ancestors,
> be praised and extolled forever.
> Blessed be your glorious and holy name,
> praised and extolled forever.
> May you be blessed in the Temple of your sacred glory,
> exalted and glorified above all else forever:
> blessed on the throne of your Kingdom,
> praised and exalted above all else forever.
> Blessed, you fathomer of the great depths,
> enthroned on the cherubs,
> praised and glorified above all else forever;
> blessed in the vault of heaven,

exalted and glorified above all else forever."
(Dn 3:52-56*)

As they were singing in the fire, the king sprang to his feet in astonishment, for as he looked into the fire, he could see *four* figures walking around freely with no harm coming to them. Approaching the fire, he yelled out to them to come out.

And from the heart of the fire, out came Shadrach, Meshach and Abednego. Everyone crowded around the three men to examine them: the fire had had no effect on their bodies: not a hair of their heads had been singed, their cloaks were not scorched, no smell of burning hung about them. Nebuchadnezzar exclaimed, "Blessed be the God of Shadrach, Meshach and Abednego: he has sent his angel to rescue his servants who, putting their trust in him, defied the order of the king, and preferred to forfeit their bodies rather than serve or worship any god but their own. I therefore decree as follows: Men of all peoples, nations, and languages! Let anyone speak disrespectfully of the God of Shadrach, Meshach and Abednego, and I will have him torn limb from limb and his house razed to the ground, for there is no other god who can save like this."

Then the king showered favours on Shadrach, Meshach and Abednego.
(Dn 3:93-96*)

A Second Dream

In time, King Nebuchadnezzar had another dream - this time of a great tree providing shelter and food for all, that is cut down and transformed into a beast for seven years. Daniel interpreted the dream, saying the great tree is symbolic of his rule, and the cutting down representing a seven-year punishment.

"You are to be driven from human society, and live with the wild animals; you will feed on grass like the oxen, you will be drenched by the dew of heaven; seven times will pass over you until you have learned that the Most High rules over the kingship of men, and confers it on whom he pleases. (But)

your kingdom will be kept for you until you come to understand that heaven rules all." (Dn 4:22-23*)

Twelve months later, the dream came true. While Nebuchadnezzar was strolling on the roof of his palace, he boasted about how exceptional he was, but before his words were finished, a voice came down from heaven.

"King Nebuchadnezzar, these words are for you! 'Sovereignty is taken from you, you are to be driven from human society, and live with the wild animals; you will feed on grass like oxen, and seven times will pass over you until you have learned that the Most High rules over the kingship of men, and confers it on whom he pleases.'" (Dn 4:28-29)

Eventually, after enduring the prophecy as foretold, Nebuchadnezzar came to his senses and blessed God the Most High.

"Praise and extoll him who lives forever, for his sovereignty is an eternal sovereignty, his empire lasts from age to age. The inhabitants of the earth count for nothing: he does as he pleases with the array of heaven, and with the inhabitants of the earth. No one can arrest his hand or ask him, 'What are you doing?'" (Dn 4:31-32)

Daniel in the Lions Pit

After the reign of Nebuchadnezzar came Belshazzar, followed by Darius. While Daniel continued to serve and keep favour, many others of the king's consort were intent on usurping him. So, they hatched a plan.

They encouraged King Darius to proclaim a decree that for thirty-days no one in the realm could pray or worship any other god or person, apart from the king himself. Once passed by the king, they went about trapping Daniel, who, being ever faithful to God, would not stop praying three times a day. He was soon caught and taken before the king. Unsettled at the thought of losing Daniel, the king tried to save him, but the decree he was influenced into mandating was ironclad. Daniel was thrown into a pit with lions.

That night the king could not sleep, and at first light he hurried to the pit and shouted, *"Daniel, servant of the living God, is your God, whom you serve continually, able to deliver you from the lions?"*

Then Daniel said to the king, *"O king, live forever! My God has sent his angel, and has shut the lions' mouths, and they have not hurt me, because innocence was found in me before him; and also before you, O king, I have done no harm."*

Then the king was exceedingly glad and commanded that they should take Daniel up out of the den. So Daniel was taken up out of the den, and no kind of harm was found on him, because he had trusted in his God.

The king commanded, and they brought those men who had accused Daniel, and they cast them into the den of lions – them, their children, and their wives; and the lions mauled them, and broke all their bones in pieces before they came to the bottom of the den. (Dn 6:20-24)

Daniel's Vision

Daniel received a vision in which he saw four beasts emerging from the sea. The first was like a lion with eagle wings; the second like a bear with three ribs in its mouth; the third like a leopard with four heads and four birdlike wings; the fourth was different from the rest and was terrifying, fearful, and strong, with iron teeth and ten horns.

> *"I gazed into the visions of the night.*
> *And I saw, coming on the clouds of heaven,*
> *one like a son of man.*
> *He came to the one of great age*
> *and was led into his presence.*
> *On him was conferred sovereignty,*
> *glory and kingship,*
> *and men of all peoples, nations and languages became*
> *his servants.*
> *His sovereignty is an eternal sovereignty,*

> which shall never pass away,
> nor will his empire ever be destroyed." (Dn 7:13-14*)

Greatly disturbed by what he saw, Daniel sensed a person standing nearby. He interpreted the vision for him.

"*These great animals, which are four, are four kings, who will arise out of the earth. But the saints of the Most High will receive the kingdom, and possess the kingdom forever, even forever and ever.*" (Dn 7:17-18)

"*The fourth animal will be a fourth kingdom on earth, which will be different from all the kingdoms, and will devour the whole earth... As for the ten horns, ten kings will arise out of this kingdom. Another will arise after them; and he will be different from the former, and he will put down three kings. He will speak words against the Most High, and will wear out the saints of the Most High...*

"*But the judgement will be set, and they will take away his dominion, to consume and to destroy it to the end. The kingdom and the dominion, and the greatness of the kingdoms under the whole sky, will be given to the people of the saints of the Most High. His kingdom is an everlasting kingdom, and all dominions will serve and obey him.*"[147] (Dn 7:23-27)

Daniel Receives Another Vision

Daniel sees a ram with two uneven horns standing by a river. It overpowered all in its way to the North, South and West. Then from the West, he saw a goat with one majestic horn. The goat overpowered the ram and grew ever more powerful, but then its horn snapped off. In its place grew four new horns facing North, South, East, and West. One of the

---

[147] According to The Jerome Biblical Commentary, p. 455, the four beasts are the four successive pagan empires of Babylon, the Medes, Persia, and Greece. The fourth beast is the Greek kingdom. When the fourth beast is broken, i.e., when the reign of the persecutor Antiochus IV comes to an end, the splendours of all the kingdoms under heaven will be given to the people of the saints of the Most High.

four horns grew and conquered all around it. He then heard one angel speaking to another angel.

"How long will the vision about the continual burnt offering, and the disobedience that makes desolate, to give both the sanctuary and the army to be trodden under foot be?"

He said to me, *"To two thousand and three hundred evenings and mornings. Then the sanctuary will be cleansed."* (Dn 8:13-14)

Then a man from the far side of the river to Daniel yelled over to the angel, "Gabriel, interpret the vision for him."

"Understand, son of man, for the vision belongs to the time of the end."

Now as he was speaking with me, I fell into a deep sleep with my face toward the ground; but he touched me and set me upright.

He said, *"Behold, I will make you know what will be in the latter time of the indignation, for it belongs to the appointed time of the end. The ram which you saw, that had the two horns, they are the kings of Media and Persia. The rough male goat is the king of Greece. The great horn that is between his eyes is the first king. As for that which was broken, in the place where four stood up, four kingdoms will stand up out of the nation, but not with his power.*

"In the latter time of their kingdom, when the transgressors have come to the full, a king of fierce face, and understanding riddles, will stand up. His power will be mighty, but not by his own power. He will destroy awesomely, and will prosper in what he does. He will destroy the mighty ones and the holy people." (Dn: 8:17-24)

A Third Vision is Received

In the third year of King Cyrus (king of Persia), while Daniel was doing a three-week penance, he received a vision of *a man clothed in linen, whose waist was adorned with pure gold of Uphaz. His body also was like beryl, and his face as the appearance of lightning, and his eyes as flaming torches. His arms and his feet were like burnished bronze. The voice of his words was like the voice of a multitude.* (Dn 10:5-6)

An angel said, *"Daniel, you greatly beloved man, understand the words that I speak to you, and stand upright, for I have been sent to you, now."*

When he had spoken this word to me, I stood trembling.

Then he said to me, "Don't be afraid, Daniel; for from the first day that you set your heart to understand, and to humble yourself before your God, your words were heard. I have come for your words' sake..., to make you understand what will happen to your people in the latter days, for the vision is yet for many days." (Dn 10:11-14)

He said then, "Do you know why I have come to you? Now I will return to fight with the prince of Persia. When I go out, behold, the prince of Greece will come. But I will tell you that which is inscribed in the writing of truth. There is no one who holds with me against these but Michael[148] *your prince."* (Dn 10:20-21)

The End Times

The angel continued. *"At that time Michael will stand up, the great prince who stands for the children of your people; and there will be a time of trouble, such as never was since there was a nation even to that same time.*

"At that time your people will be delivered, everyone who is found written in the book. Many of those who sleep in the dust of the earth will awake, some to everlasting life, and some to shame and everlasting contempt. Those who are wise will shine as the brightness of the expanse. Those who turn many to righteousness will shine as the stars forever and ever.

"But you, Daniel, shut up the words and seal the book, even to the time of the end. Many will run back and forth, and knowledge will be increased." (Dn 12:1-4)

---

[148] The NJB footnote offers that Michael ('Who-is-like-God?') is the guardian angel of the people of God.

HAGGAI

Set in Jerusalem after the House of Judah has returned from exile in Babylon. God is becoming impatient with the progress, or lack thereof, in the rebuilding of the Temple.
Dated around 520 BC.

The Call to Rebuild the Temple

Is it a time for you yourselves to dwell in your panelled houses, while this house lies waste? Now therefore, this is what Yahweh of Armies says: "Consider your ways. You have sown much, and bring in little. You eat, but you don't have enough. You drink, but you aren't filled with drink. You clothe yourselves, but no one is warm; and he who earns wages earns wages to put them into a bag with holes in it."

This is what Yahweh of Armies says: "Consider your ways. Go up to the mountain, bring wood, and build the house. I will take pleasure in it, and I will be glorified." (Hag 1:4-8)

The spirit of all the remnant of the people was stirred by these words, and the rebuilding of the Temple began.[149]

God is pleased with the efforts and progress of the rebuilding.

"The latter glory of this house will be greater than the former," says Yahweh of Armies *"and in this place I will give peace,"* says Yahweh of Armies. (Hag 2:9)

---

[149] 520 BC

Haggai's final message from God is to Zerubbabel, the high commissioner of Judah. *"I will overthrow the throne of kingdoms. I will destroy the strength of the kingdoms of the nations. I will overthrow the chariots and those who ride in them. The horses and their riders will come down, everyone by the sword of his brother. In that day,"* says the Lord of Armies, *"I will take you, Zerubbabel my servant, the son of Shealtiel,"* says the Lord, *"and will make you like a signet ring, for I have chosen you,"* says the Lord of Armies.[150] (Hag 2:22-23)

---

[150] This passage is believed to foreshadow the future Messianic reign of Christ.

ZECHARIAH

Zechariah was a prophet sent during the period c. 520 BC, after the return of the Jews from exile. Through a series of vivid visions, his message is twofold: first, concerning the rebuilding of the Temple; and second, pointing to the hope and glory that awaits Judah in the future.

Zechariah was sent eight visions, all designed to emphasise the plan of God to restore his people to their rightful place in the world and in his heart.

The First Vision - God Understands the Plight of his People

Four horsemen said to the angel[151] presenting Zechariah with the vision, *"We have been patrolling the world, and see, the whole world is at peace and rest."* (Zec 1:11*)

The angel then asked God, *"How long will you wait before taking pity on Jerusalem and the cities of Judah, on which you have inflicted your anger for the past seventy years?"* (Zec 1:12*)

God answered, *"I feel a most jealous love for Jerusalem and Zion... I turn again in compassion to Jerusalem; my Temple there shall be rebuilt... and the measuring line will be stretched over Jerusalem. Make this proclamation too: Yahweh says this: 'My cities are once more going to be very prosperous.*

---

[151] Some commentaries report the angel to be Christ.

Yahweh will again take pity on Zion, again make Jerusalem his very own.'" (Zec 1:14-17*)

The Second Vision - God Will Destroy Their Enemies

Directly after, Zechariah was presented with a vision of four horns, followed by a vision of four blacksmiths. The angel explained the visions as: *"The horns* (are the nations that) ... *have scattered Judah (Israel) and Jerusalem,"* (Zec 2:2*) "and the blacksmiths will destroy the four nations that have risen against Judah."

The Third Vision - God Will Rebuild Jerusalem

Raising his eyes again, Zechariah saw a man with a measuring line who was preparing to measure Jerusalem with instructions, *"that Jerusalem will* (remain) *without walls, because of the multitude of men and livestock in it. For I,"* says Yahweh, *"will be to her a wall of fire around it, and I will be the glory in the middle of her."* (Zec 2:4-5*)

The Fourth Vision - God Will Forgive

Yahweh showed Zechariah, *Joshua the high priest standing before Yahweh's angel, and Satan standing at his right hand to be his adversary. Yahweh's angel said to Satan, "May Yahweh rebuke you, Satan... he who has made Jerusalem his very own."* (Zec 3:2*)

The High Priest Joshua was dressed in dirty clothes, and the angel commanded those around him to redress him in splendid and glorious clothes as a sign of God taking away his iniquity. Yahweh spoke, *"If you will walk in my ways, and if you will follow my instructions, then you also shall judge my house, and shall also keep my courts, and I will give you a place of access among these who stand by."* (Zec 3:7)

The Fifth Vision - God Empowers his Leaders

Zechariah saw a gold lampstand with seven lamps and a bowl on top, adjacent were two olive trees. The angel explained the vision, saying, *"*(The lamps), *are the seven eyes of Yahweh; they cover the whole world,"* (Zec 4:6*) *"and the trees are the two anointed ones*[152] *who stand before the Lord of the whole world."* (Zec 4:14*)

The Sixth Vision - God Will Remove Lawlessness

Again, Zechariah raised his eyes to see an enormous flying scroll, which the angel explained was a *"Curse sweeping across... the whole country... every thief will be banished...everyone who swears falsely by my name will be banished."* (Zec 5:3-4*)

The Seventh Vision - The Wicked will be Defeated

Zechariah next sees a flying basket with a woman sitting inside. The angel tells Zechariah, the woman is Wickedness, and she has been forced back into the basket. Then two other women appeared, lifted the basket, and took it away to Shinar in Babylon (the centre of the pagan world). For "if God inhabits the Jerusalem Temple, then sin and impurity must be removed - sin and sorrow are brought to Shinar."[153]

The Eighth Vision - God's Peace will Reign

The final vision is of four chariots riding between two mountains of bronze, sent out to the *four winds of the heaven, after standing before Yahweh.* (Zec 6:5*) The angel explained, *"Those going northward will make*

---

[152] The Jerusalem Bible says the two anointed ones are Joshua and Zerubbabel as mentioned in Haggai, who represent spiritual and temporal power respectively.
[153] Unkown source.

the spirit of Yahweh descend on the country of the North.[154] *And those who are far away will come and rebuild the sanctuary of Yahweh."* (Zec 6:8 & 15*)

God's plans, approach, and requirements are outlined.

"With the remnant of this people, I am not as I was in the past... For I mean to spread peace everywhere; the vine will give its fruit, the earth its increase, and heaven its dew. I am going to bestow all these blessings on the remnant of this people. Just as once you were a curse among the nations, you House of Judah (and House of Israel), so I mean to save you for you to become a blessing." (Zec 8:11-12*)

> *"These are the things that you must do.*
> *Speak the truth to one another;*
> *let the judgements at your gates be such as conduce to peace;*
> *do not secretly plot evil against one another;*
> *do not love false oaths; since all this is what I hate.*
> *It is Yahweh who speaks."* (Zec 8:16-17*)

God speaks through Zechariah about a coming messianic salvation.

> *"I am burning with jealousy for Zion,*
> *with great anger for her sake.*
> ...
> *"I am coming back to Zion*
> *and shall dwell in the middle of Jerusalem.*
> *Jerusalem will be called Faithful City*
> *and the mountain of Yahweh, the Holy Mountain."*
> (Zec 8:2-4*)

> *"Rejoice heart and soul, daughter of Zion!*
> *Shout with gladness, daughter of Jerusalem!*

---

[154] Where the exiles are.

See now, your king comes to you;
he is victorious, he is triumphant,
humble and riding on a donkey,[155]
on a colt, the foal of a donkey.
He will banish chariots from Ephraim
and horses from Jerusalem;
the bow of war will be banished.
He will proclaim peace for the nations.
His empire shall stretch from sea to sea,
from the River to the ends of the earth." (Zec 9:9-10*)

---

[155] Jesus riding into Jerusalem.

MALACHI

Malachi offers two distinct yet powerful messages from God. First is an indictment of the priests. Secondly marriage and divorce are scrutinised. The audience is the House of Judah.
Dated c. 430 BC.

Malachi begins by prophesying God's displeasure at the priests who have 'despised his name' and 'offered polluted bread' on his altar. He continues, saying: *"I will send the curse on you, and I will curse your blessings. Indeed, I have cursed them already, because you do not take it to heart. Behold, I will rebuke your offspring, and will spread dung on your faces, even the dung of your feasts; and you will be taken away with it. You will know that I have sent this commandment to you, that my covenant may be with Levi."* (Mal 2:2-4)

Next, Malachi speaks for God as he turns his attention to their continual unfaithfulness. Condemning them for their actions. *"Don't we all have one father? Hasn't one God created us? Why do we deal treacherously every man against his brother, profaning the covenant of our fathers? Judah has dealt treacherously, and an abomination is committed in Israel and in Jerusalem; for Judah has profaned the holiness of the Lord which he loves, and has married the daughter of a foreign god. The Lord will cut off the man who does this, him who wakes and him who answers, out of the tents of Jacob and him who offers an offering to the Lord of Armies."* (Mal 2:10-12)

Like other prophets before him,[156] Malachi speaks of the 'Day of the Lord'.

"*Look, I am going to send my messenger to prepare a way before me.*[157] *And the Lord you are seeking*[158] *will suddenly enter his Temple; and the angel of the covenant whom you are longing for, yes, he is coming, says Yahweh Sabaoth.*

"*Who will be able to resist the day of his coming? Who will remain standing when he appears?*" (Mal 3:1-2)

"*For the day is coming now, burning like a furnace; and all the arrogant and the evil-doers will be like stubble. The day that is coming is going to burn them up, says Yahweh Sabaoth, leaving them neither root nor stalk.*

"*But for you who fear my name, the sun of righteousness will shine out with healing in its rays; you will leap like calves going out to pasture.*

"*You will trample on the wicked, who will be like ashes under your feet on the day I am preparing, says Yahweh Sabaoth.*" (Mal 3:19-21*)

And we now come to the end of the Old Testament, the final words are left to God.

"*Remember the Law of Moses my servant, which I commanded to him in Horeb for all Israel, even statutes and ordinances.*

"*Behold, I will send you Elijah the prophet before the great and terrible day Yahweh comes. He will turn the hearts of the fathers to the children and the hearts of the children to their fathers, lest I come and strike the earth with a curse.*" (Mal 3:22-24*)

---

[156] Amos, Joel, Zephaniah, and Isaiah.
[157] Tradition suggests this is a prohecy of John the Baptist.
[158] Tradition suggests this is a prohecy of Jesus t.

THE NEW TESTAMENT

MATTHEW

The Gospel of Matthew was long considered to be the first of the four Gospels to be written (c.80 AD).[159] It is widely speculated the Gospel of Mark was used as a reference for Matthew's Gospel.

Made up of five books, Matthew's Gospel is focused mainly on delivering the message of the Kingdom of Heaven. It is written by a Jew for the Jews converting to Christianity, and in doing this, Matthew pays particular attention to showing Jesus as a fulfilment of the Old Testament Scripture. Matthew portrays Jesus as a 'New Moses'.

Matthew's Gospel is primarily focused on recording 'what Jesus says' rather than on 'what Jesus did', which is notably relevant as he focuses much of his Gospel on Jesus' formation and teaching of his apostles.

The Early Years of Jesus

Mary, the mother of Jesus, was engaged to Joseph and was still a virgin when she conceived. When Joseph became aware, he resolved to end the relationship quickly and quietly, until an angel appeared and told him, *"Joseph, son of David,*[160] *don't be afraid to take to yourself Mary as your wife, for that which is conceived in her is of the Holy Spirit. She shall give birth to a*

---

[159] Mark is now considered the first Gospel written, in c.65 AD.

[160] Matthew traces the genealogy of Joseph back 28 generations to David, and a further thirteen back to Abraham.

son. You shall name him Jesus, for it is he who shall save his people from their sins." (Mt 1:20-21)

Joseph stayed with Mary, and Jesus was born in Bethlehem, Judah.

At the same time, some wise men,[161] inspired to seek Jesus after seeing a star rise, came to King Herod in Jerusalem asking, *"Where is he who is born King of the Jews? For we saw his star in the East and have come to worship him."* (Mt 2:2)

When King Herod learned of the wise men's journey and inquiry, he was immediately suspicious and summoned his chief priests and scribes to find out more. They confirmed what the prophets had foretold.

> *You Bethlehem, land of Judah,*
> *are in no way least among the princes of Judah;*
> *for out of you shall come a governor*
> *who shall shepherd my people, Israel.*[162] (Mt 2:6)

King Herod, an evil man, wanted to protect himself and remove any potential threat to his rule, so he sent some of his own men along with the wise men under the pretence that he too wanted to pay homage to the child.

Arriving in Bethlehem, the wise men fell to their knees to give worship to the newborn Jesus, and offered gifts of gold, frankincense,[163] and myrrh.[164]

When it was time to return home, the wise men chose an alternate route that bypassed Jerusalem, for they had been warned in a dream about evil King Herod.

---

[161] Interestingly, the Bible never mentions 'three' wise men.

[162] Mic 5:2

[163] Frankincense had been traded on the Arabian Peninsula for the last 4,000 years. It is an aromatic resin used in incense and perfumes.

[164] Like frankincense, myrrh is a natural gum or resin used at the time as a perfume or incense. It was also offered, mixed with wine, to Jesus when he was on the cross.

Joseph was also warned in a dream to avoid Herod. He was told, *"Get up, take the child and his mother with you, and escape into Egypt, and stay there until I tell you, because Herod intends to search for the child and do away with him."* (Matt 2:13*)

After King Herod died, Joseph had another dream. This time he was told it was safe to return to the land of his people, the Israelites. Taking Mary and Jesus, he made his way to Nazareth in Galilee, *that it might be fulfilled that which was spoken through the prophets that he will be called a Nazarene.* (Mt 2:23)

John the Baptist

In the wilderness area of Judah, there was a preacher called John the Baptist,[165] whose message was, *"Repent, for the Kingdom of Heaven is at hand! For* (Jesus is the one) *spoken of by Isaiah the prophet, saying,*

> *"'The voice of one crying in the wilderness,*
> *make the way of the Lord ready!*
> *Make his paths straight!'"*[166] (Mt 3:2-3)

John the Baptist lived a simple life, dressing in camel hair and eating locusts and wild honey. He attracted people from all over the district who confessed their sins and were baptised.

One day, a group of Pharisees and Sadducees came to see John the Baptist. When he saw them, he yelled, *"You offspring of vipers, who warned you to flee from the wrath to come? Therefore, produce fruit worthy of repentance! Don't think to yourselves, 'We have Abraham for our father,' for I tell you that God is able to raise up children to Abraham from these stones. Even now the axe lies at the root of the trees. Therefore, every tree that doesn't produce good fruit is cut down, and cast into the fire.*

---

[165] A cousin of Jesus. His mother was Elizabeth, a relative of Mary.
[166] Is 40:3

"*I indeed baptise you in water for repentance, but he who comes after me is mightier than I, whose sandals I am not worthy to carry. He will baptise you in the Holy Spirit.*" (Mt 3:7-11)

On another day, Jesus himself came to John to be baptised, and this stunned John (for he knew who Jesus was).

"*I need to be baptised by you, and you come to me?*"

But Jesus… said to him, "*Allow it now, for this is the fitting way for us to fulfil all righteousness.*" Then he allowed him.

Once baptised, the heavens were opened to him. *He saw the Spirit of God descending as a dove, and coming on him. Behold, a voice out of the heavens said, 'This is my beloved Son, with whom I am well pleased.*' (Mt 3:14-17)

The Temptation in the Desert[167]

Jesus was then led by the Spirit into the desert to fast for forty days and nights and be tempted by the devil. One day while experiencing great hunger the devil spoke to Jesus, "*If you are the Son of God, command that these stones become bread.*"

But Jesus answered, "*It is written, 'Man shall not live by bread alone, but by every word that proceeds out of God's mouth.'*"[168]

Then the devil took him into the holy city. He set him on the pinnacle of the temple, and said to him, "*If you are the Son of God, throw yourself down, for it is written,*

> "'*For he will put his angels in charge of you,*
> *to guard you in all your ways.*
> *They will bear you up in their hands,*
> *so that you won't dash your foot against a stone.*'"[169]

---

[167] As Moses was in the wilderness for forty years, Jesus was in the wilderness for forty days.
[168] Dt 8:3
[169] Ps 91:11-12

Jesus said to him, "Again, it is written, 'You shall not tempt Yahweh your God.'"[170]

Again, the devil took him to a high mountain, and showed him all the kingdoms of the world and their glory. He said to him, "I will give you all of these things, if you will fall down and worship me."

Then Jesus said to him, "Get behind me, Satan! For it is written, 'You shall worship Yahweh your God, and you shall serve him only.'"[171]

Then the devil left him, and... angels came and served him. (Mt 4:3-11)

Jesus' ministry had begun - with the message, *"Repent! For the Kingdom of Heaven is at hand."* (Mt 4:17)

The First Apostles are Called

Walking by the Sea of Galilee, Jesus came across Simon (who would come to be called Peter) and his brother Andrew. Jesus spoke to them, *"Come after me, and I will make you fishers of men."* (Mt 4:19)

They immediately stopped what they were doing and followed Jesus.

He next saw two other brothers, James, and John[172] (the sons of Zebedee) and called out to them. They too immediately stopped what they were doing, left their boats and father to follow Jesus.

Jesus Begins his Teaching Ministry

As Jesus moved around Galilee, he began teaching in the synagogues and healing the sick. His fame spread quickly and soon hordes of people came to see and hear him; bringing along their sick to be healed.

Seeing the crowds, Jesus went to a hilltop and spoke to them.

> *"Blessed are the poor in spirit,*
> *for theirs is the Kingdom of Heaven.*

---

[170] Dt 6:16
[171] Dt 6:13
[172] The writer of The Gospel of John.

Blessed are those who mourn,
for they shall be comforted.
Blessed are the gentle,
for they shall inherit the earth.
Blessed are those who hunger and thirst for righteousness,
for they shall be filled.
Blessed are the merciful,
for they shall obtain mercy.
Blessed are the pure in heart,
for they shall see God.
Blessed are the peacemakers,
for they shall be called children of God.
Blessed are those who have been persecuted
for righteousness' sake,
for theirs is the Kingdom of Heaven.

"Blessed are you when people reproach you, persecute you, and say all kinds of evil against you falsely, for my sake. Rejoice, and be exceedingly glad, for great is your reward in heaven. For that is how they persecuted the prophets… before you." (Mt 5:3-12)

Love Your Enemies

Jesus continued, "*You have heard that it was said, 'You shall love your neighbour and hate your enemy.'*[173] *But I tell you, love your enemies, bless those who curse you, do good to those who hate you, and pray for those who mistreat you and persecute you, that you may be children of your Father who is in heaven. For he makes his sun to rise on the evil and the good, and sends rain on the just and the unjust. For if you love those who love you, what reward do you have?… Therefore you shall be perfect, just as your Father in heaven is perfect.*" (Mt 5:43-48)

---

[173] Lv 19:18

Jesus taught when giving alms, fasting, or doing charitable works, to do it quietly and secretly, and not for the accolades of those around you, but for God alone who will see them and reward them. He also said the same about praying, *"When you pray, enter into your inner room, and having shut your door, pray to your Father who is in secret; and your Father who sees in secret will reward you openly."* (Mt 6:6)

He taught them how to pray:

> "Our Father
> who art in Heaven,
> hallowed be your name;
> your Kingdom come;
> your will be done on earth as it is in Heaven.
> Give us today our daily bread;
> and forgive us our sins,
> as we forgive those who sin against us.
> Lead us not into temptation, but deliver us from evil."

God and Money

Jesus spoke about trusting completely in God. *"No one can serve two masters, for either he will hate the one and love the other, or else he will be devoted to one and despise the other. You can't serve both God and money."* (Mt 6:24)

Trust in Providence

"Therefore, I tell you, don't be anxious for your life: what you will eat, or what you will drink; nor yet for your body, what you will wear. Isn't life more than food, and the body more than clothing? See the birds of the sky, they don't sow, neither do they reap, nor gather into barns. Your heavenly Father feeds them. Aren't you of much more value than they?

"Which of you, by being anxious, can add one moment to his lifespan? Why are you anxious about clothing? Consider the lilies of the field, how they

grow. They don't toil, neither do they spin, yet I tell you that even Solomon in all his glory was not dressed like one of these. But if God so clothes the grass of the field, which today exists and tomorrow is thrown into the oven, won't he much more clothe you, you of little faith?

"Therefore, don't be anxious, saying, 'What will we eat? What will we drink?' or, 'With what will we be clothed?' For the Gentiles seek after all these things; for your heavenly Father knows that you need all these things. But seek first God's Kingdom and his righteousness; and all these things will be given to you as well. Therefore, don't be anxious for tomorrow, for tomorrow will be anxious for itself. Each day's own evil is sufficient." (Mt 6:25-34)

"Ask, and it will be given to you. Seek, and you will find. Knock, and it will be opened for you. For everyone who asks receives. He who seeks finds. To him who knocks it will be opened. Or who is there among you who, if his son asks him for bread, will give him a stone? Or if he asks for a fish, who will give him a serpent? If you then, being evil, know how to give good gifts to your children, how much more will your Father who is in heaven give good things to those who ask him!" (Mt 7:7-11)

The True Disciple

Jesus went on to say, "Not everyone who says to me, 'Lord, Lord,' will enter into the Kingdom of Heaven, but he who does the will of my Father who is in heaven. Many will tell me on that day, 'Lord, Lord, didn't we prophesy in your name, in your name cast out demons, and in your name do many mighty works?' Then I will tell them, 'I never knew you. Depart from me.'

"Everyone therefore who hears these words of mine and does them, I will liken him to a wise man who built his house on a rock. The rain came down, the floods came, and the winds blew and beat on that house; and it didn't fall, for it was founded on the rock. Everyone who hears these words of mine and doesn't do them will be like a foolish man who built his house on the sand. The rain came down, the floods came, and the winds blew and beat on that house; and it fell - and its fall was great." (Mt 7:21-27)

Jesus begins his Healing Ministry

Travelling to the Jewish town of Capernaum, Jesus was met by a centurion, who had sought him to cure his paralysed servant. Jesus did not hesitate and asked to be taken to him, so he could cure the servant. The centurion however said, *"Lord, I'm not worthy for you to come under my roof. Just say the word, and my servant will be healed."* (Mt 8:8)

Amazed, Jesus said, *"Most certainly I tell you, I haven't found so great a faith, not even in Israel."* (Mt 8:10) *"Go your way. Let it be done for you as you have believed."* (Mt 8:13)

The centurion's servant was healed.

The Calming of the Storm

Later that night while Jesus and his apostles were in a boat, *a violent storm came up on the sea, so much that the boat was covered with the waves; but he was asleep. The disciples came to him and woke him up, saying, "Save us, Lord! We are dying!"*

He said to them, "Why are you fearful, O you of little faith?" Then he got up, rebuked the wind and the sea, and there was a great calm.

The men marvelled, saying, "What kind of man is this, that even the wind and the sea obey him?" (Mt 8:23-27)

Cure of a Paralytic

Arriving on the other side of the sea, a group of townspeople brought a paralytic to Jesus. Touched by the strength of their faith, he said, *"Son, cheer up! Your sins are forgiven you."* (Mt 9:2)

This infuriated those scribes who were nearby. They said it was blasphemy. Jesus of course knew their thoughts and challenged them, *"Which is easier, to say, 'Your sins are forgiven'; or to say, 'Get up, and walk'? But that you may know that the Son of Man has authority on earth to forgive sins."*

(Then he said to the paralytic), "*Get up, and take up your mat, and go to your house.*" (Mt 9:5-6)

The paralytic man got up and went home, the crowd was amazed and *glorified God, who had given such authority to men.* (Mt 9:8)

Matthew is Called[174]

Moving on, Jesus saw a tax collector named Matthew. He called out to him to follow him. Matthew got up and followed. Later that night, Jesus sat down to eat dinner with more tax collectors and other social outcasts. This troubled the Pharisees, who couldn't understand why Jesus would associate with such people. Jesus was quick to bring them to an understanding. "*Those who are healthy have no need for a physician, but those who are sick do. But you go and learn what this means: 'I desire mercy, and not sacrifice',*[175] *for I came not to call the righteous, but sinners to repentance.*" (Mt 9:12-13)

As news of Jesus, his teachings and miracles grew, larger and larger crowds came to him.

When he saw the multitudes, he was moved with compassion for them because they were harassed and scattered, like sheep without a shepherd. Then he said to his disciples, 'The harvest indeed is plentiful, but the labourers are few. Pray therefore that the Lord of the harvest will send out labourers into his harvest.' (Mt 9:36-38)

Jesus Commissions his Twelve Apostles

He called to himself his twelve disciples, and gave them authority over unclean spirits, to cast them out, and to heal every disease and every sickness. (Mt 10:1)

His twelve apostles were Peter, and Andrew his brother; James and John, the sons of Zebedee; Philip, Bartholomew, Thomas, Matthew

---

[174] The writer of this Gospel.
[175] Hos 6:6

the tax collector; James the son of Alphaeus; Thaddaeus;[176] Simon the Zealot; and Judas Iscariot, who was to betray him.

His instructions to them were, *"Don't go among the Gentiles, and don't enter into any city of the Samaritans.*[177] *Rather, go to the lost sheep of the house of Israel. As you go, preach, saying, 'The Kingdom of Heaven is at hand!' Heal the sick, cleanse the lepers, and cast out demons. Freely you received, so freely give. Don't take any gold, silver, or brass in your money belts. Take no bag for your journey, neither two coats, nor sandals, nor staff: for the labourer is worthy of his food... Behold, I send you out as sheep among wolves. Therefore, be wise as serpents and harmless as doves."* (Mt 10:5-15)

Jesus went on to explain to his followers how the life ahead was not going to be easy. *"Brother will deliver up brother to death, and the father his child. Children will rise up against parents and cause them to be put to death. You will be hated by all men for my name's sake, but he who endures to the end will be saved. But when they persecute you in this city, flee into the next, for most certainly I tell you, you will not have gone through the cities of Israel until the Son of Man has come."* (Mt 10:21-23)

But Jesus also taught them they should not be worried *"When they deliver you up, don't be anxious how or what you will say, for it will be given you in that hour what you will say. For it is not you who speak, but the Spirit of your Father who speaks in you."* (Mt 10:19-20)

And, *"Don't be afraid of those who kill the body, but are not able to kill the soul. Rather, fear him who is able to destroy both soul and body in Hell."* (Mt 10:28)

"He who doesn't take his cross and follow after me isn't worthy of me. He who seeks his life will lose it; and he who loses his life for my sake will find it. He who receives you receives me, and he who receives me receives him who sent me." (Mt 10:38-40)

---

[176] Known as Jude in Luke's Gospel.

[177] Samaritans believed the Law like other Jews but their history goes back only to the time of the deportation, so were not considered 'real' Jews.

Jesus' Ministry Continues

After Jesus had finished teaching his disciples, he moved on to continue his teaching and preaching in other nearby towns. During this time, he spoke about his relationship with God the Father. *"All things have been delivered to me by my Father. No one knows the Son, except the Father; neither does anyone know the Father, except the Son, and he to whom the Son desires to reveal him."* (Mt 11:27)

A little later that day, while in a synagogue, a man came to Jesus asking to be cured, the Pharisees again began challenging him, asking, *"Is it lawful to heal on the Sabbath day?"*...

He said to them, "What man is there among you who has one sheep, and if this one falls into a pit on the Sabbath day, won't he grab on to it and lift it out? Of how much more value then is a man than a sheep! Therefore, it is lawful to do good on the Sabbath day." Then he told the man, "Stretch out your hand." He stretched it out; and it was restored whole, just like the other. (Mt 12:10-13)

Sensing the Pharisees would not rest until they trapped him, Jesus moved on to continue his ministry elsewhere *and commanded* (the people) *that they should not make him known, that it might be fulfilled which was spoken through Isaiah the prophet, saying,*

> *"Behold, my servant whom I have chosen,*
> *my beloved in whom my soul is well pleased.*
> *I will put my Spirit on him.*
> *He will proclaim justice to the nations.*
> *He will not strive, nor shout,*
> *neither will anyone hear his voice in the streets.*
> *He won't break a bruised reed.*
> *He won't quench a smoking flax,*
> *until he leads justice to victory.*

In his name, the nations will hope."[178] (Mt 12:16-21)

Jesus and the Devil

The Pharisees continued with their attacks on Jesus, saying it was through the devil that Jesus was able to work miracles. As always, Jesus knew their thoughts and responded. *"He who is not with me is against me, and he who doesn't gather with me, scatters. Therefore, I tell you, every sin and blasphemy will be forgiven men, but the blasphemy against the Spirit will not be forgiven. Whoever speaks a word against the Son of Man, it will be forgiven him; but whoever speaks against the Holy Spirit, it will not be forgiven him, either in this age, or in that which is to come.*

"Either make the tree good and its fruit good, or make the tree corrupt and its fruit corrupt; for the tree is known by its fruit. You offspring of vipers, how can you, being evil, speak good things? For out of the abundance of the heart, the mouth speaks. The good man out of his good treasure brings out good things, and the evil man out of his evil treasure brings out evil things. I tell you that every idle word that men speak, they will give account of it on the day of judgement. For by your words you will be justified, and by your words you will be condemned." (Mt 12:30-37)

The Sign of Jonah

Still pursuing him, the scribes and Pharisees tried again to trap Jesus, asking, *"Teacher, we want to see a sign from you."*

But he answered them, *"(Only) an evil and adulterous generation seeks after a sign, but no sign will be given to it but the sign of Jonah the prophet. For as Jonah was three days and three nights in the belly of the huge fish, so will the Son of Man be three days and three nights in the heart of the earth. The men of Nineveh will stand up in the judgement with this generation*

---

[178] Is 42:4

and will condemn it, for they repented at the preaching of Jonah; and behold, someone greater than Jonah is here." (Mt 12:39-41)

The Parable of the Darnel

Jesus taught the crowds following him many lessons using parables.

"*The Kingdom of Heaven is like a man who sowed good seed in his field, but while people slept, his enemy came and sowed darnel weeds also among the wheat, and went away. But when the blade sprang up and produced grain, then the darnel weeds appeared also. The servants of the householder came and said to him, 'Sir, didn't you sow good seed in your field? Where did these darnel weeds come from?'*

"*He said to them, 'An enemy has done this.'*

"*The servants asked him, 'Do you want us to go and gather them up?'*

"*But he said, 'No, lest perhaps while you gather up the darnel weeds, you root up the wheat with them. Let both grow together until the harvest, and in the harvest time I will tell the reapers: "First, gather up the darnel weeds, and bind them in bundles to burn them; then gather the wheat into my barn."'"* (Mt 13:24-30)

Later, after the crowds had left, his apostles asked him to explain what he meant by the parable of the darnel.

He answered them, "He who sows the good seed is the Son of Man, the field is the world, the good seeds are the children of the Kingdom, and the darnel weeds are the children of the evil one. The enemy who sowed them is the devil. The harvest is the end of the age, and the reapers are angels. As therefore the darnel weeds are gathered up and burned with fire; so will it be at the end of this age. The Son of Man will send out his angels, and they will gather out of his Kingdom all things that cause stumbling and those who do iniquity, and will cast them into the furnace of fire. There will be weeping and gnashing of teeth. Then the righteous will shine like the sun in the Kingdom of their Father. He who has ears to hear, let him hear." (Mt 13:37-43)

The Parables of the Treasure, the Pearl, and the Dragnet

Jesus went on teaching his apostles. *"The Kingdom of Heaven is like a treasure hidden in the field, which a man found and hid. In his joy, he goes and sells all that he has and buys that field.*

"Again, the Kingdom of Heaven is like a man who is a merchant seeking fine pearls, who having found one pearl of great price, he went and sold all that he had and bought it.

"Again, the Kingdom of Heaven is like a dragnet that was cast into the sea and gathered some fish of every kind, which, when it was filled, fishermen drew up on the beach. They sat down and gathered the good into containers, but the bad they threw away. So it will be in the end of the world. The angels will come and separate the wicked from among the righteous, and will cast them into the furnace of fire. There will be weeping and gnashing of teeth." (Mt 13:44-50)

A Visit to Nazareth

Moving on, Jesus returned to his hometown of Nazareth to continue his teaching, but he was not welcomed. Instead, they argued,

"Isn't he just a carpenter's son?"

"Don't we know his mother, Mary?"

"Where did he get this wisdom from; how does he perform miracles?"

Jesus said to them, *"A prophet is only despised in his own country and in his own house,"* (Mt 13:57) and he left there without doing many miracles at all.

The First Miracle of the Loaves and Fishes

Soon there came a day when the crowds around Jesus were massive. The apostles recommended they be sent home so they could find food to eat, as mealtime was nearing. Jesus said, *"They don't need to go away. You give them something to eat."*

They told him, *"We only have five loaves and two fish."*

He said, *"Bring them here to me."* *He commanded the multitudes to sit down on the grass; and he took the five loaves and the two fish, and looking up to heaven, he blessed, broke and gave the loaves to the disciples; and the disciples gave to the multitudes. They all ate and were filled. They took up twelve baskets full of that which remained left over from the broken pieces. Those who ate were about five thousand men, in addition to women and children.* (Mt 14:16-21)

Jesus Walks on Water

Jesus instructed his apostles to go on ahead in the boat while he remained alone to pray. *When evening had come, he was there alone. But the boat was now in the middle of the sea, distressed by the waves... In the fourth watch of the night, Jesus came to them, walking on the water. When the disciples saw him walking on the sea, they were troubled, saying, "It's a ghost!" and they cried out in fear. But immediately Jesus spoke to them, saying, "Cheer up! It is I! Don't be afraid."*

Peter answered him and said, "Lord, if it is you, command me to come to you on the waters."

He said, "Come!"

Peter stepped down from the boat and walked on the water to come to Jesus. But when he saw that the wind was strong, he was afraid, and beginning to sink, he cried out, saying, "Lord, save me!"

Immediately Jesus stretched out his hand, took hold of him, and said to him, "You of little faith, why did you doubt?" When they got up into the boat, the wind ceased. Those who were in the boat came to worship him, saying, "You are truly the Son of God!" (Mt 14:23-33)

Jesus Drives out a Demon

Once, while near the Gentile town of Tyre and Sidon a Canaanite woman cried from a distance, *"Have mercy Lord, my daughter is possessed by a devil, please heal her." But Jesus paid her no attention. Soon his disciples begged him to do as she asked just to get her away, but Jesus said to them,*

"I wasn't sent to anyone but the lost sheep of the house of Israel."

But she came and worshipped him, saying, "Lord, help me."

But he answered, "It is not appropriate to take the children's bread and throw it to the dogs."

But she said, "Yes, Lord, but even the dogs eat the crumbs which fall from their masters' table."

Then Jesus answered her, "Woman, great is your faith! Be it done to you even as you desire." And her daughter was healed from that hour. (Mt 15:24-28)

The Second Miracle of the Loaves and Fishes

Jesus again went up into the hills and the ever-growing crowds followed him. There he continued to heal the lame, the cripple, the blind, and all who were sick. Feeling sorry for how long they had been following him, he said to his apostles, *"I have compassion on the multitude, because they have continued with me now three days and have nothing to eat. I don't want to send them away fasting, or they might faint on the way."*

The disciples said to him, "Where could we get so many loaves in a deserted place as to satisfy so great a multitude?"

Jesus said to them, "How many loaves do you have?"

They said, "Seven, and a few small fish."

He commanded the multitude to sit down on the ground; and he took the seven loaves and the fish. He gave thanks and broke them, and gave to the disciples, and the disciples to the multitudes. They all ate and were filled. They took up seven baskets full of the broken pieces that were left over. Those who ate were four thousand men, in addition to women and children. (Mt 15:32-38)

Peter's Profession of Faith

When Jesus came into the parts of Caesarea Philippi, he asked his disciples, "Who do men say that I, the Son of Man, am?"

They said, "Some say John the Baptist, some, Elijah, and others, Jeremiah or one of the prophets."[179]

He said to them, "But who do you say that I am?"

Simon Peter answered, "You are the Christ, the Son of the living God."

Jesus answered him, "Blessed are you, Simon son of Jonah, for flesh and blood has not revealed this to you, but my Father who is in heaven. I also tell you that you are Peter,[180] *and on this rock I will build my Church, and the gates of Hell will not prevail against it. I will give to you the keys of the Kingdom of Heaven, and whatever you bind on earth will have been bound in heaven; and whatever you release on earth will have been released in heaven." Then he commanded the disciples that they should tell no one that he was Jesus the Christ.* (Mt 16:13-20)

From then onwards, after having elicited (for the first time) an explicit profession of faith, Jesus began to reveal what was ahead and how he would suffer and die at the hands of the Pharisees and scribes, but he would also be raised from the dead on the third day.[181]

Peter took him aside and began to rebuke him, saying, "Far be it from you, Lord! This will never be done to you."

But he turned and said to Peter, "Get behind me, Satan! You are a stumbling block to me, for you are not setting your mind on the things of God, but on the things of men." (Mt 16:22-23)

---

[179] Jesus claimed the title 'prophet' for himself only indirectly, yet the public openly hailed him as much. The title had messianic significance because the Jews confidently expected a revival of the spirit of prophecy as a sign of the messianic era. NJB footnote (c).

[180] In the Old Testament we saw God change the name of Abram to Abraham, and Jacob to Israel.

[181] NJB footnote (k) Mt 16:21. Adding that Jesus is also The Suffering Servant of Isaiah.

The Condition of Following Jesus

Then Jesus said to his disciples, "If anyone desires to come after me, let him deny himself, take up his cross, and follow me. For whoever desires to save his life will lose it, and whoever will lose his life for my sake will find it. For what will it profit a man if he gains the whole world and forfeits his life? Or what will a man give in exchange for his life? For the Son of Man will come in the glory of his Father with his angels, and then he will render to everyone according to his deeds. Most certainly I tell you, there are some standing here who will in no way taste of death until they see the Son of Man coming in his Kingdom." (Mt 16:24-28)

The Transfiguration

Jesus took Peter, James, and John up into the mountains, where they could be alone. While there Jesus was transfigured, *his face shone like the sun, and his garments became as white as the light. Behold, Moses and Elijah appeared to them, talking with him.* (Mt 17:2-3)

On seeing this Peter offered to make three tents, one for each of them, but while he was mid-sentence, *a voice came out of the cloud, saying, "This is my beloved Son, in whom I am well pleased. Listen to him."* (Mt 17:5)

Overcome with fear, the three apostles fell onto their faces. Jesus came to them telling them to get up and not be afraid, and he also warned them, *"Don't tell anyone what you saw, until the Son of Man has risen from the dead."* (Mt 17:9)

The Power of True Faith

One day a man came to Jesus to have his possessed son cured (the apostles had tried but could not do it). *Jesus answered, "Faithless and perverse generation! How long will I be with you? How long will I bear with you? Bring him here to me."* Jesus rebuked the demon, and it went out of him, and the boy was cured from that hour.

Then the disciples came to Jesus privately, and said, "Why weren't we able to cast it out?"

He said to them, "Because of your unbelief. For most certainly I tell you, if you have faith the size of a mustard seed, you will tell this mountain, 'Move from here to there,' and it will move; and nothing will be impossible for you. But this kind doesn't go out except by prayer and fasting." (Mt 17:17-21)

The Second Prophecy of the Passion of Christ

Moving onto Galilee Jesus told his apostles again, *"The Son of Man is about to be delivered up into the hands of men, and they will kill him, and the third day he will be raised up."* (Mt 17:22-23)

This greatly distressed them.

Brotherly Correction

Another day when Jesus was with his apostles he said, *"If your brother sins against you, go, show him his fault between you and him alone. If he listens to you, you have gained back your brother. But if he doesn't listen, take one or two more with you, that at the mouth of two or three witnesses every word may be established. If he refuses to listen to them, tell it to the assembly. If he refuses to hear the assembly also, let him be to you as a Gentile or a tax collector. Most certainly I tell you, whatever things you bind on earth will have been bound in heaven, and whatever things you release on earth will have been released in heaven. Again, assuredly I tell you, that if two of you will agree on earth concerning anything that they will ask, it will be done for them by my Father who is in heaven. For where two or three are gathered together in my name, there I am in the middle of them."*

Then Peter came and said to him, "Lord, how often shall my brother sin against me, and I forgive him? Until seven times?"

Jesus said to him, *"I don't tell you until seven times, but, until seventy times seven."* (Mt 18:15-22)

Jesus Continued his Parables

"The Kingdom of Heaven is like a certain king who wanted to settle accounts with his servants. When he had begun to settle, one was brought to him who owed him ten thousand talents. But because he couldn't pay, his lord commanded him to be sold, with his wife, his children, and all that he had, and payment to be made. The servant therefore fell down and knelt before him, saying, 'Lord, have patience with me, and I will repay you all!' The lord of that servant, being moved with compassion, released him and forgave him the debt.

"But that servant went out and found one of his fellow servants who owed him one hundred denarii[182], and he grabbed him and took him by the throat, saying, 'Pay me what you owe!'

"So his fellow servant fell down at his feet and begged him, saying, 'Have patience with me, and I will repay you!' He would not, but went and cast him into prison until he should pay back that which was due. So when his fellow servants saw what was done, they were exceedingly sorry, and came and told their lord all that was done. Then his lord called him in and said to him, 'You wicked servant! I forgave you all that debt because you begged me. Shouldn't you also have had mercy on your fellow servant, even as I had mercy on you?' His lord was angry, and delivered him to the torturers until he should pay all that was due to him. So my heavenly Father will also do to you, if you don't each forgive your brother from your hearts for his misdeeds." (Mt 18:23-35)

The Parable of the Vineyard Labourers

"The Kingdom of Heaven is like a man who was the master of a household who went out early in the morning to hire labourers for his vineyard. When he had agreed with the labourers for a denarius a day, he sent them into his vineyard. He went out about the third hour and saw others standing idle in

---

[182] If 100 denarii was said to be $1, then the servant's retired debt of 10,000 talents was equivalent to $600,000.

the marketplace. He said to them, 'You also go into the vineyard, and whatever is right I will give you.' So they went on their way. Again he went out about the sixth and the ninth hour and did likewise. About the eleventh hour he went out and found others standing idle. He said to them, 'Why do you stand here all day idle?'

"They said to him, 'Because no one has hired us.'

"He said to them, 'You also go into the vineyard, and you will receive whatever is right.'

"When evening had come, the lord of the vineyard said to his manager, 'Call the labourers and pay them their wages, beginning from the last to the first.' When those who were hired at about the eleventh hour came, they each received a denarius. When they first came, they supposed that they would receive more; and they likewise each received a denarius. When they received it, they murmured against the master of the household, saying, 'These last have spent one hour, and you have made them equal to us who have borne the burden of the day and the scorching heat!'

"But he answered one of them, 'Friend, I am doing you no wrong. Didn't you agree with me for a denarius? Take that which is yours, and go your way. It is my desire to give to this last just as much as to you. Isn't it lawful for me to do what I want to with what I own? Or is your eye evil, because I am good?' So the last will be first, and the first last. For many are called, but few are chosen." (Mt 20:1-16)

The Third Prophecy of the Passion of Christ

From here Jesus and his apostles headed towards Jerusalem, when for the third time, he told them, *"The Son of Man will be delivered to the chief priests and scribes, and they will condemn him to death, and will hand him over to the Gentiles to mock, to scourge, and to crucify; and the third day he will be raised up."* (Mt 20:18-19)

Jesus is a Servant

Among the crowds following Jesus was the mother of two of his apostles, James, and John. She approached Jesus, asking that her sons be allowed to sit by the right and left of Jesus in his Kingdom.

But Jesus answered, "You don't know what you are asking. Are you able to drink the cup that I am about to drink, and be baptised with the baptism that I am baptised with?"

They said to him, "We are able."

He said to them, "You will indeed drink my cup, and be baptised with the baptism that I am baptised with; but to sit on my right hand and on my left hand is not mine to give, but it is for whom it has been prepared by my Father." (Mt 20:22-23)

The remaining apostles overheard this and became indignant, so Jesus explained, *"You know that the rulers of the nations lord it over them, and their great ones exercise authority over them. It shall not be so among you; but whoever desires to become great among you shall be your servant. Whoever desires to be first among you shall be your bondservant, even as the Son of Man came not to be served, but to serve, and to give his life as a ransom for many."* (Mt 20:25-28)

Jesus Enters Jerusalem

Getting closer to Jerusalem, *Jesus sent two disciples, saying to them, "Go into the village ... and ... you will find a donkey tied, and a colt with her. Untie them and bring them to me. If anyone says anything to you, you shall say, 'The Lord needs them,' and immediately he will send them."*

All this was done that it might be fulfilled which was spoken through the prophet, saying,

"*Tell the daughter of Zion,*
behold, your King comes to you,
humble, and riding on a donkey,

on a colt, the foal of a donkey."[183]

The disciples did just as Jesus commanded them and brought the donkey and the colt and laid their clothes on them; and he sat on it. A very great multitude spread their clothes on the road (ahead of Jesus). Others cut branches from the trees and spread them on the road.[184] The multitudes who went in front of him, and those who followed, kept shouting, "Hosanna to the son of David! Blessed is he who comes in the name of the Lord! Hosanna in the highest!"[185] (Mt 21:1-9)

Jesus and the Pharisees

Back in the Temple again, Jesus questioned the chief priests and elders, "What do you think? A man had two sons, and he came to the first, and said, 'Son, go work today in my vineyard.' He answered, 'I will not,' but afterward he changed his mind, and went. He came to the second, and said the same thing. He answered, 'I'm going, sir,' but he didn't go. Which of the two did the will of his father?"

They said to him, "The first."

Jesus said to them, "Most certainly I tell you that the tax collectors and the prostitutes are entering into God's Kingdom before you. For John came to you in the way of righteousness, and you didn't believe him; but the tax collectors and the prostitutes believed him. When you saw it, you didn't even repent afterward, that you might believe him.'" (Mt 21:28-32)

Parable of the Wedding Feast

Jesus gave another parable. "The Kingdom of Heaven is like a certain king, who held a wedding feast for his son, and sent out his servants to call those

---
[183] Zec 9:9
[184] Celebrated on Palm Sunday.
[185] Ps 118:26

who were invited to the wedding feast, but they would not come. Again he sent out other servants, saying, 'Tell those who are invited, "Behold, I have prepared my dinner. My cattle and my fatlings are killed, and all things are ready. Come to the wedding feast!"' But they made light of it, and went their ways, one to his own farm, another to his merchandise; and the rest grabbed his servants, treated them shamefully, and killed them. When the king heard that, he was angry, and sent his armies, destroyed those murderers, and burned their city.

"Then he said to his servants, 'The wedding is ready, but those who were invited weren't worthy. Go therefore to the intersections of the highways, and as many as you may find, invite to the wedding feast.' Those servants went out into the highways and gathered together as many as they found, both bad and good. The wedding was filled with guests.

"But when the king came in to see the guests, he saw there a man who didn't have on wedding clothing, and he said to him, 'Friend, how did you come in here not wearing wedding clothing?' He was speechless. Then the king said to the servants, 'Bind him hand and foot, take him away, and throw him into the outer darkness. That is where the weeping and grinding of teeth will be. For many are called, but few are chosen.'" (Mt 22:1-14)

Meanwhile, the Pharisees, still out to trap and discredit Jesus, posed a question, *"Teacher, which is the greatest commandment of the law?"*

Jesus said to him, "You shall love Yahweh your God with all your heart, with all your soul, and with all your mind.[186] *This is the first and great commandment. The second likewise is this: You shall love your neighbour as yourself.*[187] *The whole Law and the prophets depend on these two commandments."* (Mt 22:36-40)

Jesus then went on to accuse the scribes and Pharisees of abusing their positions.

---

[186] Dt 6:5
[187] Lv 19:18

"Woe to you, scribes and Pharisees, hypocrites! For you devour widows' houses, and as a pretence you make long prayers. Therefore, you will receive greater condemnation." (Mt 23:13)

"Woe to you, scribes and Pharisees, hypocrites! For you travel around by sea and land to make one convert; and when he becomes one, you make him twice as much a son of Hell as yourselves." (Mt 23:15)

"Woe to you, scribes and Pharisees, hypocrites! For you are like whitened tombs, which outwardly appear beautiful, but inwardly are full of dead men's bones and of all uncleanness. Even so, you also outwardly appear righteous to men, but inwardly you are full of hypocrisy and iniquity." (Mt 23:27-28)

The Second Coming

Leaving the Temple, Jesus withdrew with his apostles to the Mount of Olives and spoke to them about what was to come. *"As the days of Noah were, so will the coming of the Son of Man be. For as in those days, which were before the flood, they were eating and drinking, marrying and giving in marriage, until the day that Noah entered into the ark, and they didn't know until the flood came and took them all away, so will the coming of the Son of Man be. Then two men will be in the field: one will be taken and one will be left. Two women will be grinding at the mill: one will be taken and one will be left. Watch therefore, for you don't know in what hour your Lord comes. But know this, that if the master of the house had known in what watch of the night the thief was coming, he would have watched, and would not have allowed his house to be broken into. Therefore, also be ready, for in an hour that you don't expect, the Son of Man will come."* (Mt 24:37-44)

The Last Judgement

*"But when the Son of Man comes in his glory, and all the holy angels with him, then he will sit on the throne of his glory. Before him all the nations will be gathered, and he will separate them one from another, as a shepherd separates the sheep from the goats. He will set the sheep on his right hand, but the

goats on the left. Then the King will tell those on his right hand, 'Come, blessed of my Father, inherit the Kingdom prepared for you from the foundation of the world; for I was hungry and you gave me food to eat. I was thirsty and you gave me drink. I was a stranger and you took me in. I was naked and you clothed me. I was sick and you visited me. I was in prison and you came to me.'

"Then the righteous will answer him, saying, 'Lord, when did we see you hungry and feed you, or thirsty and give you a drink? When did we see you as a stranger and take you in, or naked and clothe you? When did we see you sick or in prison and come to you?'

"The King will answer them, 'Most certainly I tell you, because you did it to one of the least of these my brothers, you did it to me.' Then he will say also to those on the left hand, 'Depart from me, you cursed, into the eternal fire which is prepared for the devil and his angels; for I was hungry, and you didn't give me food to eat; I was thirsty, and you gave me no drink; I was a stranger, and you didn't take me in; naked, and you didn't clothe me; sick, and in prison, and you didn't visit me.'

"Then they will also answer, saying, 'Lord, when did we see you hungry, or thirsty, or a stranger, or naked, or sick, or in prison, and didn't help you?'

"Then he will answer them, saying, 'Most certainly I tell you, because you didn't do it to one of the least of these, you didn't do it to me.' These will go away into eternal punishment, but the righteous into eternal life." (Mt 25:31-45)

The Last Supper

With Passover only two days away, Jesus reminded his apostles that he would soon be handed over to be crucified. Meanwhile, the chief priests were putting the final touches to their plans to capture and kill him, and they were conscious of doing it sooner rather than later as they did not want the associated commotion to disrupt the upcoming festivities.

Meanwhile Judas Iscariot went to the chief priests and agreed to a plan to hand over Jesus for thirty silver pieces.

Jesus sent some of his apostles to secure a place for their Passover meal. While together at the table Jesus said to his apostles, *"Most certainly I tell you that one of you will betray me."*

They were exceedingly sorrowful, and each began to ask him, "It isn't me, is it, Lord?"

He answered, "He who dipped his hand with me in the dish will betray me. The Son of Man goes even as it is written of him, but woe to that man through whom the Son of Man is betrayed! It would be better for that man if he had not been born."

Judas, who betrayed him, answered, "It isn't me, is it, Rabbi?"

He said to him, "You said it." (Mt 26: 21-25)

While they were eating Jesus took some bread and said, *"Take, eat; this is my body."* He took the cup, gave thanks, and gave it to them, saying, *"All of you drink it, for this is my blood of the new covenant, which is poured out for many for the remission of sins."* (Mt 26:26-28)

After dinner was over and they sang hymns, they all left for the Mount of Olives, where Jesus informed them further about what was to come. *"All of you will be made to stumble because of me tonight, for it is written, 'I will strike the shepherd, and the sheep of the flock will be scattered.'*[188] *But after I am raised up, I will go before you into Galilee."*

But Peter answered him, "Even if all will be made to stumble because of you, I will never be made to stumble."

Jesus said to him, "Most certainly I tell you that tonight, before the rooster crows, you will deny me three times."

Peter said to him, "Even if I must die with you, I will not deny you." All of the disciples also said likewise. (Mt 26:31-35)

---

[188] Zec 13:7

The Agony in the Garden

Jesus moved on to a place called Gethsemane. Taking only Peter, James and John, Jesus walked on to a quiet place where he disclosed. *"My soul is exceedingly sorrowful, even to death. Stay here and watch with me."* (Mt 26:38)

Moving a little further on, he fell to his knees to pray, *"My Father, if it is possible, let this cup pass away from me; nevertheless, not what I desire, but what you desire."* (Mt 26:39)

Returning to Peter, James, and John, Jesus was upset to find them asleep. *"What, couldn't you watch with me for one hour? Watch and pray, that you don't enter into temptation. The spirit indeed is willing, but the flesh is weak."* (Mt 26:40-41)

Jesus moved on again to pray alone, *"My Father, if this cup can't pass away from me unless I drink it, then your will be done."* (Mt 26:42)

On returning to his apostles, he again found them asleep, this time he let them be and went back to his place of prayer before returning a third time. *"You can sleep on now and take your rest. Now the hour has come when the Son of Man is to be betrayed into the hands of sinners. Get up! Let us go! My betrayer is already close at hand."* (Mt 26:45-46*)

As Jesus was still speaking, Judas approached him, along with a group of the chief priests' armed men. Judas went straight to Jesus and kissed him, for he had told the guards, *"Whoever I kiss, he is the one. Seize him."* (Mt 26:48)

Immediately, the guards came forward and arrested Jesus. This frightened the apostles, causing one to strike the ear off a guard with a sword. Jesus was quick to calm everyone down, ordering them, *"Put your sword back into its place, for all those who take the sword will die by the sword. Or do you think that I couldn't ask my Father, and he would even now send me more than twelve legions of angels? How then would the Scriptures be fulfilled that it must be so?"* (Mt 26:52-54)

Jesus turned to the guards saying, *"Have you come out as against a robber with swords and clubs to seize me? I sat daily in the temple teaching, and you didn't arrest me."* (Mt 26:55)

All of this happened to fulfil the Scriptures.

The Trial and Conviction of Jesus

The guards led Jesus away to the house of the high priest Caiaphas, Peter followed behind. The chief priests and Sanhedrin[189] began presenting their (false) evidence against Jesus to justify the death penalty they sought to pass. With their own false accusations, they could not succeed though, so they brought in two men to provide further false testimony. One man said, *"This man said, 'I am able to destroy the Temple of God, and to build it in three days.'"*

The high priest stood up and said to him, "Have you no answer? What is this that these testify against you?" But Jesus stayed silent. The high priest answered him, "I challenge you by the living God that you tell us whether you are the Christ, the Son of God."

Jesus said to him, "You have said so. Nevertheless, I tell you, after this you will see the Son of Man sitting at the right hand of Power, and coming on the clouds of the sky."

Then the high priest tore his clothing, saying, "He has spoken blasphemy! Why do we need any more witnesses? Behold, now you have heard his blasphemy. What do you think?"

They answered, "He is worthy of death!" Then they spat in his face and beat him with their fists, and some slapped him, saying, "Prophesy to us, you Christ! Who hit you?" (Mt 26:61-68)

While this was going on inside, Peter was outside in the courtyard. A girl came up to him and accused him of being a follower of Jesus. Peter denied it. Moving away so as not to draw attention to himself, he was

---

[189] A group of 71 members made up of elders, high priests and scribes. Their role was to oversee and rule on religious and legal law within the community.

confronted by another girl who also said he was seen with Jesus. Peter again denied the accusation. For a third time someone accused him, this time saying his Galilean accent gave him away. Peter, now getting angry and agitated, denied for a third time any knowledge of Jesus. At that exact moment the rooster crowed and Peter, feeling sick to the stomach, remembered what Jesus said earlier in the night, *"Before the rooster crows, you will deny me three times."* (Mt 26:75)

Peter left inconsolable.

As morning came, Jesus was bound and taken to see the governor, Pilate.

When Judas heard Jesus had been condemned to death, it filled him with remorse, and he went back to the chief priests to return his silver to try to undo his betrayal. The chief priests would hear none of it, so Judas tossed the silver down, ran out, and hanged himself. Left with the silver pieces, the chief priests were in a quandary about what to do with them. They knew it was blood money and could not keep it, so they bought a graveyard for foreigners which became known as the Field of Blood. This all happened in fulfilment of the Scriptures.

> *They took the thirty pieces of silver,*
> *the price of him upon whom a price had been set,*
> *whom some of the children of Israel priced,*
> *and they gave them for the potter's field,*
> *as the Lord commanded me.*[190] (Mt 27:9)

In the meantime, Jesus was with the governor Pilate, who questioned him, *"Are you the King of the Jews?"*

Jesus said to him, *"So you say."*

As he was being accused by the chief priests and elders, he answered nothing. Then Pilate said to him, *"Don't you hear how many things they testify against you?"*

---

[190] Zechariah 11:12-13; Jeremiah 19:1-13; 32:6-9.

He gave him no answer, not even one word, so that the governor marvelled greatly. (Mt 27:11-14)

While Pilate was considering the case against Jesus, his wife approached him about a dream she had, *"Have nothing to do with that righteous man, for I have suffered many things today in a dream because of him."* (Mt 27:19)

Pilate decided his safest way out was to use a festival time custom to release a condemned prisoner back to the people. At the time there was a notorious criminal called Barabbas, so Pilate gave the people a choice. Should he release Jesus or Barabbas? Influenced by the chief priests, the crowd cried out for Barabbas. Confused, Pilate asked them, "What do you want me to do with Jesus?" Their reply was unequivocal - "Crucify him!"

Realising that to disappoint the crowd was to invite riot, Pilate *took water and washed his hands before the multitude, saying, "I am innocent of the blood of this righteous person. You see to it."*

All the people answered, "May his blood be on us and on our children!"

Then he released Barabbas to them, but Jesus he flogged and delivered to be crucified. (Mt 27:24-26)

The Crucifixion

The soldiers took Jesus away, stripped him, and made him a scarlet cloak[191] and a crown made of thorns. They spat on him and mocked him saying, "Hail, King of the Jews." When they were finished, they dressed him back in his clothes and took him away to be crucified.

When they came to a place called 'Golgotha', that is to say, 'The place of a skull', they gave him sour wine to drink mixed with gall. When he had tasted it, he would not drink. When they had crucified him, they divided his clothing among them, casting lots,[192] and they sat and watched him there. They set up over his head the accusation against him written, 'This is Jesus, the King of the Jews'. (Mt 27:33-37)

---

[191] Scarlet was a colour associated with royalty.
[192] Ps 22:18

While hanging on the cross the crowds continued their jeering and mocking, saying, *"If you are the Son of God, come down from the cross!"* (Mt 27:40), and *"He saved others, but he can't save himself. If he is the King of Israel, let him come down from the cross now, and we will believe in him. He trusts in God. Let God deliver him now, if he wants him; for he said, 'I am the Son of God.'"* (Mt 27:42-43)

Between 12noon and 3pm, a vast darkness came over the land. Jesus cried out from the cross, *"Eli, Eli, lama sabachthani?" That is, 'My God, my God, why have you forsaken me?'*[193] (Mt 27:46)

As Jesus gave up his spirit, *the veil of the temple was torn in two from the top to the bottom. The earth quaked and the rocks were split. The tombs were opened, and many bodies of the saints who had fallen asleep were raised; and coming out of the tombs after his resurrection, they entered into the holy city and appeared to many.* (Mt 27:51-53)

Seeing these events unfold, some of the guards who crucified Jesus were panic-stricken and said, *"Truly this was the Son of God!"* (Mt 27:54)

At the foot of the cross were Mary Magdalene, Mary, (the mother of James and Joseph), and the mother of the two apostles, James, and John.

Jesus Rises from the Dead

A rich man called Joseph of Arimathea was given permission from Pilate to take Jesus down from the cross, to bury him before the Sabbath. Wrapping him in a shroud, he placed Jesus in a tomb he owned. Mary Magdalene and the others sat nearby watching the stone roll over the entrance to the tomb.

The following day the chief priests and Pharisees, who were concerned about Jesus' body being removed by his followers to propagate his comments that after three days he would rise again, went to see Pilate. He promptly sent soldiers to watch the tomb and also to put an official seal on it.

---

[193] Ps 22:1

After the Sabbath, Mary Magdalene, together with the mother of James, returned to the tomb so they could complete the rituals of burial (they couldn't do this on the Sabbath). As they arrived a great earthquake occurred, followed by an angel of God ascending and rolling away the stone which covered the entrance to the tomb. The guards watching the tomb were distressed and went a deathly pale colour. The angel spoke to the two women, *"Don't be afraid, for I know that you seek Jesus, who has been crucified. He is not here, for he has risen, just like he said. Come, see the place where the Lord was lying. Go quickly and tell his disciples, 'He has risen from the dead, and behold, he goes before you into Galilee; there you will see him.' Behold, I have told you."* (Mt 28:5-7)

The women immediately ran back to tell the apostles, and met Jesus along the way. The women fell to their knees and placed their hands on his feet. Jesus said, *"Don't be afraid. Go tell the others that they should go into Galilee, and there they will see me."* (Mt 28:10)

In the meantime, the guards who witnessed the events at the tomb went to tell the chief priests, who after some discussions, gave them money in payment for their lie. They were to say it was the disciples of Jesus who took him away.

Later, as the eleven gathered in Galilee as instructed, *they saw him, they bowed down to him; but some doubted. Jesus came to them and spoke to them, saying, "All authority has been given to me in heaven and on earth. Go and make disciples of all nations, baptising them in the name of the Father and of the Son and of the Holy Spirit, teaching them to observe all things that I commanded you. Behold, I am with you always, even to the end of the age."* (Mt 28:17-20)

MARK

The Gospel of Mark is believed to have been written c.65 AD and is the shortest of the four Gospels.

Historically Mark was believed to be a follower and translator for Peter (Peter's Greek was not strong enough to preach), but this has recently come under scrutiny. Mark's audience was the non-Jewish Christians living in Rome, so he didn't spend as much time as Matthew and Luke with details and connections to the Old Testament. Instead, Mark concentrates on highlighting Jesus' miracles.

He also spends little time mentioning any background of Jesus or the times they were living in.

The beginning of the Good News of Jesus Christ, the Son of God. As it is written in the prophets,

> *"Behold, I send my messenger before your face,*
> *who will prepare your way before you:*
> *the voice of one crying in the wilderness,*
> *'Make ready the way of the Lord!*
> *Make his paths straight!'"*[194] (Mk 1:1-3)

In the days of John the Baptist, Jesus came to him to be baptised. After which, John saw *the heavens parting and the Spirit descending on him like*

---

[194] Mal 3:1, Is 40:3

a dove. A voice came out of the sky, "You are my beloved Son, in whom I am well pleased." (Mk 1:10-11)

Jesus was then drawn into the desert for forty days, where he was tempted by Satan.

Jesus Calls his First Disciples

Once, as Jesus was by the Sea of Galilee, *he saw some fishermen, in particular Simon (who he called Peter) and his brother Andrew. Jesus said to them, "Come after me, and I will make you into fishers for men." Immediately they left their nets and followed him.* (Mk 1:17-18)

Further along the shore he called James and John,[195] the sons of Zebedee. Like Simon and Andrew, they also left everything to follow Jesus.

Jesus Begins to Preach

Jesus, along with his new followers, made their way to the Jewish town of Capernaum. They were in a synagogue when Jesus was approached by a possessed man. The spirit said to Jesus, *"Ha! What do we have to do with you, Jesus, you Nazarene? Have you come to destroy us? I know who you are: the Holy One of God!"*

Jesus rebuked him, saying, "Be quiet, and come out of him!"

The unclean spirit, convulsing him and crying with a loud voice, came out of him. They were all amazed, so that they questioned among themselves, saying, "What is this? A new teaching? For with authority he commands even the unclean spirits, and they obey him!" The report of him went out immediately everywhere into all the region of Galilee and its surrounding area. (Mk 1:24-28)

---

[195] The writer of the Gospel of John.

The Cure of a Leper

Sometime later after returning to Galilee, a leper came to Jesus. Kneeling down he begged him, "If you want to, you can make me clean." *Being moved with compassion, Jesus stretched out his hand and touched him, and he said to him, "I want to be made clean." When he had said this, immediately the leprosy left him and he was made clean. Jesus strictly warned him and immediately sent him out, and said to him, "See that you say nothing to anybody, but go show yourself to the priest and offer for your cleansing the things which Moses commanded, for a testimony to them."*

But he went out and began to proclaim it ... so that Jesus could no more openly enter into a city, but was outside in desert places. People came to him from everywhere. (Mk 1:40-45)

The Cure of a Paralytic

Returning to Capernaum, it didn't take long for the crowds to gather around Jesus, hungry to hear him teach. One day he was preaching in a room inside a house. The crowd outside was so large that many could not get near him. Outside were four particularly resolute people with a sick and paralytic friend. Unable to reach Jesus through the door, they went up onto the roof and removed a section so they could lower him down into the presence of Jesus. *Seeing their faith, Jesus said to the paralytic, "Son, your sins are forgiven you."*

But there were some scribes sitting there and reasoning in their hearts, "Why does this man speak blasphemies like that? Who can forgive sins but God alone?"

Immediately Jesus, perceiving in his spirit that they so reasoned within themselves, said to them, "Why do you reason these things in your hearts? Which is easier, to tell the paralytic, 'Your sins are forgiven;' or to say, 'Arise, and take up your bed, and walk?' But that you may know that the Son of Man has authority on earth to forgive sins" - *he said to the paralytic* - *"I tell you, arise, take up your mat, and go to your house."*

Everyone was amazed, saying, "We never saw anything like this!" (Mk 2:5-12)

Matthew is Called

In the following days, Jesus called a tax collector by the name of Levi (also called Matthew) to become one of his apostles, and he returned to his house for a meal. While there, the Pharisees (who were looking for ways to discredit Jesus) said to him, "Why do John's disciples and the disciples of the Pharisees fast, but your disciples don't fast?"

Jesus said to them, "Can the groomsmen fast while the bridegroom is with them? As long as they have the bridegroom with them, they can't fast. But the days will come when the bridegroom will be taken away from them, and then they will fast. No one sews a piece of unshrunken cloth on an old garment, or else the patch shrinks and the new tears away from the old, and a worse hole is made. No one puts new wine into old wineskins; or else the new wine will burst the skins, and the wine pours out, and the skins will be destroyed; but they put new wine into fresh wineskins." (Mk 2:18-22)

Confrontation with the Pharisees

On a Sabbath day some Pharisees saw Jesus and his disciples walking through a field picking corn to eat - they saw this as a chance to trap him, posing, "Why do they do that which is not lawful on the Sabbath day?"

Jesus answered, *"Did you never read what David did when he had need and was hungry - he, and those who were with him? How he entered into God's house at the time of Abiathar the high priest, and ate the bread, which is not lawful to eat except for the priests, and gave also to those who were with him?"*[196]

He said to them, "The Sabbath was made for man, not man for the Sabbath. Therefore, the Son of Man is lord even of the Sabbath." (Mk 2:25-28)

---

[196] 1 Sam 21:1–6

Jesus Appoints his Twelve Apostles

The day came when Jesus called a chosen few to his side and *he appointed twelve, that they might be with him, and that he might send them out to preach and to have authority to heal sicknesses and to cast out demons: Simon (to whom he gave the name Peter); James the son of Zebedee; and John, the brother of James,... Andrew; Philip; Bartholomew; Matthew; Thomas; James, the son of Alphaeus; Thaddaeus; Simon the Zealot; and Judas Iscariot, who also betrayed him.* (Mk 3:14-19)

The Scribes Accuse Jesus of Being a Devil

Returning home again, Jesus was confronted by scribes who had come down from Jerusalem, looking for ways to test him and hopefully prejudice him, saying, *"He has Beelzebub in him,"* and, *"By the prince of the demons he casts out the demons."*

Jesus summoned them and said to them, *"How can Satan cast out Satan? If a kingdom is divided against itself, that kingdom cannot stand. If a house is divided against itself, that house cannot stand. If Satan has risen up against himself, and is divided, he can't stand, but has an end. But no one can enter into the house of the strong man to plunder unless he first binds the strong man; then he will plunder his house.*

"Most certainly I tell you, all men's sins will be forgiven, including their blasphemies... but whoever may blaspheme against the Holy Spirit never has forgiveness, but is subject to eternal condemnation." (Mk 3:22-29)

The Parable of the Sower

Once, while Jesus was teaching, the gathering crowds surged so much he needed to get aboard a boat so he could continue. *"Listen! Behold, the farmer went out to sow. As he sowed, some seed fell by the road, and the birds came and devoured it. Others fell on the rocky ground, where it had little soil, and immediately it sprang up, because it had no depth of soil. When the sun had risen, it was scorched; and because it had no root, it withered away. Others fell among the thorns, and the thorns grew up and choked it, and it yielded no fruit. Others fell into the good ground and yielded fruit, growing up and increasing. Some produced thirty times, some sixty times, and some, one hundred times as much." He said, "Whoever has ears to hear, let him hear."* (Mk 4: 3-9)

Later that day, the followers still with Jesus and his twelve apostles asked him why he spoke to them in parables. *He said to them, "To you is given the mystery of God's Kingdom, but to those who are outside, all things are done in parables, that 'seeing they may see and not perceive, and hearing they may hear and not understand, lest perhaps they should turn again, and their sins should be forgiven them.'"* (Mk 4:11-12)

He continued, "Don't you understand this parable? How will you understand all of the parables? The farmer sows the word. The ones by the road are the ones where the word is sown; and when they have heard, immediately Satan comes and takes away the word which has been sown in them. These in the same way are those who are sown on the rocky places, who, when they have heard the word, immediately receive it with joy. They have no root in themselves, but are short-lived. When oppression or persecution arises because of the word, immediately they stumble. Others are those who are sown among the thorns. These are those who have heard the word, and the cares of this age, and the deceitfulness of riches, and the lusts of other things entering in, choke the word, and it becomes unfruitful. Those which were sown on the good ground are those who hear the word, accept it, and bear fruit, some thirty times, some sixty times, and some, one hundred times." (Mk 4:13-20)

The Parable of the Measure

"Take heed what you hear. With whatever measure you measure, it will be measured to you; and more will be given to you who hear. For whoever has, to him more will be given; and he who doesn't have, even that which he has will be taken away from him." (Mk 4:14-25)

The Parable of the Mustard Seed

"How will we liken God's Kingdom? Or with what parable will we illustrate it? It's like a grain of mustard seed, which, when it is sown in the earth, though it is less than all the seeds that are on the earth, yet when it is sown, grows up and becomes greater than all the herbs, and puts out great branches, so that the birds of the sky can lodge under its shadow." (Mk 4:30-32)

Jesus Raises Jairus' Daughter to Life

One day a ruler of the synagogue, Jairus by name, came; and seeing (Jesus), *he fell at his feet and begged him, saying, "My little daughter is at the point of death. Please come and lay your hands on her, that she may be made healthy, and live."* (Mk 5:23-24)

However, before Jesus could return with him, a friend of Jairus' came to tell him that his daughter was already dead.

But Jesus said to Jairus, *"Don't be afraid, only believe."* He allowed no one to follow him except Peter, James, and John, the brother of James. He came to the synagogue ruler's house, and he saw an uproar, weeping, and great wailing. When he had entered in, he said to them, *"Why do you make an uproar and weep? The child is not dead, but is asleep."*

They ridiculed him. But he, having put them all out, took the father of the child, her mother, and those who were with him, and went in where the child was lying. Taking the child by the hand, he said to her, *"Talitha, kum!"*[197] *which means, 'Girl, I tell you, get up!'* Immediately the girl rose up and walked, for she was twelve years old. They were amazed. He strictly ordered them that no one should know this, and commanded that something should be given to her to eat. (Mk 5:36-43)

---

[197] Aramaic; Christ's native tongue. NJB.

The Twelve are Sent Out

Returning to his hometown of Nazareth, Jesus called his twelve apostles to him *and sent them out two by two; and he gave them authority over the unclean spirits. He commanded they should take nothing for their journey, except a staff only: no bread, no wallet, no money in their purse, but to wear sandals, and not put on two tunics. He said to them, "Wherever you enter into a house, stay there until you depart from there. Whoever will not receive you nor hear you, as you depart from there, shake off the dust that is under your feet for a testimony against them. Assuredly, I tell you, it will be more tolerable for Sodom and Gomorrah on the day of judgement than for that city!"*

They went out and preached that people should repent. They cast out many demons and anointed many with oil, who were sick and healed them. (Mk 6:7-13)

John the Baptist is Beheaded

News of Jesus and his ministry was spreading far and wide, even reaching the ears of King Herod Antipas who believed the miracles were being done in the name of John the Baptist.

Herod's wife wanted John dead but struggled to persuade Herod to agree (for he feared him as a good and holy man), until one day when a rare chance arose. It was Herod's birthday, and his wife had her daughter dance before Herod. Herod was so enamoured, he said to her, *"Ask me whatever you want, and I will give it to you."* He swore to her, *"Whatever you ask of me, I will give you, up to half of my kingdom."*

She went out and said to her mother, "What shall I ask?"

She said, "The head of John the Baptist."

She came in immediately with haste to the king and requested, "I want you to give me right now the head of John the Baptist on a platter." (Mk 6:21-25)

Unwilling to go back on his promise, Herod ordered his guards to proceed.

Jesus Heals a Deaf Man

One day, the crowds presented Jesus with a man *who was deaf and had an impediment in his speech. They begged him to lay his hand on him. He took him aside from the multitude privately and put his fingers into his ears, and he spat and touched his tongue. Looking up to heaven, he sighed, and said to him, "Ephphatha!" that is, 'Be opened!' Immediately his ears were opened, and the impediment of his tongue was released, and he spoke clearly. He commanded them that they should tell no one, but the more he commanded them, so much the more widely they proclaimed it. They were astonished beyond measure, saying, "He has done all things well. He makes even the deaf hear and the mute speak!"* (Mk 7:31-37)

Jesus Heals a Blind man

He came to Bethsaida. They brought a blind man to him and begged him to touch him. He took hold of the blind man by the hand and brought him out of the village. When he had spat on his eyes, and laid his hands on him, he asked him if he saw anything.

He looked up, and said, "I see men, but I see them like walking trees."

Then again, he laid his hands on his eyes. He looked intently and was restored, and saw everyone clearly. He sent him away to his house, saying, "Don't enter into the village, nor tell anyone in the village." (Mk 8:22-26)

The First Prophecy of the Passion

For the first time, Jesus spoke to his apostles about how he was to be handed over to the elders and chief priests to be killed, but would rise again on the third day. Peter was not happy about what he was hearing and showed his disapproval to Jesus. But Jesus ... *rebuked Peter, and said, "Get behind me, Satan! For you have in mind not the things of God, but the things of men."* (Mk 8:33)

Later Jesus spoke about what a life of following him would look like. *"Whoever wants to come after me, let him deny himself, and take up his cross, and follow me. For whoever wants to save his life will lose it; and whoever will lose his life for my sake and the sake of the Good News will save it. For what does it profit a man to gain the whole world and forfeit his life? For what will a man give in exchange for his life? For whoever will be ashamed of me and of my words in this adulterous and sinful generation, the Son of Man also will be ashamed of him when he comes in his Father's glory with the holy angels."*

He said to them, *"Most certainly I tell you, there are some standing here who will in no way taste death until they see God's Kingdom come with power."* (Mk 8:34 -9:1)

The Transfiguration

Six days later, Jesus took Peter, James, and John up on a mountain where they could be alone. There Jesus was transfigured. *His clothing became glistening, exceedingly white, like snow, such as no launderer on earth can whiten them. Elijah and Moses appeared to them, and they were talking with Jesus.*

Peter said, *"Rabbi, it is good for us to be here. Let us make three tents: one for you, one for Moses, and one for Elijah." For he didn't know what to say, for they were terrified.*

A cloud came, overshadowing them, and a voice came out of the cloud, "This is my beloved Son. Listen to him."

Suddenly looking around, they saw no one with them any more, except Jesus only. (Mk 9:3-8)

The Second Prophecy of the Passion

For a second time, Jesus took the twelve aside to speak to them, *"The Son of Man is being handed over to the hands of men, and they will kill him; and when he is killed, on the third day he will rise again."*

But they didn't understand the saying and were afraid to ask him. (Mk 9:31-32)

On Leading Others Astray

Jesus warned against anyone trying to mislead others, especially children, *"It would be better for him if he were thrown into the sea with a millstone hung around his neck."* (Mk 9:42)

He also instructed those listening as to what was important in life. *"If your hand causes you to stumble, cut it off. It is better for you to enter into life maimed, rather than having your two hands and go into Hell, into the unquenchable fire. If your foot causes you to stumble, cut it off. It is better for you to enter into life lame, rather than having your two feet and be cast into Hell, into the fire that will never be quenched. If your eye causes you to stumble, pluck it out. It is better for you to enter into God's Kingdom with one eye, rather than having two eyes and be cast into the fire of Hell. For everyone will be salted with fire, and every sacrifice will be seasoned with salt. Salt is good, but if the salt has lost its saltiness, with what will you season it? Have salt in yourselves, and be at peace with one another."* (Mk 9:43-50)

The Young Rich Man

As Jesus was moving on, a man rushed up to him asking, *"Good Teacher, what shall I do that I may inherit eternal life?"*

Jesus said to him, *"Why do you call me good? No one is good except one - God. You know the commandments: Do not murder, do not commit adultery, do not steal, do not give false testimony, do not defraud, honour your father and mother."*[198]

He said to him, *"Teacher, I have observed all these things from my youth."*

---

[198] Ex 20:12-16

Jesus (looked at him lovingly), and said, "One thing you lack. Go, sell whatever you have and give to the poor, and you will have treasure in heaven; and come, follow me, taking up the cross."

But his face fell at that saying, and he went away sorrowful, for he was one who had great possessions. (Mk 10:17-22)

The Danger of Riches

Jesus looked around and said to his disciples, "How difficult it is for those who have riches to enter into God's Kingdom!"

The disciples were amazed at his words. But Jesus answered again, "Children, how hard it is for those who trust in riches to enter into God's Kingdom! It is easier for a camel to go through a needle's eye than for a rich man to enter into God's Kingdom."

They were exceedingly astonished, saying to him, "Then who can be saved?"

Jesus, looking at them, said, "With men it is impossible, but not with God, for all things are possible with God." (Mk 10:23-27)

Peter said, "(But) we have left all and have followed you."

Jesus said, "Most certainly I tell you, there is no one who has left house, or brothers, or sisters, or father, or mother, or wife, or children, or land, for my sake, and for the sake of the Good News, (who will not) *receive one hundred times more now in this time: houses, brothers, sisters, mothers, children, and land, with persecutions; and in the age to come eternal life. But many who are first will be last, and the last first."* (Mk 10:28-31)

The Third Prophecy of the Passion

While on their way to Jerusalem, and for a third time, Jesus separated his apostles from the crowds and explained to them what would happen to him in Jerusalem. *"Behold, we are going up to Jerusalem. The Son of Man will be delivered to the chief priests and the scribes. They will condemn him to death, and will deliver him to the Gentiles. They will mock him,*

spit on him, scourge him, and kill him. On the third day he will rise again."
(Mk 10:33-34)

Jesus Enters Jerusalem

Approaching the Jewish town of Bethany, near Jerusalem, Jesus called two of his apostles telling them, *"Go off to the village facing you, and as soon as you enter it you will find a tethered colt that no one has yet ridden. Untie it and bring it here. If anyone says to you, 'What are you doing?' say, 'The Master needs it and will send it back here directly'"* They went off and found a colt tethered near a door in the open street. As they untied it, some men standing there said, "What are you s doing, untying that colt?" They gave the answer Jesus had told them, and the men let them go. (Mk 11:1-3*)

They brought the young donkey to Jesus and threw their garments on it, and Jesus sat on it. Many spread their garments on the way, and others were cutting down branches from the trees and spreading them on the road. Those who went in front and those who followed cried out, "Hosanna! Blessed is he who comes in the name of the Lord! Blessed is the kingdom of our father David that is coming in the name of the Lord! Hosanna in the highest!" (Mk 11:7-10)

Jesus and the Chief Priests, Scribes and Pharisees

The following day, while teaching within the city of Jerusalem, some chief priests and scribes came to question Jesus. *"By what authority do you do these things? Or who gave you this authority to do these things?"*

Jesus said to them, *"I will ask you one question. Answer me, and I will tell you by what authority I do these things. The baptism of John - was it from heaven, or from men? Answer me."*

They reasoned with themselves, saying, "If we should say, 'From heaven;' he will say, 'Why then did you not believe him?' But dare we say, 'From men?'" - they feared the people, for all held John to really be a prophet. They answered Jesus, "We don't know."

*Jesus said to them, "Neither will I tell you by what authority I do these things." *(Mk 11:28-33)

Jesus then said, *"A man planted a vineyard, put a hedge around it, dug a pit for the wine press, built a tower, rented it out to a farmer, and went into another country. When it was time, he sent a servant to the farmer to get from the farmer his share of the fruit of the vineyard. They took him, beat him, and sent him away empty. Again, he sent another servant to them; and they threw stones at him, wounded him in the head, and sent him away shamefully treated. Again he sent another, and they killed him, and many others, beating some, and killing some. Therefore, still having one, his beloved son, he sent him last to them, saying, 'They will respect my son.' But those farmers said among themselves, 'This is the heir. Come, let's kill him, and the inheritance will be ours.' They took him, killed him, and cast him out of the vineyard. What therefore will the lord of the vineyard do? He will come and destroy the farmers, and will give the vineyard to others. Haven't you even read this Scripture:*

> *'The stone which the builders rejected*
> *was made the head of the cornerstone.*
> *This was from the Lord.*
> *It is marvellous in our eyes?'"*[199] (Mk 12:1-11)

The chief priests, scribes, and elders were infuriated by what Jesus was saying and doing, as it undermined them and their authority. They wanted to bring him to justice, but were afraid of the growing crowds who followed him everywhere, and instead they walked away.

Jesus is Questioned by the Pharisees

Still not content, the chief priests sent certain Pharisees to Jesus with more questions - optimistic of trapping him. *"Teacher, we know that you*

---
[199] Ps 118:22-23

are honest, and don't defer to anyone; for you aren't partial to anyone, but truly teach the way of God. Is it lawful to pay taxes to Caesar, or not? Shall we give, or shall we not give?"

But he, knowing their hypocrisy, said to them, "Why do you test me? Bring me a denarius, that I may see it."

They brought it.

He said to them, "Whose is this image and inscription?"

They said to him, "Caesar's."

Jesus answered them, "Render to Caesar the things that are Caesar's, and to God the things that are God's."

They marvelled greatly at him. (Mk 12:14-17)

Jesus is Questioned by the Sadducees

Then it was the Sadducees turn to try and ambush Jesus. *"Teacher, Moses wrote to us, 'If a man's brother dies and leaves a wife behind him, and leaves no children, that his brother should take his wife and raise up offspring for his brother.' There were seven brothers. The first took a wife, and dying left no offspring. The second took her, and died, leaving no children behind him. The third likewise; and the seven took her and left no children. Last of all the woman also died. In the resurrection, when they rise, whose wife will she be of them? For the seven had her as a wife."*

Jesus answered them, "Isn't this because you are mistaken, not knowing the Scriptures nor the power of God? For when they will rise from the dead, they neither marry nor are given in marriage, but are like angels in heaven. But about the dead, that they are raised, haven't you read in the book of Moses about the Bush, how God spoke to him, saying, 'I am the God of Abraham, the God of Isaac, and the God of Jacob?' He is not the God of the dead, but of the living. You are therefore badly mistaken." (Mk 12:19-27)

The Widow's Offering

One day Jesus was sitting by the treasury building watching the people leaving offerings. *Many who were rich cast in much. A poor widow came and she cast in two small coins, equal to a penny. He called his disciples to himself and said to them, "Most certainly I tell you, this poor widow gave more than all those who are giving into the treasury, for they all gave out of their abundance, but she, out of her poverty, gave all that she had to live on."* (Mk 12:41-44)

Jesus Talks About Life After he is Gone

Jesus gave his apostles this warning, *"Watch yourselves, for they will deliver you up to councils. You will be beaten in synagogues. You will stand before rulers and kings for my sake, for a testimony to them. The Good News must first be preached to all the nations. When they lead you away and deliver you up, don't be anxious beforehand or premeditate what you will say, but say whatever will be given you in that hour. For it is not you who speak, but the Holy Spirit.*

"Brother will deliver up brother to death, and the father his child. Children will rise up against parents and cause them to be put to death. You will be hated by all men for my name's sake, but he who endures to the end will be saved." (Mk 13:9-13)

No One Knows the Day

Jesus cautions to be ready for the coming of man, he warns that there will be many false prophets and others who try and *deceive the elect.* (Mk 13:23)

He says they will know the time because *"the sun will be darkened, the moon will not give its light, the stars will be falling from the sky, and the powers that are in the heavens will be shaken. Then they will see the Son of Man coming in clouds with great power and glory. Then he will send out his angels, and will gather together his chosen ones from the four winds, from the ends of the earth to the ends of the sky."* (Mk 13:24-27)

"But of that day or that hour no one knows – not even the angels in heaven, nor the Son, but only the Father. Watch, keep alert, and pray; for you don't know when the time is." (Mk 13:32)

It was coming up for the Feast of Passover, and many people were in Jerusalem to celebrate. The chief priests and scribes remained determined to stop Jesus and knew they needed to do it before the celebrations for Passover started, for they feared an uprising from his followers. Their cause was advanced when Judas Iscariot approached them with an offer to hand Jesus over.

The Last Supper

On the first day of Unleavened Bread, Jesus sent two of his disciples ahead to plan for their Passover meal. Once they were all seated around a table Jesus said, *"Most certainly I tell you, one of you will betray me – he who eats with me."*

They began to be sorrowful, and to ask him one by one, "Surely not I?" And another said, "Surely not I?"

He answered them, "It is one of the twelve, (the one) *who dips with me in the dish. For the Son of Man goes* (to his fate) *as it is written about him, but woe to that man by whom the Son of Man is betrayed! It would be better for that man if he had not been born."*

As they were eating, Jesus took bread, and when he had blessed it, he broke it and gave to them, and said, "Take, eat. This is my body."

He took the cup, and when he had given thanks, he gave it to them. They all drank of it. He said to them, "This is my blood of the new covenant, which is poured out for many. Most certainly I tell you, I will no more drink of the fruit of the vine until that day when I drink it anew in God's Kingdom." (Mk 14:18-25)

The Agony in the Garden

When the meal was over and the Psalms were sung, Jesus and his apostles retired into the hills of the Mount of Olives where Jesus said, *"All of you will be made to stumble because of me tonight, for it is written, 'I will strike the shepherd, and the sheep will be scattered.'* [200] *However, after I am raised up, I will go before you into Galilee."*

But Peter said to him, "Although all will be offended, yet I will not."

Jesus said to him, "Most certainly I tell you that you today, even this night, before the rooster crows twice, you will deny me three times."

But he spoke all the more, "If I must die with you, I will not deny you." They all said the same thing. (Mk 14:27-31)

Moving a little further on, they stopped again in a place called Gethsemane. *He said to his disciples, "Sit here while I pray." He took with him Peter, James, and John, and began to be greatly troubled and distressed. He said to them, "My soul is exceedingly sorrowful, even to death. Stay here and watch."*

He went forward a little, and fell on the ground, and prayed that if it were possible, the hour might pass away from him. He said, "Abba, Father, all things are possible to you. Please remove this cup from me. However, not what I desire, but what you desire."

He came and found them sleeping, and said to Peter, "Are you sleeping? Couldn't you watch one hour? Watch and pray, that you may not enter into temptation. The spirit indeed is willing, but the flesh is weak."

Again he went away and prayed, saying the same words. Again he returned and found them sleeping, for their eyes were very heavy... He came the third time and said to them, "Sleep on now, and take your rest. It is enough. The hour has come. Behold, the Son of Man is betrayed into the hands of sinners. Arise! Let's get going. Behold, he who betrays me is at hand." (Mk 14:32-42)

---

[200] Zec 13:7

Jesus is Arrested

While Jesus was still in the garden, Judas approached him with the men sent by the chief priests and scribes to arrest Jesus. Judas had previously told the guards that the man he kisses will be Jesus. As soon as he kissed Jesus, the guards sprang into action, causing a commotion. Jesus spoke up, *"Have you come out, as against a robber, with swords and clubs to seize me? I was daily with you in the temple teaching, and you didn't arrest me. But this is so that the Scriptures might be fulfilled."* (Mk 14:48-49)

No sooner had he finished speaking when his apostles ran away.

Jesus was taken to appear before the chief priests and the Sanhedrin, who were busy plotting a way to have him killed. They even resorted to using false witnesses, as the truth couldn't condemn him. Infuriated that Jesus would not rise to any of their accusations against him, one of the chief priests came forward saying, *"Have you no answer? What is it which these testify against you?"* But he stayed quiet, and answered nothing. Again the high priest asked him, *"Are you the Christ, the Son of the Blessed?"*

Jesus said, "I am. You will see the Son of Man sitting at the right hand of Power, and coming with the clouds of the sky."

The high priest tore his clothes and said, "What further need have we of witnesses? You have heard the blasphemy! What do you think?" They all condemned him to be worthy of death. Some began to spit on him, and to cover his face, and to beat him with fists, and to tell him, "Prophesy!" The officers struck him with the palms of their hands. (Mk 14:60-65)

Peter's Denials

While Jesus was on trial inside, Peter was outside in the courtyard. Warming himself by the fire, a servant pointed at him and claimed he was a follower of Jesus. Peter vehemently denied knowing Jesus. Feeling uneasy, he moved out of the courtyard and into the forecourt just as the rooster crowed, but the servant girls followed him and accused him again. For a second time, Peter denied being a follower. Then another person in the crowd accused him. Peter was now getting irate and emphatically denied he was the man they said. At that moment the rooster crowed for a second time and Peter cried as he remembered (to his shame) the words of Jesus *"Before the rooster crows twice, you will deny me three times."* (Mk 14:72)

Jesus on Trial

First thing in the morning, the chief priests and members of the Sanhedrin took Jesus to Pilate in the hope he would pronounce the death sentence they were looking for. Pilate questioned Jesus, yet to no avail, saying nothing apart from answering one question, *"Are you the King of the Jews?"*

Jesus answered, "So you say." (Mk 15:3)

Pilate could find no cause to sentence him to death.

Sensing it was out of spite or jealousy the chief priests wanted Jesus condemned, Pilate used the tradition of releasing a prisoner back to the people during the festival time of Passover as a way out. When he offered the choice to the people though, they overwhelmingly cried out to release a prisoner named Barabbas.[201] Bemused, Pilate asked, *"What then should I do to him whom you call the King of the Jews?"*

They cried out again, "Crucify him!"

Pilate said to them, "Why, what evil has he done?"

But they cried out exceedingly, "Crucify him!"

Pilate, wishing to please the multitude, released Barabbas to them, and handed over Jesus, (to be flogged and crucified). (Mk 15:12-15)

The Crucifixion

Jesus was led away by the Roman soldiers, who inflicted their own sense of justice on him, dressing him up in a purple robe and making him a crown from thorns. They mocked him saying, "Hail, King of the Jews!"

---

[201] Who was in prison for murder.

They then led him to the place of his crucifixion. Along the way a passer-by called Simon of Cyrene was conscripted to help Jesus carry his cross.

Jesus was crucified between two robbers with the inscription 'Jesus of Nazareth, King of the Jews', written on his cross.[202]

While Jesus was on the cross, some chief priests and scribes continued their harassment of him. Saying, *"He saved others. He can't save himself. Let the Christ, the King of Israel, now come down from the cross, that we may see and believe him."* (Mk 15:31-32)

At noon a vast darkness came over the sky and stayed for three hours, then Jesus cried out, *"Eloi, Eloi, lama sabachthani?" which is, 'My God, my God, why have you forsaken me'?*[203]

Some of those who stood by, when they heard it, said, "Behold, he is calling Elijah."

One ran, and filling a sponge full of vinegar, put it on a reed and gave it to him to drink, saying, "Let him be. Let's see whether Elijah comes to take him down."

Jesus cried out with a loud voice and gave up the spirit. The veil of the temple was torn in two from the top to the bottom. When the centurion, who stood by opposite him, saw that he cried out like this and breathed his last, he said, "Truly this man was the Son of God!" (Mk 15:34-39)

As the Sabbath vigil was approaching, a member of the council, Joseph of Arimathea, received permission from Pilate to prepare the body of Jesus for burial.[204] They took him to a tomb which was cut into stone. A large stone was rolled across the opening. Mary Magdalene, Mary (the

---

[202] Traditionally we see INRI above Jesus on the cross. This is Latin 'Iesus Nazarenus Rex Iudaeorum'.

[203] Ps 22:1

[204] The Jewish Law prohibited them from doing any work or manual labour on the Sabbath.

mother of James) and Joset noted the location as they would need to return after the Sabbath was over to complete the burial ceremony.

The Resurrection

At dawn on the morning after the Sabbath, the two Marys and this time Salome went to where Jesus was buried. As they walked, they wondered if they would have the strength to roll back the stone. When they arrived, they saw that the stone had already been rolled back. *Entering the tomb, they saw a young man sitting on the right side, dressed in a white robe; and they were amazed. He said to them, "Don't be amazed. You seek Jesus, the Nazarene, who has been crucified. He has risen! He is not here. See the place where they laid him! But go, tell his disciples and Peter, 'He goes before you into Galilee. There you will see him, as he said to you.'"*

They went out and fled from the tomb, for trembling and astonishment had come on them. They said nothing to anyone; for they were afraid. (Mk 16:5-8)

When Mary Magdalene told the apostles what she had seen, they would not believe her. Two other disciples who had an encounter with Jesus out in the country would not be believed either. It wasn't until Jesus showed himself to the eleven, that they overcame their disbelief, but not before Jesus reproached them for it.

Jesus then spoke to them, *"Go into all the world and preach the Good News to the whole creation. He who believes and is baptised will be saved; but he who disbelieves will be condemned. These signs will accompany those who believe: in my name they will cast out demons; they will speak with new languages; they will take up serpents; and if they drink any deadly thing, it will in no way hurt them; they will lay hands on the sick, and they will recover."*

So then the Lord, after he had spoken to them, was received up into heaven and sat down at the right hand of God. They went out and preached everywhere; the Lord working with them and confirming the word by the signs that followed. (Mk 16:15-20)

LUKE

The Gospel of Luke is believed to have been written between 70 AD and 90 AD.[205] It is the longest of the four Gospels. Believed to have been a companion of Paul, Luke was a non-Jewish Christian, and his Gospel was written for other non-Jewish Christians.

From the opening lines of Luke, it seems he was not happy with previous attempts to document the life and times of Jesus, so he has taken it on himself to 'do it properly'.

Luke is also the author of the Acts of the Apostles.

Since many have undertaken to set in order a narrative concerning those matters which have been fulfilled among us, even as those who from the beginning were eyewitnesses and servants of the word delivered them to us, it seemed good to me also, having traced the course of all things accurately from the first, to write to you in order, most excellent Theophilus; that you might know the certainty concerning the things in which you were instructed. (Lk 1:1-4)

The Announcement of John the Baptist

In the days of King Herod of Judea, there was a priest named Zechariah, married to Elizabeth.[206] Both were devout and loyal servants of God. They could not have any children.

---

[205] 70 AD - The fall of Jerusalem. 79 AD - Mt Vesuvius erupts. 80 AD - The Colosseum is dedicated.
[206] A relative of Mary, the Mother of Jesus.

One day while Zechariah was performing his priestly duties in the temple, an angel appeared to him saying, *"Don't be afraid, Zechariah, because your request has been heard. Your wife, Elizabeth, will bear you a son, and you shall call him John … and he will be great in the sight of the Lord, … He will be filled with the Holy Spirit, even from his mother's womb. He will turn many of the children of Israel to the Lord their God. He will go before him in the spirit and power of Elijah, 'to turn the hearts of the fathers to the children',*[207] *and the disobedient to the wisdom of the just; to prepare a people prepared for the Lord."* (Lk 1:13-17)

Zechariah doubted the angel and explained he and Elizabeth were too old to have children.[208] The angel replied, *"I am Gabriel, who stands in the presence of God. I was sent to speak to you and to bring you this good news. Behold, you will be silent and not able to speak until the day that these things will happen, because you didn't believe my words, which will be fulfilled in their proper time."* (Lk 1:19-20)

After the angel departed, Zechariah was left mute and needed to make signs to be understood. When he returned home, it was as the angel had prophesied, and Elizabeth fell pregnant.

The Annunciation and Visitation

When Elizabeth was six months pregnant, God again sent his angel Gabriel, this time to a woman called Mary from the town of Nazareth in Galilee. Mary, a virgin, was engaged to Joseph from the House of David. The angel said to Mary, *"Rejoice, you highly favoured one! The Lord is with you. Blessed are you among women!"* (Lk 1:28)

The angel continued, *"Don't be afraid, Mary, for you have found favour with God. Behold, you will conceive in your womb and give birth to a son, and you shall name him Jesus. He will be great and will be called the Son of the Most High. The Lord God will give him the throne of his ancestor David,*

---

[207] Mal 4:6
[208] This mirrors the dialogue Abram and Sarai had with an angel in Genesis.

and he will reign over the House of Jacob forever. There will be no end to his Kingdom." (Lk 1:30-33)

Mary was quick to question this, for she was still a virgin. The angel told her, *"The Holy Spirit will come on you, and the power of the Most High will overshadow you. Therefore, also the holy one who is born from you will be called the Son of God. Behold, Elizabeth, your relative also has conceived a son in her old age; and this is the sixth month with her who was called barren. For nothing spoken by God is impossible."*

Mary said, *"Behold, I am the servant of the Lord; let it be done to me according to your word."* (Lk 1:35-38)

During her pregnancy, Mary set out to visit her relative Elizabeth. When Elizabeth heard Mary's voice she said, *"Blessed are you among women, and blessed is the fruit of your womb! Why am I so favoured, that the mother of my Lord should come to me? For behold, when the voice of your greeting came into my ears, the baby leaped in my womb for joy! Blessed is she who believed, for there will be a fulfilment of the things which have been spoken to her from the Lord!"* (Lk 1:42-45)

Mary responded,

> *"My soul magnifies the Lord.*
> *My spirit has rejoiced in God my Saviour,*
> *for he has looked at the humble state of his servant.*
> *For behold, from now on, all generations will call*
> *me blessed.*
> *For he who is mighty has done great things for me.*
> *Holy is his name.*
> *His mercy is for generations and generations on those*
> *who fear him.*
> *He has shown strength with his arm.*
> *He has scattered the proud in the imagination of*
> *their hearts.*
> *He has put down princes from their thrones,*

> *and has exalted the lowly.*
> *He has filled the hungry with good things.*
> *He has sent the rich away empty.*
> *He has given help to Israel, his servant,*
> *that he might remember mercy,*
> *as he spoke to our fathers,*
> *to Abraham and his offspring forever."* (Lk 1:46-55)

The Birth of John the Baptist

After Elizabeth had given birth to her son, it became time to prepare (according to the law) to have him circumcised and named. It was assumed that the baby would be named Zechariah, after the father, but Elizabeth said, "No, his name will be John." This caught those around them off guard, as this was never done. Thinking maybe Elizabeth was mistaken, they went to ask Zechariah. As Zechariah was still mute, he wrote on a tablet that the baby would indeed be called John. At once, Zechariah could again speak, and filled with the Holy Spirit he proclaimed,

> *"Blessed be the Lord, the God of Israel,*
> *for he has visited and redeemed his people;*
> *and has raised up a horn of salvation for us*
> *in the house of his servant David*
> *(as he spoke by the mouth of his holy prophets*
> *who have been from of old),*
> *salvation from our enemies*
> *and from the hand of all who hate us;*
> *to show mercy towards our fathers,*
> *to remember his holy covenant,*
> *the oath which he swore to Abraham our father,*
> *to grant to us that we,*
> *being delivered out of the hand of our enemies,*

should serve him without fear,
in holiness and righteousness before him
all the days of our life.
And you, child, will be called a prophet of the Most High;
for you will go before the face of the Lord
to prepare his ways,
to give knowledge of salvation to his people
by the remission of their sins,
because of the tender mercy of our God,
by which the dawn from on high will visit us,
to shine on those who sit in darkness
and the shadow of death;
to guide our feet into the way of peace." (Lk 1:68-79)

The Birth of Jesus

During the reign of Caesar Augustus,[209] a census of all people was ordered. This meant everyone had to return to their ancestoral town to be registered and counted. This required Joseph and the pregnant Mary to go to Bethlehem, the town of David.

While in Bethlehem Mary gave birth, and because there were so many people in town, the only place they could find shelter was in a stable. There *she wrapped* (Jesus) *in bands of cloth and laid him in a feeding trough because there was no room for them in the inn.* (Lk 2:7)

At the same time there were shepherds in the countryside calmly tending to their flocks, when to their amazement an angel appeared to them and said, *"Don't be afraid, for behold, I bring you good news of great joy which will be to all the people. For there is born to you today, in David's City, a Saviour, who is Christ the Lord. This is the sign to you: you will find a baby wrapped in strips of cloth, lying in a feeding trough."* Suddenly, there was with the angel a multitude of the heavenly army praising God and saying,

---

[209] 27 BC - 14 AD

> *"Glory to God in the highest,*
> *on earth peace, good will toward men."* (Lk 2:10-14)

As soon as the angel left, they set out for Bethlehem to see for themselves the things the angel had said. When they arrived, they *found both Mary and Joseph, and the baby was lying in the feeding trough. When they saw it, they announced widely the saying which was spoken to them about this child. All who heard it wondered at the things which were spoken to them by the shepherds. But Mary kept all these sayings, pondering them in her heart. The shepherds returned, glorifying and praising God for all the things that they had heard and seen, just as it was told them.* (Lk 2:15-20)

The Circumcision and Presentation of Jesus

The time came when Jesus was to be taken to the Temple in Jerusalem,[210] as the Law required.[211] In the temple at the time was a man called Simeon, who said to Mary, *"Behold, this child is appointed for the falling and the rising of many in Israel, and for a sign which is spoken against. Yes, a sword will pierce through your own soul, that the thoughts of many hearts may be revealed."* (Lk 2:34-35)

When all that was needed to be done was over, the family returned to Nazareth in Galilee where Jesus grew and *became strong in spirit, being filled with wisdom, and the grace of God was upon him.* (Lk 2:40)

At the age of twelve, Jesus returned to Jerusalem with Joseph and Mary to celebrate the feast of Passover (a journey they undertook every year). This time, however, as they prepared to return home, Jesus was missing. It took three days before they could find him. He was found in the Temple, listening to and questioning the learned men there. All who heard him were astonished. Mary, who had suffered over the three days

---

[210] Aged 40 days.
[211] Lv 12:2-4

looking for him, asked Jesus why he would do such a thing. He answered, *"Why were you looking for me? Didn't you know that I must be in my Father's house?"* *They didn't understand the saying which he spoke to them.* (Lk 2:49)

The Ministry of John the Baptist

In the fifteenth year of Tiberius Caesar's reign,[212] when Pontius Pilate was Governor of Judea and Herod was tetrarch of Galilee,[213] the word of God came to John the Baptist, son of Zechariah, to begin his ministry of baptism for repentance of sins, as prophesied by Isaiah.

> *The voice of one crying in the wilderness,*
> *"Make ready the way of the Lord.*
> *Make his paths straight.*
> *Every valley will be filled.*
> *Every mountain and hill will be brought low.*
> *The crooked will become straight,*
> *and the rough ways smooth.*
> *All flesh will see God's salvation."*[214] (Lk 3:4-6)

During his ministry, masses came to him for baptism, and they asked him, "What must we do?"

He answered them, "He who has two coats, let him give to him who has none. He who has food, let him do likewise."

Tax collectors also came to be baptised, and they said to him, "Teacher, what must we do?"

He said to them, "Collect no more than that which is appointed to you."

Soldiers also asked him, saying, "What about us? What must we do?"

---

[212] Circa 29 AD.
[213] Similar to a mayor.
[214] Is 40:3-5

*He said to them, "Extort from no one by violence, neither accuse anyone wrongfully. Be content with your wages." * (Lk 3:11-14)

John was so revered among the people that they even thought he might be the Christ, but John quickly set them straight. *"I indeed baptise you with water, but he comes who is mightier than I, the strap of whose sandals I am not worthy to loosen. He will baptise you in the Holy Spirit and fire."* (Lk 3:16)

One day while John was by the river, Jesus came to him to be baptised, and *the Holy Spirit descended in a bodily form like a dove on him; and a voice came out of the sky, saying, "You are my beloved Son. In you I am well pleased."* (Lk 3:22)

Leaving the Jordan, where he was baptised, Jesus went into the desert where he was tempted by the devil for forty days.

Jesus Begins his Ministry

Returning to Nazareth, Jesus went into the synagogue for the Sabbath. He was handed a scroll containing the words of the prophet Isaiah. Jesus found a section and read it aloud.

> *"The Spirit of the Lord is on me,*
> *because he has anointed me to preach good news to the poor.*
> *He has sent me to heal the broken hearted,*
> *to proclaim release to the captives,*
> *recovering of sight to the blind,*
> *to deliver those who are crushed,*
> *and to proclaim the acceptable year of the Lord."*[215]
> (Lk 4:18-19)

---

[215] Is 61:1-2

When he finished, he added that the text he just read was being fulfilled through him at that very moment. Those in the synagogue were equally astounded and enraged and quickly forced him out of town.

The First Apostles are Called

While by the Lake of Gennesaret, as he was being pressed by the crowds who were eager to hear him speak, Jesus got into the boat of a local fisherman, Simon, and asked him to set out a small distance from the shore. From there, Jesus spoke to the crowds.

Later, he asked Simon to go out further into the lake and recast his nets. Simon was reluctant, as he had already been out for a good part of the day with no luck - but he did it anyway. To Simon's astonishment, when the nets were drawn back in, they were bursting with fish, so much so that he needed to call for help from other fishermen to secure the catch. *When Simon Peter saw this he fell at the knees of Jesus saying, "Leave me, Lord; I am a sinful man." For he and all his companions were completely overcome by the catch they had made; so also were James and John, sons of Zebedee, who were Simon's partners. But Jesus said to Simon, "Do not be afraid; from now on it is men you will catch." Then, bringing their boats back to land, they left everything and followed him.* (Lk 5:8-11*)

Jesus Cures on the Sabbath

The scribes and Pharisees were suspicious and worried about Jesus' teachings and stalked him in the hope to discredit him. One Sabbath, while Jesus was in the synagogue, a man with a withered right hand approached him to be healed. The scribes and Pharisees watched on intently, sensing they could catch him by curing on the Sabbath.[216] *Jesus knew their thoughts; and he said to the man with the withered hand, "Rise up and stand in the middle." He arose and stood. Then Jesus said to them, "I*

---

[216] Contravening their 'Laws'.

will ask you something: Is it lawful on the Sabbath to do good, or to do harm? To save a life, or to kill?" He looked around at them all, and said to the man, "Stretch out your hand." He did, and his hand was restored as sound as the other. But they were filled with rage and talked with one another about what they might do to Jesus. (Lk 6:8-11)

The Twelve Apostles

It was about this time that Jesus, after a night spent in prayer, chose his apostles. Simon, (whom he renamed Peter), his brother Andrew, James, John, Philip, Bartholomew, Levi, who became Matthew, Thomas, James son of Alphaeus, Simon called the zealot, Judas son of James, and Judas Iscariot who was to betray Jesus.

The Beatitudes

Returning to the crowds, Jesus addressed his apostles and the crowds.

> *"Blessed are you who are poor, for God's Kingdom is yours.*
> *Blessed are you who hunger now, for you will be filled.*
> *Blessed are you who weep now, for you will laugh.*
>
> *"Blessed are you when men hate you,*
> *and when they exclude and mock you,*
> *and throw out your name as evil, for the Son of Man's sake.*
> *Rejoice in that day and leap for joy,*
> *for behold, your reward is great in heaven,*
> *for their fathers did the same thing to the prophets.*
>
> *"But woe to you who are rich!*
> *For you have received your consolation.*
> *Woe to you, you who are full now, for you will be hungry.*
> *Woe to you who laugh now, for you will mourn and weep.*

> *Woe, when men speak well of you,*
> *for their fathers did the same thing to the false prophets."*
> (Lk 6:20-26)

Jesus continued,

> *"Be merciful, even as your Father is also merciful.*
> *Don't judge, and you won't be judged.*
> *Don't condemn, and you won't be condemned.*
> *Set free, and you will be set free.*

"Give, and it will be given to you: good measure, pressed down, shaken together, and running over, will be given to you. For with the same measure you measure it will be measured back to you." (Lk 6:36-38)

He spoke a parable to them. "Can the blind guide the blind? Won't they both fall into a pit? A disciple is not above his teacher, but everyone when he is fully trained will be like his teacher. Why do you see the speck of chaff that is in your brother's eye, but don't consider the beam that is in your own eye? Or how can you tell your brother, 'Brother, let me remove the speck of chaff that is in your eye,' when you yourself don't see the beam that is in your own eye? You hypocrite! First remove the beam from your own eye, and then you can see clearly to remove the speck of chaff that is in your brother's eye." (Lk 6:39-42)

Jesus Raises a Widow's Son

Soon afterwards, while in the town of the Jewish town of Nain, Jesus saw a funeral procession - the only son of a widow. Jesus felt pity for her saying. *"Don't cry."* He came near and touched the coffin, and the bearers stood still. He said, "Young man, I tell you, arise!" He who was dead sat up and began to speak. Then he gave him to his mother.

Fear took hold of all, and they glorified God, saying, "A great prophet has arisen among us!" and, "God has visited his people!" This report went *out concerning him in the whole of Judah and in all the surrounding region.* (Lk 7:13-17)

Jesus' Testimony

Eventually, the news of Jesus' ministry reached John the Baptist, who sent one of his followers to Jesus with the question, "Are you the one who is to come, or do we need to wait for another?" Jesus answered, *"Go and tell John the things which you have seen and heard: that the blind receive their sight, the lame walk, the lepers are cleansed, the deaf hear, the dead are raised up, and the poor have good news preached to them. Blessed is he who finds no occasion for stumbling in me."* (Lk 7:22-23)

The Penitent Woman

One night while at dinner, a woman came to Jesus and began crying tears onto his feet and anointing them with oil. Also at the table was a Pharisee who knew the woman. The Pharisee thought to himself that if Jesus was a real prophet, he would know of the woman's poor reputation and not let her come near him. Jesus knew what the Pharisee was thinking, so turned to Simon and said, *"A certain lender had two debtors. The one owed five hundred denarii, and the other fifty. When they couldn't pay, he forgave them both. Which of them therefore will love him most?"*

Simon answered, *"He, I suppose, to whom he forgave the most."*

He said to him, *"You have judged correctly."* Turning to the woman, he said to Simon, *"Do you see this woman? I entered into your house, and you gave me no water for my feet, but she has wet my feet with her tears, and wiped them with the hair of her head. You gave me no kiss, but she, since the time I came in, has not ceased to kiss my feet. You didn't anoint my head with oil, but she has anointed my feet with ointment. Therefore, I tell you, her sins, which are many, are forgiven, for she loved much. But one to whom little is forgiven, loves little."* He said to her, *"Your sins are forgiven."*

Those who sat at the table with him began to say to themselves, "Who is this who even forgives sins?"

He said to the woman, "Your faith has saved you. Go in peace." (Lk 7:41-50)

The Mission of the Apostles

Jesus called his apostles to him and *gave them power and authority over all demons, and to cure diseases. He sent them out to preach God's Kingdom and to heal the sick. He said to them, "Take nothing for your journey – no staff, nor wallet, nor bread, nor money. Don't have two tunics each. Into whatever house you enter, stay there, and depart from there. As many as don't receive you, when you depart from that city, shake off even the dust from your feet for a testimony against them."*

They departed and went throughout the villages, preaching the Good News and healing everywhere. (Lk 9:2-6)

The First Prophecy of the Passion

One day while Jesus *was praying alone, the apostles were near him, and he asked them, "Who do the multitudes say that I am?"*

They answered, "John the Baptist, but others say, 'Elijah', and others, 'that one of the old prophets has risen again.'"

He said to them, "But who do you say that I am?"

Peter answered, "The Christ of God."

But he warned them and commanded them to tell this to no one, saying, "The Son of Man must suffer many things, and be rejected by the elders, chief priests, and scribes, and be killed, and the third day be raised up." (Lk 9:18-22)

He said to all, "If anyone desires to come after me, let him deny himself, take up his cross, and follow me. For whoever desires to save his life will lose it, but whoever will lose his life for my sake will save it. For what does it profit a man if he gains the whole world, and loses or forfeits his own self? For whoever will be ashamed of me and of my words, of him will the Son of Man be ashamed when he comes in his glory, and the glory of the Father, and of the holy angels." (Lk 9:23-26)

The Transfiguration

Soon after, Jesus took Peter, James, and John up into the mountains to pray. While they were there, Jesus' appearance suddenly changed, *his face was altered, and his clothing became white and dazzling. Behold, two men were talking with him, who were Moses and Elijah, who appeared in glory and spoke of his departure, which he was about to accomplish at Jerusalem.* (Lk 9:29-31)

Peter (and the others) saw Jesus talking to Moses and Elijah. He asked Jesus if they should make three tents for them - without knowing or understanding what was going on. As Peter was speaking, a loud voice came from the clouds. *"This is my beloved Son. Listen to him!"*

When the voice came, Jesus was found alone. They were silent, and told no one in those days any of the things which they had seen. (Lk 9:35-36)

The Second Prophecy of the Passion

Everywhere Jesus went, the crowds were full of admiration for him and all his miracles. Aware of this, he spoke for the second time to his apostles about his Passion. *"Let these words sink into your ears, for the Son of Man will be delivered up into the hands of men."* But they didn't understand... *It was concealed from them, that they should not perceive it, and they were afraid to ask him about* (it). (Lk 9:44-45)

Jesus Commissions Some Disciples

In preparation of his journey to Jerusalem, Jesus sent seventy disciples out ahead of him, saying, *"The harvest is rich but the labourers are few, so ask the Lord of the harvest to send labourers to his harvest. Start off now, but remember, I am sending you out like lambs among wolves. Carry no purse, no haversack, no sandals. Salute no one on the road. Whatever house you go into, let your first words be, 'Peace to this house!' And if a man of peace lives there, your peace will go and rest on him: if not, it will come back to you. Stay in the same house, taking what food and drink they have to offer, for the labourer deserves his wages; do not move from house to house. Whenever you go into a town where they make you welcome, eat what is set before you. Cure those in it who are sick, and say, 'The Kingdom of God is very near to you.' But whenever you enter a town and they do not make you welcome, go out into the streets and say, 'We wipe off the very dust of your town that clings to our feet, and leave it with you. Yet be sure of this: the Kingdom of God is very near.'*

"Anyone who listens to you listens to me; anyone who rejects you rejects me, and those who reject me reject the one who sent me." (Lk 10:2-11*)

When the seventy returned to Jesus, they were excited with the success they had. *"Lord, even the demons are subject to us in your name!"*

He said to them, *"I saw Satan having fallen like lightning from heaven. Behold, I give you authority to tread on serpents and scorpions, and over all the power of the enemy. Nothing will in any way hurt you. Nevertheless, don't rejoice in this, that the spirits are subject to you, but rejoice that your names are written in heaven."* (Lk 10:17-20)

The Great Commandment

One day a lawyer questioned Jesus, *"Teacher, what shall I do to inherit eternal life?"*

He said to him, *"What is written in the law? How do you read it?"*

He answered, *"You shall love the Lord your God with all your heart, with all your soul, with all your strength, and with all your mind;*[217] *and your neighbour as yourself."*[218]

He said to him, *"You have answered correctly. Do this, and you will live."*

But he, desiring to justify himself, asked Jesus, *"Who is my neighbour?"*

---

[217] Dt 6:5
[218] Lv 19:18

Jesus answered, "A certain man was going down from Jerusalem to Jericho, and he fell among robbers, who both stripped him and beat him, and departed, leaving him half dead. By chance a certain priest was going down that way. When he saw him, he passed by on the other side. In the same way a Levite also, when he came to the place and saw him, passed by on the other side. But a certain Samaritan[219]*, as he travelled, came to where he was. When he saw him, he was moved with compassion, came to him, and bound up his wounds, pouring on oil and wine. He set him on his own animal, brought him to an inn, and took care of him. On the next day, when he departed, he took out two denarii, gave them to the host, and said to him, 'Take care of him. Whatever you spend beyond that, I will repay you when I return.' Now which of these three do you think seemed to be a neighbour to him who fell among the robbers?"*

He said, "He who showed mercy on him."

Then Jesus said to him, "Go and do likewise." (Lk 10:25-37)

Martha and Mary

One day while in the house of two sisters Mary and Martha,[220] Mary was sitting at the feet of Jesus when Martha, busy with serving everyone, said to Jesus, *"Lord, do you not care that my sister is leaving me to do the serving all by myself?"* But the Lord answered, *"Martha, Martha,"* he said, *"You worry and fret about so many things, and yet few are needed, indeed only one. It is Mary who has chosen the better part; it is not to be taken from her."* (Lk 10:40-42*)

---

[219] At this time the Jews and Samaritans deplored each other.
[220] The sisters of Jesus' friend Lazarus (who he later raises from the dead).

Effective Prayer

"I tell you, keep asking, and it will be given you. Keep seeking, and you will find. Keep knocking, and it will be opened to you. For everyone who asks, receives. He who seeks finds. To him who knocks it will be opened.

"Which of you fathers, if your son asks for bread, will give him a stone? Or if he asks for a fish, he won't give him a snake instead of a fish, will he? Or if he asks for an egg, he won't give him a scorpion, will he? If you then, being evil, know how to give good gifts to your children, how much more will your heavenly Father give the Holy Spirit to those who ask him?" (Lk 11:9-13)

Jesus and Satan

Another time when Jesus was casting out a devil, the people who witnessed it were wonder-struck, with some believing it was through Satan that Jesus could cast out devils. To test him, they asked for a sign from heaven. Jesus told them, *"Every kingdom divided against itself is brought to desolation. A house divided against itself falls. If Satan also is divided against himself, how will his kingdom stand? For you say that I cast out demons by Satan. But if I cast out demons by Satan, by whom do your* (experts) *cast them out? Therefore, they will be your judges. But if I by God's finger cast out demons, then God's Kingdom has come to you…*

"He who is not with me is against me. He who doesn't gather with me scatters." (Lk 11:17-23)

Courage under Persecution

Back with his apostles and the faithful crowds Jesus said, *"Beware of the yeast of the Pharisees, which is hypocrisy. There is nothing covered up that will not be revealed, nor hidden that will not be known. Therefore, whatever you have said in the darkness will be heard in the light. What you have spoken in the ear in the inner rooms will be proclaimed on the housetops.*

"I tell you, my friends, don't be afraid of those who kill the body, and after that have no more that they can do. But I will warn you whom you should fear. Fear him who after he has killed, has power to cast into Hell. Yes, I tell you, fear him.

"Aren't five sparrows sold for two coins? Not one of them is forgotten by God. (Yet) *the very hairs of your head are all counted. Therefore, don't be afraid. You are* (worth more than hundreds of) *sparrows.*

"I tell you, everyone who confesses me before men, the Son of Man will also confess before the angels of God; but he who denies me in the presence of men will be denied in the presence of God's angels. Everyone who speaks a word against the Son of Man will be forgiven, but those who blaspheme against the Holy Spirit will not be forgiven. When they bring you before the synagogues, the rulers, and the authorities, don't be anxious how or what you will answer or what you will say; for the Holy Spirit will teach you in that same hour what you must say." (Lk 12:1-12)

Trust in God Alone

A man in the crowd came forward and asked Jesus, *"Teacher, tell my brother to divide the inheritance with me."*

But he said to him, "Man, who made me a judge or an arbitrator over you?" He said to them, "Beware! Keep yourselves from covetousness, for a man's life doesn't consist of the abundance of the things which he possesses."

He spoke a parable to them, saying, "The ground of a certain rich man produced abundantly. He reasoned within himself, saying, 'What will I do, because I don't have room to store my crops?' He said, 'This is what I will do. I will pull down my barns, build bigger ones, and there I will store all my grain and my goods. I will tell my soul, "Soul, you have many goods laid up for many years. Take your ease, eat, drink, and be merry."'

"But God said to him, 'You foolish one, tonight your soul is required of you. The things which you have prepared - whose will they be?' So is he who lays up treasure for himself, and is not rich toward God." (Lk 12:13-21)

Entering Through the Narrow Door

Continuing his journey towards Jerusalem, someone came to Jesus with the question, *"Lord, are they few who are saved?"*

He said to them, *"Strive to enter in by the narrow door, for many will seek to enter in and will not be able. When once the master of the house has risen up and has shut the door, and you begin to stand outside and to knock at the door, saying, 'Lord, Lord, open to us!' then he will answer and tell you, 'I don't know you or where you come from.' Then you will begin to say, 'We ate and drank in your presence, and you taught in our streets.' He will say, 'I tell you, I don't know where you come from. Depart from me, all you workers of iniquity.' There will be weeping and gnashing of teeth when you see Abraham, Isaac, Jacob, and all the prophets in God's Kingdom, and yourselves being thrown outside. They will come from the East, West, North, and South, and will sit down in God's Kingdom. Behold, there are some who are last who will be first, and there are some who are first who will be last."* (Lk 13:23-30)

Parable of Humility

One night while having dinner with a leading Pharisee Jesus *spoke a parable to those who were invited, when he noticed how they chose the best seats, and said to them, "When you are invited by anyone to a wedding feast, don't sit in the best seat, since perhaps someone more honourable than you might be invited by him, and he who invited both of you would come and tell you, 'Make room for this person.' Then you would begin, with shame, to take the lowest place. But when you are invited, go and sit in the lowest place, so that when he who invited you comes, he may tell you, 'Friend, move up higher.' Then you will be honoured in the presence of all who sit at the table with you. For everyone who exalts himself will be humbled, and whoever humbles himself will be exalted."* (Lk 14:7-11)

Bearing your Cross

Soon after, Jesus spoke to the crowds that accompanied him everywhere. *"If anyone comes to me, and doesn't disregard his own father, mother, wife, children, brothers, and sisters, yes, and his own life also, he can't be my disciple. Whoever doesn't bear his own cross and come after me, can't be my disciple."* (Lk 14:26-27)

Among the crowds were Pharisees and scribes who were always undermining Jesus by saying, "This man associates with sinners." So, Jesus taught them many more parables.

The Parable of the Lost Sheep

"Which of you men, if you had one hundred sheep and lost one of them, wouldn't leave the ninety-nine in the wilderness and go after the one that was lost, until he found it? When he has found it, he carries it on his shoulders, rejoicing. When he comes home, he calls together his friends and his neighbours, saying to them, 'Rejoice with me, for I have found my sheep which was lost!' I tell you that even so there will be more joy in heaven over one sinner who repents, than over ninety-nine righteous people who need no repentance." (Lk 15:4-7)

The Parable of the Prodigal Son

He also said, *"A certain man had two sons. The younger of them said to his father, 'Father, give me my share of your property.' So he divided his livelihood between them. Not many days after, the younger son gathered all of this together and travelled into a far country. There he wasted his property with riotous living. When he had spent all of it, there arose a severe famine in that country, and he began to be in need. He went and joined himself to one of the citizens of that country, and he sent him into his fields to feed pigs. He wanted to fill his belly with the pods that the pigs ate, but no one gave him any. But when he came to himself, he said, 'How many hired servants of my father's have bread enough to spare, and I'm dying with hunger? I will get up and go to my father, and will tell him, "Father, I have sinned against heaven and in your sight. I am no more worthy to be called your son. Make me as one of your hired servants."'*

"He arose and came to his father. But while he was still far off, his father saw him and was moved with compassion, and ran.., and kissed him. The son said to him, 'Father, I have sinned against heaven and in your sight. I am no longer worthy to be called your son.'

"But the father said to his servants, 'Bring out the best robe and put it on him. Put a ring on his hand and sandals on his feet. Bring the fattened calf, kill it, and let's eat and celebrate; for this, my son, was dead and is alive again. He was lost and is found.' Then they began to celebrate.

"Now his elder son was in the field. As he came near to the house, he heard music and dancing. He called one of the servants to him and asked what was going on. He said to him, 'Your brother has come, and your father has killed the fattened calf, because he has received him back safe and healthy.' But he was angry and would not go in. Therefore, his father came out and begged him. But he answered his father, 'Behold, these many years I have served you, and I never disobeyed a commandment of yours, but you never gave me a goat, that I might celebrate with my friends. But when this your son came, who has devoured your living with prostitutes, you killed the fattened calf for him.'

"He said to him, 'Son, you are always with me, and all that is mine is yours. But it was appropriate to celebrate and be glad, for this, your brother, was dead, and is alive again. He was lost, and is found.'" (Lk 15:11-32)

The Rich Man and Lazarus

Turning to his disciples, Jesus said, *"Now there was a certain rich man, and he was clothed in purple and fine linen, living in luxury every day. A certain beggar, named Lazarus, was taken to his gate, full of sores, and desiring to be fed with the crumbs that fell from the rich man's table. Yes, even the dogs came and licked his sores. The beggar died, and he was carried away by the angels to Abraham's bosom. The rich man also died and was buried. In Hell, he lifted up his eyes, being in torment, and saw Abraham far off, and Lazarus at his bosom. He cried and said, 'Father Abraham, have mercy on me, and send Lazarus, that he may dip the tip of his finger in water and cool my tongue! For I am in anguish in this flame.'*

"But Abraham said, 'Son, remember that you, in your lifetime, received your good things, and Lazarus, in the same way, bad things. But here he is now comforted and you are in anguish. Besides all this, between us and you there is a great gulf fixed, that those who want to pass from here to you are not able, and that no one may cross over from there to us.'

"He said, 'I ask you therefore, father, that you would send him to my Father's house – for I have five brothers – that he may testify to them, so they won't also come into this place of torment.'

"But Abraham said to him, 'They have Moses and the prophets. Let them listen to them.'

"He said, 'No, father Abraham, but if one goes to them from the dead, they will repent.'

"He said to him, 'If they don't listen to Moses and the prophets, neither will they be persuaded if one rises from the dead.'" (Lk 16:19-31)

The Coming of the Kingdom of God

Being asked by the Pharisees when God's Kingdom would come, he answered them, "God's Kingdom doesn't come with observation; neither will they say, 'Look, here!' or, 'Look, there!' for behold, God's Kingdom is within you." (Lk 17:20-21)

"Don't go away or follow after them, for as the lightning, when it flashes out of one part under the sky, shines to another part under the sky, so will the Son of Man be in his day. But first, he must suffer many things and be rejected by this generation. As it was in the days of Noah, even so it will also be in the days of the Son of Man. They ate, they drank, they married, and they were given in marriage until the day that Noah entered into the ship, and the flood came and destroyed them all." (Lk 17:23–27)

The Need to Pray Continually

He also spoke a parable to them that they must always pray and not give up, saying, "There was a judge in a certain city who didn't fear God and didn't respect man. A widow was in that city, and she often came to him, saying, 'Defend me from my adversary!' He wouldn't for a while; but afterward he said to himself, 'Though I neither fear God nor respect man, yet because this widow bothers me, I will defend her, or else she will wear me out by her continual coming.'"

The Lord said, "Listen to what the unrighteous judge says. Won't God avenge his chosen ones who are crying out to him day and night, and yet he exercises patience with them? I tell you that he will avenge them quickly. Nevertheless, when the Son of Man comes, will he find faith on the earth?" (Lk 18:1-8)

The Parable of the Pharisee and the Publican

"Two men went up into the temple to pray; one was a Pharisee, and the other was a tax collector. The Pharisee stood and prayed by himself like this: 'God, I thank you that I am not like the rest of men: extortionists, unrighteous, adulterers, or even like this tax collector. I fast twice a week. I give tithes of all that I get.' But the tax collector, standing far away, wouldn't even lift up his eyes to heaven, but beat his breast, saying, 'God, be merciful to me, a sinner!' I tell you, this man went down to his house justified rather than the other; for everyone who exalts himself will be humbled, but he who humbles himself will be exalted." (Lk 18:10-14)

The Danger of Riches

Amongst the crowds one day was a member of one of the leading families of the town. Jesus spoke to him. *"How hard it is for those who have riches to enter into God's Kingdom! For it is easier for a camel to enter in through a needle's eye than for a rich man to enter into God's Kingdom."*

Those who heard it said, *"Then who can be saved?"*

But he said, "The things which are impossible with men are possible with God." (Lk 18:24-27)

This concerned the apostles, and Peter spoke up and asked, "What about us?" as they had all left everything to follow Jesus. Jesus replied, "Most certainly I tell you, there is no one who has left house, or wife, or brothers, or parents, or children, for God's Kingdom's sake, who will not receive many times more in this time, and in the world to come, eternal life." (Lk 18:29-30)

The Third Prophecy of the Passion

Jesus took the apostles aside and spoke (for the third time) privately to them about what was going to happen to him. *"Behold, we are going up to Jerusalem, and all the things that are written through the prophets concerning the Son of Man will be completed. For he will be delivered up to the Gentiles, will be mocked, treated shamefully, and spit on. They will scourge and kill him. On the third day, he will rise again."*

They understood none of these things. This saying was hidden from them, and they didn't understand the things that were said. (Lk 18:31-34)

Jesus Enters Jerusalem

As Jesus got close to Jerusalem, near Bethphage, he called two of his apostles and sent them into a nearby village with instructions to find a colt no one had yet ridden. Jesus rode on the colt as he entered Jerusalem, and the crowds joyfully proclaimed.

> *"Blessed is the King who comes in the name of the Lord!*[221]
> *Peace in heaven, and glory in the highest!" (Lk 19:38)*

---

[221] Ps 118:26

Jesus spent his days in the Temple teaching (much to the continuing irritation of the scribes and Pharisees), while at night he would retire to the Mount of Olives.

The scribes and Pharisees saw Jesus being in Jerusalem as an opportunity to once and for all put an end to him. This opportunity presented itself in the person of Judas Iscariot, who by now was possessed by Satan. A scheme where Judas would be paid to hand over Jesus was agreed.

The Last Supper

As the day of Passover approached, Jesus sent Peter and John off to secure a room for them to eat the Passover meal. When all was done and the apostles were all seated at the table, Jesus spoke to them, *"I have earnestly desired to eat this Passover with you before I suffer, for I tell you, I will no longer by any means eat of it until it is fulfilled in God's Kingdom."* He received a cup, and when he had given thanks, he said, *"Take this and share it among yourselves, for I tell you, I will not drink at all again from the fruit of the vine, until God's Kingdom comes."*

He took bread, and when he had given thanks, he broke and gave it to them, saying, "This is my body which is given for you. Do this in memory of me." Likewise, he took the cup after supper, saying, "This cup is the new covenant in my blood, which is poured out for you. But behold, the hand of him who betrays me is with me on the table. The Son of Man indeed goes as it has been determined, but woe to that man through whom he is betrayed!"

They began to question among themselves which of them it was who would do this thing. (Lk 22:15-23)

An argument broke out amongst the apostles, about which of them should be seen as the greatest, Jesus responded, *"Among pagans it is the kings who lord it over them, and those who have authority over them are given the title Benefactor. This must not happen with you. No; the greatest among you must behave as if he were the youngest, and the leader as if he were the one who serves. For who is the greater: the one at table or the one who serves?*

"You are the men who have stood by me faithfully in my trials; and now I confer a Kingdom on you, just as my Father conferred one on me: you will eat and drink at my table in my Kingdom, and you will sit on thrones to judge the twelve tribes of Israel." (Lk 22:26-30*)

Jesus spoke to Peter, *"Simon, Simon! Satan, you must know, has got his wish to sift you all like wheat; but I have prayed for you, Simon, that your faith may not fail, and once you have recovered, you in your turn must strengthen your brothers."*

Peter said to him, *"Lord, I am ready to go with you both to prison and to death!"*

Jesus said, *"I tell you,* (by the time the roosters crows today, you will have denied me three times.)*"* (Lk 22:31-34)

Jesus then returned his attention to the apostles, telling them, *"When I sent you out without purse, bag, and sandals, did you lack anything?"*

They said, *"Nothing."*

Then he said to them, *"But now, whoever has a purse, let him take it, and likewise a bag. Whoever has none, let him sell his cloak, and buy a sword. For I tell you that this which is written must still be fulfilled in me: 'He was counted with transgressors'.*[222] *For that which concerns me is being fulfilled."* (Lk 22:35-37)

The Agony in the Garden

After dinner Jesus went back to the Mount of Olives as he did on the previous evenings in Jerusalem. Before leaving them to go off alone to pray, he told them, *"Pray not to be put to the test."* (Lk 22:40)

Alone, Jesus prayed, *"Father, if you are willing, remove this cup from me. Nevertheless, not my will, but yours, be done."*

An angel from heaven appeared to him, strengthening him. Being in agony, he prayed more earnestly. His sweat became like great drops of blood falling down on the ground.

---

[222] Is 53:12

When he rose up from his prayer, he came to the apostles and found them sleeping because of grief, and said to them, "Why do you sleep? Rise and pray that you may not enter into temptation." (Lk 22:42-46)

Judas Betrays Jesus

Before long Judas and some high priests' guards appeared. Judas approached Jesus to kiss him. Jesus said, *"Judas, do you betray the Son of Man with a kiss?"* (Lk 22:49)

In the commotion, one apostle cut the ear off a guard. Jesus immediately told them to stop, and he healed the man's ear.

Turning to one of the guards, Jesus said, *"Have you come out as against a robber, with swords and clubs? When I was with you in the temple daily, you didn't stretch out your hands against me. But this is your hour, and the power of darkness."* (Lk 22:52-53)

Peter's Denials

As they led Jesus away to the high priests' house Peter followed and waited by a fire with other onlookers, when someone spoke up, *"This man... was with him."*

He denied Jesus, saying, *"Woman, I don't know him."*

After a little while someone else saw him and said, *"You also are one of them!"*

But Peter answered, *"Man, I am not!"*

After about one hour had passed, another confidently affirmed, saying, *"Truly this man also was with him, for he is a Galilean!"*

But Peter said, *"Man, I don't know what you are talking about!"* Immediately, while he was still speaking, a rooster crowed. The Lord turned and looked at Peter. Then Peter remembered the Lord's word, how he said to him, *"Before the rooster crows you will deny me three times."* He went out, and wept bitterly. (Lk 22:56-62)

Meanwhile, the men guarding Jesus blindfolded him, and while beating and mocking him, said, "You're a prophet, tell us who hit you?"

Jesus on Trial

At daybreak Jesus was taken to appear before the Sanhedrin, where he was questioned, *"If you are the Christ, tell us."*

But he said to them, "If I tell you, you won't believe, and if I ask, you will in no way answer me or let me go. From now on, the Son of Man will be seated at the right hand of the power of God."

They all said, "Are you then the Son of God?"

He said to them, "You say it, because I am."

They said, "Why do we need any more witnesses? For we ourselves have heard from his own mouth!" (Lk 22:67-71)

The Sanhedrin, intent on having Jesus killed, took him to Pilate (for they themselves could not condemn him to death). They told Pilate they had found him guilty of inciting revolt, refusing to pay tribute to Caesar and calling himself a king.

Pilate turned to Jesus asking him directly, *"Are you the King of the Jews?"*

He answered him, "So you say." (Lk 23:3)

He gestured back to the chief priest and crowds and said he found no case against him. But they continued pressing him for a sentence. Eventually Pilate thought of a way out; after he overheard the crowds mention that Jesus was a Galilean. He told them to go before Herod Antipas, because as a Galilean it was his jurisdiction.

It delighted Herod to meet Jesus, as he had heard much about him and the miracles he performed. Herod probed Jesus with questions, but got no reply. He then mocked and humiliated him before sending him back to Pilate.

Pilate was frustrated when he saw Jesus before him again - as he couldn't find any case against him, and nor could Herod it seemed; but to appease the growing crowds and their need for justice he ordered Jesus to be flogged as his only punishment.

The crowds wanted blood though, and a flogging wasn't enough. This dismayed Pilate as he was eager to free Jesus, but the unappeasable crowd began a chant of, "Crucify him! Crucify him!" For the third time, Pilate addressed the people, *"Why? What evil has this man done? I have found no capital crime in him. I will therefore chastise him and release him."* (Lk 23:22)

The crowd would not let up, so Pilate gave in and handed Jesus over to be crucified.

The Crucifixion

A large crowd continued to surround Jesus, even as he was carrying his cross to Calvary. Seeing many women crying, he said, *"Daughters of Jerusalem, don't weep for me, but weep for yourselves and for your children. For behold, the days are coming in which they will say, 'Blessed are the barren, the wombs that never bore, and the breasts that never nursed.' Then they will begin to tell the mountains, 'Fall on us!' and tell the hills, 'Cover us.'* [223] *For if they do these things in the green tree, what will be done in the dry?"* (Lk 23:28-31)

Reaching his place of crucifixion, as he hung on his cross, Jesus said, *"Father, forgive them, for they don't know what they are doing."* (Lk 23:34)

Looking up on the cross were some religious leaders, who persisted with their mocking, saying, "He saved others but he can't save himself", and "Aren't you a king?"[224]

At the same time, two other men were being crucified, one of them yelled across to Jesus, *"If you are the Christ, save yourself and us!"*

But the other answered, and rebuking him said, *"Don't you even fear God, seeing you are under the same condemnation? And we indeed justly, for we*

---

[223] Hos 10:8

[224] On the cross above Jesus was an inscription 'This is the King of the Jews'.

receive the due reward for our deeds, but this man has done nothing wrong." He said to Jesus, "Lord, remember me when you come into your Kingdom."

Jesus said to him, "Assuredly I tell you, today you will be with me in Paradise." (Lk 23:39-43)

At about noon a vast darkness came over the skies and remained for three hours. *The sun was darkened, and the veil of the temple was torn in two. Jesus, crying with a loud voice, said, "Father, into your hands I commit my spirit!" Having said this, he breathed his last.* (Lk 23:45-46)

One of the Roman centurions, after witnessing his death, *glorified God, saying, "Certainly this was a righteous man."* (Lk 23:47)

A man named Joseph of Arimathea was granted permission by Pilate to take Jesus down from the cross and bury him quickly as it needed to be done before the approaching Sabbath.

The Resurrection

At dawn on the first day of the week, Mary of Magdala, Joanna, and Mary the mother of James, went to where Jesus was buried - to finish the burial rite.[225] When they got there, they found the tombstone rolled away and the body of Jesus was gone. Standing there dumbfounded, two men in brightly coloured clothes appeared to them and said, *"Why do you seek the living among the dead? He isn't here, but is risen. Remember what he told you when he was still in Galilee, saying that the Son of Man must be delivered up into the hands of sinful men and be crucified, and the third day rise again?"* (Lk 24:5-7)

They promptly made their way back to where the apostles were and reported what had happened. Their story was not believed until Peter raced to the tomb himself and discovered Jesus was gone.

That same day two disciples were travelling to Emmaus, a town seven miles from Jerusalem. Along the way, as they were going over the events of the day, Jesus appeared to them (but they did not recognise him). He

---

[225] Spices and ointments.

asked them what it was they were talking about. They answered, "You must be the only person in town who doesn't know what has taken place over the last few days." When Jesus asked them to clarify what they meant, they told him, *"The things concerning Jesus the Nazarene, who was a prophet mighty in deed and word before God and all the people; and how the chief priests and our rulers delivered him up to be condemned to death and crucified him. But we were hoping that it was he who would redeem Israel. Yes, and besides all this, it is now the third day since these things happened. Also, certain women of our company amazed us, having arrived early at the tomb; and when they didn't find his body, they came saying that they had also seen a vision of angels, who said that he was alive. Some of us went to the tomb and found it just like the women had said, but they didn't see him."*

He said to them, *"Foolish people, and slow of heart to believe in all that the prophets have spoken! Didn't the Christ have to suffer these things and to enter into his glory?" Beginning from Moses and from all the prophets, he explained to them in all the Scriptures the things concerning himself.* (Lk 24:19-27)

As they got close to Emmaus, Jesus motioned his continuation another way, but they urged him to stay with them as night was approaching. Sitting down for dinner, Jesus took the bread, broke it, and gave a blessing. Immediately the two men recognised Jesus. They rebuked themselves for not knowing earlier, saying to each other, "When he spoke to us about the Scriptures, didn't our hearts rejoice?"

Without delay they returned to those in Jerusalem telling them all they saw and heard, especially about the realisation when they saw Jesus break bread. While they were still coming to terms with the events Jesus appeared and said, *"Peace be to you."* But they were terrified and filled with fear, and supposed that they had seen a spirit.

He said to them, *"Why are you troubled? Why do doubts arise in your hearts? See my hands and my feet, that it is truly me. Touch me and see, for a spirit doesn't have flesh and bones, as you see that I have."* When he had said this, he showed them his hands and his feet. While they still didn't believe for joy, and wondered, he said to them, *"Do you have anything here to eat?"*

They gave him a piece of a broiled fish and some honeycomb. He took them, and ate in front of them. He said to them, "This is what I told you while I was still with you, that all things which are written in the Law of Moses, the prophets, and the Psalms concerning me must be fulfilled."

Then he opened their minds, that they might understand the Scriptures. He said to them, "Thus it is written, and thus it was necessary for the Christ to suffer and to rise from the dead the third day, and that repentance and remission of sins should be preached in his name to all the nations, beginning at Jerusalem. You are witnesses of these things. Behold, I send out the promise of my Father on you. But wait in the city of Jerusalem until you are clothed with power from on high."[226] (Lk 24:36-49)

On Jesus' last day, he took the apostles out along the way to the Jewish town of Bethany. He raised his hands and gave them a blessing, and while he was doing this he was taken up to heaven.

---

[226] Referring to the Holy Spirit.

JOHN

It is widely held that the author of the Gospel of John was John, son of Zebedee, one of the twelve apostles of Jesus.

Because of its varied style and content, it was once held that the fourth Gospel writer did not know of, or have access to, the first three gospels of Matthew, Mark, and Luke. Recently this theory has been under review.

Originally written in Greek, it is thought to have been written no later than 110 AD. The opinion of catholic.com 'is that the Gospel was written for the Christians of the second and third generations in Asia Minor' with the purpose that those who read it may believe that Jesus is the Christ, the Son of God, and that believing they may have life in his name. (Jn 20:31)

In the beginning was the Word, and the Word was with God, and the Word was God.... All things were made through him. Without him, nothing was made that has been made. (Jn 1:1-3)

He was in the world, and the world was made through him, and the world didn't recognise him. He came to his own, and those who were his own didn't receive him. But as many as received him, to them he gave the right to become God's children. (Jn 1:10-13)

From his fullness we all received grace upon grace. (Jn 1:16)

John the Baptist

John the Baptist *came as a witness, that he might testify about the light, so that all might believe through him. He was not the light, but was sent that he might testify about the light. The true light that enlightens everyone, was coming into the world.* (Jn 1:7-9)

One day some priests and Pharisees were sent to see and question John the Baptist, asking him who he was, was he the Christ, Elijah, or a prophet? John answered, *"I am the voice of one crying in the wilderness, 'Make straight the way of the Lord,'"*[227] (Jn 1:23)

They questioned him further, asking that if he wasn't the Christ, Elijah or indeed a prophet, why was he baptising people? John replied, *"I baptise in water, but among you stands one whom you don't know. He is the one who comes after me, who is preferred before me, whose sandal strap I'm not worthy to loosen."* (Jn 1:26-27)

Soon after Jesus came to John to be baptised, and as he approached, John said, *"Behold, the Lamb of God, who takes away the sin of the world! This is he of whom I said, 'After me comes a man who is preferred before me, for he was before me.'"* (Jn 1:29-30)

Jesus Calls the First Disciples

The next day, a follower of John the Baptist, called Andrew, left John to follow Jesus. The following morning Andrew met his brother Simon and told him, "We have found the Messiah!"

Jesus spoke to Simon. *"You are Simon, the son of Jonah. You shall be called Cephas." (which is, Peter).* (Jn 1:42)

The following day, Jesus called Philip, and Philip went to his friend Nathanael, telling him, *"We have found him of whom Moses in the Law and also the prophets, wrote: Jesus of Nazareth, the son of Joseph."* (Jn 1:45)

---

[227] Is 40:3

The Wedding at Cana

Three days later, Jesus, his disciples and Mary his mother were at a wedding. During the ceremony, Mary came to tell Jesus that the parents of the bride had run out of wine. Jesus said to his mother, *"Woman, what does that have to do with you and me? My hour has not yet come."* (Jn 2:4)

Mary paid no attention to his answer, telling the wedding servants to do whatever her son Jesus said. Jesus told the servants, *"Fill the water pots with water.... Now draw some out and take it to the ruler of the feast."...*

When the steward of the feast tasted the water now become wine, and having no knowledge where it came from (but the servants who had drawn the water knew), the steward of the feast called the bridegroom and said to him, "Everyone serves the good wine first, and when the guests have drunk freely, then that which is worse. You have kept the good wine until now!" This was the first of the signs Jesus did... and revealed his glory; and his disciples believed in him. (Jn 2:7-11)

Jesus' Anger with the Temple Vendors

One day while in the Temple at Jerusalem, the sight of animals being sold[228] and the business of the money changers taking place angered Jesus. He scattered and flipped over the tables. Those who saw this asked him under whose authority he acted this way. What sign could he show them? Jesus replied, *"Destroy this temple, and in three days I will raise it up."*

The Jews said, "It took forty-six years to build this temple! Will you raise it up in three days?" But he spoke of the temple of his body. When therefore he was raised from the dead, his disciples remembered that he had said this, and they believed the Scripture and the word which Jesus had said. (Jn 2:19-22)

---

[228] According to Jewish law, worshippers were required to offer animal sacrifices for atonement, thanksgiving, and other religious rituals. Many pilgrims travelled long distances to the temple and found it impractical to bring their own animals, so merchants provided a convenient way for them to purchase suitable offerings, such as doves, sheep, and oxen.

Jesus and Nicodemus

One night, a Pharisee named Nicodemus said to Jesus that he knew he was from God because of the signs he showed. Jesus said to him, *"Most certainly I tell you, unless one is born anew, he can't see God's Kingdom."* (Jn 3:3)

Nicodemus was confused, wondering how it was possible for a man to go back into the womb and be reborn. Jesus clarified his meaning. *"Most certainly I tell you, unless one is born of water and Spirit, he can't enter into God's Kingdom. That which is born of the flesh is flesh. That which is born of the Spirit is spirit. Don't marvel that I said to you, 'You must be born anew.'"* (Jn 3:5-7)

Nicodemus continued to try and understand Jesus, asking, "How can these things be?"

Jesus answered him, *"If I told you earthly things and you don't believe, how will you believe if I tell you heavenly things? No one has ascended into heaven but he who descended out of heaven, the Son of Man, who is in heaven.*

"As Moses lifted up the serpent in the wilderness,[229] *even so must the Son of Man be lifted up, that whoever believes in him should not perish, but have eternal life.*

"For God so loved the world, that he gave his only born Son, that whoever believes in him should not perish, but have eternal life.

"For God didn't send his Son into the world to judge the world, but that the world should be saved through him.

"He who believes in him is not judged. He who doesn't believe has been judged already, because he has not believed in the name of the only born Son of God.

"This is the judgement, that the light has come into the world, and men loved the darkness rather than the light, for their works were evil." (Jn 3:9, 12-19)

---

[229] Nm 21:9

Jesus Reveals Himself to the Samaritans[230]

Leaving Jerusalem, Jesus headed out for Galilee via a Samaritan town. Stopping by a well, Jesus saw a woman and asked her for some water. The Samaritan woman said to him, *"How is it that you, being a Jew, ask for a drink from me, a Samaritan woman?" (For Jews have no dealings with Samaritans.)*

Jesus answered her, "If you knew the gift of God, and who it is who says to you, 'Give me a drink,' you would have asked him, and he would have given you living water."

The woman said to him, "Sir, you have nothing to draw with, and the well is deep. So where do you get that living water? Are you greater than our father Jacob, who gave us the well and drank from it himself, as did his children and his livestock?"

Jesus answered her, "Everyone who drinks of this water will thirst again, but whoever drinks of the water that I will give him will never thirst again." (Jn 4:9-14)

The woman said to him, "I know that Messiah is coming, he who is called Christ. When he has come, he will declare to us all things."

Jesus said to her, "I am he, the one who speaks to you." (Jn 4:25-26)

The woman enthusiastically raced back into town and returned with scores of people.

The Pharisees Question Jesus

Coming back to Jerusalem, Jesus healed a man who had been tormented for thirty-eight years. As it was on a Sabbath, the local Jews were angry with him; for according to their laws, no one was allowed to do any work on the Sabbath. Jesus knew their thoughts and declared, *"My Father is still working, so I am working, too."* (Jn 5:17)

---

[230] Samaritans believed the Law like other Jews but their history goes back only to the time of the deportation, so they were not considered 'real' Jews.

Hearing that breaking the Sabbath wasn't his only sin, but that he also spoke of God as his own father, they became even more incensed, to the point they wanted him dead. Jesus spoke up, *"Most certainly, I tell you, the Son can do nothing of himself, but what he sees the Father doing. For whatever things he does, these the Son also does likewise. For the Father has affection for the Son, and shows him all things that he himself does. He will show him greater works than these, that you may marvel. For as the Father raises the dead and gives them life, even so the Son also gives life to whom he desires. For the Father judges no one, but he has given all judgement to the Son, that all may honour the Son, even as they honour the Father. He who doesn't honour the Son doesn't honour the Father who sent him.*

"Most certainly I tell you, he who hears my word and believes him who sent me has eternal life, and doesn't come into judgement, but has passed out of death into life." (Jn 5:19-24)

Jesus condemned the Pharisees, saying that while they prided themselves on knowing and following the Scriptures - they fail to see in the same Scriptures the foretelling of Jesus.

"You search the Scriptures, because you think that in them you have eternal life; and these are they which testify about me. Yet you will not come to me, that you may have life. I don't receive glory from men. But I know you, that you don't have God's love in yourselves. I have come in my Father's name, and you don't receive me. If another comes in his own name, you will receive him." (Jn 5:39-43)

Jesus is the Bread of Life

While in the Jewish town of Capernaum, Jesus spoke to the crowds following him, *"I am the bread of life. Whoever comes to me will not be hungry, and whoever believes in me will never be thirsty. For I have come down from heaven, not to do my own will, but the will of him who sent me."* (Jn 6:35, 38)

"Most certainly I tell you, he who believes in me has eternal life. I am the bread of life. Your fathers ate the manna in the wilderness and they died.[231] *This is the bread which comes down out of heaven, that anyone may eat of it and not die. I am the living bread which came down out of heaven. If anyone eats of this bread, he will live forever. Yes, the bread which I will give for the life of the world is my flesh."*

The Jews therefore contended with one another, saying, "How can this man give us his flesh to eat?"

Jesus therefore said to them, "Most certainly I tell you, unless you eat the flesh of the Son of Man and drink his blood, you don't have life in yourselves. He who eats my flesh and drinks my blood has eternal life, and I will raise him up at the last day." (Jn 6:47-54)

Jesus Encounters the Pharisees in Jerusalem

Knowing the Jews in Jerusalem wanted him dead, Jesus left for Galilee and stayed there until the Feast of Tabernacles approached. The apostles came to Jesus to make plans to return to Jerusalem to celebrate, but Jesus sent them on without him as he knew the Pharisees were still seeking his death - but his time had not yet come.

After his apostles left, however, Jesus quietly went into town.

By the time the festival was half over, Jesus was again in the Temple preaching. As always, those who heard him were touched by his knowledge and wisdom, questioning how it could be so. Jesus gave them this answer, *"My teaching is not mine, but his who sent me. If anyone desires to do his will, he will know about the teaching... Didn't Moses give you the law, and yet none of you keeps the law?"* (Jn 7:16,17,19)

Hearing Jesus was in town, the Pharisees dispatched Temple police to arrest him.

---

[231] Exodus.

Meanwhile, the crowds were debating amongst themselves whether Jesus was indeed the promised Messiah. Those who were against him declared he couldn't be the Messiah because they knew him and where he came from. As the Scripture said, no one will know where he comes from. Those in favour, said his miracles were a sign that it was true, adding they needed no more signs other than what Jesus had already given.

On the last day of the festival Jesus cried out with emotion, *"If anyone is thirsty, let him come to me and drink! He who believes in me, as the Scripture has said, from within him will flow rivers of living water."* (Jn 7:37-38)

Meanwhile, some guards sent to arrest Jesus returned to the chief priests and Pharisees empty handed. When confronted, they replied they had never heard anyone speak with such authority as him. The Pharisees were outraged and accused them of being duped, as only they themselves knew the Law and could teach in the Temple.

The following day Jesus went back to the Temple, where the Pharisees were ready with a trap. They brought to him a woman accused of adultery. *"Teacher, we found this woman in adultery, in the very act. Now in our law, Moses commanded us to stone such women.*[232] *What then do you say about her?" They said this testing him, that they might have something to accuse him of.* (Jn 8:4-6)

Jesus looked up and said to them, *"He who is without sin among you, let him throw the first stone at her."* (Jn 8:7)

Hearing this, they all dispersed until Jesus remained alone with the woman. Turning to her he said, *"Woman, where are your accusers? Did no one condemn you?"*

She said, *"No one, Lord."*

Jesus said, *"Neither do I condemn you. Go your way. From now on, sin no more."* (Jn 8:10-11)

---

[232] Lev 20:10, Dt 22:22

When Jesus again spoke, he said, *"I am the light of the world. He who follows me will not walk in the darkness, but will have the light of life."* (Jn 8:12)

Jesus singled out some unbelieving Jews who were in the crowds. *"I am going away, and you will seek me, and you will die in your sins. Where I go, you can't come."* (Jn 8:21)

"When you have lifted up the Son of Man, then you will know that I am he, and I do nothing of myself, but as my Father taught me, I say these things. He who sent me is with me. The Father has not left me alone, for I always do the things that are pleasing to him." (Jn 8:27-29)

Many came to believe in him that day.

The Jews Question Jesus' Teachings

In the crowds following Jesus were also some Jews who believed in him, but these Jews did not understand Jesus when he told them, *"If you remain in my word, then you are truly my disciples. You will know the truth, and the truth will make you free."*[233] (Jn 8:32)

For they were sons of Abraham, not slaves, so how could they be set free?

Jesus helped them to understand by saying, *"Most certainly I tell you, everyone who commits sin is the slave of sin. A slave doesn't live in the house forever. A son remains forever. If therefore the Son makes you free, you will be free indeed. I know that you are Abraham's offspring, yet you seek to kill me, because my word finds no place in you. I say the things which I have seen with my Father; and you also do the things which you have seen with your father."* (Jn 8:34-38)

Taking umbrage, they said, "But our father is Abraham."

Jesus again helped them to understand, *"If you were Abraham's children, you would do the works of Abraham. But now you seek to kill me, a man who has told you the truth which I heard from God. Abraham did not do this."* (Jn 8:39-40)

---

[233] Ps 119:45

Getting annoyed, they replied, "We have only one father, God."

Jesus clarified, *"If God were your father, you would love me, for I came out and have come from God. For I have not come of myself, but he sent me. Why don't you understand me? Because you cannot hear my word. Your father is the devil, and you want to do the desires of your father."* (Jn 8:42-44)

The Jews were now getting furious at the way Jesus was speaking to them and accused him of being possessed by the devil. Jesus responded, *"I don't have a demon, but I honour my Father and you dishonour me. But I don't seek my own glory. There is one who seeks and judges. Most certainly, I tell you, if a person keeps my word, he will never see death."* (Jn 8:49-51)

This was the last straw for the Jews. They challenged Jesus, saying, *"Abraham died, as did the prophets; and you say, 'If a man keeps my word, he will never taste of death.' Are you greater than our father, Abraham, who died? The prophets died. Who do you make yourself out to be?"*

Jesus answered, *"If I glorify myself, my glory is nothing. It is my Father who glorifies me, of whom you say that he is our God. You have not known him, but I know him. If I said, 'I don't know him,' I would be like you, a liar. But I know him and keep his word. Your father Abraham rejoiced to see my day. He saw it and was glad."*

The Jews therefore said to him, *"You are not yet fifty years old! Have you seen Abraham?"*

Jesus said to them, *"Most certainly, I tell you, before Abraham came into existence, I Am."*[234] (Jn 8:52-58)

Hearing this, they picked up stones to throw at Jesus, but he slipped away.

It wasn't long before the Pharisees caught up with Jesus again, and he spoke to them, *"Most certainly, I tell you, one who doesn't enter by the door into the sheepfold, but climbs up some other way, is a thief and a robber. But one who enters in by the door is the shepherd of the sheep. The gatekeeper opens the gate for him, and the sheep listen to his voice. He calls his own sheep by name and leads them*

---

[234] Ex 3:14

out. *Whenever he brings out his own sheep, he goes before them; and the sheep follow him, for they know his voice. They will by no means follow a stranger, but will flee from him; for they don't know the voice of strangers."* (Jn 10:1-5)

"I am the door. If anyone enters in by me, he will be saved, and will go in and go out and will find pasture. The thief only comes to steal, kill, and destroy. I came that they may have life, and may have it abundantly." (Jn 10:9-10)

"I am the good shepherd.[235] *I know my own, and I'm known by my own; even as the Father knows me, and I know the Father. I lay down my life for the sheep. I have other sheep which are not of this fold.*[236] *I must bring them also, and they will hear my voice. They will become one flock with one shepherd. Therefore, the Father loves me, because I lay down my life,*[237] *that I may take it again. No one takes it away from me, but I lay it down by myself. I have power to lay it down, and I have power to take it again. I received this commandment from my Father."* (Jn 10:14-18)

As was often the case, the words of Jesus created division. Some said the devil possessed him, others questioned how a devil could cure and heal the way Jesus did.

Jesus Claims to be the Son of God

At the time of Hanukkah, Jesus again went to the Temple in Jerusalem. This time the Jews asked him the question, "Why do you keep us in suspense? If you are the Christ, can you just tell us plainly and simply?"

Jesus gave them this answer, *"I told you, and you don't believe. The works that I do in my Father's name, these testify about me. But you don't believe, because you are not of my sheep, as I told you. My sheep hear my voice, and I know them, and they follow me. I give eternal life to them. They will never perish, and no one will snatch them out of my hand. My Father who has*

---

[235] Is 40:11; Ez 34:11-12,15,22
[236] Is 56:8
[237] Is 53:7-8

given them to me is greater than all. No one is able to snatch them out of my Father's hand. I and the Father are one." (Jn 10:25-29)

Again the Jews picked up stones to throw at Jesus, but before they could throw anything he asked them, "For which deed do you try to stone me?"

To which they answered, "It isn't because of anything you do but because of your blasphemy. You are only a man, yet you say you are God."

Jesus told them, *"If I don't do the works of my Father, then don't believe me. But if I do them, though you don't believe me, believe the works, that you may know and believe that the Father is in me, and I in the Father."* (Jn 10:37-38)

He then left to the far side of the Jordan.

The Resurrection of Lazarus

There came a time when two sisters Mary and Martha sent a message to Jesus about their brother Lazarus, saying, "The man you love, our brother is ill." On receiving the message, Jesus said, *"This sickness is not to death, but for the glory of God, that God's Son may be glorified by it."* (Jn 11:4)

Notwithstanding this, and his love for the whole family, Jesus remained where he was for the next two days.

Jesus said to his apostles, *"Lazarus is dead. I am glad for your sake that I was not there, so that you may believe. Nevertheless, let's go to him."* (Jn 11:14-15)

By the time Jesus got to the home of Lazarus, he had already been dead for four days. Martha went to meet Jesus and said, *"Lord, if you would have been here, my brother wouldn't have died. Even now I know that whatever you ask of God, God will give you."*

Jesus said to her, "Your brother will rise again."

Martha said to him, *"I know that he will rise again in the resurrection at the last day."*

Jesus said to her, "I am the resurrection and the life. He who believes in me will still live, even if he dies. Whoever lives and believes in me will never die. Do you believe this?"

She said to him, "Yes, Lord. I have come to believe that you are the Christ, God's Son, he who comes into the world." (Jn 11:21-27)

Mary came to Jesus and said, *"Lord, if you would have been here, my brother wouldn't have died."*

When Jesus saw her weeping, and the Jews weeping who came with her, he groaned in the spirit and was troubled, and said, "Where have you laid him?"

They told him, "Lord, come and see."

Jesus wept. (Jn 11:32-35)

Standing outside the tomb, Jesus ordered them to remove the stone. *Jesus lifted his eyes and said, "Father, I thank you that you have listened to me. I know that you always listen to me, but because of the multitude standing around I said this, that they may believe that you sent me." When he had said this, he cried with a loud voice, "Lazarus, come out!"*

He who was dead came out, bound hand and foot with wrappings, and his face was wrapped around with a cloth.

Jesus said to them, "Free him, and let him go." (Jn 11:41-44)

Like many of Jesus' miracles, word soon got back to the chief priests and Pharisees, who continued to see him as a threat. Caiaphas, the high priest, said to his colleagues, *"Do you consider that it is advantageous for us that one man should die for the people, and that the whole nation not perish?"* (Jn 11:50)

From that day on, Caiaphas planned ways for Jesus to be killed, so he could no longer walk around in the open. He left with his apostles for the Jewish town of Ephraim.

Jesus Returns to Jerusalem for the Third Time

For the third time in his ministry, the feast of Passover approached and the people of Jerusalem, including the chief priests and Pharisees, were all wondering if Jesus would attend. After stopping by the house of Mary, Martha, and Lazarus, Jesus went towards Jerusalem. As he was getting near, the crowds gathered to await his arrival. *They took the branches of the palm trees and went out to meet him, and cried out, "Hosanna! Blessed is he who comes in the name of the Lord,*[238] *the King of Israel!"*

Jesus, having found a young donkey, sat on it. As it is written, 'Don't be afraid, daughter of Zion. Behold, your King comes, sitting on a donkey's colt'.[239] (Jn 12:13-15)

All this emphasised further to the chief priests and Pharisees - they had to kill Jesus.

Amongst the crowds were some recent converts who asked the apostle Philip if they could see Jesus, but Jesus replied, *"The time has come for the Son of Man to be glorified. Most certainly I tell you, unless a grain of wheat falls into the earth and dies, it remains by itself alone. But if it dies, it bears much fruit. He who loves his life will lose it. He who hates his life in this world will keep it to eternal life. If anyone serves me, let him follow me. Where I am, there my servant will also be. If anyone serves me, the Father will honour him.*

"Now my soul is troubled. What shall I say? 'Father, save me from this time?' But I came to this time for this cause. Father, glorify your name!"

Then a voice came out of the sky, saying, "I have both glorified it and will glorify it again." (Jn 12:23-28)

Hearing this, some in the crowd thought it was a clap of thunder, others the voice of an angel. Jesus responded, *"This voice hasn't come for my sake, but for your sakes. Now is the judgement of this world. Now the prince of this world will be cast out. And I, if I am lifted up from the earth, will draw all people to myself."*[240] (Jn 12:30-32)

Though they had witnessed many signs and wonders, they still did not believe in Jesus. *Nevertheless, even many of the* (leaders) *believed in*

---

[238] Ps 118:25-26
[239] Zec 9:9
[240] Is 6:10

him, *but because of the Pharisees they didn't confess it, so that they wouldn't be put out of the synagogue, for they loved men's praise more than God's praise.* (Jn 12:42-43)

Jesus added, *"Whoever believes in me, believes not in me, but in him who sent me. He who sees me sees him who sent me. I have come as a light into the world, that whoever believes in me may not remain in the darkness."* (Jn 12:44-46)

He went on to say, *"For I spoke not from myself, but the Father who sent me gave me a commandment, what I should say and what I should speak. I know that his commandment is eternal life. The things therefore which I speak, even as the Father has said to me, so I speak."* (Jn 12:49-50)

The Last Supper

The Feast of Passover was approaching, and Jesus sat down to supper with his apostles (the devil had already entered the mind of Judas Iscariot, so he would betray Jesus). Jesus knew what was to come. He also knew his Father had put everything into his hands.

Jesus started by washing the feet of his apostles, but by the time he came around to Peter, he would not accept it and could not understand why Jesus would lower himself like this. Jesus told him, *"If I don't wash you, you have no part with me."*

Peter said to him, *"Lord, not only my feet, but also my hands and my head!"* (Jn 13:8-9)

When he was finished, Jesus asked his apostles if they understood what he had just done. He wanted them to know that *a servant is not greater than his master, neither is one who is sent greater than he who sent him.* (Jn 13:16)

He also said, *"I have given you an example, that you should also do as I have done to you."* (Jn 13:15)

Jesus spoke again about his imminent betrayal quoting Scripture, *"Someone who shares my table rebels against me."*[241] (Jn 13:18)

The apostles spoke among themselves, asking, "Who is it?"

Jesus told John it would be the person he hands his piece of bread to - it was Judas Iscariot. Jesus even said to Judas, "What you do, do quickly." Even so, the other apostles did not fully understand.

After Judas left, Jesus spoke, *"Where I am going, you can't come, so now I tell you. A new commandment I give to you, that you love one another. Just as I have loved you, you must also love one another. By this everyone will know that you are my disciples, if you have love for one another."* (Jn 13:33-35)

Peter asked why he couldn't go where Jesus was going, adding he would follow him anywhere, even if it meant losing his life. Jesus replied, *"Will you lay down your life for me? Most certainly I tell you, the rooster won't crow until you have denied me three times."* (Jn 13:38)

Jesus continued, *"Don't let your heart be troubled. Believe in God. Believe also in me. In my Father's house there are many rooms. If it weren't so, I would have told you. I am going to prepare a place for you... You know where I go, and you know the way."* (Jn 14:1-4)

Thomas spoke up asking Jesus, *"(If) we don't know where you are going. How can we know the way?"*

Jesus said to him, "I am the way, the truth and the life. No one comes to the Father, except through me." (Jn 14:5-6)

Still not comprehending what Jesus was saying, Phillip said, "Show us the Father."

Jesus said, *"Have I been with you such a long time, and do you not know me, Philip? He who has seen me has seen the Father. How do you say, 'Show us the Father'? Don't you believe that I am in the Father, and the Father is in me? The words that I tell you, I speak not from myself; but the Father who lives in me does his works.*

---

[241] Ps 41:9

"Believe me that I am in the Father, and the Father is in me; or else believe me for the very works' sake. Most certainly I tell you, he who believes in me, the works that I do, he will do also; and he will do greater works than these, because I am going to my Father. Whatever you will ask in my name, I will do it, that the Father may be glorified in the Son. If you will ask anything in my name, I will do it.

"If you love me, keep my commandments.

"I will pray to the Father, and he will give you another Counsellor, that he may be with you forever: the Spirit of truth, whom the world can't receive, for it doesn't see him and doesn't know him. You know him, for he lives with you and will be in you. I will not leave you orphans. I will come to you." (Jn 14:9-18)

Jesus continued his teaching on the Holy Spirit and about following him. "I have said these things to you while still living with you. But the Counsellor, the Holy Spirit, whom the Father will send in my name, will teach you all things, and will remind you of all that I said to you. Peace I leave with you. My peace I give to you; not as the world gives, I give to you. Don't let your heart be troubled, neither let it be fearful." (Jn 14:25-28)

"This is my commandment, that you love one another, even as I have loved you. Greater love has no one than this, that someone lay down his life for his friends. You are my friends if you do whatever I command you." (Jn 15:12-14)

"If the world hates you, know that it hated me before it hated you. If you were of the world, the world would love its own. But because you are not of the world, since I chose you out of the world, therefore the world hates you. Remember the word that I said to you: 'A servant is not greater than his master.' If they persecuted me, they will also persecute you. If they kept my word, they will also keep yours. But they will do all these things to you for my name's sake, because they don't know him who sent me. If I had not come and spoken to them, they would not have had sin; but now they have no excuse for their sin." (Jn 15:18-22)

"I have said these things to you so that you wouldn't be caused to stumble. They will put you out of the synagogues. Yes, the time is coming that whoever kills you will think that he offers service to God. They will do these things because they have not known the Father nor me. But I have told you these things so that when the time comes, you may remember that I told you about them." (Jn 16:1-4)

"Nevertheless, I tell you the truth: It is to your advantage that I go away; for if I don't go away, the Counsellor won't come to you. But if I go, I will send him to you. When he has come, he will convict the world about sin, about righteousness, and about judgement." (Jn 16:7-8)

Jesus, raising his eyes to heaven, said. "Father, the time has come. Glorify your Son, that your Son may also glorify you." (Jn 17:1)

"As you sent me into the world, even so I have sent them into the world. For their sakes I sanctify myself, that they themselves also may be sanctified in truth." (Jn 17:18-19)

"Not for these only do I pray, but for those also who will believe in me through their word, that they may all be one; even as you, Father, are in me, and I in you, that they also may be one in us; that the world may believe that you sent me. The glory which you have given me, I have given to them, that they may be one, even as we are one." (Jn 17:20-22)

Jesus is Arrested

When Jesus had finished saying all he needed, he took his apostles into a garden he had taken them to before, and while he was there Judas appeared with the guards sent by the chief priests and Pharisees. Jesus surrendered himself peacefully, but Peter wasn't going without a fight. He drew his sword and cut off the right ear of a guard named Malchus. Jesus healed the guard and told Peter, *"Put the sword into its sheath. The cup which the Father has given me, shall I not surely drink it?"* (Jn 18:11)

Peter and John followed behind Jesus as the guards took him away. Waiting outside the chief priest's home while Jesus was inside, a maid saw Peter and asked him if he was a disciple of Jesus. Peter said, "I am not," and returned to warming himself by the fire.

Shortly after, another person approached Peter with the same challenge, "Aren't you a disciple of Jesus?" Peter again denied it.

One of the high priest's servants (the brother of Malchus) said, "Didn't I see you in the garden with Jesus?" For a third time, Peter denied knowing Jesus, and then the cock crew.

Before Pilate

Meanwhile, Jesus was inside the house of Caiaphas, the chief priest, being interrogated about his teachings. Jesus asked them, *"I spoke openly to the world. I always taught in synagogues and in the temple where the Jews always meet. I said nothing in secret. Why do you ask me? Ask those who have heard me what I said to them. Behold, they know the things which I said."* (Jn 18:20-21)

Jesus' response prompted a nearby guard to slap him across the face, yelling, "That is no way to speak to the high priest!"

In the morning, they took Jesus to the Praetorium to see Pilate. It perplexed Pilate why Jesus was before him. The Jews said it was because they couldn't legally sentence anyone to death. Pilate asked Jesus why he was being handed over. Jesus responded, *"My Kingdom is not of this world. If my Kingdom were of this world, then my servants would fight, that I wouldn't be delivered to the Jews. But now my Kingdom is not from here."*

Pilate therefore said to him, "Are you a king then?"

Jesus answered, *"You say that I am a king. For this reason I have been born, and for this reason I have come into the world, that I should testify to the truth."* (Jn 18:36-37)

The high priests were not inside with Pilate and Jesus, as they believed they would be defiled if they entered his house, so Pilate came outside to where they were waiting and told them he could find no case against Jesus, but he agreed to have him scourged. To add further humiliation, the soldiers made a crown of thorns for Jesus' head and wrapped him in a purple robe while mockingly chanting, "Hail, King of the Jews!"[242]

Assuming the scourging would appease the priests, Pilate again presented Jesus to them, but it was not enough. The chief priests and guards shouted out, "CRUCIFY HIM! CRUCIFY HIM!" Pilate said no as he could find no guilt. He advised them if they wanted him dead to do it themselves. The chief priests pointed out that under their Law they could not sentence anyone to death, so it had to be him. Their reason for the death sentence was because Jesus claimed to be the Son of God.

Pilate withdrew to speak to Jesus again, but this time, Jesus was not as forthcoming. Frustrated, Pilate said, *"Don't you know that I have power to release you and have power to crucify you?"*

Jesus answered, *"You would have no power at all against me, unless it were given to you from above. Therefore, he who delivered me to you has greater sin."* (Jn 19:10-11)

This firmed the resolve of Pilate to release him, but he was no match for the determined chief priests who would only settle with Jesus' death. Speaking to the crowds, Pilate said, *"Behold, your King!"*

They cried out, "Away with him! Away with him! Crucify him!"

Pilate said to them, "Shall I crucify your King?"

The chief priests answered, "We have no king but Caesar!"

So then he delivered him to them to be crucified. (Jn 19:14-16)

The Crucifixion

Carrying his own cross, Jesus went to Golgotha, where he was crucified with two other men, one on either side.

Pilate arranged for a notice to be fixed to the cross. It read, JESUS OF NAZARETH, THE KING OF THE JEWS. This aggrieved the Jewish high priests greatly.

---

[242] In Rome at the time, purple was identified with victory and triumph.

After the soldiers had finished nailing Jesus to the cross, they took his clothes and gambled for them. This was to fulfil Scripture: *They parted my garments among them. They cast lots for my clothing.*[243] (Jn 19:24)

Standing at the foot of the cross were John (the apostle Jesus loved), and Jesus' mother, Mary. Jesus said to his mother, *"Woman, behold, your son!"* Then he said to the disciple, *"Behold, your mother!"* (Jn 19:26-27)

Knowing his death was near, and in fulfilment of the Scriptures, Jesus said, *"I am thirsty!"* Now a vessel full of vinegar was set there; so they put a sponge full of the vinegar on hyssop and held it to his mouth. When Jesus therefore had received the vinegar, he said, *"It is finished!"* Then he bowed his head and gave up his spirit. (Jn 19:28-30)

It was the custom at the time to break the legs of the crucified to bring on final death, but when the soldiers came to Jesus, they saw he was already dead, so instead, they pierced his side with a lance. Water and blood flowed. This was to fulfil the Scripture that said, *no bone of him will not be broken.*[244] (Jn 19:36)

And also, they will look on him whom they pierced.[245] (Jn 19:37)

Later, Joseph of Arimathea was granted permission from Pilate to take Jesus down from the cross and bury him. They buried Jesus according to the customs of the Jews.

Jesus is Risen

Two days later, early on Sunday morning, Mary Magdalene went to the tomb only to find the stone which was blocking it had been rolled away. She hurried back to Peter, informing him about what she had found. Peter and the others immediately ran to the place where Jesus was buried and saw for themselves that the tomb was empty. All they saw was Jesus' burial linen cloth lying on the ground.

---

[243] Ps 22:18
[244] Ex 12:46; Ps 34:20
[245] Zec 12:10

Till this moment, they had failed to understand the teaching of Scripture, that he must rise from the dead. (Jn 20:9)

The apostles returned home, but Mary stayed. Crying, she entered the tomb only to see two angels. When she turned around to leave, she saw Jesus (although she did not recognise him). Jesus spoke to Mary, saying, *"Woman, why are you weeping? Who are you looking for?"*

She, supposing him to be the gardener, said to him, "Sir, if you have carried him away, tell me where you have laid him, and I will take him away."

Jesus said to her, "Mary."

She turned and said to him, "Rabboni!" which is to say, 'Teacher'!

Jesus said to her, "Don't touch me, for I haven't yet ascended to my Father; but go to my brothers and tell them, 'I am ascending to my Father and your Father, to my God and your God.'" (Jn 20:15-17)

Mary did as asked and returned to tell the apostles what she had seen and heard.

That same night, the apostles were hiding together in a locked room (for they feared further action from the chief priests), when Jesus appeared. He said to them, *"Peace be to you. As the Father has sent me, even so I send you."* When he had said this, he breathed on them, and said to them, *"Receive the Holy Spirit! If you forgive anyone's sins, they have been forgiven them. If you retain anyone's sins, they have been retained."* (Jn 20:21-23)

There was one apostle not in the room the night Jesus appeared, his name was Thomas. When he was told what happened, he said that unless he saw for himself the holes in his hands and side, he would not believe it to be true. Eight days later, when they again were gathered in the same locked room, Jesus once again appeared, saying, "Peace be with you." Jesus spoke directly to Thomas, *"Reach here your finger and see my hands. Reach here your hand and put it into my side. Don't be unbelieving, but believing."*

Thomas answered him, "My Lord and my God!"

Jesus said to him, "Because you have seen me, you have believed. Blessed are those who have not seen and have believed." (Jn 20:27-29)

Jesus Commissions Peter

There was a third time Jesus showed himself to his apostles. It took place on a day when Peter and the others were out fishing by the Sea of Tiberias. Throughout the entire night, they caught nothing. As daylight appeared, they saw a man standing on the shore (it was Jesus, but they did not realise it). He asked them how their fishing had gone, and they responded appropriately. Jesus advised them to throw their nets again, and this time the catch was so big they couldn't haul it in. John declared to Peter, "It is the Lord!" Peter hastily jumped from the boat to go to him.

When the boat with the rest of the apostles eventually came to shore, there was a fire going with bread and fish cooking. Jesus invited them to eat breakfast. None of the apostles dared inquire of him, "Who are you?" knowing it was the Lord. *Then Jesus came and took the bread, gave it to them, and the fish likewise. (Jn 21:13)*

When they had finished eating, Jesus spoke to Peter. *"Simon, son of Jonah, do you love me more than these?"*

He said to him, "Yes, Lord; you know that I love you."

He said to him, "Feed my lambs." He said to him again a second time, "Simon, son of Jonah, do you love me?"

He said to him, "Yes, Lord; you know that I love you."

He said to him, "Tend my sheep." He said to him the third time, "Simon, son of Jonah, do you have affection for me?"

Peter was grieved because he asked him the third time, "Do you have affection for me?" He said to him, "Lord, you know everything. You know that I love you."

Jesus said to him, "Feed my sheep." (Jn 21:15-17)

ACTS OF THE APOSTLES

The Book of Acts is seen as the second part of a two-part book, the first being the Gospel of Luke.

In Acts of the Apostles, we see the fruits of the Holy Spirit.

Acts tells the story of a normal man (Paul), or normal people (i.e. not divine like Jesus) who carry on divinely, just as Jesus did. We see people being healed and resurrected.

It shows the continuation of Jesus' ministry under the guidance of the Holy Spirit and the real-life struggles of Christians spreading the Good News. It isn't always successful or easy, in fact the opposite is often true.

The Ascension of Jesus

For forty days after his resurrection, Jesus continued to appear to his apostles. During this time he promised the coming of the Holy Spirit, saying, *"For John indeed baptised in water, but you will be baptised in the Holy Spirit not many days from now."* (Acts 1:5)

The apostles asked Jesus about the future, and if he would restore Israel to its former glory. Jesus answered, "That is between me and my Father. All you need to concern yourselves with is being my witnesses throughout the world."

Once Jesus had finished speaking, a cloud took him from their sight, and while *they were looking into the sky..., two men stood by them in white clothing, who said, "You men of Galilee, why do you stand looking into the sky? This Jesus, who was received up from you into the sky, will come back in the same way as you saw him going into the sky."* (Acts 1:9-11)

Pentecost

Soon after, when the apostles were all together, they agreed they needed to replace Judas Iscariot. A vote took place, and they chose Matthias to complete the twelve apostles again.

As Pentecost came, all the apostles were together in a room when *suddenly there came from the sky a sound like the rushing of a mighty wind, and it filled all the house where they were sitting. Tongues like fire appeared and were distributed to them, and one sat on each of them. They were all filled with the Holy Spirit and began to speak with other languages, as the Spirit gave them the ability to speak.* (Acts 2:2-4)

Leaving the room, the apostles began preaching, and miraculously everyone listening could understand them, even though there were a multitude of nationalities present with different languages spoken, including *Parthians, Medes, Elamites, and people from Mesopotamia, Judah, Cappadocia, Pontus, Asia, Phrygia, Pamphylia, Egypt, the parts of Libya around Cyrene, visitors from Rome, both Jews and proselytes, Cretans, and Arabians.* (Acts 2:9-11)

Peter Addresses the Crowds

Peter came forward to address the astonished crowd. *"You men of Judah and all you who live in Jerusalem, let this be known to you, and listen to my words. This is what has been spoken through the prophet Joel:*

> *'It will be in the last days, says God,*
> *that I will pour out my Spirit on all flesh.*
> *Your sons and your daughters will prophesy.*
> *Your young men will see visions.*
> *Your old men will dream dreams.*

> *Yes, and on my servants and on my handmaidens in those days,*
> *I will pour out my Spirit, and they will prophesy.*
> *I will show wonders in the sky above,*
> *and signs on the earth beneath."*[246] (Acts 2:14-19)

"*Men of Israel, listen to what I am going to say: Jesus the Nazarene was a man commended to you by God by the miracles and portents and signs that God worked through him when he was among you, as you all know. This man, who was put into your power by the deliberate intention and foreknowledge of God, you took and had crucified by men outside the Law. You killed him, but God raised him to life, freeing him from the pangs of Hades; for it was impossible for him to be held in its power.*" (Acts 2:22-24*)

"*Being therefore exalted by the right hand of God, and having received from the Father the promise of the Holy Spirit, he has poured out this which you now see and hear.*" (Acts 2:33)

"*Let all the house of Israel therefore know that God has made him both Lord and Christ, this Jesus whom you crucified.*" (Acts 2:36)

The crowds were cut to the heart on hearing Peter, and asked him what it is they must do. Peter told them to, "*Repent and be baptised, every one of you, in the name of Jesus Christ for the forgiveness of sins, and you will receive the gift of the Holy Spirit.*" (Acts 2:38)

That day, three thousand people believed.

Peter Cures a Lame Man

One day, as Peter and John were going to the temple, they saw a man who for forty years was carried to the temple entrance every day to beg. Peter spoke to him, "*I have no silver or gold, but what I have I give you. In the name of Jesus Christ of Nazareth, get up and walk!*" (Acts 3:6)

The man rose and walked away.

---

[246] Joel 2:28-32

The people who witnessed this were amazed and unable to explain what happened. They all gathered around Peter and John. Peter told them, *"You men of Israel, why do you marvel at this man? Why do you fasten your eyes on us, as though by our own power or godliness we had made him walk? The God of Abraham, Isaac, and Jacob, the God of our Fathers, has glorified his Servant Jesus, whom you delivered up and denied in the presence of Pilate, when he had determined to release him... faith in his name has made this man strong."* (Acts 3:12-13,16)

"Now, brothers, I know that you did this in ignorance, as did also your rulers. But the things which God announced by the mouth of all his prophets, that Christ should suffer, he has fulfilled. Repent therefore, and turn again, that your sins may be blotted out, so that there may come times of refreshing from the presence of the Lord, and that he may send Christ Jesus, who was ordained for you before, whom heaven must receive until the times of restoration of all things, which God spoke long ago by the mouth of his holy prophets." (Acts 3:17-21)

As it was with Jesus, the preaching of Peter and John angered the high priests. They were soon arrested and locked up.

Peter and John are Brought Before the Sanhedrin

The following day, Peter and John were brought before a council of high priests for interrogation and were asked by what authority they preached and healed. Peter (filled with the Holy Spirit) answered, *"You rulers of the people and elders of Israel, if we are examined today concerning a good deed done to a crippled man, by what means this man has been healed, may it be known to you all, and to all the people of Israel, that it is in the name of Jesus Christ of Nazareth, whom you crucified, whom God raised from the dead, that this man stands here before you. He is 'the stone, which was regarded as worthless by you, the builders, which has become the head of the corner.*[247]

---

[247] Ps 118:22

There is salvation in no one else, for there is no other name under heaven that is given among men, by which we must be saved!" (Acts 4:8-12)

The priests were astonished and confused. They knew they were followers of Jesus, but they were uneducated men, so how could they speak so eloquently; and how could they cure the man standing before them? All they could agree on was to ban them from speaking in the name of Jesus again. Peter boldly responded, *"Whether it is right in the sight of God to listen to you rather than to God, judge for yourselves, for we can't stop telling the things which we saw and heard."* (Acts 4:19-20)

After their release, they went back to their community and told everyone about the events and the warning issued to them. Being of one mind, they all prayed, *"Grant to your servants to speak your word with all boldness, while you stretch out your hand to heal; and that signs and wonders may be done through the name of your holy Servant Jesus."* (Acts 4:29-30)

They were all filled with the Holy Spirit and began to praise and proclaim the name of Jesus.

All the faithful regularly met to praise God, and while the nonbelievers would not join them, they did bring along their sick, believing if the shadow of Peter fell on them, they would be healed. This news spread far and wide. Soon people from all around arrived with their sick; all were cured.

The Apostles are Arrested

The high priests became increasingly irate with the continued preaching and healing by the apostles (despite receiving warnings to stop), until they could take no more and had them arrested and put into jail. *But an angel of the Lord opened the prison doors by night, and released them, adding, "Go stand and speak in the temple to the people all the words of this life."* (Acts 5:19-20)

The following morning the high priests sent for the prisoners, only to be told they were not there, even though the doors remained locked, and the guards were in place! While the news of the escape was being communicated, another man addressed the high priests, telling them he saw the apostles outside preaching. Infuriated, they ordered them to be recaptured and brought back. The high priests reinforced on them the strict instructions not to preach in the name of Jesus. Peter replied, *"We must obey God rather than men. The God of our fathers raised up Jesus, whom you killed, hanging him on a cross. God exalted him with his right hand to be a Prince and a Saviour, to give repentance to Israel, and remission of sins. We are his witnesses of these things; and so also is the Holy Spirit, whom God has given to those who obey him."* (Acts 5:29-32)

This inflamed them so much they wanted to put them all to death, but had them flogged instead, while reissuing the warning not to preach in the name of Jesus.

Honoured at having suffered in the name of Jesus, they continued to proclaim the Good News of Jesus in the temple and in homes every day.

Stephen

From among the faithful arose a man called Stephen. Filled with the Holy Spirit, he performed many miracles. Some members from a local synagogue tried to debate with him but could not win, so they devised a plot against him. They found a false witness to testify that Stephen was heard blaspheming. He was arrested and taken to the Sanhedrin, where the false accusations were repeated.

One of the high priests asked Stephen if there was any truth to the accusations. Stephen replied beginning with a vivid retelling of the origins of God's calling of Abraham, Isaac, and Jacob, the coming of Jesus, his ministry, his death, and his resurrection. He concluded with the proclamation, *"You stiff-necked and uncircumcised in heart and ears, you always resist the Holy Spirit! As your fathers did, so you do. Which of the prophets didn't your fathers persecute? They killed those who foretold the coming of the Righteous One, of whom you have now become betrayers and murderers. You received the Law as it was ordained by angels and didn't keep it!"* (Acts 7:51-53)

They were infuriated by his speech, but Stephen was not finished. Gazing towards heaven he said, *"Behold, I see the heavens opened and the Son of Man standing at the right hand of God!"* (Acts 7:56)

The high priests had had enough and they ordered him to be stoned to death.

Among the approving witnesses to Stephen's death was a young man called Saul.

Saul and his Conversion

From that day forward, a bitter persecution of the new church commenced. At the forefront was Saul, who *worked for the complete destruction of the Church; he went from house to house arresting both men and women and sending them to prison.* (Acts 8:3*)

Not content with persecuting the church solely in Jerusalem, Saul sought approval from the high priests to travel to Damascus to continue *breathing threats and slaughter against the disciples of the Lord.* (Acts 9:1)

While travelling to Damascus, Saul was startled by a heavenly voice that spoke to him, *"Saul, Saul, why do you persecute me?"*

He said, *"Who are you, Lord?"*

The Lord said, "I am Jesus, whom you are persecuting. But rise up and enter into the city, then you will be told what you must do." (Acts 9:4-6)

Those travelling with Saul at the time were dumbfounded, for they could hear a voice but did not know where it came from.

Saul was left blind.

His companions took Saul the rest of the way to Damascus, where he remained blind for three days.

At the same time in Damascus, a man called Ananias, who had also been spoken to by God, was instructed to find Saul. This terrified Ananias, as he had heard of Saul and the enthusiasm he brought to his role of persecutor. God told him, *"Go your way, for he is my chosen vessel to bear my name before the nations and kings, and the children of Israel.*

For I will show him how many things he must suffer for my name's sake." (Acts 9:15-16)

Ananias did as God asked, and finding Saul he said, *"Brother Saul, the Lord, who appeared to you on the road by which you came, has sent me that you may receive your sight and be filled with the Holy Spirit."* (Acts 9:17)

Saul's sight was restored, and he was baptised.

Within a few days, Saul was out preaching in the synagogues, proclaiming Jesus as the Son of God. Naturally, all those who heard him were astounded and confused, for they knew of his reputation. Like many prophets before and after him, the local Jews plotted to kill Saul, but with the help of his companions, he escaped to Jerusalem.

Once in Jerusalem, Saul hoped for acceptance from the church but instead was met with more resistance, for even the apostles found it difficult to believe in his conversion. In time, however, he was accepted, and he preached fearlessly. It wasn't long before another plot to kill him emerged, and this time he escaped to Tarsus.

Peter Cures a Paralytic and Raises the Dead

A lull in persecution soon followed, and the church grew and flourished, filled with the Holy Spirit.

One day, while preaching in the townships of Lydda and Sharon, Peter approached a paralytic man named Aeneas and said, *"Jesus Christ heals you. Get up and make your bed!"* (Acts 9:34)

He immediately got up, and everybody in the towns was converted.

Leaving Lydda, Peter made his way to Jaffa, where the local church had reached out to him about the death of a faithful woman, Tabitha. When Peter arrived, they took him to the room where she lay. He went to Tabitha and said, "Get up!" Tabitha rose and took Peter's hand.

Peter Visits a Roman Officer

Another day while praying, Peter received a vision in which God told him to visit a centurion called Cornelius. The vision and the message disturbed Peter, as it was forbidden for a Jew to associate with pagans. God explained otherwise, *"What God has cleansed, you must not call unclean."* (Acts 10:15)

When Peter arrived at the house of Cornelius, he said, *"You yourselves know how it is an unlawful thing for a man who is a Jew to join himself or come to one of another nation, but God has shown me that I shouldn't call any man unholy or unclean. Therefore, I also came without complaint when I was sent for."* (Acts 10:28-29)

"Truly I perceive that God doesn't show favouritism; but in every nation he who fears him and works righteousness is acceptable to him." (Acts 10:34-35)

While Peter was speaking, the Holy Spirit came down on everyone there, even the pagans. They all praised God in many strange languages. Afterward, Peter directed them all to be baptised.

Returning to Jerusalem, the local Jews were not happy with Peter and the news of his meeting with the uncircumcised pagans, but when he explained his visions from God, they calmed down and gave glory to God.

The Church Takes Hold in Antioch

The church in Jerusalem heard the Good News was taking a foothold in Antioch, so they sent Barnabas along. Finding God was truly working there, Barnabas gave them his blessings and moved on to Tarsus, where Saul was evangelising. They both returned to Antioch and stayed there for a year.

It was during this time that the disciples of Jesus were first called Christians.

Peter Put in Prison

The persecution of the Christians escalated as Herod Agrippa took an interest. He started by beheading James[248] and then ordered the arrest of Peter.

The night before his trial, while in prison and chained between two guards, Peter received a visit from an angel. Tapping Peter on the shoulder, the angel said, *"Get dressed and put on your sandals." He did so. He said to him, "Put on your cloak and follow me."* (Acts 12:8)

Not sure if he was dreaming or not, Peter obliged and followed the angel, past the guards, through the city gates and out into the street. Once the angel left, Peter knew it was not a dream, but it was God who delivered him from Herod.

Peter made his way to the home of Mary, the mother of Mark.[249] Everyone there was stunned, for they knew Peter was in prison about to face trial. He asked them to tell James[250] and the others.

When Herod discovered Peter had escaped, the guards responsible were killed.

Saul's First Missionary Journey

Meanwhile in Antioch the Holy Spirit appeared to the church there with a message. *"Separate Barnabas and Saul for me, for the work to which I have called them."* (Acts 13:2)

The two of them set out west for Cyprus, stopping first at Salamis, then Paphos. While in Paphos, a Jewish magician called Bar-Jesus caused difficulty for both Paul[251] and Barnabas. Paul would have none of it though and rebuked him, *"You son of the devil, full of all deceit and all cunning, you enemy of all righteousness, will you not cease to pervert the right*

---

[248] The apostle and brother of John.
[249] The writer of the second Gospel.
[250] The writer of the Letter from James in the New Testament.
[251] From here on Saul is called Paul.

ways of the Lord? Now, behold, the hand of the Lord is on you, and you will be blind, not seeing the sun for a season!"

Immediately a mist and darkness fell on him. He went around seeking someone to lead him by the hand. Then the proconsul, when he saw what was done, believed, being astonished at the teaching of the Lord. (Acts 13:10-12)

From Cyprus they headed northwest to the coastal town of Perga in Pamphylia,[252] then onto Antioch in Pisidia.[253] On arrival, they began preaching in the local synagogues.

Paul Preaches to the Jews

"Men of Israel, and you who fear God, listen. The God of this people chose our fathers, and exalted the people when they lived as foreigners in the land of Egypt, and with an uplifted arm, he led them out of it. For a period of about forty years he put up with them in the wilderness. When he had destroyed seven nations in the land of Canaan, he gave them their land for an inheritance for about four hundred and fifty years. After these things, he gave them judges until Samuel the prophet. Afterward they asked for a king, and God gave to them Saul the son of Kish, a man of the tribe of Benjamin, for forty years. When he had removed him, he raised up David to be their king." (Acts 13:17-22)

Paul continued, *"What the people of Jerusalem and their rulers did, though they did not realise it, was in fact to fulfil the prophecies read on every Sabbath. Though they found nothing to justify his death, they condemned him and asked Pilate to have him executed. When they had carried out everything that Scripture foretells about him they took him down from the tree and buried him in a tomb. But God raised him from the dead, and for many days he appeared to those who had accompanied him from Galilee to Jerusalem: and it is these same companions of his who are now his witnesses before our people.*

---

[252] Perga is today in modern day Turkey.
[253] Different to the Antioch in Syria which is where they left from.

"We have come here to tell you the Good News. It was to our ancestors that God made the promise but it is to us, their children, that he has fulfilled it, by raising Jesus from the dead." (Acts 13:26-33*)

The people were so moved by Paul's message that they appealed to him to repeat it the following Sabbath. This time the entire town (Jews and pagans) came out to hear him. The local Jews became resentful[254] and sought to contradict Paul's message with blasphemies. Paul admonished them, saying, *"It was necessary that God's word should be spoken to you (Jews) first. Since indeed you thrust it from yourselves, and judge yourselves unworthy of eternal life, behold, we turn to the Gentiles. For so has the Lord commanded us, saying, 'I have set you as a light for the Gentiles, that you should bring salvation to the uttermost parts of the earth.'"*[255] (Acts 13:46-47)

Paul's Mission Continues to Iconium

Eventually Paul and Barnabas were expelled from Antioch, and they moved on to Iconium, where they again went to preach in the synagogues. Many Jews and pagans came to believe, but at the same time some Jews were corrupting the minds of the pagans. A strong discord grew in the city, for as Paul and Barnabas continued to spread the Good News, the discontented Jews created havoc. Ultimately, they had to flee south, going to the towns of Lystra and Derbe to continue their mission.

In Lystra, Paul cured a man who had never walked in his life. When the locals saw this, they revered Paul and Barnabas as gods, calling Barnabas, 'Zeus'[256] and Paul, 'Hermes'.[257]

When Paul and Barnabas discovered this, and the sacrifices they were intending to make, they put a stop to it. *"Men, why are you doing these things? We also are men of the same nature as you, and bring you good*

---

[254] They resented the Good News being shared with non Jews.
[255] Is 49:6
[256] The pagan supreme god.
[257] The messenger of the gods.

news, *that you should turn from these vain things to the living God, who made the sky, the earth, the sea, and all that is in them."* (Acts 14:15)

The crowds were not dissuaded.

It did not help their cause when some Jews from Antioch and Iconium arrived to create further division. Paul was stoned and thrown outside the city gates.[258] The following day, he left with Barnabas for Derbe. Here they won many more souls for God before retracing their steps back to Antioch in Pisidia via Lystra and Iconium.

In Antioch they encouraged the faith of the church saying, *"We all have to experience many hardships before we enter the Kingdom of God"* (Acts 14:22*)

In each of the churches Paul visited, he appointed elders.[259]

Trouble in Jerusalem

During the time when many pagans were being converted to Christianity, arguments developed in Jerusalem over whether they needed to be circumcised to be fully converted. Peter spoke to clarify the church's position, *"Brothers, you know that a good while ago God made a choice among you that by my mouth the nations should hear the word of the Good News and believe. God, who knows the heart, testified about them, giving them the Holy Spirit, just like he did to us. He made no distinction between us and them, cleansing their hearts by faith. Now therefore why do you tempt God, that you should put a yoke on the neck of the disciples which neither our fathers nor we were able to bear? But we believe that we are saved through the grace of the Lord Jesus, just as they are."* (Acts 15:7-11)

James added, *"Peter has reported how God first visited the nations to take out of them a people for his name. This agrees with the words of the prophets. As it is written,*

---

[258] The Jews believed they had stoned Paul to death.
[259] Paul's first missionary journey was 45-49 AD.

'After these things, I will return.
I will again build the tabernacle of David, which
has fallen.
I will again build its ruins.
I will set it up
that the rest of men may seek after the Lord;
all the Gentiles who are called by my name,
says the Lord, who does all these things.' [260]

"All of God's works are known to him from eternity. Therefore, my judgement is that we don't trouble those from among the Gentiles who turn to God, but that we write to them that they abstain from the pollution of idols, from sexual immorality, from what is strangled, and from blood." (Acts 15:14-20)

A letter was sent along with some delegates to Antioch to deliver this message so all the churches would be of the same mind.

Paul Begins his Second Missionary Journey and meets Timothy[261]

Soon after, Paul and Barnabas separated. Paul went with Silas north to Lycaonia, while Barnabas travelled with John Mark west to Cyprus.

Travelling through Lystra, Paul met a man called Timothy,[262] who became his travelling companion. Together they visited numerous towns, instructing the people and the churches to grow in faith.

Paul Goes into Prison

One night Paul received a vision from God, summoning him to take the Good News to Macedonia. Heading west to the port of Troas, he and

---

[260] Amos 9:11-12
[261] See letters to and from Timothy.
[262] The New Testament letters 1, 2 Timothy are addressed to him.

Silas sailed across the Aegean Sea to Neapolis and then onto the Roman colony of Philippi in Macedonia.

One day a slave-girl prophetess, who was well regarded by her masters (she made them money telling fortunes), started to follow Paul and Silas. Every day as she followed them, she would shout, *"These men are servants of the Most High God, who proclaim to us a way of salvation!"* (Acts 16:17)

Knowing the truth however, Paul rebuked her. *"I command you in the name of Jesus Christ to come out of her!"* (Acts 16:18)

Immediately the (evil) spirit left her. When her masters found out she could no longer tell fortunes, and therefore not make them money, they dragged Paul and Silas before the courts to have them charged. They were stripped, flogged, and thrown into jail.

That night while in prison, there was a great earthquake. All the prison doors flew open. When the jailer regained his composure, he assumed his prisoners would have fled, so he tried to kill himself. Before he could go through with it, Paul alerted him that they were still there. Shocked, the guard went into the cell and fell to his knees before them, asking, *"Sirs, what must I do to be saved?"*

They said, *"Believe in the Lord Jesus Christ, and you will be saved, you and your household." They spoke the word of the Lord to him, and to all who were in his house.* (Acts 16:30-32)

At daybreak orders were sent for Paul and Silas to be released.

Paul's Travels Take him to Athens

Paul and Silas continued their travels and left Philippi for Thessalonica before arriving in Beroea. In both places they went to the synagogues to preach and interpret through Scripture how Jesus was to suffer, die and rise from the dead. As usual, trouble was never far away, as the Jews who were closed to the truth stirred up dissension. Eventually, Paul had to be secreted away south to Athens. Silas and Timothy followed soon after.

While Paul was waiting in Athens, he continued his mission of teaching and debating with anyone who would listen. Eventually he was invited to speak to the local Councilmen, as even they were curious to know more about his message.

Paul was happy to answer. *"You men of Athens, I perceive that you are very religious in all things. For as I passed along and observed the objects of your worship, I also found an altar with this inscription: 'To an unknown God'. What therefore you worship in ignorance, I announce to you. The God who made the world and all things in it, he, being Lord of heaven and earth, doesn't dwell in temples made with hands. He isn't served by men's hands, as though he needed anything, seeing he himself gives to all life and breath and all things. He made from one blood every nation of men to dwell on all the surface of the earth."* (Acts 17:22-26)

"Now he commands that all people everywhere should repent, because he has appointed a day in which he will judge the world in righteousness by the man whom he has ordained; of which he has given assurance to all men, in that he has raised him from the dead." (Acts 17:30-31)

The Church Grows in Corinth[263]

Paul's next stop was Corinth, where for eighteen months he continued his ministry to convert Jews and Greeks by preaching that Jesus was the Christ. Many Jews however would not listen to his message and tried unsuccessfully to accuse him before the courts, saying he was breaking the law.

This completed Paul's second missionary journey.[264]

---

[263] While in Corinth Paul writes his first letter to the Thessalonians.
[264] Paul's second missionary journey was 50-52 AD.

Paul Begins his Third Missionary Journey

Moving on, Paul travelled south to Cenchreae, crossed the Aegean Sea to Ephesus before sailing to Caesarea and then overland to Antioch in Syria.[265]

It wasn't long before Paul set out from Antioch again, travelling west through Galatia to Ephesus, where he met up with several disciples. *He said to them, "Did you receive the Holy Spirit when you believed?"*

They said to him, "No, we haven't even heard that there is a Holy Spirit."
He said, "Into what then were you baptised?"
They said, "Into John's baptism."
Paul said, "John indeed baptised with the baptism of repentance, saying to the people that they should believe in the one who would come after him, that is, in Jesus."

When they heard this, they were baptised in the name of the Lord Jesus. When Paul had laid his hands on them, the Holy Spirit came on them and they spoke with other languages and prophesied. They were about twelve men in all. (Acts 19:2-7)

The Church is Formed in Ephesus[266]

Paul continued his ministry in Ephesus for two years, and many people from Asia were able to hear the Good News. *God worked special miracles by the hands of Paul, so that even handkerchiefs or aprons were carried away from his body to the sick, and the diseases departed from them, and the evil spirits went out.* (Acts 19:11-12)

---

[265] It is around this time Paul writes his 2nd letter to the Thessalonians.
[266] While in Ephesus Paul writes his two letters to the Corinthians and also a letter to the Galatians.

Paul Brings a Man Back to Life Before Departing for Jerusalem

One night in Troas, while Paul was in an upstairs room preaching, a young man called Eutychus, who was sitting by the window listening, fell out and died. *Paul went down and fell upon him, and embracing him said, "Don't be troubled, for his life is in him."*

When he had gone up, had broken bread, and eaten, and had talked with them a long while, even until break of day, he departed. They brought the boy in alive and were greatly comforted. (Acts 20:10-12)

Paul then made plans to depart for Jerusalem, leaving the church with these words.[267]

"You yourselves know, from the first day that I set foot in Asia, how I was with you all the time, serving the Lord with all humility, with many tears, and with trials which happened to me by the plots of the Jews; how I didn't shrink from declaring to you anything that was profitable, teaching you publicly and from house to house, testifying both to Jews and to Greeks, repentance toward God and faith toward our Lord Jesus. Now, behold, I go bound by the Spirit to Jerusalem, not knowing what will happen to me there; except that the Holy Spirit testifies in every city, saying that bonds and afflictions wait for me. But these things don't count; nor do I hold my life dear to myself, so that I may finish my race with joy, and the ministry which I received from the Lord Jesus, to fully testify to the Good News of the grace of God.

"Now, behold, I know that you all, among whom I went about preaching God's Kingdom, will see my face no more. Therefore, I testify to you today that... I gave you an example, that so labouring you ought to help the weak, and to remember the words of the Lord Jesus, that he himself said, 'It is more blessed to give than to receive.'" (Acts 20:18-35)

After crossing the Mediterranean and reaching Tyre, Paul spent time with Philip the evangelist. During his stay there a prophet named Agabus spoke to Paul, warning him not to go to Jerusalem, saying, *"The*

---

[267] Paul also sent his letter to the Romans.

Jews at Jerusalem will bind (him), *and will deliver him into the hands of the Gentiles."* (Acts 21:11)

Paul, however, was willing to accept whatever God ordained for him. Replying, *"What are you doing, weeping, and breaking my heart? For I am ready not only to be bound, but also to die at Jerusalem for the name of the Lord Jesus… The Lord's will be done."*[268] (Acts 21:13-14)

Paul is Back in Jerusalem and Back in Prison

Some Jews from Asia had arrived in Jerusalem to stir up the crowds against Paul, saying he taught to break away from the laws of Moses and also profaned the temple by allowing Greeks to enter. Their lies were believed, and the people dragged Paul out of the temple. Before they could beat him to death, the local centurions intervened and took him away. Before they could do any harm, Paul was able to convince the local tribune that the allegations were false and was allowed to set the record straight. He recounted the story of his early persecution of the Jews, his subsequent conversion on the road to Damascus and the warning from God to flee Jerusalem and go to the pagans.

Paul Before the Sanhedrin

Paul's explanations were not enough though, and the fired-up crowd screamed for his blood. He was seized by a centurion who strapped him down to prepare for a flogging. Just in time Paul yelled out that he was in fact a Roman citizen and therefore it was illegal to flog him. They released him.

The following day, Paul sought justice and vindication against the false charges brought against him and demanded to meet the chief priests and the entire Sanhedrin.

---

[268] Paul's third (and final) missionary journey was 53-58 AD.

Still under guard by the Roman soldiers, Paul told the Sanhedrin he had a clear conscience in all he had done and said it in the name of Jesus. This caused the high priest Ananias to scoff, and he ordered Paul to be hit. Paul challenged Ananias and his authority to make such an order, which further riled up the Sanhedrin.

Looking around him, Paul surmised the Sanhedrin was composed of half Pharisees and half Sadducees. As a Pharisee himself, Paul appealed to them. *"Men and brothers, I am a Pharisee, a son of Pharisees. Concerning the hope and resurrection of the dead, I am being judged!"*

When he had said this, an argument arose between the Pharisees and Sadducees, and the crowd was divided. For the Sadducees say that there is no resurrection, nor angel, nor spirit; but the Pharisees confess all of these. A great clamour arose, and some scribes of the Pharisees' part stood up, and contended, saying, "We find no evil in this man. But if a spirit or angel has spoken to him, let's not fight against God!" (Acts 23:6-9)

This caused a great ruckus, and the guards were forced to remove Paul for his own safety.

(That) *night, the Lord stood by him and said, "Cheer up, Paul, for as you have testified about me at Jerusalem, so you must testify also at Rome."* (Acts 23:1-11)

A Group of Jews Conspire Against Paul

The following day, a group of forty Jews made a vow they would not eat or drink until Paul was dead. They conspired with the Sanhedrin to ask the tribune to bring Paul to them on the pretext that they wanted to question him further. Their plan was to ambush and kill him along the route. Luckily for Paul, his nephew heard of the plot and made it known to the tribune, who arranged for Paul to be quietly removed from the city and taken to Caesarea, where Felix, the governor, would hear the case against him.

Five days later, the high priest Ananias travelled from Jerusalem to Caesarea to petition Felix in the case against Paul. He said, *"I entreat you to bear with us and hear a few words. For we have found this man to be a plague, an instigator of insurrections among all the Jews throughout the world, and a ringleader of the sect of the Nazarenes. He even tried to profane the temple, and we arrested him. By examining him yourself you may ascertain all these things of which we accuse him."* (Acts 24:4-8)

Paul refuted the accusations that he was in any way a troublemaker, saying, *"What I do admit to you is this: it is according to the Way which they describe as a sect that I worship the God of my ancestors, retaining my belief in all points of the Law and in what is written in the prophets; and I hold the same hope in God as they do that there will be a resurrection of good men and bad men alike. In these things, I, as much as they, do my best to keep a clear conscience at all times before God and man."* (Acts 24:14-16*)

"After several years I came to bring alms to my nation and to make offerings; it was in connection with these that they found me in the Temple; I had been purified, and there was no crowd involved, and no disturbance. But some Jews from Asia... these are the ones who should have appeared before you and accused me of whatever they had against me. At least let those who are present say what crime they found me guilty of when I stood before the Sanhedrin... It is about the resurrection of the dead that I am on trial before you today." (Acts 24:17-21*)

Felix held Paul in prison (but with many freedoms) for the next two years,[269] until he was succeeded by Porcius Festus, who, like Felix, was harassed by the Jews to convict Paul. Over the ensuing months, they presented Paul before Festus in Caesarea, then King Agrippa, where he stoically defended himself and proclaimed the Good News of Jesus. He explained his early persecution of the Jews, his conversion, and subsequent missions. Neither man could find any guilt. They then dispatched him on a trouble-filled boat journey to Rome,[270] where he was to appear before Caesar himself.

---

[269] This was the maximum period allowed for a prisoner to be kept without any charge or conviction.

[270] Stopping at Adramyttium, Sidon, Myra, Fair Havens, Malta, Syracuse, Rhegium, and Puteoli.

In Rome,[271] Paul continued to preach to the Roman Jews in the hope he could bring to them the truth of the Good News. Sadly, it was as he had experienced before; they were not willing to listen. He left them with a quote from Isaiah.

> *"Go to this people and say,*
> *in hearing, you will hear,*
> *but will in no way understand.*
> *In seeing, you will see,*
> *but will in no way perceive.*
> *For this people's heart has grown callous.*
> *Their ears are dull of hearing.*
> *Their eyes they have closed.*
> *Lest they should see with their eyes,*
> *hear with their ears,*
> *understand with their heart,*
> *and would turn again,*
> *then I would heal them.*[272]

"Be it known therefore to you that the salvation of God is sent to the nations, and they will listen." (Acts 28:26-28)

Paul remained in Rome for the following two years.

---

[271] During his time in Rome Paul wrote his letters to the Philippians, Ephesians, Colossians and Philemon.

[272] Is 6:9-10

ROMANS

In this letter Paul is preparing the local church in Rome for a visit which he had always intended but would not eventuate as planned. Paul teaches that salvation does not come from following the Law, but from following the life and words of Jesus, the son of God.[273]

This epistle of St Paul 'has affected later Christianity more than any other New Testament book'.[274]

Written sometime around 58 AD.

Paul opens his letter by stressing there are no excuses for not knowing God, explaining that throughout history he has continually sought to make himself known. But eventually he relented and left them to their own demise.

The anger of God is being revealed from heaven against all the impiety and depravity of men who keep truth imprisoned in their wickedness. For what can be known about God is perfectly plain to them since God himself has made it plain. Ever since God created the world, his everlasting power and deity - however invisible - have been there for the mind to see in the things he has made. That is why such people are without excuse: they knew God and yet refused to honour him as God or to thank him; instead, they made nonsense out of logic and their empty minds were darkened.

---

[273] Brown, R. E., Fitzmyer, J. A., & Murphy, R. E. (1989). The Jerome Biblical commentary. Dallas, TX: CDWord Library. Introduction to the Letter to the Romans.
[274] Ibid.

The more they called themselves philosophers, the more stupid they grew, until they exchanged the glory of the immortal God for a worthless imitation, for the image of mortal man, of birds, of quadrupeds and reptiles. That is why God left them to their filthy enjoyments and the practices with which they dishonour their own bodies, since they have given up divine truth for a lie and have worshipped and served creatures instead of the creator who is blessed forever. (Rom 1:18-25*)

He warns the church against judging the pagans, especially if they are going to act like pagans themselves. He advises them not to assume they are saved just because of 'some' of their actions. They are to always remember that the goodness of God is in his desire to accept their repentance, so they need to repent continually or risk the same judgement as the pagans.

So no matter who you are, if you pass judgement you have no excuse. In judging others you condemn yourself, since you behave no differently from those you judge. We know that God condemns that sort of behaviour impartially: and when you judge those who behave like this while you are doing exactly the same, do you think you will escape God's judgement? (Rom 2:1-3*)

Paul explains that the Law itself cannot save them. They can't just say, yes, I know the Law[275] and then not live it. For the pagan who does not know the Law yet lives virtuously will be saved. Just as the Jew who knows it and doesn't live it will be punished.

God has no favourites... It is not listening to the Law but keeping it that will make people holy in the sight of God. For instance, pagans who have never heard of the Law but are led by reason to do what the Law commands may not actually 'possess' the Law, but they can be said to 'be' the Law. They can point to the substance of the Law engraved on their hearts - they can call a witness, that is, their own conscience - they have accusation and defence, that

---

[275] The Law is the Ten Commandments and the first 5 books of the Old Testament.

is, their own inner mental dialogue ... on the day when, according to the Good News I preach, God, through Jesus Christ. (Rom 2:11,13-16*)

You preach against stealing, yet you steal; you forbid adultery, yet you commit adultery; you despise idols, yet you rob their temples. By boasting about the Law and then disobeying it, you bring God into contempt. (Rom 2:21-23*)

Paul clarifies that not even circumcision will save them, if it is the physical act only. It is what is in their heart that matters, not how they look.

He tells the Roman Church that even though God has promised salvation and even though he is an eternally forgiving God; it doesn't mean he won't punish sin. Paul instructs not to rely on the forgiveness of God as a 'get out of jail free card' and so sin with impunity, in the expectation that forgiveness will be given. It doesn't work that way.

Paul sets about explaining the distinction between living by the Law and living by faith. *All the law does is to tell us what is sinful.* (Rom 3:20*)

A man is justified by faith and not by doing something the Law tells him to do. (Rom 3:28*)

He explains that if they only had the Law to live by (like their Old Testament forebears) then they can, and will, break the Law and therefore open themselves up to punishment. Faith, however, is above the Law.

The *Law involves the possibility of punishment for breaking the law - only where there is no law can that be avoided. That is why what fulfils the promise depends on faith, so that it may be a free gift and be available to all.* (Rom 4:15-16*)

It is this faith, faith in Jesus, that should be their claim. But in knowing this they also need to know that as Jesus suffered, so too will they. However, because Jesus died for us all while we were still sinners, he will not forsake us in the future.

Being therefore justified by faith, we have peace with God through our Lord Jesus Christ; through whom we also have our access by faith into this grace in which we stand. We rejoice in hope of the glory of God. Not only this, but we also rejoice in our sufferings, knowing that suffering produces perseverance; and perseverance, proven character; and proven character, hope; and hope doesn't disappoint us, because God's love has been poured into our hearts through the Holy Spirit who was given to us.

For while we were yet weak, at the right time Christ died for the ungodly. For one will hardly die for a righteous man. Yet perhaps for a good person someone would even dare to die. But God commends his own love toward us, in that while we were yet sinners, Christ died for us.

Much more then, being now justified by his blood, we will be saved from God's wrath through him. For if while we were enemies, we were reconciled to God through the death of his Son, much more, being reconciled, we will be saved by his life. (Rom 5:1-10)

Paul describes how sin entered the world through Adam, and that Adam was a prefigure of Jesus. For as Adam brought sin and death into the world, so Jesus brought salvation, and his gift of salvation far surpasses the sin of Adam.

As sin entered into the world through one man, and death through sin, so death passed to all men because all sinned. (Rom 5:12)

So then as through one trespass, all men were condemned; even so through one act of righteousness, all men were justified to life. For as through the one man's disobedience many were made sinners, even so through the obedience of the one, many will be made righteous. The law came in that the trespass might abound; but where sin abounded, grace abounded more exceedingly, that as sin reigned in death, even so grace might reign through righteousness to eternal life through Jesus Christ our Lord. (Rom 5:18-21)

Paul turns to baptism and how it fits in.

Don't you know that all of us who were baptised into Christ Jesus were baptised into his death? We were buried therefore with him through baptism into death, that just as Christ was raised from the dead through the glory of the Father, so we also might walk in newness of life.

> *For if we have become united with him in the likeness of his death, we will also be part of his resurrection; knowing this, that our old man was crucified with him, that the body of sin might be done away with, so that we would no longer be in bondage to sin. For he who has died has been freed from sin. But if we died with Christ, we believe that we will also live with him, knowing that Christ, being raised from the dead, dies no more. Death no longer has dominion over him! For the death that he died, he died to sin one time; but the life that he lives, he lives to God. Thus consider yourselves also to be dead to sin, but alive to God in Christ Jesus our Lord.* (Rom 6:3-11)
>
> *Therefore, don't let sin reign in your mortal body, that you should obey it in its lusts. Also, do not present your members to sin as instruments of unrighteousness, but present yourselves to God as alive from the dead, and your members as instruments of righteousness to God. For sin will not have dominion over you, for you are not under law, but under grace.* (Rom 6:12-14)
>
> *For the wages of sin is death, but the free gift of God is eternal life in Christ Jesus our Lord.* (Rom 6:23)

Paul continues teaching about the Law and sin, revealing that sin only exists because of the Law. He stresses that when we act outside the Law, this is sin living in us. Paul reveals that while in his mind he serves the Law of God, with his body he too is under the law of sin.

But the Law does not sentence us to sin and death - because of Jesus, who has set us free. God has dealt with sin once and for all by sending his only Son. So, we must live in this new 'spiritual' life. The spirit we receive makes us call God our father. So as children of God, we become his heirs and therefore co-heirs with Jesus, where we not only share in his suffering but also his glory. Nothing we suffer here on earth can approach the glory waiting for us.

1 CORINTHIANS

Paul founded the church in Corinth during his second missionary journey (around 57 AD). At that time, Corinth was a hotbed of every kind of vice, and as such, the fledgling church and the newly converted Christians were struggling to live out their newfound faith.

In this first letter Paul looks to address some of their specific problem areas while also encouraging and uplifting them.

Paul begins by admonishing the Corinthians for developing the habit of attributing the source of their conversion, and therefore their loyalty to the person who brought the Good News to them, rather than Jesus. *Each one of you says, "I follow Paul," "I follow Apollos," "I follow Cephas," and, "I follow Christ." Is Christ divided? Was Paul crucified for you? Or were you baptised into the name of Paul?* (1Cor 1:12-13)

Paul then moves on to discussing true and false wisdom, or God's wisdom against the world's wisdom.

For the word of the cross is foolishness to those who are dying, but to us who are being saved it is the power of God. For it is written,

> *'I will destroy the wisdom of the wise.*
> *I will bring the discernment of the discerning to nothing.'*[276]

---

[276] Ps 33:10

Where is the wise? Where is the scribe? Where is the debater of this age? Hasn't God made foolish the wisdom of this world? For seeing that in the wisdom of God, the world through its wisdom didn't know God, it was God's good pleasure through the foolishness of the preaching to save those who believe. For Jews ask for signs, Greeks seek after wisdom, but we preach Christ crucified, a stumbling block to Jews and foolishness to Greeks, but to those who are called, both Jews and Greeks, Christ is the power of God and the wisdom of God; because the foolishness of God is wiser than men, and the weakness of God is stronger than men. (1Cor 1:18-25)

We are different from the world. *We received not the spirit of the world, but the Spirit, which is from God, that we might know the things that were freely given to us by God. We also speak these things, not in words which man's wisdom teaches but which the Holy Spirit teaches, comparing spiritual things with spiritual things.* (1Cor 2:12-13)

Paul provides an insight into what his life is like, and thus by extension what his fellow Christians can expect.

For I think that God has put us, the apostles, last of all, like men sentenced to death. For we are made a spectacle to the world, both to angels and men. We are fools for Christ's sake, but you are wise in Christ. We are weak, but you are strong. You have honour, but we have dishonour. Even to this present hour we hunger, thirst, are naked, are beaten, and have no certain dwelling place. We toil, working with our own hands. When people curse us, we bless. Being persecuted, we endure. Being defamed, we entreat. We are made as the filth of the world, the dirt wiped off by all, even until now. (1Cor 4:9-13)

Next Paul condemns the news that someone in the community is committing sexual immorality by sleeping with their father's wife. He writes they must remove this evildoer from them.

Paul answers some questions sent to him concerning marriage, celibacy, and virginity, as the views on these matters as Christians are totally opposed to the views as held by pagans. Paul clarifies that his decision to remain celibate is his own choice and not mandated by God, and others in the church should not feel they need to follow in his path.

Again, because the Corinthians had come from a mostly pagan background Paul teaches how, as Christians, they are to turn away from their old idols, and food eating rituals, *for we know that no idol is anything in the world, and that there is no other God but one.* (1Cor 8:4)

You can't both drink the cup of the Lord and the cup of demons. You can't both partake of the table of the Lord and of the table of demons. Or do we provoke the Lord to jealousy? Are we stronger than he? (1Cor 10:21-22)

Whether therefore you eat or drink, or whatever you do, do all to the glory of God. (1Cor 10:31)

Paul moves on to revealing some of himself. Why he does what he does and tries to instil in the Corinthian church the devotion he has.

For if I preach the Good News, I have nothing to boast about, for necessity is laid on me; but woe is to me if I don't preach the Good News. For if I do this of my own will, I have a reward. But if not of my own will, I have a stewardship entrusted to me. What then is my reward? That when I preach the Good News, I may present the Good News of Christ without charge, so as not to abuse my authority in the Good News.

For though I was free from all, I brought myself under bondage to all, that I might gain the more. To the Jews I became as a Jew, that I might gain Jews; to those who are under the law, as under the law, that I might gain those who are under the law; to those who are without law, as without law (not being without law toward God, but under law toward Christ), that I might win those who are without law. To the weak I became weak. I have become all things to all men, that I may by all means save some. Now I do this for the sake of the Good News, that I may be a joint partaker of it.

Don't you know that those who run in a race all run, but one receives the prize? Run like that, so that you may win. Every man who strives in the games exercises self-control in all things. Now they do it to receive a corruptible crown, but we are incorruptible. I therefore run like that, not aimlessly.

I fight like that, not beating the air, but I beat my body and bring it into submission, lest by any means, after I have preached to others, I myself should be disqualified. (1Cor 9:16-27)

Paul offers some encouragement in the face of trials and hardships, which can and will befall them. *Therefore, let him who thinks he stands be careful that he doesn't fall. No temptation has taken you except what is common to man. God is faithful, who will not allow you to be tempted above what you are able, but will with the temptation also make the way of escape, that you may be able to endure it.* (1Cor 10:12-13)

Paul addresses the celebration of the Lord's Supper and in particular news made known to him about how the Corinthians are weakening its relevance and reverence. *For I received from the Lord that which also I delivered to you, that the Lord Jesus on the night in which he was betrayed took bread. When he had given thanks, he broke it and said, "Take, eat. This is my body, which is broken for you. Do this in memory of me." In the same way he also took the cup after supper, saying, "This cup is the new covenant in my blood. Do this, as often as you drink, in memory of me." For as often as you eat this bread and drink this cup, you proclaim the Lord's death until he comes.*

Therefore, whoever eats this bread or drinks the Lord's cup in a way unworthy of the Lord will be guilty of the body and the blood of the Lord. (1Cor 11:23-27)

Paul then talks about the spiritual gifts of the Holy Spirit. *Now concerning spiritual things... I don't want you to be ignorant. You know that when you were heathen, you were led away to those mute idols... Therefore I make known to you that no man speaking by God's Spirit says, "Jesus is accursed." No one can say, "Jesus is Lord," but by the Holy Spirit.* (1Cor 12:1-3)

Now there are various kinds of gifts, but the same Spirit. There are various kinds of service, and the same Lord. There are various kinds of workings, but the same God who works all things in all. But to each one is given the manifestation of the Spirit for the profit of all. For to one is given through the

Spirit the word of wisdom, and to another the word of knowledge according to the same Spirit, to another faith by the same Spirit, and to another gifts of healings by the same Spirit, and to another workings of miracles, and to another prophecy, and to another discerning of spirits, to another different kinds of languages, and to another the interpretation of languages. But the one and the same Spirit produces all of these, distributing to each one separately as he desires. (1Cor 12:4-11)

Before dropping the subject of the gifts of the Holy Spirit, Paul puts some context around them, saying they are nothing without love.

If I speak with the languages of men and of angels, but don't have love, I have become a sounding brass or a clanging cymbal. If I have the gift of prophecy, and know all mysteries and all knowledge, and if I have all faith, so as to remove mountains, but don't have love, I am nothing. (1Cor 13:1-2)

Love is patient and is kind. Love doesn't envy. Love doesn't brag, is not proud, doesn't behave itself inappropriately, doesn't seek its own way, is not provoked, takes no account of evil; doesn't rejoice in unrighteousness, but rejoices with the truth; bears all things, believes all things, hopes all things, and endures all things. Love never fails. (1Cor 13:4-8)

In short, there are three things that last: faith, hope and love; and the greatest of these is love. (1Cor 13:13*)

Next, Paul talks about how the spiritual gifts serve the church community. In particular, he mentions the gift of tongues and prophecy and urges them to place higher importance on the gift of prophecy, for it can benefit and uplift the entire community. The gift of tongues, whilst it is a significant conduit between the person and God, it is less beneficial to the community - unless it can be interpreted.

He also adds that *other languages are a sign, not to those who believe, but to the unbelieving; but prophesying is a sign, not to the unbelieving, but to those who believe. If therefore the whole assembly is assembled together and all speak with other languages, and unlearned or unbelieving people come in, won't they say that you are crazy? But if all prophesy, and someone unbelieving* or unlearned comes in, he is reproved by all, and he is judged by all. And thus the secrets of his heart are revealed. So he will fall down on his face and worship God, declaring that God is among you indeed.* (1Cor 14:22-25)

Paul then talks about the resurrection of Jesus and his followers. *Now if Christ is preached, that he has been raised from the dead, how do some among you say that there is no resurrection of the dead? But if there is no resurrection of the dead, neither has Christ been raised. If Christ has not been raised, then our preaching is in vain and your faith also is in vain. Yes, we are also found false witnesses of God, because we testified about God that he raised up Christ, whom he didn't raise up if it is true that the dead are not raised. For if the dead aren't raised, neither has Christ been raised. If Christ has not been raised, your faith is vain; you are still in your sins.* (1Cor 15:12-17)

For since death came by man, the resurrection of the dead also came by man. For as in Adam all die, so also in Christ all will be made alive. (1Cor 15:21-22)

Paul next describes how the resurrection will work, stating we will be brought to life in Christ. *When the end comes, he will deliver up the Kingdom to God the Father, when he will have abolished all rule and all authority and power. For he must reign until he has put all his enemies under his feet. The last enemy that will be abolished is death. For, 'He put all things in subjection under his feet'.*[277] *... When all things have been subjected to him, then the Son will also himself be subjected to him who subjected all things to him, that God may be all in all.* (1Cor 15:23-28)

Then he progresses into a more human explanation of how the resurrection will work.

But someone will say, "How are the dead raised?" and, "With what kind of body do they come?" You foolish one, that which you yourself sow is not made alive unless it dies. That which you sow, you don't sow the body that will be,

---

[277] Ps 110:1

but a bare grain, maybe of wheat, or of some other kind. But God gives it a body even as it pleases him, and to each seed a body of its own. All flesh is not the same flesh, but there is one flesh of men, another flesh of animals, another of fish, and another of birds. There are also celestial bodies and terrestrial bodies; but the glory of the celestial differs from that of the terrestrial. There is one glory of the sun, another glory of the moon, and another glory of the stars; for one star differs from another star in glory.

So also is the resurrection of the dead. The body is sown perishable; it is raised imperishable. It is sown in dishonour; it is raised in glory. It is sown in weakness; it is raised in power. It is sown a natural body; it is raised a spiritual body. There is a natural body and there is also a spiritual body. (1Cor 15:35-44)

If the soul has its own embodiment, so does the spirit have its own embodiment. The first man, Adam, as Scripture says, became a living soul; but the last Adam has become a life-giving spirit. That is, first the one with the soul, not the spirit, and after that, the one with the spirit. The first man, being from the earth, is earthly by nature; the second man is from heaven. (1Cor 15:44-47*)

Or else, brothers, put it this way: flesh and blood cannot inherit the Kingdom of God: and the perishable cannot inherit what lasts forever. (1Cor 15:50*)

When this perishable nature has put on imperishability, and when this mortal nature has put on immortality, then the words of Scripture will come true: Death is swallowed up in victory. Death, where is your victory? Death, where is your sting? (1Cor 15:54-55*)

2 CORINTHIANS

In this letter, Paul spends considerable time defending himself, his message, and his authority to preach. Since his last visit to the Corinthians there has been a bit of a vacuum left and there are many 'arch-apostles' looking to fill it with messages differing from Paul's message of Christ's death and resurrection.

Here, Paul shows vulnerability, hoping the Corinthians see he truly loves them and wants only what is best for their eternal souls. He also addresses some news that has reached him.

Paul opens his letter with an explanation of why he had to change his plans to revisit them. He writes he does not follow his own human plans, but God's.

Paul moves on to talk about the trials and tribulations of his apostolate.

> *We are only the earthenware jars that hold this treasure, to make it clear that such an overwhelming power comes from God and not from us. We are in difficulties on all sides, but never cornered; we see no answer to our problems, but never despair; we have been persecuted, but never deserted; knocked down, but never killed; always, wherever we may be, we carry with us in our body the death of Jesus, so that the life of Jesus, too, may always be seen in our body.* (2Cor 4:7-10*)

> *And so it is with the fear of the Lord in mind that we try to win people over. God knows us for what we really are, and I hope that in your consciences you know us too. This is not another attempt to commend ourselves to you:*

we are simply giving you reasons to be proud of us, so that you will have an answer ready for the people who can boast more about what they seem than what they are. If we seemed out of our senses, it was for God; but if we are being reasonable now, it is for your sake. And this is because the love of Christ overwhelms us when we reflect that if one man has died for all, then all men should be dead; and the reason he died for all was so that living men should live no longer for themselves, but for him who died and was raised to life for them. (2Cor 5:11-15*)

From now onward, therefore, we do not judge anyone by the standards of the flesh. Even if we did once know Christ in the flesh, that is not how we know him now. And for anyone who is in Christ, there is a new creation; the old creation has gone, and now the new one is here. It is all God's work. (2Cor 5:16-18*)

Paul reflects on how he has been treated as a man of God.

We do nothing that people might object to, so as not to bring discredit on our function as God's servants. Instead, we prove we are servants of God by great fortitude in times of suffering: in times of hardship and distress; when we are flogged, or sent to prison, or mobbed; labouring, sleepless, starving. We prove we are God's servants by our purity, knowledge, patience and kindness; by a spirit of holiness, by a love free from affectation; by the word of truth and by the power of God. (2Cor 6:3-7*)

Paul implores the Corinthians not to believe the false reports about him which are being spread. He also addresses news which has reached him in Macedonia about a previous letter he sent to the Corinthians, one that was harsh, yet he insists they needed it. Whilst he apologises for the initial hurt it caused them, he urges them to reflect instead on the ultimate good which has come from it.

Then Paul raises the matters of collections, or almsgiving. He begins by telling how generous the Macedonians are - even though they have very little.

He reminds the Corinthians how well off they are, and implies their generosity should far outweigh that of the Macedonians. *Remember how generous the Lord Jesus was: he was rich, but he became poor for your sake, to make you rich out of his poverty.* (2Cor 8:9*)

Paul also addresses accusations made by other missionaries, or arch-apostles, that he is spreading himself too thin, travelling too widely, and because of that they boast they are more effective than he is.

We… are not going to boast without a standard to measure against: taking for our measure the yardstick, which God gave us to measure with, which is long enough to reach to you. We are not stretching further than we ought; otherwise we should not have reached you, as we did come all the way to you with the Gospel of Christ. (2Cor 10:13-14*)

He warns them against believing anything they hear being preached that does not centre on Christ.

I am afraid… (you)… may get corrupted and turned away from simple devotion to Christ. Because any new comer has only to proclaim a new Jesus, different from the one that we preached, or you have only to receive a new spirit, different from the one you have already received, or a new gospel, different from the one you have already accepted – and you welcome it with open arms: As far as I can tell, these arch-apostles have nothing more than I have. I may not be a polished speechmaker, but as for knowledge, that is a different matter; surely we have made this plain, speaking on every subject in front of all of you. (2Cor 11:3-6*)

He then lists his credentials against the others, who are spreading a different message to him.

But if anyone wants some brazen speaking – I am still talking as a fool – then I can be as brazen as any of them, and about the same things. Hebrews, are they? So am I. Israelites? So am I. Descendants of Abraham? So am I. The servants of Christ? I must be mad to say this, but so am I, and more than they: more, because I have worked harder, I have been sent to prison more often, *and whipped so many times more, often almost to death. Five times I had the thirty-nine lashes from the Jews; three times I have been beaten with sticks; once I was stoned; three times I have been shipwrecked and once adrift in the open sea for a night and a day.* (2Cor 11:21-25*)

Paul explains how the grace of an apostolate is sufficient. The greater the weakness of the apostle, the clearer it will be that his power comes from God. This weakness is the greatest thing an apostle has to boast of, because it is the indisputable condition for possessing the strength of Christ. So he can rejoice in his trials and sufferings, since anything that proves his human weakness, at the same time proves that the strength of Christ is at work within him.

To stop me from getting too proud, I was given a thorn in the flesh, an angel of Satan to beat me and stop me from getting too proud! About this thing, I have pleaded with the Lord three times for it to leave me, but he has said, "My grace is enough for you: my power is at its best in weakness." (2Cor 12:7-8*)

Paul continues to defend his message and his authority to instruct faithfully in Christ. He knows other arch-apostles are trying to defame him and he knows the Corinthians are wavering, however he implores them to stay faithful to him and the message of Christ that he teaches.

GALATIANS

In this letter, Paul defends his ministry against those who try to bring him down. Criticism abounds that Paul isn't a real apostle because he never 'knew' Jesus, only the eleven did. As a result, people try to discredit his teachings to the Gentiles, particularly because Paul teaches that they can receive the Good News and become Christians without undergoing the rite of circumcision and practising the Law, as the traditional Jews do.

Written sometime around 57 AD.

Paul opens his letter by addressing things he has heard about how the Galatians have let their faith slip away. It seems there have been other missionaries visiting them, preaching a different message from Paul.

I am astonished at the promptness with which you have turned away from the one who called you and have decided to follow a different version of the Good News. Not that there can be more than one Good News; it is merely that some troublemakers among you want to change the Good News of Christ; and let me warn you that if anyone preaches a version of the Good News different from the one we have already preached to you, whether it be ourselves or an angel from heaven, he is to be condemned. (Gal 1:6-8*)

Paul explains his message is not a human one, but a divine one. He recounts his conversion and how he was the most zealous persecutor of Christ and his followers, but God specifically chose to reveal his son

Jesus to him and commissioned him with the proclamation of the Good News to the pagan nations.

Paul firms up his authority to preach to the pagans by telling a story of one of his visits to Jerusalem, where the leading locals challenged him. They maintained the Good News was for the Jews only. But Paul explained that *the same person whose action had made Peter the apostle of the circumcised had given me a similar mission to the pagans.* (Gal 2:8*)

Paul also reassures the Galatian converts that their journey to righteousness is no harder or easier than that of those born Jewish.

Though we were born Jews and not pagan sinners, we acknowledge that what makes a man righteous is not obedience to the Law, but faith in Jesus Christ. We had to become believers in Christ Jesus no less than you had, and now we hold that faith in Christ rather than fidelity to the Law is what justifies us, and that no one can be justified by keeping the Law. (Gal 2:15-16*)

Through the Law I am dead to the Law, so that now I can live for God. I have been crucified with Christ, and I live now not with my own life but with the life of Christ who lives in me. (Gal 2:19-20*)

Paul delves into the antipathy between the Christians who were once Jews and those who were once pagans. There have been seeds of division sown amongst the Galatians suggesting that unless they also observe the Law, they cannot be true followers of Christ.

Are you people in Galatia mad? Has someone put a spell on you, in spite of the plain explanation you have had of the crucifixion of Jesus Christ? Let me ask you one question: was it because you practised the Law that you received the Spirit, or because you believed what was preached to you? (Gal 3:1-2*)

Does God give you the Spirit so freely and work miracles among you because you practise the Law, or because you believed what was preached to you? (Gal 3:5*)

Paul reveals that in living only by the Law, you are doomed. For everyone will break the Law and sin, so if it is only the Law you live by, then forget it! He reminds them that is why Christ came.

Christ redeemed us from the curse of the Law by being cursed for our sake. (Gal 3:13*)

Before faith came, we were allowed no freedom by the Law; we were being looked after until faith was revealed. The Law was to be our guardian until the Christ came and we could be justified by faith. Now that that time has come, we are no longer under that guardian. (Gal 3:23-25*)

On and on he goes, he won't lose the Galatians to these other preachers.

Let me put this another way: an heir, even if he has actually inherited everything, is no different from a slave for as long as he remains a child. He is under the control of guardians and administrators until he reaches the age fixed by his father. Now before we came of age, we were as good as slaves to the elemental principles of this world, but when the appointed time came, God sent his Son, born of a woman, born a subject of the Law, to redeem the subjects of the Law and to enable us to be adopted as sons. The proof that you are sons is that God has sent the Spirit of his Son into our hearts: the Spirit that cries, "Abba, Father," and it is this that makes you a son, you are not a slave anymore; and if God has made you son, then he has made you heir.

Once you were ignorant of God and enslaved to 'gods' who are not really gods at all; but now that you have come to acknowledge God – or rather, now that God has acknowledged you – how can you want to go back to elemental things like these, that can do nothing and give nothing, and be their slaves? You and your special days and months and seasons and years! You make me feel I have wasted my time with you. (Gal 4:1-11*)

Paul challenges why they have discarded his message to them, saying when he was last there they *would even have gone so far as to pluck out your eyes and give them to me. Is it telling you the truth that has made me your enemy?* (Gal 4:16-17*)

He laments he will need to return to them and do it all over again; he likens it to going *through the pain of giving birth to you all over again until Christ is formed in you.* (Gal 4:19*)

Moving on, Paul discusses living in the freedom of Jesus and how the works of the flesh are opposite to the fruits of the spirit, saying that *if you are guided by the Spirit you will be in no danger of yielding to self-indulgence, since self-indulgence is the opposite of the Spirit, ... If you are led by the Spirit, no law can touch you. When self-indulgence is at work, the results are obvious: fornication, gross indecency, and sexual irresponsibility; idolatry and sorcery; feuds and wrangling, jealousy, bad temper, and quarrels; disagreements, factions, envy; drunkenness, orgies, and similar things. I warn you now, as I warned you before: those who behave like this will not inherit the Kingdom of God. What the Spirit brings is very different: love, joy, peace, patience, kindness, goodness, trustfulness, gentleness, and self-control.* (Gal 5:16-23*)

Paul leaves them with...*It is only self-interest that makes them want to force circumcision on you – they want to escape persecution for the cross of Christ – they accept circumcision but do not keep the Law themselves; they only want you to be circumcised so that they can boast of the fact. As for me, the only thing I can boast about is the cross of our Lord Jesus Christ, through whom the world is crucified to me, and I to the world. It does not matter if a person is circumcised or not; what matters is for him to become an altogether new creature.* (Gal 6:12-15*)

EPHESIANS

It is probable that this letter is not actually to the church community in Ephesus (as Paul's other epistles were) but to a broader range of churches throughout Paul's missionary journeys. This does not diminish its message of encouragement - that as pagans they are no longer separated from the salvation of Christ. There is now hope through Jesus.
    Written c.61 AD.

Paul's letter opens with how we (God's creation) became separated from God through sin, and how Christ rejoined us through his dying for us (while we were still sinners) which finally brought together God's plan. *He has let us know the mystery of his purpose, the hidden plan he so kindly made in Christ from the beginning, to act upon when the times had run their course to the end: that he would bring everything together under Christ, as head, everything in the heavens and everything on earth.* (Ep 1:9-10)

God loved us with so much love that he was generous with his mercy: when we were dead through our sins, he brought us to life with Christ - it is through grace that you have been saved - and raised us up with him and gave us a place with him in heaven, in Christ Jesus. This was to show for all ages to come, through his goodness towards us in Christ Jesus, how infinitely rich he is in grace. Because it is by grace that you have been saved, through faith; not by anything of your own, but by a gift from God; not by anything that you have done, so that nobody can claim the credit. We are God's work of art. (Ep 2:4-10)

He asserts it was Jesus, through his act of dying on the cross, that bridged the gap between the pagan and Jew, between the circumcised and uncircumcised. Through Jesus, we are all now one spirit. *You had no Christ and were excluded from membership of Israel, aliens with no part in the covenants with their Promise; you were immersed in this world, without hope and without God. But now in Christ Jesus, you that used to be so far apart from us have been brought very close, by the blood of Christ. For he is the peace between us.* (Ep 2:12-14)

In his own person he killed the hostility. Later he came to bring the good news of peace, peace to you who were far away and peace to those who were near at hand. (Ep 2:16-17)

Paul reveals he has *been entrusted by God with the grace he meant for* (them). (Ep 3:2)

This mystery that has now been revealed through the Spirit to his holy apostles and prophets was unknown to any men in past generations; it means that pagans now share the same inheritance, that they are parts of the same body, and that the same promise has been made to them, in Christ Jesus, through the gospel. (Ep 3:5-6)

Next Paul implores the church in Ephesus to *lead a life worthy of your vocation. Bear with one another charitably, in complete selflessness, gentleness and patience. Do all you can to preserve the unity of the Spirit by the peace that binds you together. There is one Body, one Spirit, just as you were all called into one and the same hope when you were called. There is one Lord, one faith, one baptism, and one God who is Father of all, over all, through all and out of his infinite glory, may he give you the power through his Spirit for your hidden self to grow strong, so that Christ may live in your hearts within all.* (Ep 4:1-6)

Paul encourages them to stay strong and continue the fight against their old pagan ways, to stay away from lying, stealing and anger, to reject the lives they lived before hearing the message of Christ.

> *You must give up your old way of life; you must put aside your old self, which gets corrupted by following illusory desires. Your mind must be renewed by a spiritual revolution so that you can put on the new self that has been created in God's way, in the goodness and holiness of the truth.* (Ep 4:22-24)

He summarises his message asking them to *imitate God, as children of his that he loves, and follow Christ by loving as he loved you.* (Ep 5:1) And *try to discover what the Lord wants of you.* (Ep 5:10)

Paul next turns his consideration to the morals of the home and about how the way husbands treat their wives and wives treat their husbands has a connection with Christ and his Church. Paul analogises that a wife is to her husband as the Church is to Christ.[278]

> *Give way to one another in obedience to Christ. Wives should regard their husbands as they regard the Lord, since as Christ is head of the Church and saves the whole body, so is a husband the head of his wife; and as the Church submits to Christ, so should wives to their husbands, in everything. Husbands should love their wives just as Christ loved the Church and sacrificed himself for her to make her holy. He made her clean by washing her in water with a form of words, so that when he took her to himself she would be glorious, with no speck or wrinkle or anything like that, but holy and faultless. In the same way, husbands must love their wives as they love their own bodies; for a man to love his wife is for him to love himself. A man never hates his own body, but he feeds it and looks after it; and that is the way Christ treats the Church, because it is his body – and we are its living parts. For this reason, a man must leave his father and mother and be joined to his wife, and the two will become one body.*[279] (Ep 5:21-31)

Paul delivers a similar message of obedience for children, workers (slaves) and employers (masters).

---

[278] This passage may be a familiar one. It is amongst the most popular readings heard at Christian weddings.
[279] Gen 2:24

Finishing up, Paul issues a warning against evil, encouraging his readers to *put God's armour on so as to be able to resist the devil's tactics. For it is not against human enemies that we have to struggle, but against the sovereignties and the powers who originate the darkness in this world, the spiritual army of evil in the heavens.* (Ep 6:11-12)

Also carry the shield of faith so that you can use it to put out the burning arrows of the evil one. And then you must accept salvation from God to be your helmet and receive the word of God from the Spirit to use as a sword. Pray all the time asking for what you need. (Ep 6:16-18)

PHILIPPIANS

Written while under house arrest in Rome (c.56 AD), Paul understands that in his absence, the faith of the new churches will be tested. He thanks the Philippians for being strong in their faith, and discusses how happily he accepts his imprisonment, knowing it is being used as a source of strength and resolve by other preachers of the Good News.

Paul opens his letter by thanking the Philippians for being strong in their faith. It seems they hold a special place in his heart.

He discusses his house arrest in Rome and how happily he accepts it, knowing it is being used as a source of strength and resolve by other preachers of the Good News.

Paul writes he is happy if by his death, or life, Christ is glorified - he doesn't care which. *For to me to live is Christ, and to die is gain. But if I live on in the flesh, this will bring fruit from my work; yet I don't know what I will choose. But I am hard pressed between the two, having the desire to depart and be with Christ, which is far better. Yet to remain in the flesh is more needful for your sake.* (Ph 1:21-24)

He sends encouragement to the Philippians, telling them to *let your way of life be worthy of the Good News of Christ, that whether I come and see you or am absent, I may hear of your state, that you stand firm in one spirit, with one soul striving for the faith of the Good News; and in nothing frightened by the adversaries, which is for them a proof of destruction, but to you of salvation, and that from God.* (Ph 1:27-28)

Moving his attention to unity amongst the Philippians, Paul advises them that *in your minds you must be the same as Christ Jesus.* (Ph 2:5*)

Expanding by telling them to *make my joy full by being like-minded, having the same love, being of one accord, of one mind; doing nothing through rivalry or through conceit, but in humility, each counting others better than himself; each of you not just looking to his own things, but each of you also to the things of others.* (Ph 2:2-4)

Paul commends them to be like Jesus, *who, existing in the form of God, didn't consider equality with God a thing to be grasped, but emptied himself, taking the form of a servant, being made in the likeness of men. And being found in human form, he humbled himself, becoming obedient to the point of death, yes, the death of the cross. Therefore God also highly exalted him, and gave to him the name which is above every name, that at the name of Jesus every knee should bow, of those in heaven, those on earth, and those under the earth, and that every tongue should confess that Jesus Christ is Lord, to the glory of God the Father.* (Ph 2:6-11)

The next subject which Paul touches on is common in all his letters, that is the right of pagans to enjoy the salvation brought by Christ - without the need of being raised under the Law or being circumcised. He explains he was such a person, a true Jew, raised under the Law, but he does not rely on that, in fact he now considers it a disadvantage to his journey in Christ. *All I want is to know Christ and the power of his resurrection and to share his sufferings by reproducing the pattern of his death. That is the way I can hope to take my place in the resurrection of the dead.* (Ph 3:10-11*)

My brothers, be united in following my rule of life. Take as your models everybody who is already doing this and study them as you used to study us. I have told you often, and I repeat it today with tears, there are many who are behaving as the enemies of the cross of Christ. They are destined to be lost... For us, our homeland is in heaven, and from heaven comes the Saviour we are waiting for, the Lord Jesus Christ, and he will transfigure these wretched bodies of ours into copies of his glorious body. (Ph 3:17-20)

Paul leaves the Philippians with one last piece of advice - to be happy; to be tolerant; not to worry - but pray to God for anything they need; to remain pure and noble and continue doing all the things he taught them.

The letter finishes with Paul thanking them for their recent help, and while he truly appreciates it, he puts it into context by saying. *Not that I speak because of lack, for I have learned in whatever state I am, to be content in it. I know how to be humbled, and I also know how to abound. In any and all circumstances I have learned the secret both to be filled and to be hungry, both to abound and to be in need. I can do all things through Christ who strengthens me. However you did well that you shared in my affliction.* (Ph 4:11-14)

COLOSSIANS

Another of St Paul's letters written while he was imprisoned. This one dates c.62 AD. Paul has never visited the Church at Colossae but he gets reports given to him.

In this letter Paul writes to reassure them, to instruct them, and also to reinforce a doctrine which is being eroded away by those against the conversion of pagans.

Paul opens by encouraging the new Church in Colossae, telling them they are not alone nor are they unknown to him. (I) *have never failed to pray for you.* (Col 1:9*) (Since) *having heard of your faith in Christ Jesus and of the love which you have toward all the saints.* (Col 1:4)

For not long ago, you were foreigners and enemies, in the way that you used to think and the evil things that you did: but now he has reconciled you, by his death. (Col 1:21-22)

Instructing them, that God has *made us fit to be partakers of the inheritance of the saints in light, who delivered us out of the power of darkness, and translated us into the Kingdom of the Son of his love, in whom we have our redemption, the forgiveness of our sins.* (Col 1:12-14)

Paul takes this opportunity to impart some formal teaching about Christ to the Colossians.

> *He is the image of the invisible God,*
> *the firstborn of all creation.*

> *For by him all things were created in the heavens and on the earth,*
> *visible things and invisible things...*
> *All things have been created through him and for him.*
> *He is before all things,*
> *and in him all things are held together.*
> *He is the head of the body, the assembly,*
> *who is the beginning,*
> *the firstborn from the dead,*
> *that in all things he might have the preeminence.*
> *For all the fullness was pleased to dwell in him,*
> *and through him to reconcile all things to himself by him,*
> *whether things on the earth or things in the heavens,*
> *having made peace through the blood of his cross.*
> (Col 1:15-20)

You must be rooted in him and built on him and held firm by the faith you have been taught. (Col 2:7*)

In him you were also circumcised with a circumcision not made with hands, in the putting off of the body of the sins of the flesh, in the circumcision of Christ, having been buried with him in baptism, in which you were also raised with him through faith in the working of God, who raised him from the dead. You were dead through your trespasses and the uncircumcision of your flesh. He made you alive together with him, having forgiven us all our trespasses, wiping out the handwriting in ordinances which was against us. He has taken it out of the way, nailing it to the cross. (Col 2:11-14)

The new 'Christian' churches all suffer the persecution of coming from pagan stock and Paul is saddened by this as their conversion and salvation was the mission given to him by God.

It makes me happy to suffer for you... I became the servant of the Church when God made me responsible for delivering God's message to you. (Col 1:24-25*)

Let no one therefore judge you in eating or drinking, or with respect to a feast day or a new moon or a Sabbath day, which are a shadow of the things to come; but the body is Christ's. (Col 2:16-17)

But *set your mind on the things that are above, not on the things that are on the earth. For you died, and your life is hidden with Christ in God.* (Col 3:2-3)

He urges them to exercise control over their earthly practises such as *sexual immorality, uncleanness, depraved passion, evil desire, and covetousness, which is idolatry. For these things' sake the wrath of God comes on the children of disobedience. You also once walked in those, when you lived in them, but now you must put them all away: anger, wrath, malice, slander, and shameful speaking out of your mouth.* (Col 3:5-8)

There is only Christ: he is everything and he is in everything. You are God's chosen race, his saints: he loves you, and you should be clothed in sincere compassion, in kindness and humility, gentleness and patience. Bear with one another: forgive each other as soon as a quarrel begins. The Lord has forgiven you: now you must do the same. (Col 3:11-13*)

1 THESSALONIANS

Written c.51 AD, and after Paul's first of two visits. In the letter, Paul shares his happiness over their conversion, and also recaps some of the messages he gave them whilst there. He also tries to set them straight about the second coming of Christ or the 'parousia'.

Paul begins his letter by telling the Thessalonians how widespread their conversion story is. He asserts that since they turned from their pagan ways and accepted God the news has spread far and wide throughout Macedonia, Achaia, and further, with many drawing inspiration from them. *You are and you will be the crown of which we shall be proudest in the presence of our Lord Jesus when he comes; you are our pride and our joy.* (1Th: 2:19-20*)

He reminds them before his arrival in Thessalonica he was *grossly insulted at Philippi, and it was our God who gave us the courage to proclaim his Good News to you in the face of great opposition.* (1Th 2:2*)

But he also reasserts that his ministry is a commission given to him by God, and it is one he accepts *like a mother feeding and looking after her own children.* (1Th 2:7*)

Another reason why we constantly thank God for you is that as soon as you heard the message that we brought you as God's message, you accepted it for what it really is, God's message and not some human thinking, and it is still a living power among you who believe it. For you, my brothers, have been like the churches of God in Christ Jesus which are in Judea, in suffering the same treatment from your own countrymen as they have suffered from the

Jews, the people who put the Lord Jesus to death, and the prophets too. And know they have been persecuting us, and acting in a way that cannot please God and makes them the enemies of the whole human race, because they are hindering us from preaching to the pagans and trying to save them. They never stop trying to finish off the sins they have begun, but retribution is overtaking them at last. (1Th 2:13-16*)

Paul explains the reason behind sending Timothy to visit them, also pointing out that he wanted to come himself, but it just wasn't possible.

He was concerned and wanted to *prevent any of you from being unsettled by the present troubles. As you know, these are bound to come our way: when we were with you, we warned you that we must expect to have persecutions to bear, and that is what has happened now, as you have found out.* (1Th 3:3-4*)

Paul continues his letter, urging the Thessalonians to make *more progress in the kind of life that you are meant to live: the life that God wants, as you learned from us, and as you are already living it.* (1Th 4:1*)

What God wants is for you all to be holy. He wants you to keep away from fornication, not giving way to selfish lust like the pagans who do not know God. (1Th 4:3&5*)

For we have been called by God to be holy, not to be immoral. (1Th 4:7*)

Paul speaks about the living and the dead and the coming of Christ. *We want you to be quite certain, brothers, about those who have died, to make sure that you do not grieve about them, like the other people who have no hope. We believe that Jesus died and rose again, and that it will be the same for those who have died in Jesus: God will bring them with him. We can tell you this from the Lord's own teaching, that any of us who are left alive until the Lord's coming will not have any advantage over those who have died. At the trumpet of God, the voice of the archangel will call out the command and the Lord himself will come down from heaven; those who have died in Christ will be the first to rise, and then those of us who are still alive will be taken up in the* *clouds, together with them, to meet the Lord in the air. So we shall stay with the Lord forever.* (1Th 4:13-17*)

Know very well that the Day of the Lord is going to come like a thief in the night. It is when people are saying, "How quiet and peaceful it is" that the worst suddenly happens, as suddenly as labour pains come on a pregnant woman; and there will be no way for anybody to evade it. (1Th 5:2-3*)

God never meant us to experience the Retribution, but to win salvation through our Lord Jesus Christ, who died for us so that, alive or dead, we should still live united to him. (1Th 5:9-10*)

Paul finishes by encouraging them to be at peace with themselves, to be *happy at all times; pray constantly; and for all things give thanks to God, because this is what God expects you to do in Christ Jesus.* (1Th 5:17-18*)

2 THESSALONIANS

Also written from Corinth, after receiving a reply from his first letter. Paul needs to continue his message regarding the second coming as there is still unease in the community.

Like 1 Thessalonians, Paul opens his letter by declaring how proud he is about the strength of their faith, but he also reminds them that faith and persecution go hand in hand. The purpose of persecution is that it *shows that God's judgement is just, and the purpose of it is that you may be found worthy of the Kingdom of God; it is for the sake of this that you are suffering now.* (2Th 1:5*)

Paul reminds them that at the Parousia[280] *God will rightly repay with injury those who are injuring you, and reward you, who are suffering now.* (2Th 1:6-7*)

He even goes into some detail of what it will look like. *He will come in flaming fire to impose the penalty on all who do not acknowledge God and refuse to accept the Good News of our Lord Jesus. It will be their punishment to be lost eternally, excluded from the presence of the Lord and from the glory of his strength on that day when he comes to be glorified among his saints and seen in his glory by all who believe in him.* (2Th 1:8-10*)

Next Paul turns to the 'when' of the Parousia, saying it is not now. He explains it cannot happen until a series of events precede it. Paul calls it

---

[280] Judgement Day. The second coming. The second advent. The Jerome Biblical Commentary p234.

the 'Great Revolt' and writes it must take place first. During the Great Revolt a Rebel will appear. This Rebel is the Antichrist, the servant of Satan. He will rebel against all forms of religion and will bestow divine honours on himself.

Paul concedes that while there is currently some form of rebellion going on, it is not 'The' Rebel at work, for there is *one who is holding it back.* (2Th 2:7*) And they must be removed first. *But when the Rebel comes, Satan will set to work: there will be all kinds of miracles and a deceptive show of signs and portents, and everything evil that can deceive those who are bound for destruction because they would not grasp the love of the truth which could have saved them. The reason why God is sending a power to delude them and make them believe what is untrue is to condemn all who refused to believe in the truth and chose wickedness instead.* (2Th 2:9-12*)

Paul's letter concludes with a word of guidance. *My brothers never grow tired of doing what is right. If anyone refuses to obey what I have written in this letter, take note of him and have nothing to do with him, so that he will feel that he is in the wrong; though you are not to regard him as an enemy but as a brother in need of correction.* (2Th 3:13-15*)

1 TIMOTHY

In this letter to Timothy, Paul is building up his spirit. Throughout the letter, he encourages him and reminds him of his calling. *You must aim to be saintly and religious, filled with faith and love, patient and gentle. Fight the good fight of the faith and win for yourself the eternal life to which you were called when you made your profession and spoke up for the truth in front of many witnesses.* (1Tim 6:11-12*)

Written c.65 AD.

Paul begins his letter to Timothy by clarifying why he asked him to stay behind in Ephesus while he left for Macedonia. It was to *insist that certain people stop teaching strange doctrines and taking notice of myths and endless genealogies,* (1Tim 1:3*) which are *only likely to raise irrelevant doubts instead of furthering the design of God which are revealed in faith. The only purpose of this instruction is that there should be love, coming out of a pure heart, a clear conscience and a sincere faith. There are some people who have gone off the straight course and taken a road that leads to empty speculation; they claim to be doctors of the Law, but they understand neither the arguments they are using nor the opinions they are upholding.* (1Tim 1:4-7*)

He stresses it needs to be understood that while the Law is good, it's laws are not for the good but for the *criminals and revolutionaries, for the irreligious and the wicked, for the sacrilegious and the irreverent; they are for people who kill their fathers or mothers and for murderers, for those who are immoral with women or with boys or with men, for liars and for perjurers - and for everything else that is contrary to the sound teaching that goes with the Good News of the glory of the blessed God, the gospel that was entrusted to me.* (1Tim 1:9-11*)

Paul shares some wisdom with Timothy - which he should believe without doubt; *that Christ Jesus came into the world to save sinners, of whom I am chief. However, for this cause I obtained mercy, that in me first, Jesus Christ might display all his patience for an example of those who were going to believe in him for eternal life.* (1Tim 1:15-16*)

Moving on, Paul outlines what it is he wants Timothy to know about prayer, that *in every place ... I want the men to lift their hands up reverently in prayer.* (1Tim 2:8*) He writes that the offering of prayers *is good and acceptable in the sight of God our Saviour, who desires all people to be saved and come to full knowledge of the truth. For there is one God and one mediator between God and men, the man Christ Jesus, who gave himself as a ransom for all, the testimony at the proper time.* (1Tim 2:3-6)

Paul's next instruction applies to the roles of women, presiding elders and deacons in the church community.

A woman ought not to speak, because Adam was formed first and Eve afterward, and it was not Adam who was led astray but the woman who was led astray and fell into sin. Nevertheless, she will be saved by childbearing, provided she lives a modest life and is constant in faith and love and holiness. (1Tim 2:12-15*)

A presiding elder and deacon *must be without reproach, the husband of one wife, temperate, sensible, modest, hospitable, good at teaching; not a drinker, not violent, not greedy for money, but gentle, not quarrelsome, not covetous; one who rules his own house well, having children in subjection with all reverence; (for how could someone who doesn't know how to rule his own house take care of God's assembly?)* (1Tim 3:2-5)

Paul pauses to encourage Timothy in his role. He reminds him he has *a spiritual gift which was given to you when the prophets spoke and the body of elders laid their hands on you; do not let it lie unused.* (1Tim 4:14*)

He also warns him to be resolute, knowing *in later times some will fall away from the faith, paying attention to seducing spirits and doctrines of demons, through the hypocrisy of men who speak lies, branded in their own conscience as with a hot iron, forbidding marriage and commanding to abstain from foods which God created to be received with thanksgiving by those who believe and know the truth. For every creature of God is good, and nothing is to be rejected if it is received with thanksgiving. For it is sanctified through the word of God and prayer.* (1Tim 4:1-5)

Have nothing to do with godless myths and old wives' tales. Train yourself spiritually. Physical exercises are useful enough, but the usefulness of spirituality is unlimited, since it holds out the reward of life here and now and of the future life as well. (1Tim 4:7-8*) *For to this end we both labour and suffer reproach, because we have set our trust in the living God, who is the Saviour of all men, especially of those who believe.* (1Tim 4:10)

In some pastoral advice, Paul advises Timothy not to speak harshly to anyone older than himself, but instead treat them as he would his mother or father. Widows are also singled out, with Paul explaining that *if anyone doesn't provide for his own, and especially his own household, he has denied the faith and is worse than an unbeliever.* (1Tim 5:8)

But godliness with contentment is great gain. For we brought nothing into the world, and we certainly can't carry anything out. But having food and clothing, we will be content with that. But those who are determined to be rich fall into a temptation, a snare, and many foolish and harmful lusts, such as drown men in ruin and destruction. For the love of money is a root of all kinds of evil. Some have been led astray from the faith in their greed, and have pierced themselves through with many sorrows. (1Tim 6:6-10)

Charge those who are rich in this present age that they not be arrogant, nor have their hope set on the uncertainty of riches, but on the living God, who richly provides us with everything to enjoy; that they do good, that they be rich in good works, that they be ready to distribute, willing to share. (1Tim 6:17-18)

2 TIMOTHY

Written from prison, this letter could be seen as Paul's attempt to leave Timothy with guidance and wisdom as he suspects his time with him was coming to an end. Written c. 67AD.

Paul opens by calling Timothy a *dear child of mine,* (2Tim 1:2*) and telling him *he always remembers him in my prayers; I remember your tears and long to see you again to complete my happiness ... I am reminded of the sincere faith which you have.* (2Tim 1:3-4*)
    For this cause, I remind you that you should stir up the gift of God which is in you through the laying on of my hands. For God didn't give us a spirit of fear, but of power, love, and self-control. Therefore don't be ashamed of the testimony of our Lord, nor of me his prisoner; but endure hardship for the Good News according to the power of God. (2Tim 1:6-8)

Writing from prison in Rome, Paul empowers Timothy to continue the spreading of the Good News.
    The things which you have heard from me among many witnesses, commit the same things to faithful men who will be able to teach others also. (2Tim 2:2)
    But with responsibility comes danger, and Paul tells him to *put up with your share of difficulties, like a good soldier of Christ Jesus.* (2Tim 2:3*) *You are well aware, then, that anybody who tries to live in devotion to Christ is certain to be attacked.* (2Tim 3:12*)

For if we died with him, we will also live with him. If we endure, we will also reign with him. If we deny him, he also will deny us. If we are faithless, he remains faithful; for he can't deny himself. (2Tim 2:11-13)

Give diligence to present yourself approved by God, a workman who doesn't need to be ashamed, properly handling the Word of Truth. (2Tim 2:15)

Paul warns Timothy against the false teachers who are emerging, particularly naming Hymenaeus and Philetus *who have erred concerning the truth, saying that the resurrection is already past, and overthrowing the faith of some.* (2Tim 2:18)

He also warns him about the last days, saying *that in the last days, grievous times will come. For men will be lovers of self, lovers of money, boastful, arrogant, blasphemers, disobedient to parents, unthankful, unholy, without natural affection, unforgiving, slanderers, without self-control, fierce, not lovers of good, traitors, headstrong, conceited, lovers of pleasure rather than lovers of God, holding a form of godliness but having denied its power.* (2Tim 3:1-5)

But you remain in the things which you have learned and have been assured of, knowing from whom you have learned them. (2Tim 3:14)

For all Scripture is inspired by God and can profitably be used for teaching, for refuting error, for guiding people's lives and teaching them to be holy. This is how the man who is dedicated to God becomes fully equipped and ready for any good work. (2Tim 3:16-17*)

Paul leaves Timothy with a creed: *I command you therefore before God and the Lord Jesus Christ, who will judge the living and the dead at his appearing and his Kingdom: preach the word; be urgent in season and out of season; reprove, rebuke, and exhort with all patience and teaching. For the time will come when they will not listen to sound doctrine, but having itching ears, will heap up for themselves teachers after their own lusts, and will turn away their ears from the truth, and turn away to fables. But you be sober in all things, suffer hardship, do the work of an evangelist, and fulfil your ministry.* (2Tim 4:1-5)

TITUS

Paul writes to Titus, who remained behind in Crete to oversee the appointment of elders throughout the region. Paul spells out the type of characteristics that are needed amongst the elders. That is, they must have irreproachable character, be married only once, and have faithful and obedient children. They must not be arrogant or hot-headed, avoid violence and heavy drinking, and not profit from their ministry.

Written c.65 AD.

Paul (like in so many of his letters) warns Titus against the false teachers who are stirring up division, particularly those who preach that salvation only comes to those who uphold the old Jewish traditions. *They have got to be silenced: men of this kind ruin whole families, by teaching things that they ought not to, and doing it with the vile motive of making money.* (Tit 1:11*)

He goes on to tell Titus that he *will have to be severe in correcting them and make them sound in the faith so that they stop taking notice of Jewish myths and doing what they are told to do by people who are no longer interested in the truth.* (Tit 1:13-14*)

Paul commissions Titus to *preach the behaviour that goes with healthy doctrine.* (Tit 2:1) He specifically details the qualities needed for men and women, old and young, and even slaves.

For the grace of God has appeared, bringing salvation to all men, instructing us to the intent that, denying ungodliness and worldly lusts, we would live soberly, righteously, and godly in this present age; looking for the blessed hope and appearing of the glory of our great God and Saviour, Jesus Christ. (Tit 2:11-13)

But when the kindness of God our Saviour and his love toward mankind appeared, not by works of righteousness which we did ourselves, but according to his mercy, he saved us through the washing of regeneration and renewing by the Holy Spirit, whom he poured out on us richly through Jesus Christ our Saviour; that being justified by his grace, we might be made heirs according to the hope of eternal life. (Tit 3:4-7)

I want you to be quite uncompromising in teaching all this, so that those who now believe in God may keep their minds constantly occupied in doing good works. All this is good, and will do nothing but good to everybody. (Tit 3:8*)

Paul concludes his letter saying he has sent Artemas and Tychicus to meet up with Titus and that he will await all three of them in Nicopolis, where they will spend the winter.

PHILEMON

Paul addresses this letter not only to Philemon but also Apphia and Archippus.

The letter serves as a recommendation for the letter carrier, Onesimus. Onesimus was a slave of Philemon who ran away to Rome, where he was converted by Paul. Paul asks Philemon to welcome Onesimus back not as a slave but as a brother in Christ.

I appeal to you for my child Onesimus, whom I have become the father of in my chains, who once was useless to you, but now is useful to you and to me. I am sending him back. Therefore receive him, that is, my own heart, whom I desired to keep with me, that on your behalf he might serve me in my chains for the Good News. But I was willing to do nothing without your consent, that your goodness would not be as of necessity, but of free will. For perhaps he was therefore separated from you for a while that you would have him forever, no longer as a slave, but more than a slave, a beloved brother – especially to me, but how much rather to you, both in the flesh and in the Lord. (Ph 1:10-16)

Paul also asks him to obtain a room for him as he hopes to revisit in the not too distant future.

HEBREWS

Originally attributed to Paul, but no longer, the Letter to the Hebrews differs from the preceding letters in the New Testament because it resembles a sermon to the Jewish-Christian community as a whole, rather than a letter to a specific regional church.

The letter explains the role of Christ's sacrifice and how it fulfils the messages and promises of the Old Testament. Christ is the new Covenant between God and humanity, superseding the Old Testament Covenant. The letter assures us that Christ's sacrifice was a 'once and for all' sacrifice - nothing more is needed to bring us back into the arms of God our Father. Jesus did it all; he reopened the door to God and heaven forever.

It was most likely written after 63 AD and before 70 AD.

At various times in the past and in various different ways, God spoke to our ancestors through the prophets; but in our own time, the last days,[281] he has spoken to us through his Son, the Son that he has appointed to inherit everything and through whom he made everything there is. (Heb 1:1-2*)

---

[281] John F. McConnell in his introduction to the Epistle to the Hebrews states that The days we are living in are 'these last days'; now that God has spoken to us in the one who is Son, nothing can remain to be said. No greater revelation is to be expected.

The writer begins by demonstrating through Scripture[282] that Jesus is truly man and also the Son of God. *God has never said to any angel: "You are my Son, today I have become your father;"[283] or: "I will be a father to him and he a son to me."[284] Again, when he brings the First-born into the world, he says: "Let all the angels of God worship him."[285]* (Heb 1:5-7*)

He did not appoint angels to be rulers of the world to come, and that world is what we are talking about. Somewhere there is a passage that shows us this. It runs: 'What is man that you should spare a thought for him, the son of man that you should care for him? For a short while you made him lower than the angels; you crowned him with glory and splendour. You have put him in command of everything.[286] *Well then, if he has put him in command of everything, he has left nothing which is not under his command. At present, it is true, we are not able to see that everything has been put under his command, but we do see in Jesus one who was for a short while made lower than the angels and is now crowned with glory and splendour because he submitted to death; by God's grace he had to experience death for all mankind.* (Heb 2:5-9*)

The author illustrates that since all God's children are flesh and blood, so too did Jesus share *equally in it, so that by his death he could take away all the power of the devil who had power over death, and set free all those who had been held in slavery all their lives by the fear of death.* (Heb 2:14-15*)

It was essential that he should in this way become completely like his brothers so that he could be a compassionate and trustworthy high priest of God's religion, able to atone for human sins. That is, because he has himself been through temptation he is able to help others who are tempted. (Heb 2:17-18*)

In other words, just as God made Jesus his Son perfect through suffering, so he can use our sufferings to make us perfect - for he is also our Father.

---

[282] Which is the one thing the Jews could not dispute.
[283] Ps 2:7
[284] 2 Sam 7:14
[285] Dt 32:43
[286] Ps 8: 4-6

The writer continues using the Old Testament to reason out how and why Moses and the old covenant was superseded by Jesus and the new covenant. *That is why all you who are holy brothers and have had the same heavenly call should turn your minds to Jesus... He was faithful to the one who appointed him, just like Moses, who stayed faithful in all his house; but he has been found to deserve a greater glory than Moses.* (Heb 3:1-3*)

It is true that Moses was faithful in the house of God, as a servant, acting as witness to the things which were to be divulged later; but Christ was faithful as a son, and as the master in the house. (Heb 3:5-6*)

Next the writer references Psalm 95, where God reveals how the disbelief of certain elements within the Israelites, who journeyed with Moses through the desert, resulted in them being barred from entering the Promised Land. He urges them to *keep encouraging one another so that none of you is hardened by the lure of sin, because we shall remain co-heirs with Christ only if we keep a grasp on our first confidence right to the end.* (Heb 3:13-14*)

The Holy Spirit says, *If only you would listen to him today; do not harden your hearts, as happened in the Rebellion, on the Day of Temptation in the wilderness, when your ancestors challenged me and tested me, though they had seen what I could do for forty years. That was why I was angry with that generation and said: 'How unreliable these people who refuse to grasp my ways!' And so, in anger, I swore that not one would reach the place of rest I had for them." Take care, brothers, that there is not in any one of your community a wicked mind, so unbelieving as to turn away from the living God.* (Heb 3:7-12*)

The word of God is something alive and active: it cuts like any double-edged sword but more finely: it can slip through the place where the soul is divided from the spirit;... it can judge the secret emotions and thoughts. No created thing can hide from him; everything is uncovered and open to the eyes of the one to whom we must give account of ourselves. (Heb 4:12-13*)

A grim warning is issued to anyone who turns from God and commits 'deliberate infidelities, which pave the way for apostasy'.[287] *As for those people who were once brought into the light, and tasted the gift from heaven, and received a share of the Holy Spirit, and appreciated the good message of God and the powers of the world to come and yet in spite of this have fallen away – it is impossible for them to be renewed a second time. They cannot be repentant if they have wilfully crucified the Son of God and openly mocked him.* (Heb 6:4-6*)

He leaves them with hope though; *but you, my dear people, in spite of what we have just said, we are sure you are in a better state and on the way to salvation. God would not be so unjust as to forget all you have done, the love that you have for his name or the services you have done, and are still doing, for the saints.* (Heb 6:9-10*)

The writer moves into a long and in parts detailed explanation of how Jesus is a high priest in the order of Melchizedek. (Melchizedek was the priest who visited Abraham after his recapturing of Sodom.[288]) Abraham offers Melchizedek a tenth of his booty. The writer draws analogues of how Abraham's tithe offering impacts the lawful tithe offering from the house of Israel to the priests of the house of Levi. He reasons that if Abraham paid the tithe not out of any duty or law, then it is more meaningful than the ones the Israelites pay because the Law prescribes it. The writer goes on to say how Jesus, being from the house of Judah, is not (or cannot) be a priest like the Levitical priests, who earn their priesthood through the swearing of an oath, but instead, is of the order of Melchizedek, who earned his priesthood through God swearing on oath. And God's oaths cannot be broken. *For the Law appoints high priests who are men subject to weakness; but the promise on oath, which came after the Law, appointed the Son who is made perfect forever.* (Heb 7:28*)

---

[287] The epistle to the Hebrews John F McConnell p31.
[288] See Gen 14.

The new ministry that Christ has been given is *of a far higher order, and to the same degree it is a better covenant of which he is the mediator, founded on better promises. If that first covenant had been without a fault, there would have been no need for a second one to replace it. And in fact God does find fault with them; he says:*

"See, the days are coming – it is the Lord who speaks when I will establish a new covenant with the House of Israel and the House of Judah, but not a covenant like the one I made with their ancestors on the day I took them by the hand to bring them out of the land of Egypt. They abandoned that covenant of mine, and so I on my side deserted them. It is the Lord who speaks. No, this is the covenant I will make with the House of Israel when those days arrive–it is the Lord who speaks. I will put my laws into their minds and write them on their hearts. Then I will be their God and they shall be my people. There will be no further need for neighbour to try to teach neighbour, or brother to say to brother, 'Learn to know the Lord.' No, they will all know me, the least no less than the greatest, since I will forgive their iniquities and never call their sins to mind."[289]

By speaking of a new covenant, he implies that the first one is already old. Now anything old only gets more antiquated until in the end it disappears. (Heb 8:6-13*)

The writer now discusses the connections between the 'first covenant' - the one established with Moses, and the 'second covenant, or new covenant' - the one established by Jesus' sacrifice. He explains how the laws of worship related to the meeting tent of Moses' time. Inside the tent were two compartments, the first where the priest would go every day in performing his duties; and the second, where the stone tablets of the Ten Commandments were - and was considered the earthly dwelling place of God. The priest would only enter the second tent once a year

---

[289] Jer 31:31-34

- on the Day of Atonement.[290] On that day, he would sprinkle the blood of a sacrificed animal,[291] *because according to the Law almost everything has to be purified with blood; and if there is no shedding of blood, there is no remission.* (Heb 9:22*)

He mentions that none of the gifts and sacrifices offered under these regulations can possibly bring any worshipper to perfection in his inner self; they are rules about the outward life. (Heb 9:9-10*)

By contrast, the new covenant which replaces the old one is born by Christ's willing death on the cross where he offered himself *only once to take the faults of many on himself.* (Heb 9:28*) Christ's offering is more perfect because it was freely given. *His death took place to cancel the sins that infringed the earlier covenant.* (Heb 9:15*)

The writer explains that just as the high priest had the right of access to the second tent with the blood of the sacrificed animal, so Jesus' life, offered in sacrifice, gives all the right of access to the heavenly dwelling place of God.[292] Unlike the high priest who commemorated the Day of Atonement sacrifice once every year, Christ had to sacrifice himself only once, for he was a perfect offering.

All the priests stand at their duties every day, offering over and over again the same sacrifices which are quite incapable of taking sins away. He, on the other hand, has offered one single sacrifice for sins, and then taken his place forever, at the right hand of God, where he is now waiting until his enemies are made into a footstool for him. By virtue of that one single offering, he has achieved the eternal perfection of all whom he is sanctifying. (Heb 10:11-14*)

---

[290] The Jerome Biblical Commentary (p396) says that one the Day of Atonement two sacrifices are offered by the high priest: one to expiate his sins and those of his family, the other to expiate those of the people.

[291] The Jerome Biblical Commentary (p396) says the purpose of slaughtering the animal was to release its blood. The blood was the element in which life resided.

[292] The Jerome Biblical Commentary (p397).

The writer delivers a warning, this time to anyone who after accepting the sacrifice of Jesus, makes a deliberate decision to walk away from it.

If, after we have been given knowledge of the truth, we should deliberately commit any sins, then there is no longer any sacrifice for them. There will be left only the dread prospect of judgement and of the raging fire that is to burn rebels. Anyone who disregards the Law of Moses is ruthlessly put to death on the word of two or three witnesses; and you may be sure that anyone who tramples on the Son of God, and who treats the blood of the covenant which sanctified him as if it were not holy, and who insults the Spirit of grace, will be condemned to a far severer punishment. (Heb 10:26-29*)

He reminds the readers that in the same way they needed to develop 'thick skins' to suffer the insults and injuries of being faithful to God, so too will they need to continue with this strength of perseverance (and more) in following Christ - for the reward offered by the new covenant is far greater than the old.

Remember all the sufferings that you had to meet after you received the light, in earlier days; sometimes by being yourselves publicly exposed to insults and violence, and sometimes as associates of others who were treated in the same way. For you not only shared in the sufferings of those who were in prison, but you happily accepted being stripped of your belongings, knowing that you owned something that was better and lasting. Be as confident now, then, since the reward is so great. You will need endurance to do God's will and gain what he has promised. (Heb 10:32-36*)

After delivering such a powerful warning, the writer moves onto more pleasant things, detailing the long history of faithfulness among the Jews and how God is always steadfast to his promises.

Only faith can guarantee the blessings that we hope for.

It is by faith that we understand that the world was created by one word from God.

It was through his faith that Noah, when he had been warned by God of something that had never been seen before, felt a holy fear and built an ark to save his family.

It was by faith that Abraham obeyed the call to set out for a country that was the inheritance given to him and his descendants, and that he set out without knowing where he was going. By faith he arrived, as a foreigner, in the Promised Land, and lived there as if in a strange country, with Isaac and Jacob, who were heirs with him of the same promise.

It was equally by faith that Sarah, in spite of being past the age, was made able to conceive, because she believed that he who had made the promise would be faithful to it.

All these died in faith, before receiving any of the things that had been promised.

It was by faith that Abraham, when put to the test, offered ... to sacrifice his only son even though the promises had been made to him and he had been told: It is through Isaac that your name will be carried on.

It was by faith that this same Isaac gave his blessing to Jacob and Esau for the still distant future. By faith Jacob, when he was dying, blessed each of Joseph's sons.

It was by faith that Moses, when he was born, was hidden by his parents for three months.

It was by faith that, when he grew to manhood, Moses refused to be known as the son of Pharaoh's daughter and chose to be ill-treated in company with God's people rather than to enjoy for a time the pleasures of sin. He considered that the insults offered to the Anointed were something more precious than all the treasures of Egypt.

It was by faith that he kept the Passover and sprinkled the blood to prevent the Destroyer from touching any of the first-born sons of Israel. It was by faith they crossed the Red Sea as easily as dry land, while the Egyptians, trying to do the same, were drowned.

It was through faith that the walls of Jericho fell down when the people had been around them for seven days.

Is there any need to say more? (Heb 11:1-32*) with omissions.

With so many witnesses, ...we too then, should throw off everything that hinders us, especially the sin that clings so easily, and keep running steadily in the race we have started. Let us not lose sight of Jesus, who leads us in our faith and brings it to perfection: for the sake of the joy, which was still in the future, he endured the cross, disregarding the shamefulness of it, and from now on has taken his place at the right of God's throne. Think of the way he stood up to such opposition from sinners, and then you will not give up for want of courage. In the fight against sin, you have not yet had to keep fighting to the point of death. (Heb 12:1-4*)

The letter winds up with a reassuring message of God as our Father, explaining how, if through the love of our earthly fathers we are raised and reprimanded, how much more will God our Father love and train and reprimand us.

Have you forgotten that encouraging text in which you are addressed as sons? 'My son, when the Lord corrects you, do not treat it lightly; but do not get discouraged when he reprimands you. For the Lord trains the ones that he loves and he punishes all those that he acknowledges as his sons. Suffering is part of your training; God is treating you as his sons.[293] *Has there ever been any son whose father did not train him? If you were not getting this training, as all of you are, then you would not be sons but bastards.* (Heb 12:5-8*)

Of course, any punishment is most painful at the time, and far from pleasant; but later, in those on whom it has been used, it bears fruit in peace and goodness. So hold up your limp arms and steady your trembling knees and smooth out the path you tread; then the injured limb will not be wrenched, it will grow strong again. (Heb 12:11-13*)

In conclusion, the author delivers an uplifting and glorious image of the future that lays ahead.

---

[293] Ps 3:11-12

What you have come to is nothing known to the senses: not a blazing fire or a gloom turning to total darkness, or a storm...But what you have come to is Mount Zion and the city of the living God, the heavenly Jerusalem where the millions of angels have gathered for the festival, with the whole Church in which everyone is a 'first-born son' and a citizen of heaven. You have come to God himself, the supreme Judge, and been placed with the spirits of the saints who have been made perfect; and to Jesus, the mediator who brings a new covenant and a blood for purification ... Make sure that you never refuse to listen when he speaks. (Heb 12:18-25*)

We have been given possession of an unshakable kingdom. Let us therefore hold on to the grace that we have been given and use it to worship God in the way that he finds acceptable, in reverence and fear. For our God is a consuming fire. (Heb 12:28-29*)

JAMES

This is not so much a letter as it is a series of short sermons with a strong Jewish undertone. It was written for the Jewish-Christians or as he writes in the opening verse 'the twelve tribes of the Dispersion', as opposed to the letters of St Paul, which were written for the Gentile Christian. This text is believed to date around 58 AD.

James is thought to be the brother of Jesus as mentioned in Mark's Gospel (6:3), who at the time was the head of the Jerusalem Community.

James begins by saying that trials will always be a part of Christian life, but *count it all joy,... when you fall into various temptations, knowing that the testing of your faith produces endurance.* (Jm 1:2-3)

And while enduring trials, he encourages the reader to *ask of God, who gives to all liberally and without reproach, and it will be given to him. But... ask in faith, without any doubting, for he who doubts is like a wave of the sea, driven by the wind and tossed. For that man shouldn't think that he will receive anything from the Lord. He is a double-minded man, unstable in all his ways.* (Jm 1:5-8)

Blessed is a person who endures temptation, for when he has been approved, he will receive the crown of life which the Lord promised to those who love him. (Jm 1:12)

With trials also come temptations, but when they come, don't say, "*I am tempted by God,*" for *God can't be tempted by evil, and he himself tempts no one. But each one is tempted when he is drawn away by his own lust and enticed.* (Jm 1:13-14)

James also warns against being a passive Christian, cautioning that to *listen to the word and not obey is like looking at your own features in a mirror and then, after a quick look, going off and immediately forgetting what you looked like. But the man who looks steadily at the perfect law of freedom… will be happy in all that he does.* (Jm 1:23-25*)

Nobody must imagine that he is religious while he still goes on deceiving himself and not keeping control over his tongue; anyone who does this has the wrong idea of religion. Pure, unspoiled religion, in the eyes of God our Father is this: coming to the help of orphans and widows when they need it, and keeping oneself uncontaminated by the world. (Jm 1:26-27*)

James moves on to to tell a story about judging people by their looks, or by class distinction. It is about a man entering a synagogue poorly dressed, while another one comes in wearing expensive robes. They shuffled the poorly dressed man to the back, while the other was escorted to the front. He explains how this is wrong and against God's will, for *didn't God choose those who are poor in this world to be rich in faith and heirs of the Kingdom which he promised to those who love him?* (Jm 2:5)

The right thing to do is to keep the supreme Law of Scripture: you must love your neighbour as yourself; but as soon as you make distinctions between classes of people, you are committing sin, and under condemnation for breaking the Law. (Jm 2:8-9*)

The next issue raised is how faith without good works will not save you. He paints the picture of a brother or sister who *needs clothes and has not enough food to live on, and one of you says to them, "I wish you well; keep yourself warm and eat plenty," without giving them these bare necessities of life, then what good is that? Faith is like that: if good works do not go with it, it is quite dead.* (Jm 2:15-17*)

For faith can be proven by showing good deeds, but without them it cannot. *For as the body apart from the spirit is dead, even so faith apart from works is dead.* (Jm 2:26)

James counsels against speaking ill of others for *the tongue is a whole wicked world in itself: it infects the whole body; catching fire itself from hell, it sets fire to the whole wheel of creation.* (Jm 3:6*) *With it we bless our God and Father, and with it we curse men who are made in the image of God. Out of the same mouth comes blessing and cursing. My brothers, these things ought not to be so.* (Jm 3:9-10)

James writes about giving in to God, for *the nearer you go to God, the nearer he will come to you.* (Jm 4:8*) *When you do pray and don't get it, it is because you have not prayed properly, or you have prayed for something to indulge your own desires.* (Jm 4:3*)

Don't you know that friendship with the world is hostility toward God? (Jm 4:4)

James signs off by counselling that if *any among you are suffering? Let him pray. Is any cheerful? Let him sing praises. Is any among you sick? Let him call for the elders of the assembly, and let them pray over him, anointing him with oil in the name of the Lord; and the prayer of faith will heal him who is sick, and the Lord will raise him up. If he has committed sins, he will be forgiven. Confess your sins to one another and pray for one another, that you may be healed. The insistent prayer of a righteous person is powerfully effective.* (Jm 5:13-16)

1 PETER

This letter is written by the apostle Peter, who was the Bishop of Rome at the time. It was written for *the chosen ones who are living as foreigners in the Dispersion in Pontus, Galatia, Cappadocia, Asia, and Bithynia,* (1Pt 1:1) **during a time of trial and persecution of the Christian Church, to reassure them of the victory won by Christ.**

Peter opens his letter by reaffirming the victory won by Christ is *an incorruptible and undefiled inheritance that doesn't fade away, reserved in Heaven for you, who by the power of God are guarded through faith for a salvation ready to be revealed in the last time. In this you greatly rejoice, though now for a little while, if need be, you have been grieved in various trials.* (1Pt 1:4-6)

Peter reveals that trials will be coming - *that the proof of your faith, which is more precious than gold that perishes, even though it is tested by fire, may be found to result in praise, glory, and honour at the revelation of Jesus Christ.* (1Pt 1:7)

You did not see him, yet you love him; and still without seeing him, you are already filled with a joy so glorious that it cannot be described, because you believe; and you are sure of the end to which your faith looks forward, that is, the salvation of your souls. (1Pt 1:8-9*)

Peter urges them to be holy in all of (their) *behaviour.* (1Pt 1:15)

He reminds the reader of the price paid by Christ and the inheritance that awaits them through God the Father. *Remember, the ransom that was* *paid to free you from the useless way of life your ancestors handed down was not paid in anything corruptible, neither in silver nor gold, but in the precious blood of a lamb without spot or stain, namely Christ... Through him you now have faith in God, who raised him from the dead and gave him glory for that very reason – so that you would have faith and hope in God.* (1Pt 1:18-21*)

You are a chosen race, a royal priesthood, a holy nation, a people for God's own possession, that you may proclaim the excellence of him who called you out of darkness into his marvellous light. (1Pt 2:9)

Peter commends the reader to follow in Christ's footsteps and also to bear any burdens (justly or unjustly) which come our way, just as Christ suffered. *You see, there is some merit in putting up with the pains of unearned punishment if it is done for the sake of God, but there is nothing meritorious in taking a beating patiently if you have done something wrong to deserve it. The merit, in the sight of God, is in bearing it patiently when you are punished after doing your duty.* (1Pt 2:19-20*)

The bottom line is, this is what Christians are called to do, for Jesus *had done nothing wrong, and there had been no perjury in his mouth. He was insulted and did not retaliate with insults; when he was tortured, he made no threats but he put his trust in the righteous judge. He was bearing our faults in his own body on the cross, so that we might die to our faults and live for holiness; through his wounds you have been healed. You had gone astray like sheep but now you have come back to the shepherd and guardian of your souls.* (1Pt 2:22-25*)

No one can hurt you if you are determined to do only what is right; if you do have to suffer for being good, you will count it a blessing. There is no need to be afraid or to worry about them. Simply reverence the Lord Christ in your hearts, and always have your answer ready for people who ask you the reason for the hope that you all have. (1Pt 3:13-15*)

But because you are partakers of Christ's sufferings, rejoice, that at the revelation of his glory you also may rejoice with exceeding joy. If you are insulted for the name of Christ, you are blessed, because the Spirit of glory and of God rests on you. On their part he is blasphemed, but on your part he is glorified. (1Pt 4:13-14) *If it is hard for the righteous to be saved, what will happen to the ungodly and the sinner?*[294] (1 Peter 4:18)

Humble yourselves therefore under the mighty hand of God, that he may exalt you in due time, casting all your worries on him, because he cares for you.

Be sober and self-controlled. Be watchful. Your adversary, the devil, walks around like a roaring lion, seeking whom he may devour. Withstand him steadfast in your faith, knowing that your brothers who are in the world are undergoing the same sufferings. But may the God of all grace, who called you to his eternal glory by Christ Jesus, after you have suffered a little while, perfect, establish, strengthen, and settle you. To him be the glory and the power forever and ever. Amen. (1Pt 5:6-11)

---

[294] Is 8:2-13

2 PETER

This general letter to Christian communities, covers the Parousia, as it becomes apparent it will not happen in the lifetime of the current generation, while also re-embedding strong Christian doctrine.

In Peter's second letter he continues the theme of the first letter by reiterating its purpose - *that is to awaken a true understanding in you by giving you a reminder: recalling to you what was said in the past by the holy prophets and the commandments of the Lord and Saviour, which you were given by the apostles.* (2Pt 3:2*)

He reminds the reader that through the divine power of Jesus, *he has given us all the things that we need for life and for true devotion, bringing us to know God himself.* (2Pt 1:3*)

Yes, and for this very cause adding on your part all diligence, in your faith supply moral excellence; and in moral excellence, knowledge; and in knowledge, self-control; and in self-control, perseverance; and in perseverance, godliness; and in godliness, brotherly affection; and in brotherly affection, love. (2Pt 1:5-7)

Therefore, be more diligent to make your calling and election sure. For if you do these things, you will never stumble. (2Pt 1:10)

Peter then recounts the venerable day when he, along with James and John, saw Jesus transfigured on the mountain.[295] *It was not any cleverly invented myths that we were repeating when we brought you the knowledge*

---

[295] Mt 17; Mk 9; Lk 9

of the power and the coming of our Lord Jesus Christ; we had seen his majesty for ourselves. He was honoured and glorified by God the Father, when the Sublime Glory itself spoke to him and said, "This is my Son, the Beloved; he enjoys my favour." We heard this ourselves, spoken from heaven, when we were with him on the holy mountain. (2Pt 1:16-18*)

As in many of Paul's letters, Peter addresses the troubles besetting the Christians - that of false and misleading teachers. *As there were false prophets in the past history of our people, so too you will have your false teachers, who will insinuate their own disruptive views and disown the Master who purchased their freedom.* (2Pt 2:1*)

He assures them that their time will come, and they will be held accountable, for *when angels sinned, God did not spare them.* (2Pt 2:4*) *Nor did he spare the world in ancient times: it was only Noah he saved.* (2Pt 2:5*) *The cities of Sodom and Gomorrah, these too he condemned and reduced to ashes; he destroyed them completely, as a warning to anybody lacking reverence in the future; he rescued Lot, however, a holy man who had been sickened by the shameless way in which these vile people behaved.* (2Pt 2:6-7*)

These are all examples of how the Lord can rescue the good from the ordeal, and hold the wicked for their punishment until the day of Judgement, especially those who are governed by their corrupt bodily desires and have no respect for authority. (2Pt 2:9-10)

But Peter also warns that a similar fate awaits anyone who turns away from God after once accepting his truth. *Anyone who has escaped the pollution of the world once by coming to know our Lord and Saviour Jesus Christ, and who then allows himself to be entangled by it a second time and mastered, will end up in a worse state than he began in. It would even have been better for him never to have learned the way of holiness, than to know it and afterward desert the holy rule that was entrusted to him. What he has done is exactly as the proverb rightly says: The dog goes back to his own vomit.*[296] (2Pt 2:20-22*)

---

[296] Pr 26:11

Another recurring theme from other letters of the New Testament is the debate over when the 'end times', or 'second coming' will be. Peter reminds them *that during the last days there are bound to be people who will be scornful, the kind who always please themselves in what they do, and they will make fun of the promise and ask, "Well, where is this coming?"* (2Pt 3:3-4*)

Peter urgently reiterates, do not *forget this one thing, beloved, that one day is with the Lord as a thousand years, and a thousand years as one day. The Lord is not slow concerning his promise, as some count slowness; but he is patient with us, not wishing that anyone should perish, but that all should come to repentance. But the day of the Lord will come as a thief in the night, in which the heavens will pass away with a great noise, and the elements will be dissolved with fervent heat; and the earth and the works that are in it will be burned up.* (2Pt 3:8-10)

What we are waiting for is what he promised: the new heavens and new earth, the place where righteousness will be at home. So then, my friends, while you are waiting, do your best to live lives without spot or stain so that he will find you at peace. Think of our Lord's patience as your opportunity to be saved. (2Pt 3:13-15*)

1 JOHN

This letter was written by John the Apostle, and writer of the Gospel of John to the Christian Churches in Asia so that *you who believe in the name of the Son of God, that you may know that you have eternal life.* (1Jn 5:13)

John opens by sharing the four conditions which must be met in order to live in the light of Christ.

Firstly, we must break from sin. *If we say that we have no sin, we deceive ourselves, and the truth is not in us. If we confess our sins, he is faithful and righteous to forgive us our sins and to cleanse us from all unrighteousness.* (1Jn 1:8-9)

Second, we must keep his commandments. *Anyone who says, "I know him," and doesn't keep his commandments, is a liar, and the truth isn't in him.* (1Jn 2:4)

But when anyone does obey what he has said, God's love comes to perfection in him. (1Jn 2:5*)

Thirdly, John writes we must detach ourselves from this world. *Don't love the world or the things that are in the world. If anyone loves the world, the Father's love isn't in him. For all that is in the world—the lust of the flesh, the lust of the eyes, and the pride of life—isn't the Father's, but is the world's. The world is passing away with its lusts, but he who does God's will remains forever.* (1Jn 2:15-17)

Finally, we must beware of false teachers and prophets. *You were told that an Antichrist must come, and now several antichrists have already appeared.* (1Jn 2:18*) *The man who denies that Jesus is the Christ, is the liar, he is Antichrist; and he is denying the Father as well as the Son.* (1Jn 2:22*)

John then reveals three conditions that must be met to live as children of God.

The first condition, like that already mentioned, is to break from sin, for *Jesus appeared in order to abolish sin, and that in him there is no sin; anyone who lives in God does not sin, and anyone who sins has never seen him or known him,* (1Jn 3:5-6) *to lead a sinful life is to belong to the devil, since the devil was a sinner from the beginning. It was to undo all that the devil has done that the Son of God appeared.* (1Jn 3:8)

Again, mirroring the first set of conditions, the second condition to live as a child of God *is that we are to love one another.* (1Jn 3:11)

My little children, let's not love in word only, or with the tongue only, but in deed and truth. And by this we know that we are of the truth and persuade our hearts before him, because if our heart condemns us, God is greater than our heart, and knows all things. (1Jn 3:18-20)

This is his commandment, that we should believe in the name of his Son, Jesus Christ, and love one another, even as he commanded. He who keeps his commandments remains in him, and he in him. By this we know that he remains in us, by the Spirit which he gave us. (1Jn 3:23-24)

The third condition is to be on the watch for false teachers and those who oppose the will of God. *Beloved, don't believe every spirit, but test the spirits, whether they are of God, because many false prophets have gone out into the world. By this you know the Spirit of God: every spirit who confesses that Jesus Christ has come in the flesh is of God, and every spirit who doesn't confess that Jesus Christ has come in the flesh is not of God; and this is the spirit of the Antichrist, of whom you have heard that it comes.* (1Jn 4:1-3)

John next moves onto the topics of love and faith.

Beloved, let's love one another, for love is of God; and everyone who loves has been born of God and knows God. He who doesn't love doesn't know God, for God is love. By this God's love was revealed in us, that God has sent his only born Son into the world that we might live through him. (1Jn 4:7-10)

If a man says, "I love God," and hates his brother, he is a liar; for he who doesn't love his brother whom he has seen, how can he love God whom he has not seen? This commandment we have from him, that he who loves God should also love his brother. (1Jn 4:20-21)

He who believes in the Son of God has the testimony in himself. He who doesn't believe God has made him a liar, because he has not believed in the testimony that God has given concerning his Son... He who has the Son has the life. He who doesn't have God's Son doesn't have the life. (1Jn 5:10,12)

The letter concludes with: *We know that whoever is born of God doesn't sin, but he who was born of God keeps himself, and the evil one doesn't touch him. We know that we are of God, and the whole world lies in the power of the evil one. We know that the Son of God has come and has given us an understanding, that we know him who is true; and we are in him who is true, in his Son Jesus Christ. This is the true God and eternal life.* (1Jn 5:18-20)

2 JOHN

Addressed to a 'dear lady', it is believed that this term is used as a personification of the Church. Love and truth are the chief themes of the letter.[297]

I rejoice greatly that I have found some of your children walking in truth, even as we have been commanded by the Father. Now I beg you, dear lady, not as though I wrote to you a new commandment, but that which we had from the beginning, that we love one another. This is love, that we should walk according to his commandments. This is the commandment, even as you heard from the beginning, that you should walk in it.

For many deceivers have gone out into the world, those who don't confess that Jesus Christ came in the flesh. This is the deceiver and the Antichrist. Watch yourselves, that we don't lose the things which we have accomplished, but that we receive a full reward. Whoever transgresses and doesn't remain in the teaching of Christ doesn't have God. He who remains in the teaching has both the Father and the Son. If anyone comes to you and doesn't bring this teaching, don't receive him into your house, and don't welcome him, for he who welcomes him participates in his evil deeds.

Having many things to write to you, I don't want to do so with paper and ink, but I hope to come to you and to speak face to face, that our joy may be made full. The children of your chosen sister greet you. Amen. (2Jn 4-13)

---

[297] NAB, Thomas Nelson Publishers 1970.

3 JOHN

The shortest book in the Bible, 3 John highlights the importance of living truthfully, and supporting those who work for the Gospel. Written c. 95 AD.

The elder to Gaius the beloved, whom I love in truth.

Beloved, I pray that you may prosper in all things and be healthy, even as your soul prospers. For I rejoiced greatly when brothers came and testified about your truth, even as you walk in truth. I have no grater joy than this: to hear about my children walking in truth. Beloved, you do a faithful work in whatever you accomplish for those who are brothers and strangers. They have testified about your love before the assembly. You will do well to send them forward on their journey in a way worthy of God, because for the sake of the Name they went out, taking nothing from the Gentiles. We therefore ought to receive such, that we may be fellow workers for the truth.

I wrote to the assembly, but Diotrephes, who loves to be first among them, doesn't accept what we say. Therefore, if I come, I will call attention to his deeds which he does, unjustly accusing us with wicked words. Not content with this, he doesn't receive the brothers himself, and those who would, he forbids and throws out of the assembly.

Beloved, don't imitate that which is evil, but that which is good. He who does good is of God. He who does evil hasn't seen God. Demetrius has the testimony of all, and of the truth itself; yes, we also testify, and you know that our testimony is true.

I had many things to write to you, but I am unwilling to write to you with ink and pen; but I hope to see you soon. Then we will speak face to face. Peace be to you. The friends greet you. Greet the friends by name.[298]

---

[298] The whole letter.

JUDE

Jude is believed to be related to one of the twelve apostles. The letter warns believers about individuals who have infiltrated the Christian community and are distorting the Gospel.

In this letter, Jude, a servant of Jesus Christ and brother of James, writes to a Christian Community with an *appeal to you to fight hard for the faith which has been once and for all entrusted to the saints. (Because) certain people have infiltrated among you, and they are the ones you had a warning about, in writing, long ago, when they were condemned for denying all religion, turning the grace of our God into immorality, and rejecting our only Master and Lord, Jesus Christ.* (Jude 1:3-4)

Jude points out that punishment awaits those who anger God. *I should like to remind you... how the Lord rescued the nation from Egypt, but afterward he still destroyed the men who did not trust him. Next let me remind you of the angels who had supreme authority but did not keep it and left their appointed sphere; he has kept them down in the dark, in spiritual chains, to be judged on the great day. The fornication of Sodom and Gomorrah and the other nearby towns was equally unnatural, and it is a warning to us that they are paying for their crimes in eternal fire.*

I tell you, the Lord will come with his saints in their tens of thousands, to pronounce judgement on all mankind and to sentence the wicked for all the wicked things they have done, and for all the defiant things said against him by irreligious sinners. They are mischief-makers, grumblers governed only by their own desires, with mouths full of boastful talk, ready with flattery for other people when they see some advantage in it. (Jude 1:14-16)

Jude restates what the apostles said about the end times - *there are going to be people who sneer at religion and follow nothing but their own desires for wickedness.* (Jude 1:18)

Glory be to him who can keep you from falling and bring you safe to his glorious presence, innocent and happy. To God, the only God, who saves us through Jesus Christ our Lord, be the glory, majesty, authority and power, which he had before time began, now and forever. Amen. (Jude 1:24-25)

THE BOOK OF REVELATION

Some things to consider while reading Revelation which may help.

- When a <u>woman</u> is mentioned, it represents *a people*.
- <u>Horns</u>, symbolise *power*.
- <u>Eyes</u>, symbolise *knowledge*, while <u>wings</u> are *mobility*.
- <u>Trumpets</u> signify a *superhuman or divine voice*.
- A <u>sharp sword</u> is the *Word of God*.
- <u>White robes</u> signify the *world of glory*, while <u>white</u> alone indicates the *joy of victory*.
- <u>Purple</u> is for *luxury or kingship*. <u>Black</u> is *death*.
- A <u>long robe</u> is the *priesthood*.
- <u>Crowns</u> signify *dominion, kingship, royalty*.
- <u>The sea</u> is an *evil element, source of insecurity and death*.
- The number seven (7) signifies fullness and perfection.
- The number twelve (12) is for the twelve tribes of Israel and signifies faith and completion.
- The number four (4) is for the whole world (north, south, east, west); cosmic order.
- Babylon = Rome = Satan
- The Beast = Rome = Satan

The book is not to be read as a prophetic vision for the future Church, but as reflective of the events happening in the Church at the time of writing (c.95 AD).

It was written during a time when Christians were being persecuted by Rome. The Temple of Jerusalem had been destroyed, and the Jews scattered,[299] so that they could look forward to a 'happy messianic future'.[300]

The basic message of Revelation is that the risen Christ, identified with Jesus of Nazareth, is Lord of this world's history.[301] It is also an unravelling of the Old Testament prophecies in light of the New Testament.[302] It sets the scene that Christ's final victory is yet to be won - the final battle between good and evil yet to happen.

Prologue

This is the Revelation of Jesus Christ, which God gave to his servant John to show to his servants the things which must happen soon, which he sent and made known by his angel to his servant, John, who testified to God's word and of the testimony of Jesus Christ, about everything that he saw. (Rev 1:1-3)

John opens stating: *"I am your brother and share your sufferings, your kingdom, and all you undure."* (Rev 1:9*) He adds that the visions he is about to reveal came to him while he was in the Roman Penal Colony island of Pathos.

John sees a door open in heaven, and hears a voice like a trumpet saying, *"Come up here: I will show you what is to come in the future."* (Rev 4:1*)

---

[299] A new catholic commentary p 1268.
[300] Ibid.
[301] A new catholic commentary p 1267.
[302] Ibid.

He receives messages for the seven churches[303] of Asia. The voice singles out each of the churches and delivers messages. Each is unique yet contain similar themes of commendations for the good life they are living, balanced with warnings and consequences for unfaithfulness.

Each message ends the same. "If anyone has ears to hear, let him listen to what the Spirit is saying to the churches."

The Vision of the Throne and the Lamb

John is shown a vision of the future in which he sees God sitting on a throne holding a scroll with seven seals. Encircling God are twenty-four elders in white robes and gold crowns singing praises to God. Beside them are seven burning lamps and the seven spirits of God. Between John and the throne are four animals.[304] Each animal had six eyes and they sang to God all day.

"You are our Lord and our God, you are worthy of glory and honour and power, because you made all the universe and it was only by your will that everything was made and exists." (Rev 4:11*)

An angel came forward asking if there was anyone who could break open the seals, but there was no one in heaven, on earth, or in hell who could. John wept. Then he saw a Lamb, (which appeared to have been sacrificed) standing between the throne of God and the four animals.

The Lamb took the scroll from God's right hand, and as he did the four animals (the whole world) and the twenty-four elders (all the church) prostrated themselves and sang a new hymn.

> *"You are worthy to take the book*
> *and to open its seals,*
> *for you were killed,*

---

[303] Ephesus, Smyrna, Pergamum, Thyatira, Sardis, Philadelphia, and Laodicea

[304] One was like a lion, one like a bull, one like an eagle, and one with a human face. Also representing the whole world.

> *and bought us for God with your blood*
> *out of every tribe, language, people, and nation,*
> *and made us kings and priests to our God;*
> *and we will reign on the earth."* (Rev 5:9-10)

The seven seals of the scroll were opened one by one.

The Opening of the Six Seals

When the first seal was broken, *a white horse appeared, and the rider on it was holding a bow; he was given the victor's crown, and he went away to go from victory to victory.* (Rev 6:2*)

When the second seal was broken, *out came another horse, bright red, and its rider was given this duty: to take away peace from the earth and set people killing each other.* (Rev 6:4*)

On the opening of the third seal, *a black horse appeared, and its rider was holding a pair of scales;... saying, "A ration of corn for a day's wages, and three rations of barley for a day's wages, but do not tamper with the oil or the wine."* (Rev 6:5-6*)

After the fourth seal was broken, *another horse appeared, deathly pale, and its rider was called Plague, and Hades followed at his heels. They were given authority over a quarter of the earth, to kill by the sword, by famine, by plague and wild beasts.* (Rev 6:8*)

The fifth seal revealed *underneath the altar the souls of all the people who had been killed on account of the word of God, for witnessing to it. They shouted aloud, "Holy, faithful Master, how much longer will you wait before you pass sentence and take vengeance for our death on the inhabitants of the earth?" Each of them was given a white robe, and they were told to be patient a little longer, until the roll was complete and their fellow servants and brothers had been killed just as they had been.* (Rev 6:9-11*)

The breaking of the sixth seal unleashed *a violent earthquake, and the sun went ... black...; the moon turned red..., and the stars of the sky fell onto the earth...; the sky disappeared like a scroll rolling up and all the mountains* *and islands were shaken from their places. Then all the earthly rulers…, the rich people and the men of influence, the whole population, slaves and citizens, took to the mountains to hide in caves and among the rocks. They said to the mountains and the rocks, "Fall on us and hide us away from the One who sits on the throne and from the anger of the Lamb. For the Great Day of his anger has come, and who can survive it?"* (Rev 6:12-17*)

The Sealing of the Faithful, and the Opening of the Seventh Seal

Standing at the four corners of the earth, holding the four winds of the world back, (Rev 7:1*) John saw another angel appear with a message for the four angels. *"Wait before you do any damage on land or at sea or to the trees, until we have put the seal on the foreheads of the servants of our God."* (Rev 7:3*)

Then I heard how many were sealed: a hundred and forty-four thousand,[305] *out of all the tribes of Israel.* (Rev 7:3-4*)

Next, innumerable people from all over the world appeared. Dressed in white robes and standing in front of the Lamb they shouted out, *"Salvation be to our God, who sits on the throne, and to the Lamb!"* (Rev 7:10)

All the angels responded, *"Amen! Blessing, glory, wisdom, thanksgiving, honour, power, and might, be to our God forever and ever! Amen."* (Rev 7:12)

Finally, the seventh seal was broken by the Lamb and there was an exalted silence in heaven, until seven trumpets were given to seven angels, then an eighth angel came to the golden altar carrying a golden censer.

The Seven Trumpets and Two Troubles

Following the prayers and incense offering, the seven angels with the seven trumpets readied themselves.

---

[305] Twelve thousand from each of the twelve tribes.

The first sounded, and there followed hail and fire, mixed with blood, and they were thrown to the earth. One-third of the earth was burned up, and one-third of the trees were burned up, and all green grass was burned up. (Rev 8:7)

The second angel sounded, and something like a great burning mountain was thrown into the sea. One-third of the sea became blood, and one-third of the living creatures which were in the sea died. One-third of the ships were destroyed. (Rev 8:8-9)

The third angel sounded, and a great star fell from the sky, burning like a torch, and it fell on one-third of the rivers, and on the springs of water… One-third of the waters became wormwood. Many people died from the waters, because they were made bitter. (Rev 8:10-11)

The fourth angel sounded, and one-third of the sun was struck, and one-third of the moon, and one-third of the stars, so that one-third of them would be darkened; and the day wouldn't shine for one-third of it, and the night in the same way. (Rev 8:12)

Before the fifth trumpet was blown, there was a warning issued from a high-flying eagle. *"Woe! Woe! Woe to those who dwell on the earth, because of the other blasts of the trumpets of the three angels, who are yet to sound!"* (Rev 8:13)

At the sounding of the fifth trumpet the first of three troubles began. A star was seen falling from heaven,[306] it was given the key to the Abyss.[307] Once it was unlocked, smoke poured out and up into the sky. From the smoke dropped locusts with stings like scorpions. Their leader was an emperor, the angel of the Abyss, whose name was Destruction.[308]

The locusts attacked only those who did not belong to God. The sting didn't kill them, instead it gave *them pain for five months, and the pain was to be the pain of a scorpion's sting. When this happens, men will*

---

[306] Most likely Satan.
[307] The place where the fallen angels were imprisoned.
[308] Satan.

long for death and not find it anywhere; they will want to die and death will evade them. (Rev 9:5-6*)

At the sounding of the sixth trumpet, the angel was told to release four angels who had been chained up in preparation for this moment. Their army numbered twenty million mounted men, and their order was to destroy one-third of mankind. *By these three plagues, one-third of mankind was killed: by the fire, the smoke, and the sulphur, which proceeded out of their mouths.* (Rev 9:18)

The rest of mankind, who were not killed with these plagues, didn't repent of the works of their hands, that they wouldn't worship demons, and the idols of gold, and of silver, and of brass, and of stone, and of wood, which can't see, hear, or walk. They didn't repent of their murders, their sorceries, their sexual immorality, or their thefts. (Rev 9:20-21)

Next John saw *a powerful angel coming down from heaven wrapped in a cloud, with a rainbow over his head.* Rev (10:1*) The angel was holding a small unrolled scroll, when seven claps of thunder erupted. As John prepared to write down what was going to be said, a voice from heaven told him, *"Keep the words of the seven thunders secret and do not write them down."* (Rev 10:4*)

John was then told to take and eat the scroll.

Then John was given a measuring rod and told to *measure God's sanctuary, and the altar, and the people who worship there.* (Rev 11:1*). He was told that the outer court of the sanctuary would be overrun by pagans for forty-two months, but during this time God will send two witnesses to prophecy, and consume their enemies, control the weather and bring plague as often as they like.

Eventually the two witnesses will be killed by a *beast that comes out of the Abyss.* (Rev 11:7*) For three and a half days their unburied bodies will be laughed at and ridiculed by men of every people, race, language, and nation, because they had been a *plague to the people of the world.* (Rev 11:10*) After the three and a half days, God raised them back to life and they ascended to heaven on a cloud.

This was the second of the three troubles, the third quickly followed.

The seventh and final trumpet finally sounded. An angel spoke, *"The kingdom of the world has become the Kingdom of our Lord and of his Christ. He will reign forever and ever!"* (Rev 11:15*) This was followed by the twenty-four elders proclaiming, *"We give you thanks, Lord God, the Almighty, the one who is and who was, because you have taken your great power and reigned."* (Rev 11:17*) *"The time has come to destroy those who are destroying the earth."* (Rev 11:18*)

The Vision of the Woman, the Dragon, and the Beasts

The next vision given to John was of a pregnant woman wearing a twelve star crown and in the midst of childbirth.[309] A seven headed, ten horned red dragon appeared and tried to eat the newborn baby boy, *the son who was to rule all the nations with an iron sceptre, and the child was taken straight up to God and to his throne, while the woman escaped into the desert.* (Rev 12:5-6*)

Then a war broke out between the angel Michael and his armies against *the great dragon, ... known as the devil or Satan, who had deceived all the world, was hurled down to the earth and his angels were hurled down with him.* (Rev 12:9*)

---

[309] According to the New Jerusalem Bible the woman is essentially an image of Israel as the mother of the messianic Saviour. The son born to her is, like Moses, snatched from the dragon of water and taken up to the throne, while she herself escapes into the desert for 42 months (recalling the 42 years of Israel's desert wanderings). The Messiah here is seen under the type of Moses. It seems improbable that John intended any allusion to the physical birth of the Messiah.

Once the devil found himself on earth he began to pursue the woman again, but she was given eagle wings and was able to escape.

John then witnessed a new beast rising from the seas, this one was like a leopard, with bear claws and a lion's mouth. The dragon handed over its power, throne, and kingdom, to the beast. For forty-two months the beast was allowed to boast and blaspheme against God all it wanted. *It was given to him to make war with the saints and to overcome them. Authority over every tribe, people, language, and nation was given to him. All who dwell on the earth will worship him, everyone whose name has not been written from the foundation of the world in the book of life of the Lamb who has been killed.* (Rev 13:7-8)

Emerging next was a second beast with two horns that looked like a lamb but sounded like a dragon. This beast was a servant of the first and it went throughout the whole world making all the people worship its master. *And it worked great miracles…* (and) *was able to win over the people of the world.* (Rev 13:13-14*)

He compelled everyone – small and great, rich and poor, slave and citizen – to be branded on the right hand or on the forehead, and made it illegal for anyone to buy or sell anything unless he had been branded with the name of the beast or with the number of its name. There is need for shrewdness here: if anyone is clever enough, he may interpret the number of the beast: it is the number of a man, the number 666. (Rev 13:16-18*)

The Lamb and the Seven Last Plagues

Next was a vision of a Lamb standing on Mt Zion, overlooking God's Holy City, surrounded by one hundred and forty-four thousand people. The people had the name of the Lamb and his father on their foreheads.

John *saw an angel flying in mid heaven, having an eternal Good News to proclaim to those who dwell on the earth – to every nation, tribe, language, and people. He said with a loud voice, "Fear the Lord, and give him glory, for the hour of his judgement has come. Worship him who made the heaven, the earth, the sea, and the springs of waters!"* (Rev 14:6-7)

Another angel appeared, this one was proclaiming, "The pagan world has fallen, all those hostile to God have fallen."

...a third, followed them, saying with a great voice, "If anyone worships the beast and his image, and receives a mark on his forehead or on his hand, he also will drink of the wine of the wrath of God,... He will be tormented with fire and sulphur in the presence of the holy angels and in the presence of the Lamb... They have no rest day and night, those who worship the beast and his image, and whoever receives the mark of his name.

"Here is the perseverance of the saints, those who keep the commandments of God and the faith of Jesus." (Rev 14:9-12)

What I saw next, in heaven, was a great and wonderful sign: seven angels were bringing the seven plagues that are the last of all, because they exhaust the anger of God. (Rev 15:1*)

The seven angels were then given seven golden bowls full of the wrath of God, who lives forever and ever. The temple was filled with smoke from the glory of God and from his power. No one was able to enter into the temple until the seven plagues of the seven angels would be finished. (Rev 15:7-8)

That is to say, once the final judgement of God comes, no one can stop it or intercede until it is completed.

The Third Trouble

The seven angels were ordered to empty their bowls of God's anger over the earth.

The first bowl caused virulent sores to grow on all those marked with the sign of the beast.

The second bowl turned all the seas into blood.

Likewise, the third bowl turned all the rivers and springs into blood.

The fourth bowl caused the sun to scorch the earth.

The fifth poured out his bowl on the throne of the beast, and his kingdom was darkened. They gnawed their tongues because of the pain, and they blasphemed the God of heaven because of their pains and their sores. (Rev 16:10-11)

When the sixth bowl was emptied, it started a war between the kings of the East[310] and the beast. It is the war of the Great Day of God the Almighty. *They called the kings together at the place called… Armageddon.* (Rev 16:16*)

Then the seventh angel emptied his bowl into the air. A voice cried, "The end has come." This was followed by violent earthquakes. Islands and mountains disappeared. Hail fell. And the people cursed God for sending such a plague.

When all this was over, one of the seven angels approached John saying, *"Come here and I will show you the punishment given to the famous prostitute who rules enthroned beside abundant waters, the one with whom all the kings of the earth have committed fornication, and who has made all the population of the world drunk with the wine of her adultery."* (Rev 17:1-2*)

The Punishment of Babylon

John then saw a woman, dressed in scarlet and purple,[311] riding a seven headed, ten-horned beast which was covered in blasphemous words. In her hand was a cup filled with the disgusting filth of her fornication.[312] She was marked with the name 'Whore of Babylon'.[313] She was the mother of all filthy practices and was drunk on the blood of Jesus and his saints and martyrs.

---

[310] Christ's allies.
[311] Indicating the proud splendour of Rome and any other place where evil reigns. (NJB 17a footnote)
[312] Fornication is often a symbol of false religion—lack of fidelity to the God who created heaven and earth. https://www.catholic.com/tract/the-whore-of-babylon.
[313] Since the beginning of the journey of God's chosen people, Babylon has been a symbol of everything/everyone against God.

The angel explained what the vision was. "The beast that is yet to come from the Abyss, but when it does, it is doomed for destruction. When it comes, the people of the world will think of it as a miracle.

"The seven heads of the beast are seven emperors: five have been, one is here now, and one is yet to come.

"The ten horns are ten kings who are yet to come. Their time in power will be fleeting and they will support the beast in a war against the Lamb *and the Lamb will overcome them, for he is Lord of lords and King of kings; and those who are with him are called, chosen, and faithful.*" (Rev 17:14)

Next there appeared another angel who shouted with urgent authority, *"Fallen, fallen is Babylon the great, and she has become a habitation of demons, a prison of every unclean spirit!"* (Rev 18:2)

Songs of Victory

After this John *heard something like the voice of a great multitude, ...saying, "Hallelujah! For the Lord our God, the Almighty, reigns! Let's rejoice and be exceedingly glad, and let's give the glory to him. For the wedding of the Lamb has come, and his wife has made herself ready."* (Rev 19:6-7)

Then heaven opened and a white horse known by the name of 'The Word of God' appeared. On it was a rider called 'Faithful and True' and the armies of heaven followed it. The rider and armies defeated all the kings of the earth and captured the beast along with the false prophet *who had worked miracles on the beast's behalf and by them had deceived all who had been branded with the mark of the beast and worshipped his statue.* (Rev 19:20*) Together they were thrown alive into a fiery lake of burning sulphur.

The Thousand Year Reign and Final Judgement

Next, John saw an angel coming down from heaven, who had the key of the abyss in his hand. He seized the dragon (who is Satan) and bound him for a thousand years, so he couldn't deceive anyone.

Then he saw some thrones, and sitting on them were those given power to judge, those *who had been beheaded... for having preached God's word, and those who refused to worship the* (devil) - *they came to life, and reigned with Christ for a thousand years. This is the first resurrection; the rest of the dead did not come back to life until the thousand years were over.* (Rev 20:4*)

After the thousand years, Satan will be released and will come out to deceive the whole world, but God will reign down fire and devour them. Satan will be thrown into a *lake of fire and sulphur, where the beast and the false prophet are also. They will be tormented day and night forever and ever.* (Rev 20:10)

John saw the book of life open and the dead were judged out of the things that were written in the books, according to their works.... *Death and Hades gave up the dead who were in them. They were judged, each one according to his works. Death and Hades were thrown into the lake of fire. This is the second death, the lake of fire. If anyone was not found written in the book of life, he was cast into the lake of fire.* (Rev 20:11-15)

The New Heavenly Jerusalem

I saw a new heaven and a new earth, for the first heaven and the first earth have passed away, and the sea is no more. I saw the holy city, New Jerusalem, coming down out of heaven from God, prepared like a bride adorned for her husband. I heard a loud voice out of heaven saying, "Behold, God's dwelling is with people; and he will dwell with them, and they will be his people, and God himself will be with them as their God. He will wipe away every tear from their eyes. Death will be no more; neither will there be mourning, nor crying, nor pain any more. The first things have passed away."

He who sits on the throne said, "Behold, I am making all things new." He said, "Write, for these words of God are faithful and true." He said to me, "I am the Alpha and the Omega, the Beginning and the End. I will give freely to him who is thirsty from the spring of the water of life. He who overcomes, I will give him these things. I will be his God, and he will be my son. But for the cowardly, unbelieving, sinners, abominable, murderers, sexually immoral, sorcerers, idolaters, and all liars, their part is in the lake that burns with fire and sulphur, which is the second death." (Rev 21:1-8)

Conclusion

Finally, the angel said to John, *"He who acts unjustly, let him act unjustly still. He who is filthy, let him be filthy still. He who is righteous, let him do righteousness still. He who is holy, let him be holy still."* (Rev 22:11)

And we now come to the end of the New Testament, and like in the Old Testament, where the final words were left to God, here they are left to Jesus.

"I, Jesus, have sent my angel to make these revelations to you for the sake of the churches. I am of David's line, the root of David and the bright star of the morning... This is my solemn warning to all who hear the prophecies in this book: if anyone adds anything to them, God will add to him every plague mentioned in the book; if anyone cuts anything out of the prophecies in this book, God will cut off his share of the tree of life and of the holy city which are described in the book. The one who guarantees these revelations repeats his promise: I shall indeed be with you soon. Amen; come, Lord Jesus." (Rev 22:16-20*)

I pray that this book has encouraged you to explore the Bible. The Bible is the sacred text of God, containing profound insights into the nature of God the Father, his only Son, Jesus, and the Holy Spirit. It serves as a guiding creed, leading us to a deeper understanding of the Trinity, and our eternal destiny in Heaven.

Thank you and God Bless
Peter
thestoryofgod@icloud.com

REFERENCE MATERIALS

1. Brown, R. E., Fitzmyer, J. A., & Murphy, R. E. (1989). *The Jerome Biblical Commentary*. Dallas, TX: CDWord Library.
2. Brown, Raymond Edward. (1965). *The Book of Deuteronomy*. Liturgical Press.
3. Castelot, John J. (1968). *1st & 2nd Book of Chronicles*. Liturgical Press.
4. Denzer, George. (1966). *Books of Haggai, Zechariah, Malachi, Joel*. Liturgical Press.
5. Duggan, Michael W. (1991). *The Consuming Fire: A Christian Introduction to the Old Testament*. Ignatius Press.
6. Ellis, Peter F. (1966). *1st Kings, 2nd Kings*. Liturgical Press.
7. Faley, Roland J. (1966). *Genesis 12:1-50*. Liturgical Press.
8. Flanagan, Neal. (1968). *The Books of Amos, Hosea & Micah*. Liturgical Press.
9. Hunt, Ignatius. (1965). *The Books of Joshua & Judges*. Liturgical Press.
10. *The Jerusalem Bible*. (1966). London: Darton, Longman & Todd.
11. King, Philip J. (1966). *The Book of Numbers*. Liturgical Press.
12. Lussier, Ernest. (1965). *The Book of Proverbs & the Book of Sirach*. Liturgical Press.
13. McKenzie, John L. (1965). *Dictionary of the Bible*.

14. *McNamara, M. (1968). The Book of Isaiah Chapters 1-39. Liturgical Press.*
15. *Moriarty, Frederick L. (1966). Ezra & Nehemiah. Liturgical Press.*
16. *Murphy, Roland E. (1968). Introduction to the Wisdom Literature of the Old Testament. Liturgical Press.*
17. *Power, F. J., Pujolas, M., & McLarnon, D. H. (1978). Guide to Reading the New Testament. Messenger of the Sacred Heart.*
18. *Schoenberg, Martin. (1966). The 1st & 2nd Books of the Maccabees. Liturgical Press.*
19. *Stuhlmueller, Carroll. (1965). The Book of Isaiah - Chapters 40-66. Liturgical Press.*
20. *Vawter, Bruce. (1968). Introduction to the Prophetical Books. Liturgical Press.*
21. *Get Catholic Answers. Retrieved from www.catholic.com/*
22. *Confraternity of Christian Doctrine. (1970). The New American Bible. Thomas Nelson, Inc.*
23. *Catholic News Agency web site. www.catholicnewsagency.com/resource/56232/baruch*

EXPLANATIONS OF SOME FREQUENT BIBLICAL WORDS

The **Sadducees** were a priestly aristocracy who believed exclusively in the Torah. Unlike the Pharisees, they did not believe in the resurrection of the body nor in angels or spirits. They were more strict and rigid than the Pharisees in their observance of the Law. Additionally, they were supporters of living in harmony with the Roman occupiers. They were in charge of maintaining the Temple in Jerusalem.

The **Pharisees** were laypeople who were in opposition to the Sadducees. They believed in the Torah, but unlike the Sadducees, they also followed oral traditions handed down by the elders over time. They were very strict and rigid in their observance of the Law.

In McKenzie, John L. (1965), Dictionary of the Bible, p. 669 it states. 'It would be inaccurate to say the Pharisees were the only group of Jews...mortally opposed to Jesus, but their responsibility for His death seems to have been less (than)... the priests and Sadducees. The basic fault of the Pharisees was their refusal to admit that Judaism could develop beyond themselves.' Paul was a Pharisee.

The **scribes** were experts in the interpretation and application of the Jewish Law (Torah) and were skilled in reading and writing. They played a crucial role in preserving and transmitting the oral traditions and legal interpretations that accompanied the written Law. They held significant influence within Jewish society as legal scholars, and they were often closely associated with the Pharisees, sharing their emphasis on strict adherence to both the written and oral Law.

The **chief priests** were responsible for overseeing the operations of the Temple in Jerusalem. They were involved in interpreting and enforcing religious laws and traditions, particularly those related to Temple worship. They held significant authority within the religious hierarchy, often working closely with the Sanhedrin, and played a key role in major religious decisions, including matters of sacrifice and ritual purity.

The **Sanhedrin,** was a Jewish legal and judicial body made up of members from the ranks of priests, elders, and scholars, representing different factions within Judaism, such as the Pharisees and Sadducees. It held significant authority in religious and civil matters. The Sanhedrin was responsible for interpreting the Law, adjudicating legal disputes, and overseeing religious practices. The Sanhedrin played a central role in the events leading up to the crucifixion of Jesus.

The **Philistines** were repeated adversaries of the Israelites. They are prominent in the story of David and Goliath (Goliath was a Philistine) and Samson (it was the Philistines who wanted to uncover the secret to his strength). Additionally, it was the Philistines who stole the Ark of the Covenant. Their origin is uncertain.

Assyria becomes prominent in the Old Testament story when it defeats the northern Kingdom of Israel c. 731 BC. It is frequently mentioned by prophets of the Old Testament in the context of divine judgement and as a tool of God's wrath against disobedient nations. At one time in its history its capital was Nineveh - the city to which Jonah was sent.

Babylon was a city to the East of Jerusalem, and reached prominence around the 600 - 550 BC (the end years of the House of Judah), and is the place of deportation for the House of Judah, a truly significant turning point in Jewish history. Its most notable king was Nebuchadnezzar II. Not only is he known for conquering Jerusalem, but also taking Daniel and other young Israelites captive, and attempting to assimilate them into Babylonian culture, as told in the Book of Daniel. The fall of Babylon and the end of Nebuchadnezzar's reign are significant events. In c. 538 BC, the Persian King Cyrus the Great conquered Babylon, fulfilling prophecies and marking the return of the exiles to Jerusalem.

Samaria was the capital of the Northern Kingdom of Israel at the time of its defeat by Assyria c. 722 BC. It was founded by King Omri around 880 BC and became the political and religious centre of the northern tribes. Prophets such as Elijah, Elisha, Amos, and Hosea often directed their messages to the rulers in Samaria, condemning idolatry, injustice, and moral decay. After the exile of the House of Judah, the capital, Samaria, was repopulated with people from different regions. These 'immigrants' blended with the local inhabitants, took on their religious values and became known as '**Samaritans**'. They considered themselves Jews because they followed the same religious teachings as the original Jews but were not accepted as they were not 'genetically' part of them. They did have their own version of the Pentateuch (the first five books of the Bible), which is slightly different from the Jewish Torah, and followed unique religious traditions and a distinct cultural identity.

Jerusalem holds a long and close history with the Israelites of the Old Testament and the Jews of the New Testament. Briefly mentioned around the time of Abraham, it comes to prominence during the reign of King David when he made it the capital of the Kingdom of Israel (also known as the City of David). The 'First Temple' was built there by Solomon.

After Solomon's death, the kingdom split into the Northern Kingdom (Israel) and the Southern Kingdom (Judah). Jerusalem remained the capital of Judah.

Jerusalem was sacked and the inhabitants deported around 586 BC. After the Babylonian Captivity, the Persian king Cyrus the Great conquered Babylon, fulfilling prophecies and marking the return of the Israelites to Jerusalem. The Second Temple was eventually built on the same site as the First Temple. It is this Temple that Jesus visits in the Gospels.

The Roman Empire occupied Jerusalem from 63 BC to 135 AD.

Hebrews, Israelites, and Jews - what's the difference?

They all refer to the same people but cover different periods in time. In the Old Testament the word 'Hebrew' is often used by foreigners like the Philistines and Egyptians.

After the Exodus and for the balance of the Old Testament they are called Israelites (after Israel, the father of the twelve tribes).

After their return from exile in Babylon, they begin to be called Jews (which comes from the name of the tribe of Judah). **'Jew'** is used in the Old Testament after this, and throughout the New Testament.

www.ingramcontent.com/pod-product-compliance
Lightning Source LLC
Chambersburg PA
CBHW071717230426
43670CB00008B/1037